The Modern Papacy

LONGMAN HISTORY OF THE PAPACY

General Editor: A.D. Wright

This ambitious new series will cover the history of the Papacy from early medieval times through to the present day in five substantial volumes. Each, written by a leading scholar in the field, is designed to meet the needs of students and general readers, as well as those of the specialist.

The first volume to be published is:

The Modern Papacy since 1789
Frank J. Coppa

The Modern Papacy since 1789

Frank J. Coppa

LONGMAN
London and New York

Addison Wesley Longman Limited
Edinburgh Gate,
Harlow, Essex CM20 2JE,
United Kingdom
and Associated Companies throughout the world

*Published in the United States of America
by Addison Wesley Longman Inc., New York*

First published 1998

ISBN 0 582 096308 PPR
0 582 096294 CSD

Visit Addison Wesley Longman on the world wide web at http://www.awl-he.com

British Library Cataloguing in Publication Data

A catalogue record for this book is available from the British Library

Library of Congress Cataloging-in-Publication Data

Coppa, Frank J.
The Modern Papacy since 1789 /Frank J. Coppa.
p. cm. — (Longman history of the papacy)
Includes bibliographical references and index.
ISBN 0-582-09630-8 (PPR). — ISBN 0-582-09629-4 (CSD)
1. Papacy—History—1799–1870. 2. Papacy—History—19th century.
3. Papacy—History—20th century. I. Title. II. Series.
BX1386.C58 1998
262'.13'09034—dc21 98-18988
CIP

Set by 35 in 10/12pt Bembo
Produced by Addison Wesley Longman Singapore (Pte) Ltd.
Printed in Singapore

Contents

List of maps

Abbreviations used in notes

AAS	*Acta Apostolicae Sedis* (Rome, 1909–)
ASR	Archivio di Stato di Roma
ASS	*Acta Sanctae Sedis* (Rome, 1865–1908)
ASV	Archivio Segreto del Vaticano
AVR	Thomas E. Hachey, ed., *Anglo-Vatican Relations 1914–1939: Confidential Reports of the British Minister to the Holy See* (Boston, 1972)
Bull Rom Cont	*Bullarii romani continuatio*, ed. Andreas Barberi (Rome, 1835–57)
Carlen, *PE*	Claudia Carlen, ed., *The Papal Encyclicals*, 5 vols (Wilmington, NC, 1981)
Carlen, *PP*	Claudia Carlen, ed., *Papal Pronouncements. A Guide: 1740–1978*, 2 vols (Ann Arbor, MI, 1990)
Mag Bull Rom	*Magnum Bullarium Romanum* (Rome, 1843)
Mag Bull Rom Cont	*Magnum Bullarium Romanum* (Graz, Austria, 1964)
TESP	Eucardio Momigliano, ed., *Tutte le encicliche dei sommi Pontefici* (Milan, 1959)

CHAPTER 1

Introduction: the papacy in an age of ideologies

The papacy, the supreme authority of the Catholic church, is an old, enduring, and unique institution. It flourished during the Middle Ages, was a participant in the Renaissance, the Reformation, the French Revolution, and the industrial age, witnessing the rise and fall of communism. During its long tenure, it invented the notion of 'deniability', while promoting its infallibility. Leopold von Ranke, in his *History of the Popes*, presented the papacy as a crucial historical phenomenon. Thomas Babington Macaulay, in his Essay on the Protestant historian's study, stressed the popes' centrality in the church, their impact on events, and their remarkable ability to appropriate new movements.[1] He echoed sentiments earlier expressed by Napoleon.

Bonaparte considered the papacy 'one of the greatest offices of the world', whose military equivalence he estimated as a 'corps of 200,000 men'.[2] If there had been no pope, Napoleon mused, it would have been necessary to invent one. Nevertheless, Bonaparte charged that the papacy confused spiritual authority and political aims, and he insisted that priests refrain from meddling in politics.[3] The papacy functions both as head of a global spiritual realm and as a political organization exchanging diplomatic representation, sending nuncios and internuncios to other states, and receiving ambassadors and ministers from other nations. From the middle of the eighth century until the Italian seizure of Rome in 1870, the papacy governed a state in central Italy, dividing the peninsula and blocking Italian unification. Many perceived the popes as fathers of princes as well as vicars of Christ.

The papal claim of primacy and universal jurisdiction, which commenced during the Roman empire, persists to the present. Interest in it has likewise prevailed. The communication revolution, which triumphed in Rome when Guglielmo Marconi established Vatican radio in 1931, made it possible for the papacy to remain in constant touch with the hierarchy and faithful worldwide,

1 G.P. Gooch, *History and Historians in the Nineteenth Century* (Boston, 1965), p. 279.
2 John McManners, *The French Revolution and the Church* (New York, 1970), p. 141.
3 *Letter and Documents of Napoleon*, ed. John Eldred Howard (New York, 1961), p. 188.

rendering its control all the more feasible and formidable. Long before then, some resented the expanding papal power. During the Reformation, Luther attacked the papacy as an unnecessary human contrivance.[4] Later, too, there were those who decried papal primacy. The noted Catholic historian Lord Acton, though loyal to the church, proved critical of papal centralization. Returning from Rome, he warned that power corrupts and absolute power corrupts absolutely. In the 1930s, when Pierre Laval pleaded with Stalin to conciliate the pope, the Soviet dictator dismissively inquired about the number of divisions the pope directed. Possessing none, Rome nonetheless wielded tremendous moral influence and considerable diplomatic clout. Perhaps this is why the *duce* warned the Nazis to avoid the hostility of the pope, cautioning that the church warranted eternal surveillance.[5]

The papacy, the office and position of the bishop of Rome, exercising both spiritual and temporal authority, has long been a distinctive feature and cohesive factor in the existence of Catholicism. While the study of the papacy in isolation cannot explain the development of the church, its role has been crucial and its history often coterminous with that of Western civilization. As successor of Peter and vicar of Christ, bishop of Rome, patriarch of the west, and head of the universal church, the pope's powers, according to the first Vatican council, are both ordinary and immediate, while his jurisdiction is universal. According to canon law, only the pope can convoke an ecumenical council and only he, or his delegate, can preside over it. In the diplomatic realm, he ranks as first of Christian princes, while his ambassadors enjoy precedence over other members of the diplomatic community.

Although a pope cannot impose his successor, he can make appointments to the college of cardinals[6] which will select him, and from which all popes since Urban VI (1378–89) have come. Catholicism, conceded the historian and political figure Adolphe Thiers, could not exist without the pope.[7] Paul VI (1963–78) agreed, asserting in his first encyclical, *Ecclesiam suam*, that without the papacy the Catholic church would not be Catholic, and its unity would vanish.[8] The dogmatic constitution on the church, *Lumen gentium*, which

4 *Luther's Works*, ed. Eric W. Gritsch (Philadelphia, 1958), XXXIX, pp. 98–5, 101–3.

5 Annual Report of 1929, in Thomas E. Hachey, ed., *Anglo-Vatican Relations 1914–1939: Confidential Reports of the British Minister to the Holy See* (Boston, 1972), p. 172 (hereafter cited as *AVR*); Galeazzo Ciano, *L'Europa verso La Catastrofe* (Verona, 1948), II, pp. 81, 527.

6 Since the early modern period the number in the sacred college was fixed at 70, although there was often a smaller number. Thus at the end of 1923 there were 64 cardinals, 33 of whom were Italian and the remaining 31 coming from outside the peninsula. John XXIII increased its membership to 87 and his successor Paul VI raised the number to 138, making the sacred college far more international than it had been.

7 Nassau William Senior, *Conversations with Distinguished Persons During the Second Empire from 1860 to 1863*, ed. M.C.M. Simpson (London, 1880), II, p. 175.

8 Paul had earlier issued letters, but *Ecclesiam Suam* was his first official circular letter sent to the bishops worldwide on matters affecting the universal church. Presently, the term encyclical epistle is used to characterize letters addressing a particular issue to the bishops of a single country or of a particular area. Claudia Carlen, ed., *The Papal Encyclicals* (Raleigh, NC, 1990), (hereafter cited as Carlen, *PE*), I, pp. xvii–xviii.

emerged from the second Vatican council, reconfirmed the pope's role as the visible head of the church.[9]

The word 'pope' derives from the Greek word *pappas*, meaning father, and applied to the bishop of Rome as *pater patriarcharum* or father of patriarchs – the bishops of the major cities of the empire. The title of supreme pontiff or *Pontifex maximus* emerged from pagan Rome. Thomas Hobbes depicted the papacy as the ghost of the deceased Roman empire, on whose grave it was crowned. 'The papacy is a Latin institution', wrote Gregorovius, who lived in Rome in the nineteenth century, 'and will only cease to exist with the extinction of the Latin race.'[10] Contemporary social scientists have concurred that church and papal structures aped those of the empire, observing that aspects of the cult of the emperor were simply transferred to the pope.[11] It is known that the Roman emperor, as the high priest of the pagan Roman religion, served as the virtual bridge between the present and the afterlife. Not surprisingly, some believe the triple tiara worn by the pontiffs symbolize their authority in heaven, on earth, and in the underworld.

The authority of the pope was to be challenged by the mania for modernization and the rush toward renovation during which politics as well as economics sought emancipation from religious supervision. The papal response required both the leadership of a 'father' and the reconciliation of a 'bridge builder', to move from the *ancien régime* to the revolutionary age. Increasingly, Providence was overshadowed by progress, while naturalism sought to ban the supernatural from the realm of thought. As early as 1775, Pius VI condemned the attacks on orthodoxy by the spirit of modernity and the Enlightenment's critique of faith.[12] Dechristianization proceeded in the state, school and family, as human thought, tackling contemporary problems, shifted from religious and philosophic speculation to the political, social and economic problems of society. The fifteen popes from Pius VI (1775–99) to John Paul II (1978–) have had to confront momentous developments.

The outbreak of the American and French Revolutions, shadowed by the take off of the Industrial revolution in Great Britain, and the publication of Adam Smith's *Wealth of Nations* in 1776, contributed to the transformation of Europe and the world. Together they ushered in the modern age. As the discovery of the steam engine and the new puddling furnace created profound social and economic changes, the American, French and Napoleonic revolutions provoked extraordinary political upheavals in the Western world and the vast reaches of Asia and Africa upon which they impinged. The currents unleashed by these revolutions challenged the traditional political order and the

9 Austin Flannery, ed., *Vatican Council II: The Conciliar and Post Conciliar Documents* (Grand Rapids, 1992), I, p. 370.

10 Friedrich Althaus, ed., *The Roman Journals of Ferdinand Gregorovius, 1852–1874*, trans. Mrs Gustavus W. Hamilton (London, 1906), p. 280.

11 Jean-Guy Vaillancourt, *Papal Power: A Study of Vatican Control over Lay Catholic Elites* (Berkeley, 1980), pp. 25–6.

12 *Inscrutabile*, 25 December 1775, in Carlen, *PE*, I, p. 171.

prevailing religious establishment, leaving little time or inclination for things of the spirit. The emergence of liberalism, constitutionalism, nationalism, republicanism and *laissez-faire* economics, and later Darwinism, democracy, socialism and secularism, presented a potential threat to the Catholic community, and its temporal and spiritual leadership, the papacy.

In the twentieth century the crisis continued with the development of Americanism, modernism, racism, fascism, communism and totalitarianism. Feminism, the sexual revolution, the population explosion, the increasing intrusion of the scientific mindset into realms long under religious scrutiny, environmental hazards, and even the threat of a nuclear holocaust challenged the papacy. Rome had to adjust to the new world order where science challenged revealed religion and where orthodoxy was denounced as a repressive check upon progress. The papacy found itself challenged by both the claims of the radically autonomous individual and the social agnosticism of the national state.

In retrospect, the pre-revolutionary age was perceived as a golden one, in which faith appeared to be the cornerstone of social life, Catholicism shaped the lives of the population from cradle to grave, and the state bolstered the institutional church. This retrospective proved more nostalgic than historic. While the masses still adhered to the faith in Catholic countries during the course of the eighteenth century, the political and intellectual classes proved hostile to the papacy. The age of absolutism and the consolidation of national states combined to restrict the influence of Rome over the national churches.

In France, state intervention assumed the form of Gallicanism; in Germany, Febronianism; in Austria and Lombardy, Josephism; and in Tuscany, Jansenism.[13] Clement XI's condemnation of Pasquier Quesnel's Jansenist works in the *Unigenitus* of 1713 did not end the hostility to papal power or the attacks on Roman ceremonies and wealth. Benedict XIV (1740–58) found it necessary to exhort the French bishops to obey the strictures of *Unigenitus*.[14] The French faithful, in turn, were influenced by Richerism, after the thought of Edmond Richer, who called for decentralization in the church, championing the rights of the parish priests *vis-à-vis* the bishops and the pope.[15] The papacy conceded some control of the church to the French by the concordat of 1516, and to the Spanish Bourbons by the concordat of 1753. Catholic governments inspired by absolutism were hostile to the exercise of papal authority within their territories, championing a regalism that sought control over ecclesiastical matters. Among other things, the Catholic powers insisted that Rome diminish the number of religious holidays, which the pope felt constrained to do for Spain in 1742, and for Austria, Naples and Tuscany in 1748.

13 On the impact of Jansenism, Gallicanism, Febronianism and Josephism within the eighteenth century see E. Preclin and E. Jarry, *Les luttes politiques et doctrinales aux XVII siècle* (Paris, 1956).
14 *Con quanta consolazione*, of 1741, in *Tutte le Encicliche dei Sommi Pontifici*, ed. Eucardio Momigliano (Milan, 1959), pp. 23–5 (hereafter cited as *TESP*).
15 E.E.Y. Hales, *The Catholic Church in the Modern World* (Garden City, NY, 1958), pp. 25–7; Giuseppe Hergenrother, *Storia universale della Chiesa*, ed. G.P. Kirsch, trans. P. Enrico Rosa (Florence, 1911), p. 197.

The Catholic powers contested the very office of the papacy in 1740 when their rivalry delayed the papal election for half a year, the longest conclave of the century. A number of European monarchs exercised an unhealthy influence over the college of cardinals, with four of them – the Holy Roman Emperor, and the kings of France, Spain and Portugal – retaining the right to veto a potential pontiff. In 1758 the French vetoed the election of Cardinal Cavalchini in the last public use of the exclusion in the eighteenth century.

In Germany, the thought and work of Bishop Nikolaus von Hontheim (1701–90), who wrote under the pen name of Justinus Febronius, was influenced by the Gallican articles of 1682. Branding the authority of the papacy a usurpation, he claimed it provoked most of the problems plaguing the church. In place of papal centralization, he proposed episcopal decentralization, reducing the papacy to a centre of unity exercising only limited, delegated authority. The popes, in his view, had to renounce their claims to primacy either voluntarily or under collective episcopal coercion. In 1767 the republic of Venice favoured publication of an Italian edition of Hontheim's work, while other editions were distributed in Spain, France, the Low Countries and Germany. Condemned by Pope Clement XIII (1758–69), and retracted by the author, Hontheim's call for episcopal autonomy found resonance in the states of Europe, and support from the emperor and the metropolitans of Germany, who challenged papal power. Similar positions were assumed by the archbishop electors and the archbishop of Salzburg in the twenty-three articles of the *Punctuation of Ems of 1786*, which restricted the jurisdiction of papal nuncios, while judging papal briefs and resolutions invalid without episcopal endorsement.

Joseph II (1741–90), who succeeded Maria Theresa in 1780, and championed royalism, concurred with much of the Febronian programme limiting papal power, which he considered a rival authority within his state. Upon assuming power, Joseph ended direct communication between the bishops and the pope, and placed ecclesiastical decrees under secular control and censure, requiring that all papal pronouncements and documents receive his *placet* before publication in his dominions. Arguing that papal influence extended only to the spiritual life of the church, Joseph insisted that the training and organization of clericals was subject to state jurisdiction. Joseph interjected the state into the education of clerics, confiscating the property of the clergy, while reorganizing the dioceses and parishes of his lands without papal consultation.

Hoping to moderate this 'reformist' programme, Pius VI, the 'holy traveller' and one of the few popes to leave Rome since the sixteenth century, ventured to Vienna in 1782 to plead with the emperor for revocation of this legislation. Although Pius received a rapturous reception by the faithful en route, and was cordially entertained in Vienna, the emperor refused to abandon his programme. The failure of the Vienna visit exposed the impotence of the papacy, which reached its nadir. By the concordat of 1784, the pope was constrained to make additional concessions to Joseph, transferring to him as duke of Milan the authority to name candidates to the bishoprics as well as the leadership of the religious orders in the duchies of Milan and Mantua.

Spurred by the success of his older brother Joseph, Grand Duke Leopold of Tuscany (1765–90) likewise took steps to oppose the historic doctrines of the church and restrict the influence of the papacy in his duchy. The grand duke abolished the right of asylum, suppressed convents, and subjected ecclesiastical lands to taxes. By 1782, Leopold abolished the inquisition and favoured Jansenist tendencies within the church. Supported by Scipione de Ricci, the bishop of Pistoia and Prato, who shared his determination to limit the influence of Rome, much of Josephist regalism was imposed on the Tuscan church. Under the patronage of the grand duke, the synod of Pistoia (1786) accepted the four Gallican articles of 1682, curtailing the papacy's control over the Tuscan church.

In the succeeding decade hostile actions were initiated against the papacy in Venice and Naples, and other parts of the Italian peninsula. The republic of St Mark, without Rome's approval, orchestrated the reform of the religious orders in its territories. The Venetian zeal in limiting ecclesiastical privileges and suppression of convents nearly led to a complete break with the papacy in the latter half of the eighteenth century. In Naples, Pietro Giannone's *History of Naples* (1723) became the standard of the anti-papal party. The southern kingdom developed a school of jurists adverse to the 'pretensions' of the papacy, placing numerous impositions on papal prerogatives by the concordat of 1741. In 1788 Naples abolished all symbols of vassalage towards the Roman See. Throughout the peninsula, save for Savoy, there was an increased agitation against the Jesuits.

The Society of Jesus, fanatically devoted to the papacy, was criticized for its loyalty to Rome. Counting among its enemies the Jansenists, the rationalists, the apostles of absolutism, the doctors of the Sorbonne in Paris, and all those opposed to papal power, the campaign against the Order intensified in the mid-eighteenth century. The minister of King Joseph of Portugal, Sebastiao José de Carvalho, the marquis of Pombal, charging that the Jesuits were implicated in the assassination attempt on his monarch while resisting his reformism, expelled the Order in 1759. It led to a rupture of relations between Portugal and the Holy See in 1760. The Paris parlement followed suit in 1762 and suppressed the Order in France. Shortly thereafter, the Jesuits, opposed by the ministers Pedro Aranda and Manuel de Roda, were banished from Spain in 1767, and by Bernardo Tanucci from Naples, and from Parma and Piacenza the following year. The pontificate of Clement XIV (1769–74) was dominated by the pressure of the powers to dissolve the Jesuits, and in 1773 by the brief of 21 July, a reluctant pope complied.[16] Only in Catherine's Russia, beyond the pale of enlightened pressure, did the Society continue its corporate existence on the 'outskirts of civilized Europe'. In the west, ardent apostles of the age of reason perceived the dissolution as the first step towards the obliteration of the papacy.

The church, and especially the papacy, were ridiculed by the *philosophes* in France, Portugal, Spain and Naples, who branded Christianity and its hierarchy

16 Carlen, *PE*, I, p. 141.

the implacable enemy of progress, rationality and humanity. Attached to the cult of science, the *philosophes* discredited mysteries, miracles, relics and prophecies.[17] The *illuministi* in Italy shared the beliefs and sentiments of the French *philosophes*. Rationalism, likewise, swept through Germany. The philosophical revolution, which denounced the papacy, found its great champion in François-Marie Arouet, better known as Voltaire (1694–1778), who sought to discredit the Christian world and replace it with a modern, secular one. Denis Diderot (1713–74), born into a pious family, moved from Catholicism to scepticism and agnosticism, finally settling upon atheism. He and his assistant Jean d'Alembert (1712–83), collaborators in the publication of the *Encyclopédie* after 1750, were irreligious as well as atheistic, replacing the terms God and Providence with nature. In his encyclical *Christianae reipublicae* of 25 November 1766, Clement XIII denounced the 'contagious and depraved plague of books' which he believed polluted the waters of belief while eroding the foundations of faith. These 'outrageous books', he charged, sought to 'shatter the head of the Church'.[18] His denunciation of this 'immoral' literature did not stop its flow. The Enlightenment thus produced difficulties for the church which blossomed during the course of the revolutionary age which ensued, unleashing anticlericalism, economic transformation and political upheaval.

The revolt of the American colonies (1775–81), following their struggle over 'taxation without representation', and justified by the broad precepts of the Enlightenment, did not prove detrimental to the Catholic church or its leader. The Catholic minority in the colonies, no more than 20,000, rallied to the national cause as did Catholic France and Spain. In 1780 the assembly of the French clergy contributed 30,000,000 *livres* to support the revolutionaries. George Washington, appreciative of Catholic support, admonished his soldiers not to participate in anti-Catholic manifestations, which he deemed 'immature and childish'. Benjamin Franklin, in turn, informed the papal nuncio in Paris, Prince Doria Pamphili, of the American determination to assure liberty of conscience. This materialized in the first amendment to the Constitution in the Bill of Rights.[19]

Although contrary to integralism which sought the union of throne and altar favoured by the papacy, Rome recognized that the separation of church and state suited conditions in the United States. American separatism mirrored the experience of Rhode Island, New Jersey, Pennsylvania and Delaware, where church and state were already separate. Furthermore, in light of the overwhelmingly Protestant majority in these states, separatism might prove useful

17 Peter Gay, *The Party of Humanity: Essays in the French Englightenment* (New York, 1971), pp. 44–6; H. Daniel-Rops, *The Church in the Eighteenth Century*, trans. John Warrington (Garden City, NY, 1966), pp. 63–6; for an examination of the Italian reformers see Franco Venturi's *Settecento riformatore. I: Da Muratori a Beccaria* (Turin, 1969).
18 Carlen, *PE*, I, pp. 133–5.
19 Sol Bloom, ed., *History of the Formation of the Union under the Constitution* (Washington, DC, 1941), p. 557; Gene Crescenzi, 'Papa Pio VI e la libertà di culto nell' America del Nord', *Il Progresso-Due Mondi*, 25 May 1986; Daniel-Rops, *Church in the Eighteenth Century*, p. 413.

to the church in the newly formed United States. Hence Pius VI (1775–99) did not protest against the development, appointing John Carroll prefect apostolic in 1784 and bishop of Baltimore the year the French Revolution exploded. Indeed the Holy See failed to dispatch representatives to the peace congress concluding the war of the American Revolution, convinced that neither the position of the faith nor the rights of the Apostolic See were threatened.[20]

The consequences of the French Revolution proved more threatening than the American to the papacy's role as guardian of revelation and moral guide. Beginning with the confiscation of church property in 1789, followed by the civil constitution of the clergy shortly thereafter, the ensuing years witnessed a determined, often violent assault against the temporal and spiritual authority of the papacy, which culminated in 1799 in the spiriting of Pius VI from the Eternal City and the proclamation of a republic in Rome. The worship of reason and the cult of the Supreme Being were proclaimed in France as alternatives to the traditional faith as war was waged against religious authority in the name of human autonomy. Napoleon, who became first consul in 1799, sought some reconciliation with Rome, concluding a concordat with the Holy See in 1801. The agreement did not prevent the emperor from occupying the Papal States in 1808, nor its annexation in 1809. Pius VII (1800–23), like his predecessor, was dragged into exile by the French. As Napoleon's domination spread throughout Europe, the papacy appeared to be on the verge of collapse. The threat dissipated with the dissolution of Napoleon's legions in the steppes of Russia and the emperor's exile to St Helena.

The settlement of 1815 saw a reconstitution of the Papal States, the restoration of the Jesuits, and a renewed appreciation for the union of throne and altar. Ultramontanism looked to Rome 'beyond the mountains' to centralize ecclesiastical authority and assure the independence of the church. Conservatives perceived a close nexus between religion and society. The Sardinian ambassador to Russia, Joseph de Maistre (1754–1821), extolled the papacy as the senior partner in the alliance. In his manifesto of ultramontanism, *Du Pape* (1817), he praised the papacy as a mediator above all peoples and nations. Dismissing the secular power as inferior to, and dependent upon, the spiritual power of the pope, de Maistre considered legitimate sovereignty ultimately justified by the papacy. Father Gioacchino Ventura (1792–1861) concurred, claiming that only Catholicism under papal leadership provided a moral force capable of guiding political power. While their message found resonance in the romantic movement, not all justified or tolerated papal absolutism.

Franz von Baader, in 'Concerning the Separability or Inseparability of the Papacy from Catholicism' (1838), denounced spiritual bondage as no less burdensome than its secular variant. Furthermore, the revolutions of 1820, 1830, and even those of 1848 were directed against the religious order that critics charged bolstered the prevailing power structure. The revolutions of

20 Cardinal Prefect of Propaganda to the Nuncio in Paris, 15 January 1783, in Jules A. Baisnee, *France and the Establishment of the American Catholic Hierarchy: The Myth of French Interference (1783–1784)* (Baltimore, 1934), p. 45.

1830 encouraged the appearance of a liberal Catholic movement that sought to disassociate the church and the papacy from the moribund monarchical structure, giving rise to Félicité Robert de Lamennais's *Avenir* movement. At the same time, the outbreak of revolution in the Papal States, suppressed only by Austrian intervention, prompted the memorandum of the powers (1831), urging the pope to make reforms. Pope Gregory XVI (1831–46) condemned the *Avenir* movement and shelved the suggestions of the powers calling for the reform of his state. Nonetheless, criticism of the papacy continued.

The pontificate of Pius IX (1846–78), the longest in the history of the church and filled with events which dominated the second half of the nineteenth century, opened on an optimistic note as the new pope was hailed as the 'liberator' who would unite the Italian peninsula and reconcile liberty and Catholicism. The dream disappeared amidst the debris of the revolutionary upheaval of 1848, during which Pius IX determined that the revolutionaries had anti-Catholic aims in contrast to his original belief that they were the instrument of divine intervention to topple the remnants of Josephism. Pius IX fled from his subjects and witnessed the proclamation of a Roman republic guided by Mazzini and defended by Garibaldi. The pope, restored to Rome by the Catholic powers – Austria, France, Spain and Naples – concluded that his position as Supreme Pontiff was jeopardized by his experiment with constitutionalism. Following his restoration in Rome, Pius focused on his position as head of the faith. In the religious realm he adhered to traditionalism, denouncing as indifferentism the liberal call for freedom of conscience.

Pius refused to reconcile himself to the loss of his territory, which was incorporated into the kingdom of Italy proclaimed in 1861. He responded in 1864 to the call for accommodation with the new currents by issuing the encyclical *Quanta cura*, to which was appended the Syllabus of Errors.[21] Mobilizing the forces of the church to bolster the position of the papacy, he convoked the Vatican council in 1869, which the following year proclaimed the primacy and infallibility of the pope. 'In former times before I was Pope, I believed in the Infallibility,' Pius remarked, 'now however, I feel it.'[22] Opponents such as the Bavarian theologian and priest, Ignaz von Doellinger (1799–1890), charged that the proclamation lacked antiquity, universality and consent. Some still consider the claim to supremacy and infallibility the most prominent features of the papacy, setting Catholicism apart from all other churches, and acting as a barrier to Christian unity.

The combative Pius refused to sanction the loss of Rome during the Franco-Prussian War, which ended the oldest sovereignty in Europe. He was no more willing to submit to the *Kulturkampf* in Bismarck's Germany or the Los von Rom movement in Austria, which sought freedom from Rome. Pius deplored August Compte's 'theology of science', decrying the attempt to establish a

21 An English translation of the Syllabus will be found in *Dogmatic Canons and Decrees* (Rockford, IL, 1977), pp. 187–209.
22 Althaus, ed., *Roman Journals of Ferdinand Gregorovius*, p. 351.

new social and spiritual order to undermine the Catholic one, with a 'pope of positivism' replacing the Roman pontiff.

At the turn of the century Pope Leo XIII (1878–1903), striving to transcend the negativism of his two predecessors, confided to the historian Ludwig von Pastor, author of the monumental *History of the Popes from the close of the Middle Ages*, that the church did not fear public exposure.[23] Planning an accommodation with the modern world, in 1881 he opened the Vatican archives down to 1815. Leo also sought to heal the rift between Rome and democratic governments such as existed in republican France (the *ralliement*), while searching for solutions to the tribulations of the working classes in the industrial age. Citing the weaknesses of *laissez-faire*'s social indifferentism on the one hand, he condemned Marxism as a cure worse than the disease (*Rerum novarum*, 15 May 1891), on the other. His diplomatic initiatives led him to arbitrate the dispute between Spain and Germany over the Caroline Islands, to secure the opening of a Russian embassy to the Vatican, and to institute diplomatic relations with imperial Japan.

Leo's successor, Pius X (1903–14), proved less open to contemporary developments, condemning modernism, while resisting the attempt to increase the power of the laity within the church. His rejection of the synthesis between the truths of religion and those of modernity, combined with an intransigent defence of papal prerogatives, contributed to the separation of church and state in France in 1905 and in Portugal in 1911. Although his successor Benedict XV (1914–22) called for an end to the recriminations between traditionalists and modernists, Catholic clergy were still constrained to take an anti-modernist oath. It was Paul VI (1963–78), in the 1960s, who finally cancelled this imposition which had persisted since 1910!

In the twentieth century, the papacy, possessing the oldest continually existing professional diplomatic corps, flourished as a key player in international relations. Benedict XV (1914–22) proved unable to end the First World War, which found Catholics on opposing sides of the conflict. His peace proposal of 1917 earned him the suspicion of both the central powers and the allies. Although vehemently opposed to communism, during the famine of 1921 he organized a major relief programme on behalf of the Russians. Benedict's successor Pius XI (1922–39) in 1924 opened the Vatican archives through the pontificate of Gregory XVI, which ended in 1846. During the international congress of Genoa in 1922, Pius had his representative make contact with those of the Soviet Union, upsetting those on the right for the attempt to reconcile that regime with the Vatican, and those on the left for his failure to do so.

During the interwar decades (1919–39), opponents of papal power pointed to the Vatican's affinity with the far right, with some even suggesting that Catholicism had a fascist form of government, resting on the leadership principle with an infallible pope in supreme command. Pius XI's conclusion of the

23 Michele Maccarrone, 'Apertura degli Archivi della Santa Sede per I Pontificati di Pio X e di Benedetto XV (1903–1922)', *Rivista di Storia della Chiesa in Italia*, XXXIX, 2 (1985), p. 341.

Lateran Accords with Mussolini's Italy in 1929, followed by the concordat with Hitler's Germany in 1933, did little to quiet criticism. Likewise the papacy's tacit support of the authoritarian Dollfuss in Austria, and the falangist Franco in Spain, while displaying a consistent hostility and uncompromising opposition to communism, led some to equate Catholicism with fascism.

The neutrality of Pius XII (1939–58) during the Second World War, and his 'silence' in the face of the Holocaust, was subsequently exposed in Rolf Hochhuth's play *The Deputy*, which deplored the vicar of Christ's role during the war. Pius was also criticized for his encyclical *Humani generis* (Of the human race) of 1950, which rejected the new theology which challenged neo-thomism. Some found it apt that on 8 December 1954 Pius XII signed the decree for the opening of the apostolic process for the beatification of Pius IX, who had papal infallibility proclaimed.

The election of Pope John XXIII (1958–63) witnessed an attempt at *aggiornamento* to bring the church up to date without betraying its fundamental spiritual mission. The four sessions of the second Vatican council from 1962 to 1965 brought the Catholic church and the papacy to the forefront of world opinion. Conservatives charged that John, who openly endorsed democracy and championed the workers' rights to form trade unions, virtually turned the church upside down by undermining the papacy while stressing the powers of the bishops. Paul VI (1963–78), who opened the Vatican archives through the long pontificate of Pius IX (1846–78), continued John's reforms, according to some, while others believe he slammed the door on future change. Although evaluations of Paul's contribution vary, he abolished the Index of forbidden books and moderated the anti-communist crusade of the papacy, receiving the Soviet foreign minister Andre Gromyko in 1966, and the president of the 'evil empire', Nikolai Podgorny, the following year.

During the summer of 1978, the church lost two popes, Paul VI (1963–78) and his successor John Paul I (1978), bringing forth a Polish cardinal as John Paul II (1978–), terminating the Italian domination of the papacy from 1522 to 1978. John Paul II, in is first encyclical, *Redemptor hominis* (4 March 1979) (The redeemer of man), articulated a plan to prepare the church for the twenty-first century. This pope, first to enter Canterbury cathedral, first to preach in a Lutheran church, and first to enter a synagogue, was gunned down in St Peter's Square in May 1981, but survived.[24] To facilitate scholarly study of the church, John Paul II opened the Vatican archives for the pontificates of Pius X and Benedict XV, which extended from 1903 to 1922. In 1995 John Paul II authorized Reverend Leonard Boyle, prefect of the Vatican library, to conclude an accord with the International Business Machine Corporation (IBM) to open the Vatican library, founded by Pope Nicholas V (1447–55) in 1451, to the computer literate. Under the proposed arrangement, a good part of the current holdings of more than 1½ million books and over 150,000

24 Wilton Wynn, *Keepers of the Keys: John XXIII, Paul VI, and John Paul II: Three Who Changed the Church* (New York, 1988), p. 249.

manuscripts will be placed into digital form, with some of the manuscripts likely to be available on the Internet, the worldwide computer network.[25] John Paul's encyclical letter of 30 March 1995 *Evangelium vitae* (The gospel of life), on the value and inviolability of human life, is the first in the almost 2,000-year history of the encyclical to be available on disk.

In 1982 the pope met President Ronald Reagan of the United States, who had likewise survived an assassination attempt in 1981, and the two experienced a meeting of minds. By 1984, William Wilson, the president's special representative to the pope, was appointed ambassador to the Vatican. The pope and the American president supposedly conspired in a 'holy alliance' not only to support the outlawed Solidarity movement after the martial crackdown of 1981 in Poland, but sought to precipitate the end of Soviet domination of the whole of Eastern Europe. Both were to see their vision fulfilled, as well as the collapse of communism in the Soviet Union.[26]

During the height of the Vatican's crusade against communism, the papacy confronted criticism of its leadership within the church. The Jesuits, long the bulwark of papal primacy, no longer saw the ultimate leadership of the Roman church in the papacy and its worldwide hierarchy but in the 'people of God'. The more radical voices even called for a new theology to emerge from the masses below to replace the one imposed from above. In South and Central America, a number of prominent figures in the Jesuit Order called upon the church to exercise a 'preferential option' for the poor and oppressed, proposing a Christian–Marxist alliance to forge a new socialist society to replace the decadent capitalist one. The Jesuit onslaught on the capitalist establishment is enshrined in the theology of liberation.[27]

While class and social issues troubled the church in Latin America and other parts of the third world, the church in Western Europe and North America found itself under mounting criticism for its alleged gender bias, homophobia, as well as clerical domination, and the papacy for its position on such issues as priestly celibacy, birth control, abortion, and opposition to the ordination of women. Derided and denounced for its sophistry, stupidity, arrogance, bigotry and intolerance, critics charge that it took 300 years for the papacy to acknowledge that the church had erred in its seventeenth-century condemnation of Galileo. Sinead O'Connor, tearing a picture of John Paul II on national television in the United States, accused the church of the 'destruction of entire races of people'. 'It's not the man, obviously', she continued, 'it's the office and the symbol of the organization that he represents.'[28] Despite this crescendo of criticism, in 1994 John Paul II was selected *Time* 'man of the year'.[29]

25 Steve Lohr, 'I.B.M. to Help Vatican Open Its Archives to the Computing Masses', *New York Times*, 28 March 1995, D, p. 4.
26 Carl Bernstein, 'The Holy Alliance', *Time*, 24 February 1992, pp. 28–35.
27 Malachi Martin, *The Jesuits: The Society of Jesus and the Betrayal of the Roman Catholic Church* (New York, 1988), pp. 15–22.
28 *Time*, 9 November 1992, p. 78.
29 *Time*, 26 December 1994/2 January 1995.

The continuing importance of the office and its holder is also reflected in the fact that Alfred A. Knopf agreed to pay more than $6 million to the pope's charities in return for publication of his responses to questions posed by the Italian journalist Vittorio Messori.[30] Attracting a broad audience searching for guidance and moral leadership, the pope's book has sold as well as the recent translation of the Catholic church's 800-page Catechism. Despite the huge advance, Knopf has not had to endure the financial difficulties confronted by Mark Twain's Charles Webster and Company which published *The Life of Pope Leo XIII* in 1887, which failed as a venture.

The Roman Catholic church, during its two millennia, has had to confront innumerable problems and crises under the leadership of the papacy. There are those who have boasted that the popes have changed little, taking as their motto *Semper idem* (always the same), despite the tradition of electing these leaders. There has been continuity from one pope to another, yet each has emerged as a distinct figure promoting a degree of change as the papacy adjusted to the structures of the surrounding world. The papacy has sanctioned a startling shift on some issues while remaining rigidly steadfast on others. Within the last two centuries, the pontificates of Leo XIII and John XXIII have been praised for their reformism, while those of Gregory XVI, Pius IX and Pius X have been denounced for fighting a rearguard action against the contemporary world.

Despite the controversy surrounding papal policy, a consensus exists that it has involved the church in world affairs. One measure of its far-reaching influence can be gleaned from the fact that over 100 governments maintain diplomatic relations with the Holy See, which has formal diplomatic relations with most countries, and informal relations with the rest. Its nuncios, dating back to the sixteenth century, hold the rank of ambassadors and its internuncios those of ministers. Since the congress of Vienna they have been accorded the position of deans of the diplomatic corps, regardless of their years of service. These are supplemented by the apostolic delegates or the pope's representatives accredited to the clergy of the various nations. The Holy See's objectives are attained not only through formal diplomatic relations but also by means of the local bishops who provide another mechanism for communication with Rome.

During the course of the twentieth century, the ravages of two world wars exposed the weakness of excessive national sovereignty, leading to the development of mechanisms of international co-operation and collaboration. During these decades, the Catholic church, the traditional transnational organization, under the leadership of the popes, resumed an active role in international affairs.

Although the papacy's place and position in international affairs has a long history, its role had to be redefined during an age when a majority of states were no longer Catholic, and in many cases not even Christian. It had to contend with the notion that only territorial sovereignty conferred jurisdictional

30 John Paul II, *Crossing the Threshold of Hope* (New York, 1994).

legitimacy and international participation. While many of the solemn principles advocated first by the League of Nations and later adopted by the United Nations mirrored positions of the Catholic church and centuries-old Christian traditions, there were obstacles to the church's participation in an international community organized on the basis of independent, sovereign states. The creation of Vatican City in 1929 provided the Holy See with the claim to enter the concert of powers, altering in the eyes of some the weaker position it had endured at the time of the formation of the League of Nations. The popes, however, noted that some confused the Holy See with Vatican City, attributing to Vatican City recognition as an entity, juridically equal to other states, despite its tiny territory, small population, and the peculiarities of its organization. The church, on the other hand, has insisted on sovereignty for the Holy See, as the supreme organ of government of the Catholic church.

Despite the conflicting interpretations of the basis of its diplomatic role, there is a broad recognition of its longevity resulting from the papacy's willingness to reshape itself, as well as its ability to reach some accommodation with contemporary developments. Although the pope functions as the supreme authority in the pyramidal structure of the church and the Roman administration, he represents only one – albeit the first – of the five primary categories found within the church: the papacy, the Roman curia, the bishops, the priests, and the laity. The pope delegates considerable influence to the congregations, the tribunals, and the offices.[31] Thus in canon law the Apostolic See designates more than just the person of the pope, who is elected by the college of cardinals, but includes the offices and bureaux through which he conducts the business of the universal church. Those who preside over these posts by papal appointment have been collectively dubbed the Roman curia, which has been compared to the cabinets of secular governments.

The higher clergy has been convoked in council only twenty-one times during the life of the church, and only twice in the last two centuries covered in the present volume, which examines the Catholic church in the nineteenth and twentieth centuries through the prism of the papacy. This study focuses on the papal response to the modern world and its influence and impact on developments from the outbreak of the French Revolution to the collapse of communism in Eastern Europe and Russia. In the pages which follow, I have explored the forces which impinged on the papacy and its response, delving into its motivation, while exploring the consequences of its attitudes and actions.

31 Prior to the Second World War there were twelve congregations, four offices and three tribunals. The congregations consisted of (1) the Holy Office, (2) the consistorial congregation, (3) congregation of the sacraments, (4) congregation of the council, (5) congregation of the religious orders, (6) congregation of propaganda, (7) congregation of eastern churches, (8) congregation of rites, (9) ceremonial congregation, (10) congregation of extraordinary ecclesiastical affairs, (11) congregation of seminaries, universities, and studies, and (12) congregation of administration of Basilica of St Peter's. The offices included (1) the apostolic chancellory, (2) the apostolic dataria, (3) the secretariat of state, and (4) the apostolic chamber. The tribunals which attend to the administration of justice include (1) the penitentiary, (2) the sacred rota, and (3) the apostolic signatura.

Included in the volume is the papacy's reaction to the French Revolution and the Napoleonic imperium, to the revolutionary upheaval which troubled Europe from 1820 to 1848, to liberal Catholicism, to Italian and German unification, and to the *Kulturkampf*. It also traces the papacy's support of missionary efforts in the vast reaches of the 'third world' beyond Europe and the Americas, its relationship to colonialism and imperialism, its role in the First World War, its relationship with the democracies and the dictatorships in the interwar period, as well as its controversial role during the Second World War, including the so-called silence of Pope Pius XII during the Holocaust. Additional chapters examine the papacy's attitude towards internationalism, communism, the reconstruction of the post Second World War world, the crisis of authority which has troubled the church since the late 1950s, and the accommodation with the modern world initiated by the second Vatican council.

This examination of the papacy in the modern world traces this key institution within the broader framework of religious, cultural, political, social and economic events. The Holy See has had to face internal and external opposition, including the undermining of traditional forms of authority in the church as well as society at large. The problems it confronted continue to haunt humanity, including the erosion of conscience, the questions of morality in the marketplace and the limits to be placed on capitalism, the rights of the individual versus those of the community, and the rights and responsibilities of the working classes versus those of their employers. Among other things, this book seeks to explore how the papacy came to appreciate the need for an international world order to preserve the peace as well as the environment. Finally, the volume delves into the modern papacy's need to balance the welfare of the rich and the poor, the West and the 'third world', the interaction between science and religion, as well as the continuing issue of the proper relationship between church and state.

A NOTE ON SOURCES

Because the Vatican archives (ASV) are presently open only through the pontificate of Pope Benedict XV (1914–22), some 'purists' argue that a history of the modern papacy should terminate with Benedict's death. While understanding their concerns, I have not followed their advice. Most historians agree that unlimited access to these papers will most likely not change the current assessment of the controversial pontificate of Pius XII, and doubt that the discovery of a 'smoking gun' will alter the present evaluation of this pontificate. The Istituto Paolo VI in Brescia has a wealth of primary material, letters, etc., on Montini and is open to scholars. With due appreciation of the importance of the archival base of the Archivio Segreto del Vaticano, I remind the reader that these archives are supplemented by the archives of other powers and printed correspondence of their representatives to the Holy See with their home governments. Furthermore, the printed acts of the Holy See appear in the *Acta Apostolicae Sedis*, which, like the encyclical letters of the papacy, are available down to the present. In addition, one can glean much from the articles in the *Osservatore Romano*, the daily authoritative voice of the Vatican, and the Jesuit journal, *La Civiltà Cattolica*, which enjoys a close though autonomous relationship with the Holy See. Likewise, invaluable and available are the printed speeches and discourses of Popes Pius XI, Pius XII, John XXIII, Paul VI, John Paul I and John Paul II.

The memoirs of various individuals stationed at the Vatican also shed considerable light on papal developments. Some of the papers of the Vatican archive for the period of the Second World War have been published in the eleven volumes of the *Actes et documents du Saint Siège relatifs à la Seconde Guerre Mondiale*, edited by Robert Graham and others. In addition, there is a vast official printed documentary base in print for the second Vatican council, as well as the private correspondence of many of its participants during the pontificates of John XXIII and Paul VI. Finally, John Paul II has written a good deal and most of his works have been published. To be sure, the earlier period of the modern papacy has a wider archival base which together with a broader historiography provides the historian of the earlier period with greater resources than those who examine the contemporary age, particularly since the second Vatican council. Nevertheless, although some of the assumptions and assessments made concerning this later period are likely to be revised by subsequent findings and analysis, in the author's opinion, the contemporary papacy is too important to be ignored by historians.

CHAPTER 2

The chair of Peter confronts the French Revolution, 1789–1799

During the 1770s, when Louis XVI was crowned king of France (1774–93), and Giovanni Angelo Braschi of Cesena assumed the tiara as Pius VI (1775–99), Rome recognized the importance of the French church, which was far from submissive to the papacy. The French episcopacy, entirely aristocratic, retained privilege and high esteem, both socially and politically, ranking only behind the monarch. The 136 bishops of the first estate rivalled the state by possessing their own corporate organization while enjoying almost unassailable privileges. French society remained grounded on an ecclesiastical foundation and church and state were inseparable. Public assistance, health service, and education were monopolized by the church, which provided assistance to the unfortunate, poor, aged and sick. Most guilds retained a religious affiliation, while ceremonies and important events were marked by solemn processions.[1] Within France, only the Catholic church possessed the right to hold public services, and even non-believers, for the most part, did not challenge this monopoly.[2] In listing the problems facing his pontificate, Pius had railed against the French encyclopedists, although he did not specifically refer to the works of Rousseau, Voltaire and Diderot. While cataloguing the dangers confronting the faith, Pius VI did not foresee any threat from the French monarchy or any special problems within the borders of the eldest daughter of the church.[3]

The position of the French church had been challenged by royal absolutism, the decrees of the parlements, Gallicanism, Jansenism, and the works of the *philosophes*. The parlements, claiming to represent the will of the nation, reflected Jansenist sentiments by seeking to minimize papal influence. The Gallicans, in turn, viewed the church in their country as a national institution,

1 Jean François Eugene Robinet, *Le mouvement religieux à Paris pendant la Revolution (1789–1801)* (New York, 1974), I, pp. 105–9.

2 Ludwig Freiherr von Pastor, *The History of the Popes. XV: Pius VI (1775–1799)*, trans. E.F. Peeler (St Louis, MO, 1953), pp. 87–90; Henri Daniel-Rops, *The Church in an Age of Revolution 1789–1870*, trans. John Warrington (Garden City, NY, 1967), I, pp. 339–42; Owen Chadwick, *The Popes and European Revolution* (Oxford, 1981), p. 443.

3 *Inscrutabili Divinae*, 25 December 1775, in *Magnum Bullarium Romanum* (hereafter cited as *Mag Bul Rom*) (Rome, 1843), VI, pp. 184–6.

having only symbolic ties with Rome. Catholicism was also weakened by the contradiction of its privileged position in the midst of the prevailing difficulties, and by the existence of a clerical proletariat open to revolutionary sentiment. In a number of dioceses, organizations of the lower clergy emerged to redress their grievances.[4]

There was considerable rancour against the wealth of the church, an anger fuelled by the conviction that it failed to pay a fair share of taxes. Not only was the church exempt from ordinary taxation, it collected the tithe, the contribution of the faithful for the support of the church and its clergy, which increased its wealth. Furthermore, the authority of the state enforced ecclesiastical law, with public penalties prescribed for blasphemy and sacrilege. The French government also imposed a censorship of literature perceived as dangerous to the faith.[5]

The glaring and growing state deficit exposed the wanton prodigality of the court, provoking increased resentment of the privileges enjoyed by the clergy as well as the aristocracy. Early in 1787, the king convoked an assembly of notables, the first since 1626, but the aristocracy proved uncooperative, rejecting both the request for financial assistance to avert bankruptcy, and the call for fiscal reform. The French bishops contributed to the fall of Calonne and the accession of Lomenie de Brienne, archbishop of Toulouse, one of their own. The crown believed that this aristocratic cleric could influence the assembly general of the clergy of France, and that the higher clergy would prove more sympathetic and generous than their secular counterparts. De Brienne petitioned the assembly of the clergy for some eight million *livres*, but returned with only a fraction of the sum requested, as the clergy asserted its traditional right to offer what it pleased.

Complaining that the clergy and the nobility had abandoned their royal benefactor, de Brienne suggested the king appeal to the third estate by convoking the Estates-General. The affable but often irresolute Louis was energized to do so by the threat of impending national bankruptcy. The last session of this body had met in 1614, so a number of questions arose about its convocation and organization. How would elections be held, and who would be eligible? How many representatives would be accorded each estate? Would they meet separately, voting by order, or meet together and vote by head? By the end of December 1788, a number of issues had been decided, including the determination to allot the third estate a double representation, while granting the *curés* certain advantages *vis-à-vis* the hierarchy in voting regulations.

In the *cahiers de doléances* of the third estate, or petitions to the deputies for reform, most of the French regarded the parish clergy with respect. These

4 Hans Maier, *Revolution and Church: The Early History of Christian Democracy 1789–1901* (Notre Dame, 1969), pp. 97–8.

5 Gugliemo Oncken, *L'Epoca della Rivoluzione, dell' Impero e delle Guerre D'Indipendenza, 1789–1815* (Milan, 1887), I, p. 170; John McManners, *The French Revolution and the Church* (New York, 1970), pp. 5–8; Henri Daniel-Rops, *The Church in the Eighteenth Century* (Garden City, NY, 1966), p. 315.

petitions favoured granting the clergy a greater share of the immense wealth and patrimony of the first estate. Not much was said about restricting the public role or presence of the church, and even less about eliminating its role in education and public life.[6] There was remarkably little opposition to the administrative and charitable work performed by the clergy for the common good, as well as an almost total absence of determined secularism. Nonetheless, due to the interdependence of the monarchy and the church, the regime and religion, criticism of the one inevitably reflected on the other. Ecclesiastical authority was criticized for having sanctioned the absolute power of princes through the religious rite of coronation. The *cahiers* to the crown from the clergy and the third estate agreed on three fundamental points: (1) the pressing need for church reform, (2) the advisability of preserving the public position of Catholicism in France, and (3) a Gallican reaction against the power of the papacy to dominate the French church.[7]

The potentially volatile situation in Paris was neither understood nor appreciated by Rome. Giovanni Angelo Braschi, Pope Pius VI since 1775, was born in 1717 and was favoured by a series of popes. During the first years he occupied the chair of Peter, Pius VI showed himself a notorious nepotist, addicted to elegant ceremonies and grandiose projects, such as the draining of the Pontine Marshes and the restoration of the Appian Way, which bankrupted his treasury. For many, the worldly and vain pontiff personified the Roman claim that though faith was made in the Eternal City, it was exported abroad for others to believe. When this spiritual overlord of the church and Italian temporal ruler looked beyond the curia and college of cardinals dominated by his compatriots, he remained preoccupied with Joseph II's policies in Belgium and Austria, and Leopold I's in Tuscany.[8] Pius proved oblivious to the consequences of contemporary events in France, ignoring the impact they might have on the papacy. He was not alone in his indifference and incomprehension. The American minister to France, Thomas Jefferson, likewise did not foresee these developments as having any particular international importance.[9]

Few recognized in May 1789 that a revolutionary age was about to dawn, which would challenge the church, introducing a radically new society. Pius VI, who named John Carroll the first bishop in the United States that year, was preoccupied by ecclesiastical matters and the governance of his own state. Besides, domestic events in Paris did not appear to threaten Rome. The Estates-General, scheduled to open on 5 May 1789, was deemed neither an anticlerical, anti-Christian body, nor one dominated by Protestants or *philosophes*, atheists

6 For an analysis of the extent to which the parish *cahiers* reflected rural France in 1789 see Gilbert Shapiro and John Markoff, 'L'authenticité des cahiers de doléances', *Bulletin d'histoire de la Revolution Française* (1900–91), pp. 17–70.

7 Maier, *Revolution and Church*, pp. 101–2.

8 For a good review of papal preoccupation with Josephist policies in Belgium see *Documents relatifs à la juridiction des nonces et internonces des Pays-Bas pendant le régime autrichien (1706–1794)* (Rome, 1950), pp. 360–90.

9 Beckles Willson, *America's Ambassadors to France (1777–1927)* (New York, 1928), p. 31.

or anticlericals. Indeed, the first estate was assured a representation of one-fourth the deputies, or 300. Of the 296 clerical deputies elected, forty-seven were bishops, twelve canons, six vicar generals, twenty-three *abbés* or other unattached priests, with the remaining 208 simple parish priests.[10]

As early as 6 May 1789, the representatives of the third estate called upon those of the clergy and aristocracy to join with them in a national assembly to confirm credentials. The invitation was decisively rejected by the aristocrats, but the clerical delegation split almost evenly. This was not surprising in light of the deep division between those deputies drawn from the higher clergy – in 1789 all of France's bishops were aristocrats – and those from the lower, who were in a majority. Anxious to improve their lot, the lower clergy proved natural allies of the third estate.[11] The bishops of the assembly were consistently outvoted and overwhelmed by the *curé* representatives who were disposed to co-operate with the third estate. Even before 19 June 1789, when the clergy formally voted to join them, a number of clerics were meeting with the third estate, which had proclaimed itself the national assembly and sole legitimate representation of the French people. When the king closed their hall they sought refuge and temporary quarters in the church of St Louis, where they continued the defiance in the tennis court oath of 20 June. At the end of the month the king relented, accepting the fusion of the estates favoured by a substantial part of the clergy.

Many in the third estate doubted the conversion of the king and the church. On 12 July 1789 there was an assault on the house of the Lazzarists, followed two days later by an attack on the Bastille, widely perceived as a symbol of tyranny. Louis proclaimed it a riot, but others saw it as nothing less than a revolution, which Metternich considered the starting point of Europe's subsequent misfortunes.[12] The explosive atmosphere generated in mid-July pushed the assembly in August to abolish feudal rights as well as a number of clerical privileges. During the turbulent evening of 4 August 1789, the assembly abolished annates, the first year's revenue of a benefice paid to the papal curia, and other payments made to Rome. At the same time, the archbishop of Paris and the clergy renounced all the tithes collected by the French church. The clergy, like the aristocracy, was constrained to relinquish its immunity from taxation. 'Thus, there went down in one sweeping blow', wrote Jefferson who was in Paris at the time, 'all titles of rank, all the abusive privileges of feudalism, the tithes and casuals of the clergy, all provincial privileges.'[13] Some feared these steps reflected the desire not only to reform but to remodel the church.

10 Pastor, *History of the Popes*, XL, p. 111.
11 Giuseppe Hergenrother, *Storia universale della Chiesa*, ed. G.P. Kirsch, trans. P. Enrico Rosa (Florence, 1911) p. 317.
12 *Memoirs of Prince Metternich, 1773–1815*, ed. Prince Richard Metternich-Winneburg, trans. Mrs Alexander Napier (New York, 1970), I, p. 116.
13 Willson, *America's Ambassadors*, p. 37.

Following this 'night of delirium', the clergy in its assembly of 11 August proposed the continued collection of the tithe until an alternative means was found for the upkeep of the church. On 22 August the assembly created an ecclesiastical committee to resolve church–state relations. This first committee checked the more radical tendencies of the Gallicans and *philosophes*, proposing a moderate plan of clerical reform. Its sentiments were not shared by the more radical parties in the national assembly, desirous of creating a nation of individuals rather than classes, and determined to destroy the privileged position of the clergy by restricting the economic base of the church.

By this time Pius VI and part of the French episcopacy belatedly recognized the import of these revolutionary developments on the church.[14] Early in September 1789, Bishop Le Mintier of Tréguier, in Brittany, publicly denounced the dangerous ecclesiastical innovations which threatened to reduce the clergy to servility.[15] A number of French bishops, recognizing Louis's inability to provide protection, petitioned Rome. Pius, in turn, relied on the goodwill of Louis XVI to protect papal interests. On 13 September he dispatched a confidential letter to Louis, urging him to preserve the church's rights. In response, the king declared his determination to preserve the faith. But the monarch had to confront an assembly which denied him an absolute veto of legislation, while an angry mob of women brought him back from Versailles to Paris in early October. On 2 November 1789 the assembly, on the earlier suggestion of Périgord Charles Maurice Talleyrand (1754–1838), the bishop of Autun, approved the confiscation of clerical property. In December there followed orders for the auction of 400 million *livres* of ecclesiastic property, while transferring from church to state the supervision of public education.

Rome was upset to learn that the assembly in February 1790 had added fifteen new members to its ecclesiastical committee, tilting it decidedly to the left. Following the withdrawal of nine members of the episcopal minority, this second committee included six ecclesiastics and fifteen lay members.[16] Some charged that the assembly's decree of 13 February 1790, dissolving religious orders not engaged in educational or charitable efforts, while withdrawing official recognition of religious vows, threatened the spiritual life of the church while challenging its hierarchy. Abandoning his former frivolity, a determined and distraught pope denounced these measures on 29 March 1790. Pius condemned state intervention in the discipline of the church, prohibiting obedience to the pending legislation. The content of the pope's message was kept secret on the advice of Cardinal de Bernis, the French ambassador to the Holy See.

Papal restraint proved counter-productive, encouraging bolder assembly action. In April the ecclesiastical committee, inspired by Gallican sentiments,

14 André Latreille, *L'Église catholique et la Révolution française. Le pontificat de Pie VI et la crise française (1775–1799)* (Paris, 1946), pp. 93–123.
15 Jacques Godechot, *La Contre-Révolution. Doctrine et action, 1789–1804* (Paris, 1961), pp. 220–6.
16 David C. Miller, 'A.G. Camus and the Civil Constitution of the Clergy', *Catholic Historical Review*, LXXVI, 3 (July 1990), p. 490.

presented its plan for reordering the organizational church in France. The 136 bishoprics were to be reduced in number to conform to the newly created departments. Provision was made to have only ten of the former archbishops survive as rechristianed metropolitan bishops, and it was determined that towns with less than 10,000 inhabitants would henceforth support only one *curé*. Parish priests were to be elected by members of each district, and bishops chosen by the electorate of the department, which included non-Catholics. Priests were to receive canonical institution from the bishop, and the bishops from the metropolitans. Confirmation from the 'bishop of Rome' was neither required nor permitted. Finally, before receiving ordination the elected clergymen, in the presence of the community, had to swear to be faithful to the nation, to the laws, and the king, and to defend the constitution established by the nation.[17]

Archbishop Boisgelin of Aix, without referring to the specifics of the proposed civil constitution, pinpointed its fundamental flaw – it had been devised without the consultation of the church. Boisgelin complained that by acting without regard for canonical principle, the assembly had overstepped its authority. The indispensable ecclesiastical input could be acquired either by calling a national council of the Gallican church or by appealing to the pope. Since the assembly was unlikely to convoke an assembly of the clergy, which appeared as a revival of the estates, it had no recourse but to consult the pope. The deputies were unaware that Pius VI had written to Louis XVI, denouncing the growing oppression of the church in France and the decrees on the clergy. Pius also dispatched briefs to the archbishops of Bordeaux and Vienne, who were at the king's side, alerting them of the danger should the king approve these measures. Perhaps to demonstrate his concern for spiritual rather than material matters, the pope halted the collection of taxes from France, although he defended them as an incontestable right.[18] Despite these letters, the civil constitution of the clergy was approved by the assembly on 12 July 1790 and sanctioned by Louis on 22 July, the day before he received the pope's letter condemning it.

Pleading for patience and understanding, the king implored the pope to approve provisionally a number of the articles of the civil constitution pending subsequent modifications to suit Rome. The pope, perceiving he could tolerate none of the articles, sought to avoid a confrontation and proved willing to negotiate. Expecting that the troublesome issues might be resolved by time, he referred the articles to a commission of cardinals, who examined them for the next eight months while Rome remained prudently silent. Even after the cardinals had concluded that all the articles were absolutely unacceptable, Pius hesitated speaking publicly. He hoped that the assembly would revise the law, and feared that the French episcopate might not second his opposition to the measure.

17 Pastor, *History of the Popes*, XL, pp. 133, 146; J. Derek Holmes, *The Triumph of the Holy See: A Short History of the Papacy in the Nineteenth Century* (London, 1978), p. 28.
18 Carlen, *PE*, I, pp. 177–8.

In late September the assembly ordered the implementation of the law, which crystallized the opposition of the French bishops, provoking the first serious rift in the revolution. In October the bishops in the national assembly drafted a statement on the *constitution civile du clerge*, signed by all the bishops in the assembly, save Talleyrand and Gobel, which summarized their opposition and appealed to Rome for assistance and advice. In November the assembly sent troops to Avignon, which had earlier declared union with France, to exert pressure on the pope to accept the civil constitution. Additional pressure ensued in late November when the assembly warned the clergy to swear allegiance to the new ecclesiastical regulations within the next eight days or be deprived of their positions, stipends and pensions. The Rubicon had been passed; a fatal disruption in church–state relations proved inevitable.

Early in January 1791 the assembly sought to have its decree of 27 November enforced with the taking of oaths at parish masses on 2 January 1791, and the roll call of the clergy in the assembly on 4 January. Despite intense pressure and intimidation, barely one-third of the clerics in that body subscribed to the oath, including 107 priests and only two bishops. Half of the country's parish priests likewise declined to take the oath. Among those who refused to do so was Cardinal Bernis, the French representative to Rome, who was recalled. The nuncio Dugani, in turn, was forced to leave Paris. Before Dugani's departure, he transmitted to the French hierarchy the pope's address to the French episcopate of 10 March, which condemned the civil constitution. This long papal brief not only criticized this ecclesiastical legislation, but the entire train of encroachments of the national assembly which violated the concordat, sought to restrict papal jurisdiction, and impinged upon spiritual matters.[19] Some perceived it as a denunciation not only of the revolution, but of modernity.

On 13 April 1791 Pius issued an encyclical *Charitas quae* on the civil oath in France, repeating his absolute condemnation of the civil constitution of the clergy, which he declared heretical, sacrilegious, schismatic, and destructive of papal primacy. He thus rejected the arguments of Armand-Gaston Camus, a major contributor to the civil constitution, that the pope was only the symbolic head of the church.[20] Appreciating the plight of the French monarch, the pope had agreed to have a council of cardinals examine and evaluate the articles. Its conclusions confirmed his own: these articles were absolutely unacceptable.[21]

Louis, who found himself torn between the constraints of his constitutional office and his conscience, sympathized with the pope. On 21 June 1791 the royal family fled from the capital, aided by Swedish officials, but were arrested at Varennes on 25 June 1791 and forced back to Paris. This diminished the prospect of deliverance because the queen's brother, the emperor Leopold, crucial to any intervention of the powers, insisted his participation would be

19 Claudia Carlen, ed., *Quod aliquantum*, in *Papal Pronouncements. A Guide: 1740–1978* (Ann Arbor, MI, 1990), I, p. 18 (hereafter cited as Carlen, *PP*).
20 Miller, 'A.G. Camus', pp. 496–7.
21 *Charitas quae*, 13 April 1991, in *Magnum Bullarium Romanum Continuatio*. IX (Graz, Austria, 1964), pp. 11–19 (hereafter cited as *Mag Bul Rom Cont*).

contingent upon the successful escape of the royal family. The most Leopold would do was to sign, with the king of Prussia, the declaration of Pillnitz of 27 August 1791, declaring that the present situation of the king of France concerned the monarchs of Europe. It neither threatened intervention nor encouraged counter-revolution. In Rome, Pius VI was upset to learn that the assembly had approved the union of Avignon and the Venaissin with France, condemning the annexations as a violation of papal rights and international law.[22]

The opening of a decidedly anticlerical assembly on 1 October 1791, which had less than thirty clergymen out of a membership of 750, all of whom had sworn allegiance to the civil constitution, alarmed the pope. As the remains of Voltaire were escorted into the Pantheon and Honoré Gabriel de Riqueti Mirabeau thundered against religious participation in public functions, the future of the traditional church appeared problematic. Indeed Antonio Capello, the Venetian ambassador in Rome, wrote that in all preceding centuries the position of the Holy See had never been so critical.[23] Perhaps Capello exaggerated, but the danger confronting the church in France was real. At the end of November 1791 a law of proscription was passed providing that priests who refused the oath were to be stripped of their pensions, and if they persisted in their opposition within a week would be placed under special supervision and under suspicion of rebellion. These 'suspects' were liable to expulsion – or worse. On 19 December 1791 Louis vetoed this decree against the nonjuring clergy, arousing anger in the assembly and endangering the position of the monarchy.

The following year witnessed the formation of an Austrian-Prussian alliance against possible French aggression. The deplorable financial and military weakness of the Papal States, as well as the pope's determination to preserve his neutrality, precluded any papal participation in the alliance or the projected Italian confederation. Although neutral, Pius was not inactive. In March he sent agents to Paris to warn the constitutional clergy they risked excommunication unless they retracted and repented, while according extraordinary powers to those bishops who had refused to subscribe to the 'odious oath'.[24] Pius comdemned both the authors and perpetrators of the civil constitution of the clergy and those who had sworn allegiance to it. He was given a graphic if biased account of the outrages committed in the French capital by the two daughters of Louis XV, Marie Adelaide and Victoire Marie, who sought asylum in Rome. The French decision to declare war on Austria on 20 April 1792 was perceived by Rome as providential, and, like Vienna, the papacy hoped the contagion could be contained.

When Paris learned that the pope had dispatched yet another letter (13 June 1792) condemning the schismatic French clergy,[25] rumours of betrayals and invasion swept the capital. There were renewed calls to deal with the enemies

22 *Mag Bull Rom Cont*, IX, pp. 87–91.
23 Oncken, *L'Epoca della Rivoluzione*, p. 219.
24 *TESP*, p. 120; *Mag Bull Rom Cont*, IX, pp. 192–4.
25 *Ubi Lutetiam*, in *TESP*, pp. 121–7.

of the regime, and another campaign against the king and church commenced in the assembly. The agitation was compounded by the manifesto of the duke of Brunswick, the commander of the anti-French coalition, who on 25 July 1792 threatened to put Paris under siege should the royal family be harmed. It fanned popular excitement in Paris. The radicals reacted by establishing a revolutionary commune on 9 August 1792. The following day the Tuilleries was invaded, the royal family interned, and a convention convoked to decide the fate of the monarchy. Once the king was suspended, and the prospect of his veto eliminated, the assembly at the end of August 1792 decreed that all non-juring priests were to leave their country within a fortnight. Non-juring priests were constrained to go underground to avert internment or deportation. In the words of the American ambassador, terror was the order of the day.[26]

Early in September, while elections by universal manhood suffrage were held for the convention, a series of massacres erupted in France, placing pressure on the pope to approve the 'little oath'. On 3 September the latter had been imposed on all French citizens, constraining them to uphold the laws of the state. Pius VI harboured reservations even about this general oath, referring the matter to a special congregation of cardinals.[27] The September massacres took a toll of 1,000 victims, one-fourth of whom were priests, long earmarked as enemies of the regime. These massacres confirmed Rome's conviction that the attempt to establish justice by rejecting Christ and his church only provoked a blood-bath. They also contributed to the selection of a more radical convention, which abolished the monarchy on 21 September 1793, and laicized the *état civil*, making the state rather than the church responsible for the registrations of births, deaths and marriages. Rome received the news quickly by the spectacular system of communications known as the semophore of the Holy See, which involved flashing coded messages from hilltops by means of mirrors by day and flares by night. Pius was saddened to learn that the clergy, regarded as a fifth column in league with the enemy, were guillotined, deported, forced underground or into exile, while a fierce effort ensued to de-Christianize France.

The clerical exodus escalated following the loss of the king's protection. The proclamation of the republic, and the projected replacement of the Christian calendar by a revolutionary one, also provoked a new outpouring of priests to which Pius responded by creating the Opera pia della ospitalità francese to assist the flood of émigrés. Unable to protect the church in France which had been looted and shackled, the pope strove to assist its persecuted clergy.[28]

Pius VI also took measures to prevent the dissemination of revolutionary and republican propaganda within the Papal States, while he welcomed clerical émigrés and a broad range of opponents of the republic, to the consternation of the convention. The pope hesitated doing more, specifying that his

26 Willson, *America's Ambassadors*, p. 59.

27 *Responsa data de consilio selectae congregationis cardinalum diversis quaestionibus propositis a clero Galliarum*, in *Mag Bull Rom Cont*, IX, pp. 312–16.

28 *Ignotae nemini sunt*, 21 November 1792, in *Mag Bull Rom Cont*, IX, pp. 252–3.

government lacked the means to enter the coalition waging war against France. He convoked an extraordinary congregation of the cardinals in October 1792 in response to Vittorio Amadeo's plea for assistance, inviting the other Italian powers to aid Piedmont-Sardinia. This congregation repeated what the pope had earlier revealed, that the Papal States, whose troops numbered less than 10,000, could make neither a military nor a financial contribution to the enterprise. While the Papal States failed to enter the coalition against France, Paris complained that the pope favoured the enemy cause.[29] The French were not entirely mistaken, for Pius was far from neutral in sentiment and disturbed by the threatening tone of communications he received from the convention. Rome feared revolutionary retaliation by the expedition of a French naval force, relying on the *libeccio* or south-west wind which made the landing of sailing ships at its ports difficult in November.

In January 1793 the curia was annoyed by the provocative presence of the French representatives Laflotte and Bassville, who demanded that the tricolour be raised over their ambassadorial residence, and that the pope recognize the republic. The Roman poor or *trasteverini*, who were proud, clannish and fierce, vented their anger on those associated with jacobin ideas. Pius refused recognition of the government which persecuted religion and trampled upon the rights of the Holy See, but the French representatives persisted. On Sunday 13 January 1793 the audacious Frenchmen rode along the Corso, one of the main streets of Rome, in an open carriage, flaunting the republican flag and symbols, provoking the hostility of a mob which attacked the carriage and its passengers. Nicholas Bassville (1753–93), who suffered a knife wound to the stomach, died two days later. Pius, seeking to avoid a confrontation with the French republic, sent his physician to assist Bassville and urged calm, which was restored in mid-January.

Tempers flared when the Eternal City learned of the execution of Louis on 21 January 1793, which Pius condemned in a consistory or formal gathering of cardinals, claiming that the national convention had neither the authority nor the right to pass judgment on their king. At the same time, the pope decried the barbarous hostility towards the church in France which impugned Catholicism.[30] Pius deplored the 'murder' of the French monarch and was inspired by the king's last testament, composed on Christmas Day 1792, which expressed his determination to die within the bosom of the church.

Part of the French population shared the sentiments of their fallen sovereign. The peasantry in western France, devoted to the lower clergy who had long provided them with assistance and leadership, questioned the appropriation of church property, the restrictions imposed on their pastors by the civil constitution, and the imposition of the oath, which the clergy of the Vendée overwhelmingly rejected. Attached to the ritual, symbolism and ceremonies

29 *Consular Relations Between the United States and the Papal States*, ed. Leo Francis Stock (Washington, 1945), p. xxiv.
30 Consistory of 17 June 1793, in *Mag Bull Rom Cont*, IX, pp. 318–27.

of the Roman religion, they resented the subsitution of some nebulous state welfare for the clerical charity they had relied upon over the centuries. Their discontent was inflamed by the arrest of the non-juring clergy which forced the remaining 'good priests' into hiding or exile, resulting in clandestine services and nocturnal processions. The February 1793 decision of the convention to impose a levy of 300,000 men to combat the coalition of the powers ignited the smoldering situation, sparking a full-scale counter-revolutionary movement, with almost the entire countryside having recourse to arms. The peasants, singing hymns and professing their loyalty to the old faith, often wearing rosaries round their necks, hastened to re-establish the Roman religion and the old, comfortable rituals and familiar feasts. Shouting 'bring back the good priests' and 'long live the pope', they commenced a violent religious war against the revolutionary reforms decreed in Paris. A virtual civil war erupted in the Vendée and Brittany. The regime responded by increasing the persecution of the church and its clergy, forcing 30,000–40,000 of the non-juring clergy abroad.

Pius again hastened to assist those who fled the revolutionary violence.[31] At the end of January 1793, the pope invited non-juring French ecclesiastics to Rome for protection, and some 5,000 accepted the invitation. Another 6,000–8,000 fled to Catholic Spain, while another 10,000 found refuge in Protestant England. One small consolation for Rome was that the presence of some 10,000 exiled ecclesiastics in England contributed to an improved image of Catholicism in that Protestant bastion. The foreign situation remained difficult in 1793 as the republic declared war on England and Holland in early February, and Spain in March. As early as 1792, the English dispatched Sir John Cox Hippisley to Rome to co-ordinate their activities with the Holy See, appreciating the moral and political influence of the pope during these tumultuous times.[32] Although the pope's president of the congregation of the army, Cardinal Ercole Consalvi, concluded an understanding with England in opposition to France, Pius VI still proved unwilling to join the powers, refusing to provoke France unnecessarily. Fearing the reaction of the republic, the pope refused to recognize the count of Provence as Louis XVIII. Nonetheless, republicans blamed Rome for the rising in the Vendée, accusing Pius and the non-juring clergy of having inspired the counter-revolution.

The convention in France clamoured for satisfaction. Angered by the pope's opposition to the civil constitution of the clergy, his alleged encouragement of the counter-revolution in the Vendée, and the 'outrages' committed in Rome against its representatives, the committee of public safety presented an ultimatum. It demanded the dispatch of a nuncio to Paris to apologize for Bassville's murder, permission to place republican symbols on the French consulate in the Holy City, the banishment of French émigrés, both lay and clerical, immediate punishment for the instigators of the riots of 12–13 January 1793, indemnity

31 *TESP*, p. 128.
32 Cardinal Aiden Gasquet, *Great Britain and the Holy See, 1792–1806: A Chapter in the History of Diplomatic Relations between England and Rome* (Rome, 1919), p. 15.

for the victims of the 'riots', and finally the restoration of the French art academy by the Roman government. Pius uncategorically rejected these conditions.

In France, Robespierre, the Rousseau of revolutionary Paris, unleashed the terror as an emanation of virtue, calling for the liberation of the innate goodness of the people from the clutches of clerical oppression. He urged his countrymen to worship the Supreme Being in a natural religion which would welcome all believers. Its temple was the universe, its theme virtue, its programme the brotherhood of all free people. Dechristianization proceeded apace, with the implementation of the republican calendar, the suppression of Catholic religious observances, and the celebration of the feast of reason in Notre Dame in November 1793, as an anticlerical, Jacobin substitute for Christianity. The American ambassador, who viewed the spectacle of adoring masses worshipping a cross between 'an opera singer' and a scantily clad 'harlot', decried the attempt to overthrow the Christian religion by rendering it ridiculous.[33] At the end of November 1793 all churches were closed. In the countryside, the campaign against the nobility and the traditional clergy often coincided as the pews of the nobility were ripped out of churches and some tombs desecrated.[34] Proscribed as suspects, priests and nobles perished en masse upon scaffolds hastily erected throughout France. Still, Pius refused to be drawn into war. In an encyclical of 31 July 1793, Pius condemned the alleged 'manifesto of the Christian and royal army to the people of France'.[35]

The execution of Robespierre and his followers on 28 July 1794 (ninth of Thermidor) did little to console the pontiff or relieve pressure on the Papal States. In Paris, the convention formally ended the payment of clerical salaries. Although the radical dictatorship of Robespierre was replaced by the constitution of the year III (5 October 1795) which created the government of the Directory, Rome found little cause to rejoice. The new government disavowed the religion of the Supreme Being championed by the fallen dictator, but proceeded to replace it with a radical atheism. The persecution of the church continued as the new regime imposed another oath on the clergy, refused to deal with ecclesiastics, and constrained the nuncio to be called count rather than archbishop. Early in 1795, a decree prohibited the display of religious symbols in public, providing for a virtual separation of church and state in France. To make matters worse, the coalition against France was considerably weakened in 1795 when Tuscany, Prussia and Spain all sued for peace. During the negotiations for the treaty of Basel (1795), the Prussians suggested the suppression of ecclesiastical properties in Germany, ignoring the opposition of the papacy. The events of 1794–95 represented a series of further humiliations for the head of the church and the Papal States. Others appeared on the horizon as Italy succumbed to the French invasion and was exposed to the revolutionary *triennio*, 1796–99.

33 Willson, *America's Ambassadors*, p. 59.
34 John Markoff, 'Violence, Emancipation, and Democracy: The Countryside and the French Revolution', *American Historical Review*, XI, 2 (April 1995), p. 371.
35 *TESP*, pp. 128–30.

Napoleon Bonaparte (1769–1821), the youngest general in the French army, who assumed command of the army of Italy in 1796, was encouraged by the Directory to undermine both the temporal and spiritual authority of the papacy. In a dispatch of 3 February 1796, the general was invited to consider striking Rome, the centre of fanaticism. Although Napoleon promised to free the Roman people from their slavery, and to polish-off the 'old fox', he moved cautiously. In the peace of Campo Formio with Austria (1797) he obtained the left bank of the Rhine for France, compensating the German princes at the expense of ecclesiastical principalities and properties on the right bank, without consulting the pope. The French overran and plundered the papal provinces of Ravenna, Ferrara and Bologna, imprisoning the papal legates. By the winter of 1796, the French pressed south to Ancona, threatening Rome itself. Pius VI, who refused to recognize the revolutionary government of France, negotiated with it through the Spanish envoy to the Vatican.

The Papal States, which had assumed a definitive form in the middle of the eighth century, when the territories *de facto* controlled by the popes were formally conferred on the papacy by the Frankish kings, were seriously menaced by their French successors. The terms imposed by Napoleon in the armistice of Bologna were harsh, limiting the pope's temporal dominion. The agreement undermined Rome's financial basis, which provided the revenue for the papacy to fulfil its spiritual mission. Nonetheless, the Directory demanded more, pressing Napoleon to overturn the papacy, replacing it with a republic in Rome.

Under the armistice, Pius had to abandon the legations of Bologna and Ferrara to the French as well as the citadel of Ancona.[36] A tribute of 21,000,000 *scudi* was imposed, supplemented by 100 works of art – paintings, statues, busts and vases – as well as 500 precious manuscripts. Roman ports were to be open to the French fleet, while closed to enemy shipping. Pius was finally instructed to send a plenipotentiary to Paris, without delay, to conclude a formal peace, and to apologize for the 'murder' of French citizens in the Eternal City. The pope reluctantly accepted these onerous terms, dipping into the treasure of the Castel Sant' Angelo to meet the first instalment, because the armistice preserved part of the temporal power and left Rome in his hands. To quiet criticism of his alleged support of the counter-revolution in the Vendée, in July 1796 Pius issued a brief to French Catholics, urging them to remain loyal to their government while recognizing the Republic. However, the Directory's insistence that Pius revoke all the papal bulls issued since 1789, reversing its condemnation of the revolutionary religious legislation, and most notably that against the civil constitution of the clergy, met Roman resistance.

In September a frustrated Pius declared the armistice broken, suspended the shipment of booty to France, and created a citizen's army to protect the capital. Napoleon responded in January 1797, declaring war on what remained of the Papal States. Moving his forces south against only token resistance, the

36 *Consular Relations Between the United States and the Papal States*, p. xxiv.

French occupied Faenza and then Ancona, where a republic was established, while plundering and violating the shrine to Mary at Loreto, sending the venerated image of the Virgin to the museum of Egyptian antiques at Paris. 'The treasure of Loreto amounted to three million francs, they left about one million behind. I am sending you in addition the Madonna and all the relics', Napoleon wrote to the directors. 'I will grant the Pope peace provided he cedes Bologna, Ferrara, Urbino, and Ancona, and that he pays us three million for the treasure of Loreto and fifteen million that he owed us on the armistice treaty.'[37]

Panic-stricken, Pius VI sent a delegation to Napoleon at Tolentino where peace was concluded on 19 February 1797. The twenty-six articles of the treaty confirmed the harsh conditions of the armistice of Bologna, and demanded an additional 30 million *lire* indemnity, as well as 800 more cavalry horses. By its terms, the pope had to revoke any support, private or public, for the armed coalition against France and dismiss his newly enrolled troops. At the same time, he agreed to bar the ships of those states warring against the French republic from his ports while promising that the Holy See would provide compensation for the 'murder' of Bassville and release all political prisoners.[38] Pius had to renounce sovereignty over Avignon and the Venaissin county, ceding the legations of Bologna, Ferrara and the Romagna as well. To prevent the French from penetrating beyond the legations, Pius belatedly accepted the terms of Tolentino, the first pontiff to renounce by treaty part of the temporal patrimony. Napoleon, having assessed the depth of papal intransigence on religious issues and matters concerning its spiritual mission, did not press for a retraction of the condemnation of the civil constitution of the clergy.

The Directory desired more, demanding the disappearance of the temporal power. Napoleon, who inwardly questioned the policy Paris pursued toward Rome, sent assurances that it was only a matter of time before the papacy collapsed. 'In my opinion Rome cannot survive following the loss of Bologna, Ferrara, the Romagna and the 30 million lire indemnity we have imposed', the general wrote to his government. 'This ancient mechanism will self destruct.'[39] Nonetheless the general, who appreciated the influence of Rome and the traditional faith in the lives of the people of the peninsula, issued orders that religious customs and the peaceful clergy in areas under French control remain unmolested.[40]

Despite the confident expectation of the papacy's impending destruction, the treaty of Tolentino did not lead to its disappearance, nor did it end the conflict between the Directory and Pius VI. Paris deplored Rome's survival of the débâcle of Tolentino, while the Romans resented French arrogance and

37 Napoleon I, *The Corsican: A Diary of Napoleon's Life in his Own Words*, ed. R.M. Johnston (Boston, 1910), p. 57.

38 Treaty of Peace between Pope and French Republic, 19 February 1797, in *Mag Bull Rom Cont*, X, pp. 65–9.

39 Oncken, *L'Epoca della Rivoluzione*, p. 1134.

40 Napoleon Bonaparte, *Correspondance de Napoleon Ier* (Paris, 1859), II, nos 1036 and 1458.

outright looting. Subsequently the Marchese Massimi was despatched to Paris as chargé d'affaires, while Napoleon secured the appointment of his brother Joseph as ambassador to Rome. Although Napoleon hoped to use Joseph's influence to extract a papal brief facilitating the religious pacification of France, relations between Rome and Paris deteriorated. On 28 December 1797 a group of patriots took part in an anti-papal, pro-French demonstration. Dispersed by pontifical troops, they sought to regroup before the French embassy in the Corsini alla Lungora Palace. It was there that general Duphot, who was to marry Napoleon's sister, was killed in a skirmish by a corporal of the pontifical guard. Joseph fled Rome, and in January 1798 Napoleon ordered General Alexander Bethier to march on Rome to make the Papal State pay for the 'murder of Duphot'.

On 10 February 1798 the French entered Rome without opposition, occupying the Castel Sant' Angelo. Shortly thereafter, on 15 February, the anniversary of the pope's election, Berthier encouraged the deposition of the pope as head of state and the proclamation of a Roman republic. A systematic plunder ensued, which spared neither the Vatican Palace nor the apartments and the person of the pontiff. The virtual vendetta against the aged pope was orchestrated in Paris by the director Larevillere Lepaux, who sought the destruction of the spiritual as well as the temporal power of the papacy, and the triumph of the Theophilanthropist church, based on the philosophic outlook of Voltaire and the English freethinkers. On 20 February the ailing pope was brusquely removed from his capital by the French, dragged out of his state to the Augustinian convent of Siena, where he was placed under house arrest.

In June 1798 Pius was ordered out of Siena and dragged to the Carthusian monastery on the outskirts of Florence, where he remained some nine months. While here, Pius issued a bull on the election of his successor, replacing that of January 1797, and urging the college of cardinals to select a successor with minimum delay. The dean of the college, in conjunction with three or four of the most respected dignitaries, were to settle the time and place of the election, which was to be held without the traditional ceremonies in the territory of a Catholic ruler, and select the new pope by a two-thirds majority. No sooner was the bull issued, than the impending formation of a second coalition led the French to abandon Rome, which fell to the Neapolitans in November 1798. The occupation proved of short duration, with the French returning to Rome by the end of the year, pushing on to Naples in January 1799, where they established the precarious Parthenopean republic.

The French declared war not only against Austria and Russia, but the grand duchy of Tuscany as well, so the pope's residence outside of Florence was threatened. At the end of March 1799 he was thrown out of Tuscany, and dragged across the snow-covered Appenines to Bologna where he arrived in a delerium. In April the success of the Austro-Russian forces led the French to remove the old and ailing pope to Turin, and then across the border into France. The 82-year-old pontiff reached the fortress of Valence in mid-July, sick and dying, unable to be moved any further. While on his deathbed on

23 August 1799, he permitted the bishops of Spain and Spanish America the right to dispose of church property in order to help pay for the public debt.[41] He died while still a prisoner on 29 August 1799, ending his pontificate of twenty-four years and six months – the longest since that of Peter. The death of Pius VI in exile and captivity, the first pope in centuries to meet this fate, and his burial in a common graveyard, seemed to portend a fatal crisis for both the spiritual and temporal power of the papacy.

41 *Quoties animo*, 23 August 1799, in *Mag Bull Rom Cont*, IX, pp. 191–3.

CHAPTER 3

The papacy and Napoleonic France: from compromise to confrontation, 1800–1814

In 1799 Pius VI died in captivity, and the papacy seemed doomed to follow. In Paris, on the 18th of Brumaire, 9 November 1799, France threw herself into the arms of the young general who had conquered Italy and Egypt as Napoleon's *coup d'état* overturned the Directory, establishing the Consulate which placed power in his hands as the first consul.

Bonaparte, suspicious of ideologues,[1] revealed a more accommodating attitude towards the church than his predecessors. Fanaticism, he preached, was the child of persecution.[2] Concluding that the consolidation of his power could only follow a reconciliation with the Holy See, one of his first decrees was to prescribe belated funeral honours for the unfortunate Pius VI. Napoleon indicated that the honour of France required that it 'pay the highest marks of consideration to a man who occupied one of the loftiest dignities on earth'.[3] Shortly thereafter he reopened Catholic churches in France while allowing some émigré priests to return. Napoleon believed Catholic France would appreciate him more as 'saviour' than 'destroyer' of the Holy See. Napoleon also issued orders that the inhabitants of the troubled Vendée be free to practice their religion and their priests be required to take no oath except one of fidelity to the constitution.[4]

As Napoleon laboured to consolidate his power in Paris, at the end of November 1799 the cardinals of the church journeyed to Habsburg-controlled Venice for the forthcoming conclave.[5] With Rome under Neapolitan control and the legations of Bologna, Ferrara and the Romogna under Austrian rule, prospects for the Papal States remained dubious. The Austrian monarch had

1 *Memoirs of Prince Metternich, 1773–1815*, ed. Prince Richard Metternich-Winneburg, trans. Mrs Alexander Napier (New York, 1970), I, 78.

2 Barry E. O'Meara, ed., *Napoleon in Exile, or a Voice from St Helena* (New York, 1822), I, p. 219.

3 M. Adolphe Thiers, *History of the Consulate and the Empire of France under Napoleon* (Philadelphia, 1861), I, p. 55.

4 Napoleon Bonaparte, *The Corsican, A Diary of Napoleon's Life in his Own Words*, ed. R.M. Johnston (Boston, 1910), p. 121.

5 Ercole Consalvi, *Memorie sul conclave tenuto in Venezia*, in Lajos Pasztor, 'Le "Memorie sul conclave tenuto in Venezia" di Ercole Consalvi', *Archivum Historiae Pontificiae*, III (1965), pp. 239–308.

provided the site for the 34-member conclave, and most of the funds for the arrangements, while his military forces occupied papal territory as far south as Rome. Consequently the emperor's influence was considerable. Indeed the early favourite of the conclave, Cardinal Carlo Bellisomi, bishop of Cesena, was blocked by the Austrians who preferred Cardinal Mattei, the archbishop of Ferrara, and signer of the treaty of Tolentino ceding the legations.[6]

When it became apparent early in 1800 that neither Bellisomi nor Mattei could garner sufficient votes for election, a compromise candidate was sought. Weeks of intrigue within the conclave, and diplomatic manoeuvring outside, paved the way for the Benedictine monk, the moderate bishop of Imola of the noble family of Chiaramonti, to be elected on 14 March 1800 after a seven-month interregnum.[7] In deference to his predecessor and protector, the 58-year-old Gregorio Luigi Barnaba, count Chiaramonti of Cesena, chose the name Pius VII. More favourably disposed to the new order than most of the cardinals, he was considered best able to confront the precarious condition of the church and papacy. Supposedly he favoured conciliation with the revolution to preserve Christian France, which angered Vienna. Indeed rumour circulated that Austrian pique prevented his coronation in St Mark's.

Chiaramonti, in his Christmas sermon in the cathedral of Imola in 1797, had preached that revolutionary ideas were not necessarily in conflict with the church or the gospels, and that liberty, fraternity, equality and democracy could be reconciled with Christianity. He was one of the earliest proponents of rapprochement between the church and the revolutionary age. Understandably his pragmatic message pleased the French, who printed and circulated it throughout northern Italy.[8] Later in 1799 he urged the people of Imola, incorporated into the Cisalpine republic, to accept the *de facto* governing authority and preserve the peace. Once pope, his selection of Ercole Consalvi as his acting secretary of state, rather than the pro-Austrian Cardinal Flangini, and his decision to return to Rome directly, displayed his determination to preserve his freedom of action *vis-à-vis* both friends and enemies. Shortly thereafter he elevated Consalvi to the cardinalate.[9]

Recognizing that his subjects had cause for complaint, which was exploited by those scheming for revolutionary change, the new pope initiated administrative reforms.[10] In his first allocution to the cardinals, on 28 March 1800,

6 Charles van Duerm, *Un peu plus de lumière sur le conclave de Venise et sur le commencement du pontificat de Pie VII, 1799–1800* (Louvain, 1896), pp. 27–30.

7 Jean Leflon, *Pie VII. Des Abbayes bénédictines à la Papauté* (Paris, 1958), I, pp. 570–4.

8 J. Derek Holmes, *The Triumph of the Holy See: A Short History of the Papacy in the Nineteenth Century* (London, 1978), p. 41; Owen Chadwick, *The Popes and European Revolution* (Oxford, 1981), p. 455; E.E.Y. Hales, *The Catholic Church in the Modern World* (Garden City, NY, 1958), p. 54; Margaret M. O'Dwyer, *The Papacy in the Age of Napoleon and the Restoration: Pius VII, 1800–1823* (Lanham, MD, 1985), pp. 24–5; Vittorio E. Giuntella, 'Cristianesimo e democrazia in Italia al tramonto del Settecento', *Rassegna Storica del Risorgimento*, XLII (1955), p. 291.

9 *Mag Bull Rom Cont*, XI, pp. 33–4.

10 Reform decree of 31 October 1800, in *Bullarii romani continuatio*, ed. Andreas Barberi (Rome, 1835–57) (hereafter cited as *Bull Rom Cont*), *Pius VII, annum primum ad tertium* (Rome, 1846), pp. 49–79.

Pius predicted the church would overcome its tribulations. Alluding to the chilling political uncertainty and the trials of Pius VI, the new pope foresaw the eventual triumph of the church, which would survive the onslaught of its enemies and the ideological attacks upon its doctrines. An olive branch was offered to the French as Pius revealed his heartache for their suffering, imploring peace for the church.[11]

These words were not lost on the victor of the battle of Marengo of 14 June 1800, who pushed the Austrians out of Italy and sought harmony with Rome. Having shunned command of the forces in the Vendée with the gibe that it was fit for a general of the gendarmerie, while showing himself sensitive to Muslim convictions during the Egyptian campaign, Napoleon remained unwilling to sanction religious persecution. 'To-day, whatever our Paris atheists may say', he wrote home, 'I am going in full state to the *Te Deum*, that is to be sung in the cathedral of Milan.'[12] Perceiving the religious revolution in France a catastrophic failure, he announced to the faithful in the *duomo* of Milan that the French shared their religion, implying that church–state relations would be normalized. Five days after the momentous battle which re-established Gallic hegemony in Italy, Napoleon confided to Cardinal Martiniana, the archbishop of Vercelli, his proposal for commencing negotiations with the pope.

Sensing that the French had wearied of the religious conflict, Napoleon favoured a restoration of the traditional faith, considering religion a 'sort of inoculation or vacine' at once satisfying the public's need for the supernatural while safeguarding society from 'charlatans and magicians'. Motivated by the double desire of preserving order in the state while satisfying the moral needs of his people, Napoleon planned to restore Catholicism to its former position but without its political attributes. Napoleon confided to the clergy of Milan that he considered Roman Catholicism the only faith that could assure happiness to a well-ordered society and strengthen the foundations of good government. Expressing his resolve to return Catholicism to its proper place, he complained that the unfortunate treatment of the late Pius VI was orchestrated by 'the wretched intrigues of his advisers' on the one hand and 'the cruel policy of the Directoire' on the other. He pledged to remove every obstacle in the way of reconciliation between France and the papacy.[13]

Pius, for his part, moved by the prospect of restoring millions of souls to the bosom of the church, immediately seconded the idea, dispatching Monsignor Spina, one of Pius VI's companions in captivity, and the Servite Father Carlo Caselli, to negotiate, first at Vercelli and Turin, and later at Paris.[14] Napoleon, recognizing the path to domestic tranquillity required the

11 *Diu satis videmur*, 15 May 1800, in *Mag Bull Rom Cont*, XI, pp. 21–6; also see *TESP*, pp. 139–46; Erasmo Pistolesi, *Vita del Sommo Pontefice Pio VII* (Rome, 1824), I, pp. 76–80; Giuseppe Hergenrother, *Storia universale della Chiesa*, ed. G.P. Kirsch, trans P. Enrico Rosa (Florence, 1911), p. 362.

12 Bonaparte, *The Corsican*, p. 140.

13 Ibid., pp. 135, 227.

14 A. Boulay de la Meurthe, ed., *Documents sur la négociation du concordat et sur les autres rapports de la France avec le Saint-Siège en 1800 et à 1801* (Paris, 1891–1905), I, pp. 21–6.

re-establishment of Christianity in France, pointed to the Vendée as proof positive. He concluded that the concessions to the church and the restoration of the faith had been crucial in terminating the war in that troubled region. Many in Paris did not share his vision, including the foreign minister Talleyrand, an apostate bishop, whose temperament led him to champion irreligious causes, and Bishop Henri Gregoire, the acknowledged leader of the constitutional clergy.

Personally indifferent to religious practice, Napoleon was far from irreligious, perceiving in the heart of humanity an unshakeable belief in God that philosophy could neither undermine nor eradicate. If he governed the Jews, he confided, he would rebuild the temple of Solomon.[15] Since society required inequality, and since such inequality could not be supported without religion, religion was absolutely necessary for the governance of state and society. Napoleon boasted that he had pacified the Vendée by becoming a Catholic, by embracing Islam had established himself in Egypt, and by becoming ultramontane had won over public opinion in Italy.[16] He considered Catholicism, with its dogma and hierarchy, the form of worship most conducive to the preservation of tranquillity, viewing Protestantism as a source of disunity and disagreement. The deism of the *philosophes* he ridiculed as sheer speculation. The freemasons he derided as a set of imbeciles who met periodically to perform ridiculous fooleries. Many of Napoleon's advisers discouraged the conclusion of a concordat with the papacy, which they opposed as intimately linked with the Bourbons and aristocratic society. The general discarded their objections, convinced that the advantages of an agreement with Rome far outweighed the dangers.

Negotiation commenced in earnest in November 1800 on Napoleon's three basic conditions: the reinstitution of the church with a new episcopacy, the state assumption of the clergy's salaries, and the clerical renunciation of former ecclesiastical properties. While Napoleon was primarily motivated by political considerations, Pius was mainly moved by religious convictions. The pope sought to strengthen the position of the church in France and in Europe, creating twenty-seven new cardinals in February 1801.[17] In the negotiations the pope sought to end the schism in France, reconciling the Roman religion and the revolution, with both sides ignoring the thorny question of the truncated temporal power of the papacy.

The opening of the new year produced a number of stumbling blocks, including Rome's desire to have Catholicism proclaimed the religion of state and the French reluctance to make such a concession. No less troubling was Napoleon's insistence on the resignation of the entire existing episcopacy. The first consul sought to break the impasse by despatching emissaries to Rome in March 1801, instructing them to treat the pontiff as if he had 200,000 bayonets

15 André Latreille, *L'Église catholique et la Révolution française. Le pontificat de Pie VI et la crise française (1775–1779)* (Paris, 1946), II, p. 225; O'Meara, *Napoleon in Exile*, I, p. 273.
16 Bonaparte, *The Corsican*, pp. 144–5, 273.
17 *Mag Bull Rom Cont*, XI, pp. 104–5.

at his disposal. After intense bandying in which the patient Consalvi was pitted against the worldly Talleyrand, and several all-night sessions conducted under the threat that the talks would be terminated, on 15 July 1801 a bare bones agreement of two declarations and seventeen articles was approved.

In the declarations which formed a crucial preamble, the French republic recognized the Catholic Apostolic and Roman religion as that of the great majority of the French people. Article 1 provided for freedom of worship in conformity with police regulations, while articles six and seven required bishops and priests to swear an oath of loyalty to the government. Article 12 assured that property not confiscated during the revolution would be placed at the disposal of the bishops, while in article 13 the pope promised not to disturb those who had acquired confiscated ecclesiastical property. Other articles arranged for the reorganization of the church, providing for sixty dioceses in place of more than a hundred which had earlier prevailed. Provision was made for the resignation of all the existing bishops; their replacements were to be named by the first consul while canonical institution was reserved to the pope. The new bishops, in turn, were to appoint parish priests from a list approved by the government.[18]

The problem of the oath, a bone of contention in the implementation of the civil constitution of the clergy, was resolved by returning to the format employed under the old regime. In turn, the state promised to pay the salaries of the clergy. Perhaps the general hoped that the payment of clerical salaries would subordinate them to civil service status and render them less likely to resist his government's policies. The Roman faith was to enjoy full freedom of public worship and allowed to establish cathedral chapters, and its adherents permitted to create foundations on its behalf. The pardon of married priests and their reconciliation with the church was accommodated by indulgence, with Rome showing itself inclined to forgive acknowledged faults. The concordat did not mention religious orders which Napoleon and the French negotiators considered superseded and unlikely to be resurrected. This omission, coupled with the provision which granted the church liberty, would create problems in the future.

Forty days had been allowed for the governments to ratify the accord, leading Consalvi to hasten home to secure its passage. Napoleon wanted approval by 15 August 1801 so he could make nominations for bishops and archbishops at once. In mid-August 1801 Pius VII, following consultation with the sacred college, ratified the concordat and issued two encyclicals to the bishops of France, *La Chiesa di Gesù* and *Tam multa*. In the first, he related the history and rationale for the agreement, outlining its principal clauses. In the latter, he required the resignation of the entire hierarchy in the French lands, so that new appointments might be made in accordance with article 5 of the

18 The text of the concordat will be found in *Bull Rom Cont. Pius VIII*, XI, pp. 175–7. A copy of the concordat of 1801 will be found in E.E.Y. Hales, *Revolution and Papacy* (Notre Dame, 1966), pp. 298–300.

concordat.[19] This extraordinary exercise of papal power represented a death blow to Gallicanism. The accord secured for the pope not only the right to invest bishops, which he had previously possessed, but under certain conditions to depose them, which in France represented an innovation.

Neither Paris nor Rome appeared totally satisfied with the agreement, which terminated one of the most frightful persecutions ever confronted by the Catholic church. Conservative Catholic critics charged that while Pius VI sacrificed his throne to save the faith, Pius VII sacrificed the faith to save his throne. It was less than an objective assessment and misrepresented the pope's motivation. Pius VII was willing to take risks in settling church–state relations in France, just as he was willing to move towards free trade in his states.[20]

A realist in religious as well as economic issues, Pius appreciated the positive results obtained by the concordat of 1801. These included the re-establishment of the Catholic hierarchy in France,[21] the restoration of Catholic worship, and the end to the schism, while witnessing the virtual dismemberment of the remains of the constitutional church and the abandonment of the religious innovations of the revolutionaries. The centralization it sanctioned in the French church clearly reinforced the position of the papacy. Napoleon, for his part, inherited the prerogatives of the monarchy *vis-à-vis* the church and the clergy. No concessions were made to Rome regarding education and marriage, while the church ceased functioning as an estate capable of challenging the government. Furthermore, Napoleon achieved the laicization of sovereign power while depriving the royalist opposition of the most potent weapon in their arsenal.

Although Napoleon liked to say that he believed all that the church believed, he determined that in his state no religion should predominate, assuring liberty of conscience to Protestants, Jews, Muslims, Deists, as well as Catholics. He resented clerical attempts to monopolize dominion over humanity's mind, while reserving to the state dominion of the body.[22] Priests, like other ministers, were not to meddle in education, marriage and burials, confining themselves to spiritual affairs. He would not tolerate Jesuits, whom he branded the most dangerous of societies, or any other religious order. While tolerating individuals who were monks in their hearts, he would not permit any of their organizations to preserve a public presence. He equated celibacy with fanaticism, a mechanism whereby the court of Rome would 'rivet the chains of Europe by preventing the cleric from being a citizen'.[23]

Early in 1802 the rapprochement in church–state relations was reflected in Napoleon's permission for the remains of Pius VI to be returned to Rome. In April 1802 the French legislature approved the concordat, along with the organic articles or regulations for its implementation. The latter, organized

19 For the Pope's letter of 15 August 1801 on the reorganization of the Church, see *Bull Rom Cont. Pius VII*, XI, pp. 49–79, as well as Carlen, *PP*, I, p. 19.

20 Pius VII's *motu proprio* on free trade of 11 March 1801, in *Bull Rom Cont. Pius VII*, XI, pp. 109–29.

21 *Bull Rom Cont. Pius VII*, XI, pp. 245–51.

22 Bonaparte, *The Corsican*, p. 158; O'Meara, *Napoleon in Exile*, I, pp. 37, 114, 122.

23 Bonaparte, *The Corsican*, p. 228.

into four groups consisting of seventy-seven articles, were designed to preserve Gallican rights *vis-à-vis* Rome. Most of the measures in this lengthy appendix dealt with the relationship of the state to the Catholic church, establishing control of the former over the latter, while restricting the rights of the Holy See in France. Papal bulls, briefs, decrees, and even legates could not be received in France without governmental approval. Under its terms, bishops were forbidden to leave their dioceses and obliged to submit the rules of their seminaries to state authorities. They also had to accept the four Gallican declarations of 1682, which curtailed the powers of the French church while limiting the power of the pope therein.

In May 1802, while announcing the implementation of the concordat and the restoration of the Catholic religion in France, Pius praised Napoleon's efforts in achieving the religious rapprochement, but deplored the organic articles as contrary to the constitution of the church, and called for their modification.[24] Despite the flaws in the agreement, the concordat was destined to regulate church–state relations in France for over a century. 'My intention was to render everything belonging to the state and the constitution, purely civil and independent of any religion', Bonaparte later explained. 'I wished to deprive the priests of all influence and power in civil affairs; and to oblige them to confine themselves to their own spiritual matters, and meddle with nothing else.'[25] It was easier said than done.

Although Pius did not intend the agreement with France to serve as a model, its impact loomed large, as states the size of Lucca sought similar concessions. Bonaparte, who secured a peace with England in March 1802, was named consul for life in August. Declared president of the Cisalpine republic, which was rechristened the Italian republic, Bonaparte desired to regulate church–state relations in Italy. Despite the inclination of the pope to settle ecclesiastical matters in Italy unilaterally, the Vatican was constrained to sign a concordat. After bitter haggling, a 22-article agreement was concluded in September 1803. Proclaiming Catholicism the religion of state, and promising that all litigious questions would be resolved in conformity with church discipline, it proved more favourable to Rome than the French accord.[26] Following on the heels of the French concordat, it reinforced the conviction that religious affairs could only be resolved in consultation with the Holy See.

Napoleon's policies also influenced the church in Germany. By the peace of Luneville of 9 February 1801, the German empire ceded all of the ecclesiastical possessions on the left bank of the Rhine to France, confirming the 1797 spoilation of the church's ecclesiastical properties in Germany. Furthermore, the papacy had to compensate secular sovereigns who lost territory there, by surrendering many of the ecclesiastical principalities on the right bank as well,

24 Cardinal Jean Caprara, *Concordat, et recueil des bulles et brefs de N.S.P., le Pape Pie VII, sur les affaires actuelles de l'Église de France* (Liege, 1802), pp. 23–31.

25 O'Meara, *Napoleon in Exile*, I, p. 114.

26 Concordat between Pius VII and Italian Republic, 16 September 1803, in *Bull Rom Cont. Pius VII*, XII, pp. 59–62.

losing three electorates and a considerable income. Paradoxically, Napoleon's secularization of the ecclesiastical principalities of Germany, deplored by Pius at the time, worked to Rome's advantage by impoverishing the anti-Roman bishops of the Rhineland, weakening their Febronian sentiments, and constraining them to look to the pope for protection.

At the end of April 1804 the empire was proposed in France. Already perceiving himself as the heir of Charlemagne, Napoleon appreciated the symbolism of papal participation in the ceremony, proposing it to Cardinal Jean Caprara in May. In September Napoleon personally appealed to the pope to provide the sanction of religion by attending his consecration and coronation. He 'modestly' asked Pius to provide another proof of his interest in him and his great nation by participating in 'one of the most important events recorded in the annals of humanity'.[27]

In Rome, his uncle, Cardinal Joseph Fesch, one of the three newly designated French cardinals, now French ambassador, pressed Pius to accede to the request, citing the opportunity for Rome to engender goodwill. The pope, aware that his position in Rome was dependent upon Napoleon's sufferance, sought the emperor's support in Italy as well as his assistance in the normalization of relations with Russia, where he had earlier restored the Society of Jesus.[28] Pius favoured accepting Napoleon's invitation, but sought the advice and consent of the cardinals. Only after a majority of those polled approved the voyage, did he forward a positive response to Paris. At the end of October 1804, on the eve of his departure, the pope revealed he was venturing to France out of gratitude to Napoleon, who had restored the church in France, while nourishing the hope that his visit would redound to the welfare of the faith. Although the advantages to be derived from this gesture of goodwill were speculative, the disadvantages of offending the powerful and vindictive Corsican were obvious.

On 2 November 1804, accompanied by a retinue of prominent cardinals and bishops, and over 100 prelates, the pope departed Rome. He left his secretary of state, Consalvi, to preside over the administration of the Papal States, with precise instructions in case he should die or be imprisoned while away. Pius VII recalled the tribulations of his predecessor Pius VI, and perhaps intuitively nourished a premonition of his own future incarceration. Napoleon complained of the slow pace of the travellers, insisting that the pope had to accelerate his journey for he could not delay the coronation beyond 2 December 1804.[29] Pius reached Fontainebleu on 25 November 1804, where he was greeted by Napoleon. Everywhere Pius was thronged by crowds of the faithful who rendered him homage. Three days later, escorted by the French ruler, he entered Paris, receiving a rapturous reception in the capital of the revolution, denounced by conservative Catholics as the 'blasphemous centre of atheism'. Although the pope and his secretary of state pressed for the details of the

27 Bonaparte, *The Corsican*, p. 188.
28 *Restitutio societatis Jesu in regno Russiaco*, in *Mag Bull Rom Cont*, XI, pp. 106–8.
29 Bonaparte, *The Corsican*, p. 191.

ceremony, these were belatedly revealed. Nonetheless, the pope knew beforehand that he would only anoint the emperor, and Bonaparte would crown himself in the 2 December ceremony in Notre Dame.[30] Pius prevailed upon the future emperor to marry formally his long-time companion Josephine Beauharnais, presiding over the marriage ceremony before their coronation.

Following the coronation, Pius lingered in Paris until the following spring, seeking to resolve a number of outstanding church–state issues in France and the lands controlled by Napoleon. All the papal attempts to modify the organic articles in France proved abortive, although Napoleon promised to replace the revolutionary calendar with the Christian one. Since Napoleon had already planned to do so for his own political reasons, this 'concession' cost him nothing. To be sure, the papal visit proved a public relations triumph, manifested in the popular demonstrations and devotion displayed as his entourage visited the sites of the capital. Napoleon, albeit the self-proclaimed protector of the Catholic church, remained aloof and inaccessible, preoccupied with the reorganization of France and the other territories he dominated, and distracted by the prospect of England forming yet another coalition against him. Nor did the emperor appreciate sharing the adulation of the masses, even with the pope. He evaded the pope's pleas to confess his sins by claiming he was too busy at the moment, promising to do so when he was older.[31]

In March Napoleon transformed the Italian republic into the Italian kingdom, and in mid-March assumed the iron crown of Lombardy in the *duomo*, uttering the traditional phrase, '*Dio me l'ha data; guai a chi la tocca!*'. Pius permitted his legate, Cardinal Jean Caprara, to perform the ceremony on the emperor's promise that Rome would receive good news about the position of the church in the kingdom of Italy, but his actions betrayed his words. Pius objected to the French civil code, with its provision for divorce, being introduced in the Italian kingdom, which included part of the former Papal States. Pius considered its implementation incompatible with the proclamation of Catholicism as the religion of state.

Early in April the pope began the long and arduous journey home, passing roads lined with the faithful imploring the papal blessing, and going through those provinces in his state where his government had recently approved agricultural concessions and innovations.[32] He entered his capital on 16 May 1805, after an absence of more than half a year. In an address to the sacred college on 26 June, he reviewed the fruits of his venture, pointing to the imperial funds earmarked for seminaries and the missions, improvements in the salaries and pensions of the clergy, the repair of churches, as well as a renewal of funds for the maintenance of the Lateran Basilica in Rome. He reported that during his visit to Florence, he received and accepted the submission of Scipione de

30 See the correspondence of Cardinals Pacca and Gabrieli on the pope's visit to France for the coronation of Napoleon, Archivio Segreto del Vaticano (hereafter cited as ASV), Archivio Particolare Pio IX, Oggetti Vari, *n.* 909, *fascicolo* 3.
31 O'Meara, *Napoleon in Exile*, I, p. 122.
32 *Bull Rom Cont. Pius VII*, XII, pp. 137–9.

Ricci, resolving a long simmering rift. Both pope and cardinals realized that the peace established between church and state remained as precarious as that between the powers.

The curia feared the resumption of hostilities in Europe as the continental states jockeyed towards the formation of a third coalition against France, dreading the prospect of being caught in the crossfire. Sharing the cardinals' concerns, Pius resisted French pressure for entering an alliance, opting instead for neutrality.[33] Nonetheless he allowed the French emperor's troops to pass through his state on route to Naples. Napoleon proved less than grateful for the favour. Papal fear of involvement in the conflict proved justified as the French, battling the forces of Austria and Russia in 1805, paid little heed to papal impartiality and occupied Ancona.

Relations between Rome and Paris deteriorated not only because the pope refused to accept French dictates concerning the European conflict, but also because Pius disapproved of Napoleon's reorganization of the church in the kingdom of Italy, compounded by Rome's refusal to dissolve the marriage of his brother Jerome to an American Protestant, Elizabeth Patterson of Baltimore. The sacrament of marriage of Jerome Napoleon and Elizabeth Patterson occurred on Christmas Eve 1803, performed by John Carroll, archbishop of Baltimore. Disapproving of his brother's marriage, Napoleon sought to have it annulled. The emperor resented the pope's response that in accordance with canon law, the bride's Protestantism did not invalidate the marriage. Subsequently, the archbishop of Paris complied with the emperor's wish and had the marriage annulled. Napoleon did not forget or forgive the pope's refusal, failing to appreciate that Pius did not publicly condemn the action of the archbishop. After the peace of Pressburg of 26 December 1805, Napoleon determined to impose his will on Europe as well as the pope. In Germany, the French-dominated Confederation of the Rhine replaced the empire, while in southern Italy the Bourbons were pushed from power in Naples and Napoleon's brother Joseph assumed the Neapolitan throne.

Pius, bolstered by cardinals such as Ercole Consalvi, Bartolomeo Pacca and Michele di Pietro, resisted further French encroachments, denouncing the claims to power and obedience put forward in the imperial catechism of 1806. Revealing an inner strength hidden by age and infirmity, the pope insisted his neutrality be respected, the occupation of papal territory cease, and the legations returned. Napoleon refused, citing the central geographical position of the Papal States, the military situation which precipitated the French movement into Ancona, while cataloguing the abuses of the pontifical government which had rendered the occupation necessary. Napoleon envisioned himself the protector of the Holy See and in that capacity had occupied Ancona, despite the ingratitude of the Holy Father.[34] Charging that the pope had sent him a 'ridiculous letter', Napoleon indicated that he, like Charlemagne, occupied the

33 Project for a political treaty between the Holy See and the Emperor Napoleon, ASV, Archivio Particolare Pio IX, Oggetti Vari, *n.* 909, *fascicoli* 4–5.
34 Napoleon Bonaparte, *Correspondance de Napoleon Ier* (Paris, 1863), XI, p. 528.

crowns of France and of the Lombards, warning he could reduce the pope to bishop of Rome.

In mid-February 1806 Napoleon insisted that all the enemies of the empire should be enemies of the pope, including the heretical English and the schismatic Russians. The pope, after consultation with the cardinals, proved unwilling to accede to the new world order and the emperor's mandate to expel foreign subjects from his soil, observing that Napoleon was emperor of France, not of Rome. Such expulsions, the pope continued, would violate his neutrality, embroiling him in war with the present enemies of Napoleon, and all those he might make in the future. Pius presented himself as vicar of a God of peace, which meant peace towards all, including heretics and schismatics, refusing to recognize in his state any secular authority higher than his own. Napoleon ridiculed the pope's denunciations and his belief that an interdict or excommunication would really prevent him from exercising power.[35]

Relations between Rome and Paris deteriorated. In May Napoleon had his brother Joseph occupy Civitavecchia under the pretext of keeping the English out. In June Cardinal Consalvi responded by denouncing the occupation of Civitavecchia and the seizure of Benevento and Pontecorvo, which some considered irretrievably lost. The next day, in a conciliatory gesture to the French, Pius reluctantly accepted the resignation of his secretary of state, Consalvi, long sought by the French, replacing him with Cardinal Filippo Casoni, *persona grata* to Napoleon. This brought only a temporary respite in the tension between Pius and Napoleon, as the emperor protested against the former's failure to confirm a number of bishops he had nominated in compliance with the terms of the Italian concordat, and his continued refusal to align himself against France's enemies. As Napoleon abruptly closed his personal correspondence with the pope, the latter girded himself for the impending showdown.[36] Among other things, new guidelines were introduced for the election of the next pontiff.[37]

Pius and Rome received a temporary reprieve as Napoleon focused on confronting the forces of the fourth coalition. Following the Prussian defeat at Jena in October 1806, Napoleon entered Berlin in November, where he ordered the implementation of the continental system, barring all trade with Britain, as well as neutral ships that had called at British ports. He badgered the pope, who governed that 'tiny Italian duchy', no less than the other sovereigns of Europe, to adhere to and abide by the strictures of the 'protector of the Holy See', and was enraged by the pope's refusal of 12 July 1807. Ten days later, he suggested that perhaps the time had come to demote the pope to a simple bishop of the empire. Pius refused to be intimidated, indicating that in matters concerning the welfare of the church his conscience dictated his

35 Bonaparte, *The Corsican*, pp. 224, 277–8.

36 Bartolomeo Pacca, *Historical Memoirs*, trans. George Head (London, 1850), I, pp. 124–6; Joseph Schmidlin, *Histoire des papes de l'époque contemporaine*, trans. L. Marchal (Paris, 1938), I, p. 108.

37 *Bull Rom Cont, Pius VII*, XIII, pp. 92–4.

decisions. Bristling with defiance, Pius rejected Napoleon's 'request' that he join the federation, as well as the proposal that the sacred college be reconstituted, allowing the French empire to control one-third of its membership. Metternich shared the pope's suspicion of Napoleon's unlimited ambition and duplicity, warning that the French emperor would caress you one day and attack you the next. However, Vienna offered Rome scant support.[38] Most of the rulers and courts of Europe fawned upon the emperor. Unique in his defiance, Pius found himself without allies or the prospect of assistance as he championed the independence of the church and the papacy.

On 10 January 1808 Napoleon instructed Prince Eugene to dispatch troops to Rome, and the latter sent General Count Sextius de Miollis, who entered the Eternal City on 2 February, as Pius was celebrating the feast of Our Lady's purification. Locking himself in the Quirinal Palace, Pius complained of this violation to the ambassadors, as did his secretary of state, Cardinal Giuseppe Doria. In mid-March the besieged pope insisted on preserving his neutrality, while alerting the cardinals to prepare themselves for an intensification of the persecution.[39] Napoleon, lacking compassion or guilt, responded by a decree of 2 April 1808 which provided for the incorporation of the pontifical provinces of Urbino, Ancona, Macerata and the Camerino into the kingdom of Italy. In his capacity as the successor to Charlemagne, he withdrew the donations of Pepin, and the confirmation of Charlemagne.[40] Protests were launched against this both by Cardinal Gabrielli,[41] who had succeeded Cardinal Doria in March, and then by Cardinal Pacca, who succeeded Gabrielli after he was arrested and dragged to Senigallia by the French.[42] This spirited and tenacious opposition placed the pope, the sacred college, other ecclesiastics, and all loyal to Rome at risk.

In July 1808 the holy father denounced the French outrages against the temporal and spiritual power of the papacy, ignoring the pressure to join the Italian confederation within the imperial system.[43] Napoleon held Pacca responsible for the escalation of papal opposition and in September sought his arrest. The *zelante* prelate was rescued by the personal intervention of the pope, who had Pacca spirited to his private apartments. Cardinal Gabrielli, fearing for the pope's future safety, schemed with the English to despatch a frigate to transport him to Sicily, but Pius vetoed the plan. He preferred to remain in the Quirinal, paying no heed to the French cannon aimed at the windows of his apartment. Under French scrutiny, the pope tended to the

38 ASV, Segreteria di Stato Esteri, *rubrica* 247; *Memoirs of Prince Metternich*, II, pp. 158–62.
39 *Allocutio habita in consistorio die 16 martii 1808*, in *Bull Rom Cont. Pius VII*, XIII, pp. 259–72.
40 Napoleon's decree of 2 April 1808, ASV, Archivio Particolare Pio IX, Oggetti Vari, *n.* 909, *fascicolo* 1.
41 Cardinal Gabrielli to Cardinal Pacca, 14 May 1808, ASV, Archivio Particolare Pio IX, Oggetti Vari, *n.* 909, *fascicolo* 1.
42 Response of Cardinal Pacca to Napoleon's decree of 2 April, ASV, Archivio Particolare Pio IX, Oggetti Vari, *n.* 909, *fascicoli* 11, 16.
43 *Allocutio habita in consistorio secreto die 11 julii 1808*, in *Bull Rom Cont. Pius VII*, XIII, pp. 290–301.

business of the church. He divided the dioceses of archbishop John Carroll, which comprised all of the territory east of the Mississippi, with the exception of Florida and Louisiana, establishing the sees of Boston, New York and Philadelphia, while converting Baltimore into a metropolitan see. The pope's focus on ecclesiastical affairs did not deter the emperor from proceeding with his grandiose political designs.

Wishing to make Paris the seat of Catholicism while depriving the pope of all temporal power, Napoleon signed the decree of 17 May 1809, incorporating what remained of the Papal States into France, and declaring Rome a free, imperial city. It assigned the pope an annual subsidy of two million *lire* and assured him control of his private palaces. Pius dismissed the decree and declined the subsidy. In June, when the imperial decree was published in Rome, and the French flag replaced the pontifical one on the Castel Sant' Angelo, Pius unleashed the spiritual weapons at his disposal. He issued a bull of excommunication against the counsellors and executors of the spoliation of the dominion of St Peter, which he had pasted on the walls of the basilicas in Rome.[44]

On the night of 5 July 1809, four French divisions broke into the Quirinal Palace, disarmed the thirty Swiss guards, and descended from the roof to invade the papal apartments. When Pius, accompanied by Pacca, refused General Étienne Radet's demand that he renounce the temporal power, the two were driven out of Rome under military escort. Taken by coach, via a circuitous route, to the Certosa near Florence, the physically ill but emotionally stable pope was brought to southern France in a forty-day ordeal. In August he was transferred to Savona, near Genoa, where he was placed under house arrest.

The imprisoned Pius displayed a tenacity bordering on martyrdom. Unwilling to play the part of Napoleon's private chaplain, the pope refused to co-operate with his captor. Quietly at first, but with greater vigour as the captivity continued, Pius refused to sanction a series of French requests, citing his lack of liberty and access to his chief counsellors. The pope's resistance also included forbidding the clergy to take an oath of loyalty to the emperor, and refusing to confirm the bishops named by him, so that within two years some thirty dioceses were vacant. In mid-November 1809 Napoleon, seeking a veneer of legality for his ecclesiastical policy, created an ecclesiastical commission, presided over by cardinal Fesch, to propose possible solutions to the dilemma.

Napoleon's ecclesiastical commission initially rejected all alternatives to papal investiture, as Pius denounced as absolutely invalid any mechanism designed to replace it. During 1810, an angry Napoleon, determined to have the papacy transferred to France, dragged most of the cardinals to Paris along with the heads of the various religious orders and the officers of the congregations and tribunals. The Vatican archives followed in their wake. Those loyal

44 *Bull Rom Cont. Pius VII*, XIII, pp. 280–3.

to Pius, such as Consalvi, banished to Rheims, refused to take part either in the civil matrimony of 1 April, or the religious ceremony of 2 April, of Napoleon to the daughter of the Austrian emperor, Marie Louise. Bonaparte, who seldom forgot or forgave a slight, deprived these loyalists of their right to wear the cardinal's red, creating a distinction between the 'red' cardinals and the 'black'. The latter, deprived of their goods as well as of their customary habit, were exiled to the provincial cities of the empire.

Napoleon pondered the prospect of keeping the pope at Avignon where he would be treated as a spiritual sovereign. 'Henceforth the Popes shall swear allegiance to me, as they did to Charlemagne and his predecessors', Napoleon boasted. He predicted that 'they will not be inducted until after my consent, as the use was for the emperors of Constantinople to confirm them'.[45]

As the crisis continued, in January 1811 the ecclesiastical commission, reinforced by new members, who Napoleon chose for their compliance, was reconvened by Napoleon, who posed a number of questions. Since communication had ended between the pope and the subjects of the empire, to whom could he appeal for dispensations and confirmations hitherto conceded by the Holy See? If the pope persisted in his procrastination, witholding the bull of confirmation to bishops appointed by the emperor under the terms of the concordat, what legal redress existed? Regarding the pope's failure to provide canonical institution, the commission proposed an addenda to the concordat of 1801, stipulating that if papal institution were not granted within a specified period, this privilege would be transferred to a provincial council. Should the pope refuse to accept this modification, the concordat would be suspended, and a national council convoked to confront the crisis. The commission urged the emperor to negotiate with Pius to avoid this eventuality.

Napoleon followed the commission's suggestion and, early in May 1811, dispatched a deputation of three bishops to Savona, carrying letters signed by ten cardinals and an equal number of bishops, imploring peace while warning of the imminent suppression of the concordat and the convocation of a national council. On 17 June 1811 the national council, presided over by Cardinal Fesch, primate of France, opened in Notre Dame. In attendance were ninety-five French bishops, half that number of Italians, as well as a few Germans. Napoleon, who sought a decree providing for an alternative to papal institution, was furious with the scrupulosity and 'sanctimonious quibbling' of the council, which he suspended on 11 July.

Following its closure, Napoleon's agents commenced a campaign of intimidation against the council, which was reconvoked at the end of July. On 5 August 1811 the browbeaten members ratified a decree prescribing that if papal institution were not accorded within six months, the metropolitan or the oldest bishop of the province was authorized to do so. The decree was to be submitted to His Holiness for approval, and Napoleon ordered a deputation of three archbishops, five bishops and five 'red' cardinals to Savona. Pius

45 Bonaparte, *The Corsican*, p. 328.

endorsed the decree with modifications, specifying that the metropolitans should confirm installation in the name of the pope, transmitting all documentation to him. Pius wrote to Napoleon, trusting that his concessions would satisfy the emperor while eliminating the tribulations of the French church. He was stunned by the emperor's reaction. Napoleon, whose son was baptized with the title 'king of Rome', responded that he considered the concordat terminated, and would not permit any papal interference in the installation of bishops. Shortly thereafter, in October 1811, he summarily closed the national council.[46]

Napoleon's problems with the pope were compounded by his difficulties with a number of other sovereigns and states. England remained almost constantly at war with France, subsidizing a series of coalitions, protecting the Portuguese from French domination, as well as encouraging rebellion in Spain. In that Catholic country, the news of the imprisonment of the pope, combined with the opposition to the deportation of priests loyal to Rome, and the abolition of mendicant and monastic orders, fuelled the raging opposition. Catholic Spain clung to those Napoleon denounced as 'beastly friars', opposing his plan to destroy 'superstition and priestcraft'. The peasants of the Iberian peninsula resented Joseph's closing of monasteries and convents, the abolition of the inquisition, and the intimidation of the clergy. Their anger intensified the campaign against the French, requiring a force of some 200,000 men to preserve Joseph's shaky Spanish throne. In Calabria, Napoleon confronted a guerrilla campaign characterized by brutal atrocities and frequent reprisals, which one general branded 'the most monstrous of wars'. To make matters worse, at the end of December 1810 Tsar Alexander, motivated by internal considerations but also inspired by the example of Pius VII, abandoned the continental system. Napoleon could not allow this challenge to his authority, prestige and control go unpunished, rendering a future war with Russia inevitable.

On 9 June 1812, as his *grande armée* of half a million men stood poised for the attack, the emperor secretly transferred the pope from Savona, allegedly to prevent his capture by an English incursion planned by the admiralty. Under cover of darkness, the pope was unceremoniously carted off to Fontainebleu, arriving at the chateau on 19 June 1812. Pius remained a virtual prisoner, but Napoleon described him as an honoured guest. The emperor complained that though he placed fifteen carriages at his and the cardinals disposal, Pius never went out. He concluded that the pope was 'a good man, but a fanatic'.[47]

On 24 June 1812, confident of victory within three months, Napoleon led his forces across the Niemen river, confronting vast spaces and virtually no opposition in Russia. It was only at Borodino on 7 September 1812 that the Russians turned to fight, inflicting heavy casualties on the enemy, but withdrawing under cover of darkness. A week later, Napoleon entered Moscow

46 Latreille, *L'Église catholique*, II, pp. 202–25.
47 Ibid., II, p. 51.

unopposed, but found the city in flames. Expecting surrender after the first French victory, Napoleon was surprised by the obstinacy of Alexander. He attributed the failure of the expedition to the premature cold and the burning of Moscow. 'Had it not been for that fire in Moscow, I should have succeeded', he later reflected. 'I would have wintered there.'[48]

While mountains of red, rolling flames engulfed the city, and the sky was clouded by billows of black smoke, Napoleon remained in the Kremlin waiting in vain for Alexander's submission. On 17 October 1812 the French finally made preparations for withdrawal. The 'great retreat' commenced with his soldiers dispirited and confused, breaking ranks in search of warmth and fire. In one evening alone, Napoleon lamented, he lost 30,000 of his horses to the cold. In Paris, Cardinal Fesch, learning that the *grande armée* had virtually vanished in the flight while Wellington and the English had taken Madrid, commented that while his nephew was lost, the church was saved. Napoleon scrambled to rebuild his forces while mending his relations with the opposition, including the pope. Belatedly, he informed the pontiff that he earnestly sought a settlement of unresolved issues.

Napoleon and Marie Louise unexpectedly descended on Fontainebleu on 19 January 1813, showing themselves gracious and respectful to Pius. Napoleon considered the pope a 'good old man' but *testardo*, or obstinate.[49] Relying on persuasion rather than pressure, charm rather than coercion, he managed to overcome the pope's resistance and in five days emperor and pontiff hammered out the basis for an accord between church and state applicable to both France and the kingdom of Italy. The document, signed on 25 January 1813, contained eleven articles. It provided that the pope would be assured the same exercise of the pontificate as his predecessors, the dominions not yet alienated would be administered by papal agents and not subject to taxation, while the pope promised to provide canonical installation to bishops nominated by the emperor within six months.

Although Pius approved these points as the basis for a future arrangement, Napoleon regarded it as a definitive accord, labelling it the concordat of Fontainebleu. Pius immediately reconsidered his stance, because the declarations prejudiced a number of rights of the papacy and indirectly sanctioned the renunciation of the Papal States. His reservations were reinforced by the 'black' cardinals, who were now allowed to meet with the pontiff and absolutely opposed the declarations. Pius followed their position and on 24 March 1813 wrote to Napoleon retracting the transaction concluded at Fontainebleu.[50]

Napoleon, ignoring the papal disclaimer while regretting having allowed the cardinals to communicate with the pope, recalled the French cardinals from Fontainebleu and had Cardinal Di Pietro deported. Only the war in Germany restrained him from resorting to harsher measures. Following the

48 Ibid., I, p. 119.
49 O'Meara, *Napoleon in Exile*, I, p. 122.
50 Pacca, *Historical Memoirs*, II, pp. 233–83.

'battle of the nations' in October 1813, Napoleon had to withdraw to the west, and on 1 January 1814 General Blucher crossed the Rhine. Shortly thereafter Napoleon, fearing the pope would be freed by the advancing allies, ordered him back to Savona. Outraged by the betrayal of his brother-in-law, Joachim Murat, who had gone over to the allies, and who occupied Rome, the French ruler decided to take his revenge. He released the pope from custody, belatedly restoring him to full sovereignty over his states and encouraging him to return to the Eternal City.

On 11 April 1814, as Napoleon abdicated unconditionally at Fontainebleu, Pius was in Imola. Early in May, pending his return to Rome, Pius created a temporary commission to govern the Papal States.[51] He entered Rome through the Porta del Popolo on 24 May 1814, having been away for five years. In August the pope who had served as the guardian of Catholic unity restored the Society of Jesus.[52] September witnessed the opening of the congress of Vienna and the restoration, which prevailed despite Napoleon's brief return during the 'hundred days' in March–June 1815. Following Waterloo, Bonaparte was exiled to St Helena, while Pius, who had fled his capital, once again returned to Rome. For the faithful, the papal restoration, coupled with Napoleon's permanent exile, represented the triumph of the spirit over the sword.

51 *Bull Rom Cont. Pius VII*, XIII, pp. 317–18.
52 *Sollicitudo omnium ecclesiarum*, in Carlen, *PP*, I, p. 20.

CHAPTER 4

Rome: from restoration to revolution, 1815–1831

Following his release in May 1814, Pius VII (1800–23), who had been badgered and incarcerated by Napoleon, described his ordeal of over half a decade at French hands.[1] Although the papacy in general, and Pius VII in particular, achieved approval for resisting Napoleon, this appreciation did not immediately translate into compensation for Rome on the part of the victorious powers. Rome confronted a double dilemma as it sought to safeguard its religious rights and political position. For Pius VII and his successors in the nineteenth century, the spiritual and temporal powers of the papacy, though distinct, remained inseparable. Complementary in theory, in practice their needs often diverged, creating problems for the Holy See, Italy and Europe throughout the nineteenth century.

In 1814, following exile and persecution, the cardinal secretary of state's principal preoccupation remained the temporal power. He feared allied commitments would compromise the integrity of the Papal States. At the opening of 1814, the papal legations remained in Austria's possession while the marches were occupied by Naples. In mid-March 1814 the powers revealed their intention of returning the holy father to his capital, but, fearful of alienating Joachim Murat, refrained from promising a total restoration of the Papal States.[2]

The pope faced innumerable problems, including diocesan reconstruction, the reorganization of the religious orders, the restoration of the Jesuits worldwide,[3] the revitalization of missions, and the pressing need to fill numerous vacant sees. He also confronted the need to provide for education, hospital care, assistance to the poor, and other charities with diminished funds. The losses in land and income were catastrophic, threatening Rome's fiscal stability and future viability. The secularization of church estates, Cardinal Pacca confided,

1 *Bull Rom Cont. Pius VII* (Rome, 1846), XIII, p. 317.
2 John Tracy Ellis, *Cardinal Consalvi and Anglo-Papal Relations, 1814–1824* (Washington, DC, 1942), pp. 19–20, 45–6; Alan Reinerman, *Austria and the Papacy in the Age of Metternich. I: Between Conflict and Cooperation, 1809–1830* (Washington, DC, 1979), pp. 6–9; Ilario Rinieri, *Il Congresso di Vienna e la Santa Sede, 1813–15* (Rome, 1904), pp. 28–9.
3 *Bull Rom Cont. Pius VII*, XII, pp. 323–5.

had proved a mixed blessing, for while it provoked a financial nightmare, it rendered the bishops less independent and more inclined to look to Rome for leadership.

For two decades the spiritual and temporal power of the Holy See had been imperiled. Following Napoleon's fall, their future remained in jeopardy, and to protect the territorial interests of the papacy, Pius dispatched Monsignor Annibale della Genga to Paris. Consalvi, reappointed secretary of state, rushed to the French capital to assist the slow-moving monsignor, whose mental agility and diplomatic competence he questioned. The cardinal arrived in Paris in early June to find that the treaty of Paris, awarding Avignon to France, had been concluded with the younger brother of Louis XVI, the count of Provence, who assumed the throne as Louis XVIII. Determined to prevent further losses, when the representatives of the allied powers and arbiters of the future settlement departed for London, Consalvi followed. Arriving in the capital of Protestant England a few days after Alexander I of Russia and Frederick William III of Prussia, the cardinal prudently refrained from sporting the distinctive garb of his office except on extraordinary occasions. He resolved not to offend English public opinion, whose government's support he sought. Although some British ministers betrayed their deep-seated prejudices proving themselves hostile to the papacy, the prince-regent pledged his government would sustain the interests of the holy father at the approaching congress, without discussing specifics. Metternich, however, insisted that the issue of papal territory had to be settled at the conference. Thus, when the cardinal departed the English capital on 7 July, twenty-six days of negotiations had produced promises of goodwill but few concrete commitments.[4]

Cardinal Consalvi was exasperated by the news from Rome. The elderly and exhausted pope, suffering from a progressive paralysis and vertigo, dedicated himself to the religious reconstruction of the church in his states and throughout Europe, leaving much of the political restoration to the *zelanti* in the curia, who sought to revert to the old pontifical system of government. Thus Cardinal Agostino Rivaroli, assisted by Cardinal Bartolomeo Pacca, proceeded to undermine the reforms of the last decade, beginning by suppressing the French civil code. With neither prudence nor skill, the two cardinals, who decried all French innovations, restored the baronial and ecclesiastical jurisdictions, long a cause for complaint. They epitomized the resolute and implacable opposition to the modern spirit. The revived Jesuits were accorded a series of privileges, the secret societies outlawed, the Roman inquisition re-established, while the Jews were again shut in the ghetto.[5]

4 Ellis, *Cardinal Consalvi*, pp. 23–9; *Mémoires du Cardinal Consalvi, secrétraire d'état du Pape Pie VII*, ed. J. Cretineau-Joly (Paris, 1864), I, pp. 82–4; Rinieri, *Il Congresso*, pp. 129–30, 308; Charles van Duerm, ed., *Correspondance du Cardinal Hercule Consalvi avec le Prince Clement de Metternich* (Louvain, 1899), pp. 33–52.

5 Erasmo Pistolesi, *Vita del Sommo Pontefice Pio VII* (Rome, 1824), IV, pp. 7–9; Alberto Aquarone, 'La restaurazione nello Stato Pontifico ed i suoi indirizzi legislativi', *Archivio della Società Romana di Storia Patria*, LXXVIII (1955), pp. 123–5, 163; Reinerman, *Austria*, I, pp. 37–40.

In Vienna, Consalvi was preoccupied with the work of the congress called to regulate European affairs, which opened in September 1814. He faced a formidable adversary in Talleyrand, the French representative, who had been a bishop under the *ancien régime*, Napoleon's foreign minister, and had recently emerged as Louis XVIII's representative at Vienna. The cardinal also had to confront an impatient pope, whom he discreetly discouraged from venturing to the Austrian capital. Capitalizing on the goodwill that the heroic resistance of Pius had evoked throughout Europe, the growing consensus that throne and altar needed one another, Tsar Alexander's support for a papal restoration, and above all Metternich's decision to abandon Joachim Murat at the beginning of 1815, Consalvi achieved a number of victories. First, the powers agreed upon regulations establishing the rank of the various courts, assuring a precedence for the pope's representative.[6] Secondly, Metternich finally concurred that most of the pope's pre-revolutionary territory should be returned.

The war had shattered much of the optimism of the earlier age, inclining the powers to seek the consolation and protection of religion. In fact the sovereigns of Russia, Austria and Prussia sought to bolster the stipulations of the congress of Vienna with a religious foundation. On 14 September 1816, under the inspiration of Tsar Alexander, they signed the treaty of the Holy Alliance pledging their devotion to the precepts of the Christian religion. The powers perceived the pope a fellow victim of Napoleonic aggression, courting him as a valuable ally against future unrest and a pillar of the Vienna settlement. A papal restoration was deemed an integral part of the postwar order. By the final acts of the congress in June 1815, Rome regained the marches with the Camerino and their dependencies, as well as the duchy of Benevento and the principality of Ponte Corvo. The Holy See likewise resumed possession of the legations of Ravenna, Bologna and Ferrara, with the exception of that part of Ferrara on the left bank of the Po, transferred to Austria, and Avignon and the Venaissan, retained by Paris. Despite these favourable terms, Consalvi circulated a protest against the losses sustained by Rome in June 1815, confirmed by Pius in an allocution of September 1815.[7]

Consalvi's success in temporal matters was not matched by developments in the spiritual sphere. The missions worldwide were in a wretched condition. Their deterioration paralleled the decline of Spain and Portugal, followed by the revolutionary upheaval in Latin America. The loss of Canada by France, and xenophobic outbursts in the far east, aggravated an already difficult situation. Rome's problems were compounded by the dissolution of the Jesuits, who had supplied thousands of missionary priests. The revolution, which threw France into turmoil, deprived Rome of its chief source of missionaries,

6 See *Il Congresso di Vienna del 1815 e la Precedenza dei Rappresentati Pontefice nel corpo diplomatico. Relazioni del Cardinale Ercole Consalvi Segret. di Stato e Ministro Plenipotentiziario del Sommo Pontfice Pio VII al Cardinale B. Pacca Camerlengo di S.R.C. Pro-Segretario di Stato* (Rome, 1899).

7 *Allocutio habita in aula Vaticana ad diem quartam septembris 1815*, in *Bull Rom Cont, Pius VII*, XII, pp. 394–404; Pistolesi, *Vita del Sommo Pontefice Pio VII*, IV, pp. 106–16; Edward Hertslet, *The Map of Europe by Treaty* (London, 1875), I, pp. 267–8.

while Napoleon's quarrels with the pope in the decade following the conclusion of the concordat worked to undermine missionary activity.[8]

Pius VII, preoccupied with religious matters, was troubled by the revolutions in South America, which deposed the Catholic hierarchy along with the Spanish administration, as the church there fell into disarray. The agitation tore the church asunder as the lower clergy proved supportive of the revolutionary upheaval, while the aristocratic higher clergy remained loyal to Spain, provoking problems for Rome and Madrid. In January 1816 Pius dispensed a letter to the hierarchy and clergy in Spanish America, imploring them to help quell the rebellion. The effort failed, but aroused resentment among patriots. The conflict between the church and the revolution was portrayed as one between the medieval and the modern world, contributing to a violent persecution. Although a number of the new states declared Catholicism the official religion, they sought to control the church within their territories and curtail the power of the papacy within their borders. Their governments championed the historical tradition which had allowed the Spanish and Portuguese crowns sweeping powers of patronage in the new world, effectively placing the church in the colonies under Madrid and Lisbon rather than Rome. Rome challenged the right of the successor civilian authorities to inherit these powers in general, and to designate prelates in particular. This contributed to the Vatican's reluctance to formalize relations with the successor states during the subsequent decade.

The church in the young United States, whose Catholic population rose tenfold from 30,000 in 1789 to some 300,000 by the age of the restoration, was still a mission territory dependent on a European clergy. Overwhelmingly Protestant, apart from the enclave of Quebec, North America required priests, and the pope responded by alerting the superiors of the Jesuits, Vincentians and Christian Brothers of the pressing need.[9] Assistance to the church beyond Europe was provided by the return of the congregation of propaganda to Rome, the restoration of the Jesuits by the Holy See, and Louis XVIII's reinstalment of the Lazarists, fathers of the Holy Ghost, and the priests of the foreign missions. While Consalvi was immersed in political and diplomatic manoeuvres, Pius VII provided financial assistance to what eventually became the fund for the propagation of the faith, supporting mission activity.

The pope also worried about the future of the Catholics of Westphalia and the Rhineland, who were transferred to Protestant Prussia. Consalvi assured Metternich that he would not enter separate negotiations with the various German princes without the chancellor's consent. When the general German

8 H. Daniel-Rops, *The Church in an Age of Revolution 1789–1870*, trans. John Warrington (Garden City, NY, 1967), II, pp. 186–7; Frederick B. Pike, 'Latin America', in *The Oxford Illustrated History of Christianity*, ed. John McManners (Oxford, 1992), pp. 426–7; Anne Greene, *The Catholic Church in Haiti: Political and Social Change* (East Lansing, 1993), pp. 99, 4–5; Marcoes F. Mcgrath, 'Lessons of Yesterday for the New Latin America', in *The Church in the New Latin America*, ed. John J. Considine (Notre Dame, 1964), p. 13.

9 Margaret M. O'Dwyer, *The Papacy in the Age of Napoleon and the Restoration: Pius VII, 1800–1823* (New York, 1985), pp. 132, 150–1.

concordat envisioned failed to materialize, special concordats were concluded between Rome and the states of the Bund. The king of Bavaria wrote to Pius VII affirming that his constitution would be in harmony with the laws of the church and the concordat concluded with the Holy See on 5 June 1817.[10] In 1821 an agreement was finalized between the papacy and the states forming the upper Rhenish provinces.[11] These and other accords contributed to making the church in Germany more hierarchical and Roman.

The controversy over Catholic emancipation in Great Britain continued, with Castlereagh demanding some guarantee from Consalvi on the good behaviour of Britain's Catholic subjects, as well as restrictions on their correspondence with the Holy See. Consalvi did not foresee difficulties in requiring an oath by British Catholics to uphold the constitution, while acknowledging there could be some government input in the selection of bishops. However, the cardinal rejected any royal exequatur or attempt of the crown to censor papal documents, denouncing such intervention as inadmissible.[12] Nonetheless the Holy See was prepared to negotiate. Rome likewise realized that the restoration of the organizational church in Europe and the new world, which had suffered from the imprisonment and isolation of the pope, would have to be negotiated.

The readiness of the French to welcome Napoleon back exposed the weakness of the Bourbon monarchy while strengthening the clerical current, which claimed only Rome could legitimize the restoration order. Writers such as Count Joseph de Maistre, the Viscount François de Chateaubriand and Count Louis de Bonald were among the first to point to the rock of Peter as the sole salvation for postwar society. The history of the church and the papacy produced by the Danish Count von Stolberg, a convert from Protestantism, proved so favourable to Rome that the curia had it translated and published in Italian. In France and elsewhere, the lower clergy, resenting the pretensions of their bishops, likewise had recourse to the pope to defend their position.

The forces of the Quadruple Alliance defeated Napoleon at Waterloo on 18 June 1815, the very day Consalvi left Vienna for Rome. In the first week in August the British ship *Northumberland* transported Napoleon to exile in St Helena, and at the end of the year the second peace of Paris was imposed. France lost about half a million subjects, was constrained to pay an indemnity, while supporting an army of occupation, and obliged to return part of the cache of art treasures that French forces had spirited to Paris, many of which were retrieved by Rome.[13] Nine days after Napoleon's abdication and three days before the return of Louis XVIII to France, *L'Ami de la réligion et du roi: Journal ecclésiastique politique et littéraire* emerged in Paris to promote Catholic interests. Asserting that church and state should be allies in establishing an

10 *Bull Rom Cont. Pius VII*, XV, p. 121.
11 *Memoires of Prince Metternich, 1815–1829*, III, pp. 6–7.
12 Ellis, *Cardinal Consalvi*, pp. 91, 97.
13 Alessandro Ferrajoli, ed., *Lettere inedite di Antonio Canova al Cardinale Ercole Consalvi* (Rome, 1888), passim.

ordered and peaceful society, the Catholic journal pointed to the revolution of 1789 as an evil provoked by their exclusion from the political process. Its editors stressed the need to elect Catholics to the chamber of deputies to defend and promote the faith in France.[14]

The appearance of a series of Catholic newspapers, the recovery of Roman art, capping the restoration of the Papal States at Vienna, and the disillusionment with war and revolution encouraged many to find solace in the traditional faith. Some proclaimed the complete triumph of the Holy See. Consalvi, more than anyone else responsible for Rome's good fortune, remained cautious. Critical of the reaction of the *zelanti*, who were reinforced in 1816 when Pius added new prelates to the sacred college,[15] Consalvi warned that though the task of recovering the Papal States had been difficult, retaining and preserving them would prove even more so. He urged the pope to humanize and illuminate the temporal government, not liberalize it, confessing to the nuncio at Vienna that the constitutional principle was incompatible with the pontifical government. The cardinal speculated that once constitutionalism was introduced in the states of the church, there would be a clamour to extend it to the governance of the church. His fears proved prophetic.

Pius adopted Consalvi's reformism in his decree of 6 July 1816 which divided the Papal States into seventeen districts whose administration was in the hands of cardinal legates and ecclesiastical delegates, assisted by small advisory councils. A new civil and penal code, incorporating many of the French innovations, was introduced, eliminating torture and arbitrary arrest while separating the civil and criminal tribunals from the ecclesiastical courts.[16] Even the alienation of the greater part of the ecclesiastical dominion remained uncontested, with only episcopal residences and some religious houses restored. Finances were systematized and the administration and judiciary streamlined.

If fully implemented, the attempted modernization of the pontifical government would have provided for an efficient central administration which included a large number of laymen, eliminating many of the root causes of the later dissatisfaction and the need for foreign bayonets to preserve the regime. Unfortunately it was criticized and curtailed from the first. To make matters worse, the pope's fall at Castel Gandolfo in the summer of 1817 incapacitated him for over a month, allowing conservative opponents of the cardinal to undermine his reformist programme. Tiberio Pacca, governor of Rome, responded to the angry reaction of the nationalist and revolutionary sects by proposing their mass arrest, which was easier said than done. Even Metternich judged Pacca too severe. Pius, for his part, employed his remaining energy in

14 M. Patricia Dougherty, O.P., 'The Rise and Fall of *L'Ami de la Religion*: History, Purpose, and Readership of a French Catholic Newspaper', *Catholic Historical Review*, LXXVII, 1 (January 1991), pp. 27–8.

15 *Allocutio habita in concistorio secreto*, in *Bull Rom Cont. Pius VII*, XIV, pp. 240–2; Reinerman, *Austria*, I, p. 35.

16 Reform of the Public Administration of the Pontifical Administration, 6 July 1816, in *Bull Rom Cont. Pius VII*, XIV, pp. 49–79; Massimo Petrocchi, *La restaurazione, il Cardinale Consalvi, e la riforma del 1816* (Florence, 1941), pp. 265–7.

denouncing bible societies, resisting Vienna's attempts to introduce Josephist restrictions in his Italian territories, and the negotiation and ratification of concordats or other agreements with Naples, Tuscany, Piedmont, Prussia, Bavaria and France.[17] The Austrian emperor concurred with the pope's opposition to bible societies, and his chancellor shared their sentiment.[18]

The *zelanti* in Rome were reinforced by the traditionalists in France, who influenced the thought of the Catholic elite from the restoration of 1815 to the revolutionary outbursts of 1830–31. They longed for the social and religious order of the old regime, championing one king and one faith. In *Du Pape*, de Maistre not only anticipated the later proclamation of papal infallibility, but accorded the papacy an element of jurisdiction over secular sovereignties. Lamennais, who appeared near the close of the traditionalist movement, likewise interpreted the revolution as divine retribution as he described the post-revolutionary age as no longer Christian but not completely de-Christianized.[19] These men hoped to reshape European society by a renewed Christianity.

In the spring of 1819, when the Austrian emperor Francis visited Rome, Pius VII revealed his opposition to the Josephist system. Furthering centralization and papal primacy in the church, he resented the obstacles hampering Rome's leadership. He found fault with the marriage laws of the empire, the dissemination of Jansenist ideas, and the continuing Habsburg insistence that papal bulls and documents receive the royal approval before admission into the empire. The pope also revealed his irritation with the restriction of appeals to Rome. While the cautious emperor made few immediate modifications, he listened to the complaints of the holy father and apparently moderated his Josephist sentiments.[20]

Pius VII also agonized over the difficulties confronting the church in Latin America.[21] At the same time, Rome experienced difficulties in the implementation of the favourable concordat with Bavaria negotiated in 1817, which reserved questions regarding matrimony to the ecclesiastical courts, and conceded unimpeded communication of the Bavarian church with the Holy See. It also stipulated that the bishops of the ecclesiastical provinces were to enjoy unlimited power of administration in their dioceses and the superintendence of schools, while the king promised to permit the suppression of books hostile to the Catholic faith.[22] The vocal public protests against the concessions constrained the king to negotiate another arrangement which better protected the interests of the state *vis-à-vis* the church.

Problems also arose with the fourteen articles of the new French concordat, which had been signed by Consalvi for the pope, and count de Blacos for

17 *Bull Rom Cont. Pius VII*, XV, pp. 7–14, 17–31.
18 *Memoirs of Prince Metternich* (1881 ed.), III, pp. 66, 68.
19 Hans Maier, *Revolution and Church: The Early History of Christian Democracy 1789–1901* (Notre Dame, 1969), pp. 142–98.
20 Reinerman, *Austria*, I, pp. 71–2.
21 Pius VII to the Bishop of Cordoba, 27 February 1819, ASV, Epistolae ad Principes, vol. 230, f. 32–3.
22 For the Bavarian concordat see *Bull Rom Cont. Pius VII*, XIV, pp. 314–20.

Louis XVIII, and tentatively sanctioned by the *Ubi primum* of 19 July 1817.[23] Under its terms suppressed dioceses would be re-established, and the dioceses, chapters and seminaries were to be endowed with land or capital. While Pius appreciated these proposals, he balked at those which preserved the controversial Gallican liberties. Unable to secure its implementation because of the impasse over Bossuet's four articles, a papal allocution of August 1819 provided for the provisional restoration of the concordat of 1801. Under its aegis, the French educational system was brought under clerical control, with the universities and secondary schools placed under clerical supervision in 1821, followed by primary education in 1824. Catholicism recovered its preeminence as churches were reopened, public processions revived, home missions expanded, military chaplaincies instituted, and the clergy shown great respect.[24]

An accord, though not a concordat, was concluded with Prussia. By its provisions, this Protestant state, whose population was now two-fifths Catholic, recognized six bishoprics and two archbishoprics within its territory, allowing the cathedral chapters to elect them. Prussia's concessions to the church remained in sharp contrast to the hostile attitude of Danish law which prohibited Catholicism in Denmark and Schleswig-Holstein, to the dismay of Pius and Consalvi. In 1818 an agreement was concluded for the reorganization of dioceses in the kingdom of Poland.[25]

The year 1820 opened with the outbreak of revolution in Cadiz, followed by disorders in Madrid, Barcelona and Saragossa. While the Spanish revolution inspired upheaval elsewhere, the *zelanti* in Rome denounced the works on canon law and church history used in Austrian religious institutions, placing them on the Index. Nonetheless the curia in the age of Pius VII was not completely retrograde. In 1820 the Holy Office granted the *imprimatur* for the publication of Giuseppe Settele's *Astronomia*, effectively reversing Galileo's sentence of 1633, against teaching Copernicanism. Thus, the Holy See was better informed on scientific matters and more ideologically flexible than some recognized. Politically, the curia and its champions proved less forgiving.[26]

In April the pope was persuaded to write to Ferdinand VII, protesting the abolition of the Inquisition.[27] In the wake of the outbreak of a *carbonari* revolution in Naples early in July 1820, followed by one in Piedmont in March 1821, conservatives in the Papal States surmised this first challenge to the postwar order would have repercussions in Rome. Although no insurrection erupted in the States of the Church, over 400 of its citizens were precipitously incarcerated. In Vienna, the Austrian chancellor reacted caustically to the revolution in

23 *Ubi primum singulari*, 18 July 1817, in *Bull Rom Cont. Pius VII*, XIV, pp. 365–6.

24 *Conventio inter summum Pontificem Pius VII, et Christianissumum francorum regem Ludovicum XVIII*, in *Bull Rom Cont. Pius VII*, XIV, pp. 366–9.

25 *Bull Rom Cont. Pius VII*, XV, pp. 61–9.

26 For a good analysis of the 1820 close of the Copernican controversy see *Copernico, Galilei e la Chiesa: Fino della controversia gli atti del Sant'Uffizio*, ed. Walter Brandmuller and Egon Johannes Greipl (Florence, 1992).

27 Pius VII to Ferdinand VII, 30 April 1820, ASV, Epistolae ad Principes, vol. 223, fos 11 and 12.

Naples. 'A semi-barbarous people, of absolute ignorance and boundless credulity, hot-blooded as the Africans, a people who can neither read nor write, whose last word is the dagger', Metternich wrote. 'Such a people offers fine material for constitutional principles.'[28] Nonetheless, Consalvi accorded the Neapolitan constitutional regime *de facto* recognition. Metternich was not pleased.

The eastern powers, meeting in congress at Troppau in October 1820, refused to sanction the changes wrought by revolutionary upheaval and called for intervention to restore the status quo. The English rejected the Troppau protocol, while Consalvi refused the Russian suggestion that the pope mediate between Naples and the allied powers. Nor would he sanction the passage of Austrian troops through the Papal States to crush the constitutional regime, but privately promised Rome would not hinder what it could not prevent. Consalvi refused to unleash the Holy See's spiritual arsenal against a political opponent.

Conservatives in the curia seconded Metternich's entreaties, worried about the spread of freemasonry in Italy and the *charbonnerie*, its audacious French branch, fearing the political and religious consequences. The *zelanti* noted that the lodges had provided the basis of Napoleon's principal support in the peninsula and pointed to the transformation of Italian freemasonry into the *carboneria* after 1815. To elevate their opposition from the political to the religious level, they complained that carbonarism allegedly lured unsuspecting initiates by a pseudo-Catholic paraphernalia, but later dragged deluded souls into the depths of masonic pantheism and moral anarchy. In their mania to invoke spiritual condemnation for political action, the conservatives charged that revolutionaries sought to ruin religion as well as government.

Metternich and the *zelanti* tenaciously pressed Rome to condemn the *carbonari*, considering it complementary to Austria's military intervention against the Neapolitan revolution. Both the pope and his secretary of state recognized the danger represented by the revolutionary movement, but insisted that spiritual strictures could only be employed against those societies manifestly opposed to the Catholic religion, and whose practices and policies violated its principles. Hoping to placate Metternich, in April Consalvi published an edict against the *carbonari* in the Papal States which failed to satisfy the Austrian minister. Only when the Austrians uncovered the sect's initiation ceremonies, which pirated and ridiculed church ritual, did Rome respond. In mid-September 1821 Pius VII launched an excommunication against the *carbonari* and its adherents for their blasphemous misuse of Roman ritual, alleged war against the church, and antagonism towards the papacy. Justified on spiritual grounds, its real motivation was political, and as such proved a failure. While it did little to suppress or undermine the sects, it alienated Italian nationalists by identifying the papacy with Austria and reaction.[29]

28 *Memoirs of Prince Metternich* (1881 ed.), III, p. 386.
29 Alan Reinerman, 'Metternich and the Papal Condemnation of the Carbonari, 1821', *Catholic Historical Review*, LIV (April 1968), pp. 55–69; 'Ecclesiam a Jesu Christo', *Le Moniteur Universal*, 11 October 1821; *Bull Rom Cont.* (Rome, 1835–55), XV, pp. 446–8.

Rome's conservative alignment was also reflected in its refusal to accept the ambassador from the constitutional regime in Spain.[30] The Vatican reconsidered its position towards both Spain and Spanish America because Pius weighed the consequences of refusing to recognize the liberation of the latter, and because he opposed the anticlerical policies of the constitutional regime of the peninsula. In August 1822 the pope, having reassessed the Spanish-American situation, decided to dispatch an apostolic delegate to Chile, despite the outcry of the Spanish government. Resolved not to concede the *patronato* rights enjoyed by the Spanish crown over the church in Latin America to the successor republics, Pius was prepared to compromise on other issues and foreshadowed Rome's reversal on the recognition of the American republics.

Although Consalvi appreciated the support of the Holy Alliance and above all Austria, he resisted too close an association with the conservative powers and the military and diplomatic campaign to preserve the status quo. Pius insisted on the primacy of spiritual over political aims in the Roman agenda. Thus, in October, at the congress of Verona of 1822, Monsignor Giuseppe Spina, the papal representative, reasserted papal neutrality, opposing the suggestion that Austria garrison Bologna while winning the goodwill of the British by seconding their efforts against the slave trade.[31] A barrage of religious and administrative problems, including his opposition to the practice of lay trusteeship in the United States, burdened the old pope.

In early 1823 there came the disturbing news that the nuncio, Giacomo Giustiniani, was constrained to leave Madrid. Nonetheless, Pius VII wrote to the Spanish monarch in March, urging him to denounce and eliminate the slave trade.[32] His spirit was momentarily lifted in according recognition to the Society for the Propagation of the Faith. First organized in Lyons, it spread to most of France. Other positive developments followed. In April French troops crossed the border into Spain, while the pope's mission, which included the apostolic delegate Giovanni Muzi and his auditor Giovanni Maria Mastai-Ferretti, prepared to depart for Spanish America. While in Genoa, the delegation heard of the pope's fall in his apartment on 6 July 1823, damaging his thigh and hastening his demise.[33] At the same time, St Paul's outside the walls, the great Roman basilica on the site of St Paul's martyrdom, burned to the ground and allegedly news of the disaster was kept from the pope's sickbed. Pius languished for over a month, recalling the nightmare of Savona and Fontainebleu. He died of heart failure on 20 August 1823, in his eighty-first year, following a tumultuous pontificate of twenty-three and a half years. His attempt to reconcile Rome and the revolutionary age during the early part of his pontificate had ended with the papacy increasingly identified with the restoration.

30 Pius VII to Ferdinand VII, 1 May 1822, ASV, Epistolae ad Principes, vol. 23, fos 357–9.
31 Silvio Fulani, 'La Santa Sede i il Congresso di Verona', *Nuova Rivista Storica*, XXXIX (1955), pp. 465–91.
32 Pius VII to Ferdinand VII, 23 March 1823, ASV, Epistolae ad Principes, vol. 230, fos 419–22.
33 Manuscript of *Breve relazione al Cile dal Canonico Giovanni Mastai-Ferretti di Sinigaglia*, Sala Studio Manoscritti of Vatican Library.

The conclave, which opened on 2 September 1823 and continued for twenty-six days, was dominated by the *zelanti* cardinals who charged that Pius's conciliatary course towards the powers had been pursued at the expense of the papacy. They called for a pope who would champion Catholic interests against the powers as well as the revolutionaries. Metternich, on the other hand, sought a moderate replacement for Pius VII, invoking a pope that would protect not only the interests of the Holy See and religion, but the tranquillity of Italy and Europe.[34] When the intransigents were on the verge of electing Cardinal Gabriele Severoli, one of their own, Metternich reluctantly authorized Cardinal Giuseppe Albani, entrusted to represent Austrian interests in the conclave, to exercise the exclusive. This right, held by the courts of Austria, France and Spain, permitted these powers to exclude one cardinal from the election, if exercised prior to that candidate's receiving the two-thirds vote necessary for election. The frustrated cardinals supported another *zelanti*, and secured the election of Cardinal Annibale della Genga, considered a bitter opponent of Consalvi. Elected on 28 September 1823, he assumed the name Leo XII (1823–29).[35]

The new pope, though only sixty-three, suffered from poor health and fell gravely ill following his coronation, receiving the last rites. The devout Leo recovered by the end of the year, to the delight of prelates, like Lamennais, who passionately maintained that the link between throne and altar had been shattered and the church had perforce to pursue an autonomous course. The sacred college, relying on the religious revival within the faith rather than on any external political power, sought to prevent policies which subordinated the spiritual life of the church to political expediency, as had allegedly occurred during Consalvi's tenure. Reportedly, Leo was more friendly to France than Austria.[36]

In 1824 Pope Leo XII welcomed Lamennais to Rome as the herald of ultramontanism and steadfast foe of Gallicanism, rather than as the proponent of liberal Catholicism. The pope gave Lamennais rooms in the Vatican and accorded him several private audiences. Sensing his visitors fanatical commitment, Leo concluded that the Breton priest had to be handled gently. The pope, who placed a portrait of Lamennais in his room, shared some of his *zelante* views on church–state relations. In his initial encyclical of 5 May 1824 he condemned dechristianization, indifferentism, toleration and freemasonry, tracing many of the contemporary problems to the contempt for the authority of the church.[37]

Under Leo, education in the Papal States was transformed to reinforce its moral and religious message, while a decree of October 1824 revised the

34 *Memoirs of Prince Metternich, 1773–1815*, IV, 61–6.

35 Raffaele Colapietra, 'Il Diario Brunelli del Conclave del 1823', *Archivio Storico Italiano*, CXX (1962), pp. 76–146.

36 *Consular Relations Between the United States and the Papal States*, ed. Francis Stock (Washington, DC, 1945), p. 24.

37 *Ubi Primum*, in Carlen, *PP*, I, p. 21.

administrative and judicial systems, purging them of many of Consalvi's innovations. Dividing the Papal States into thirteen delegations in addition to the capital, it reorganized both the civil and criminal tribunals.[38] Rome's entire domestic programme was decidedly conservative and Leo was soon branded the 'pope of the holy alliance' and the 'pontiff of the *ancien régime*'.[39] He proved a jealous guardian of the Holy See's prerogatives, continuing the centralizing tendencies of his predecessor while abandoning his political moderation. Initially he failed to comprehend the impact of the one on the other. The contrast between Leo's energetic defence of the church, and his blatant inefficiency as a temporal ruler, proved glaring.

The Papal States were burdened by a series of intrusive, reactionary measures which restricted the sale of wine and closed cafes, taverns and theatres during Lent, capped by ridiculous edicts which sought to regulate the modesty of female dress and imprisoned males who walked too closely behind females. Jews, prevented from owning real property and restricted to the ghetto, were required to listen to a weekly Catholic sermon and, like Christians, were subject to arrest for conducting business on Sunday. Leo also imposed a strict censorship on the press, restored the judicial privileges of the higher clergy, and insisted on the use of Latin in the courts and universities. This pope restored the right of asylum to the churches while re-establishing episcopal jurisdiction in civil affairs. Rome's suspicion of innovation culminated in the suppression of the vaccination commission. Realism in art was frowned upon and naked statues removed from public view. Even the waltz, denounced as obscene, did not escape censure.

Throughout 1825 Rome's repressive measures continued and the tendency to report even trivial matters to the Inquisition swelled. Rome opened a new prison which was almost immediately filled with heretics. Leo also reinforced the *legates* entrusted with the task of controlling the 'sects' and the 'brigands'. The repression failed to provide tranquillity. Leo did not second the call for Austrian assistance to protect the papacy, relying instead on Lamennais's vision of Rome re-establishing contact with the Catholic masses of the continent and beyond. The pope's support for the Breton priest's programme was revealed by his patronage of Father Gioachino Ventura's *Giornale Ecclesiastico*, followed by the appointment of Lamennais's disciple to the chair of ecclesiastical civil law at the Sapienza, the papal university in Rome. The pope proclaimed 1825 a Holy Year, the first of the nineteenth century, drawing pilgrims from the entire Catholic world to Rome. Meanwhile the pope granted new concessions to the Society of Jesus.[40]

The powers shuddered when it appeared that Leo's papacy might abandon its association with them for the support of the Catholic masses, forging an

38 *Bull Rom Cont. Leo XII*, XVI, pp. 128–255.

39 Angelo Filipuzzi, *Pio IX e la politica Austriaca in Italia dal 1815 al 1848* (Florence, 1958), pp. 21–2, 95; Reinerman, *Austria*, I, p. 134.

40 *Bull Rom Cont. Leo XII*, XVI, pp. 449–52.

alliance of sorts between liberalism and Catholicism. Initially, this seemed to be the pope's goal as he manoeuvred to protect the prerogatives of the papacy against state impositions by relying on the support of the faithful. During the course of 1826, a number of factors led Pope Leo XII to reconsider Lamennais's ultramontanism, including the disapproval of the powers, and above all that of Metternich's Austria. Furthermore, neither the pope nor his conservative allies in the curia could find cause for complaint in the ultra-royalist programme instituted by the count of Artois who assumed the throne in France in 1824 as Charles X. The conservative monarch re-established convents for women and approved the law of sacrilege which imposed severe penalties for offences committed in churches.

Rome failed to suppress the sects and recognized that the goodwill of the Catholic masses could not easily be translated into a mechanism to defend the papacy against its phalanx of foes. The pope quietly abandoned Lamennais's notion of relying on the religious devotion of the Catholic masses instead of the armies and favours of the conservative powers. In mid-March Leo denounced the masons and other secret societies, renewing the decrees of his predecessors against them, and – reminiscent of Consalvi's earlier action – proclaiming them a threat to both throne and altar. In 1826 Leo's condemnation provoked sixteen members of the French hierarchy to criticize the papacy's intervention in political matters for spiritual reasons.

In the summer of 1826 Cardinal Tommaso Bernetti ventured to Vienna, St Petersburg, Paris and Berlin to assure them that Leo XII renounced ultramontanism. The powers reciprocated so that in Paris Charles X's government sought a more complete restoration of Catholicism. Vienna likewise made concessions, as Metternich gradually weaned his emperor away from Josephism and the Jesuits were allowed to return. Heeding the earlier admonitions of Cardinal Consalvi that schism would ensue if the papacy did not reach some accommodation with the Latin American republics, Leo XII restored the hierarchy in most of these states and commenced negotiations for the conclusion of concordats. Perhaps the reorganization of the church in Spanish America represented the most significant development of Leo XII's pontificate.

By 1827, the year the Liberals secured control of the chamber in France, Leo concluded that only Austria could preserve the legitimate order and the papal position in Italy. Consequently, the curia expressed concern in 1827 when Austrian troops were withdrawn from the kingdom of Naples, but pleased to see these restationed in Lombardy as a deterrent to revolutionary upheaval. When his secretary of state, Cardinal Giulio della Somaglia, retired the following year, Leo ignored the pressure of the *zelanti* to name the conservative Cardinal Giustiniani as his successor, selecting the more moderate Cardinal Tommaso Bernetti, a disciple of Consalvi. Like his mentor, Bernetti relied upon co-operation with Austria, while preserving Rome's official neutrality. Resolved to protect the status quo and discourage innovation at home, the pope created a congregation of vigilance to supervise the activity and conduct of all governmental, judicial and administrative employees of the Papal States.[41]

Leo sought to balance conservative policies at home with realism abroad, but his unpopular domestic course rendered him increasingly dependent upon Austrian support. Although the pope remained suspicious of the alliance of Catholics and Liberals in Ireland, Daniel O'Connell's Catholic Association worked diligently to remove the civil and religious disabilities burdening Catholics. But there were few other victories that the pope could foresee as the new year opened. The spectre of revolution hovered over the whole of Europe, theatening the political and religious order, while the discontent in the Papal States, and most notably in the legations, menaced the temporal power. Thus while prelates might praise the religious life and devotion of Leo, or the benefits of his centralizing efforts in the church, his unexpected death on 10 February 1829 left the Papal States vulnerable.[42]

Metternich was perturbed by Leo's disappearance, fearing his successor would discontinue Rome's collaboration with Austria. Thirteen days after Leo's death, on 16 February 1829, the cardinals were escorted into the conclave. In March the French ambassador, Viscount François de Chateaubriand, addressed the cardinals, stressing that the papacy had to make fundamental adjustments to the 'spirit of the age' and urging them to select a pope who would look forward rather than backwards. The conclave's official response was delivered by Cardinal Castiglioni, who observed that the church, founded on divine authority, had no need to adapt to the times, implying that the modern world should conform to its principles. The Austrian ambassador proved more diplomatic in his remarks, expressing the emperor's benevolence towards the Holy See while favouring the speedy selection of a moderate pope.[43]

The *zelanti* had learned some lessons since the election of Leo XII, recognizing that the papacy could not assert its claims against the revolutionaries and the thrones simultaneously. Thus in 1829 the rivalry among the cardinals was more personal than ideological, with the leading candidates all eschewing ultramontanism. Forty-nine days after the death of Leo XII, on 31 March 1829, the 68 year-old Francesco Saverio Castiglioni, bishop of Frascati, supported by the French and the Austrians, was elected pope. Austria had placed him at the top of the list of desirable candidates, so his election satisfied Metternich.[44] His devotion and loyalty to Pius VII had been manifest in his refusal to swear allegiance to Napoleon, which led to his exile in eastern France until 1815.

In deference to the memory of his benefactor, Pius VII, Castiglioni took the name Pius VIII (1829–30). Metternich's concern that an extremist might replace

41 Ibid., XVI, pp. 409–11.
42 Giovanni Maria Mastai's Funeral Oration for Leo XII, 21 February 1829, ASV, Fondo Particolare Pio IX, *cassetta* 9, *numero* 46.
43 Metternich, *Memoirs*, IV, p. 570; Reinerman, *Austria*, I, pp. 156–7; Rafaelle colapietra, 'Il Diario del Conclave del 1829', *Critica Storica*, I (1962), pp. 517–41.
44 *Memoirs of Prince Metternich* (1881, ed.), IV, p. 617.

Leo proved unjustified, for the new pope proved to be neither a *carbonaro* nor a *zelante*, and, unlike his predecessor, little disposed to champion Lamennais against the restoration monarchies. He showed himself well disposed towards Austria, confiding to its representative that since his family hailed from Lombardy he considered himself an Austrian subject.[45] Not surprisingly, he selected Cardinal Giuseppe Albani, attached to the Austrian empire and entrusted with its veto power during the conclave, as his secretary of state.

A moderate of Consalvi's stamp, Pius saw the need for some reforms in the Papal States, while continuing the policy of centralization in the church which has commenced with Pius VI and carried forward during the restoration. To placate the Romans, he repealed Leo's edict restricting the sale of alcoholic beverages and other burdensome regulations, appointing a congregation of cardinals to examine broader political and administrative reforms. He recognized that the appointment of bishops in South America had not been permanently resolved, and was disturbed by reports of anti-Catholicism in North America flowing from the increased Irish immigration. Mindful of the assistance of Spain in securing the restoration to his states in 1814, Pius refused to receive Pablo Francesco Vasquez whom Mexico had appointed to the Holy See. Devoting himself to the spiritual renewal of the church, and to spreading Catholicism to the world beyond Europe through his support of the missions, he left the onerous task of governing the Papal States to Cardinal Albani. Unfortunately, he also entrusted his secretary of state with the task of co-ordinating a comprehensive reform programme, which was undermined by the eighty-year-old cardinal's lack of energy and commitment to the status quo.

In April 1829 he reaped the benefits of the negotiations commenced by Consalvi and the agitation of Daniel O'Connell when George IV grudgingly approved the act of emancipation extending political rights to the Catholics of Great Britain. On 24 May 1829, in his first encyclical, Pius launched an attack on the enemies of the church and the state. Commencing with a condemnation of those who attacked the church's spiritual mission, he denounced indifferentism which claimed that salvation might be reached by means of any religion. Pius likewise warned against those who championed the private interpretation of scripture, which resulted in the reader imbibing 'lethal poison' rather than 'the saving water of salvation'. The encyclical proceeded to censure the growing menace of the secret societies, which were denounced as a threat to religious and civil society.[46] Despite the pope's reprobation, the sects flourished in the Papal States, nourished by glaring abuses in their administration.

As 1830 opened, carbonarist conspiracies threatened the tranquillity of Rome. The European situation provided little comfort, as Pius found himself in conflict with the Prussian government over the issue of mixed marriages between Protestants and Catholics. The pope criticized the Prussian civil laws regulating

45 Reinerman, *Austria*, I, p. 159; *Consular Relations Between the United States and the Papal States*, ed. Leo Francis Stock (Washington,1945), p. 24.
46 Carlen, *PE*, I, pp. 221–4.

these marriages in his apostolic letter of 25 March 1830.[47] Pius directed priests to secure promises from the partners in a mixed marriage that children would be raised as Catholics, arousing a storm of protest in Protestant Prussia. The news from Paris provided no relief for the pope, as the alliance between throne and altar under Charles X had led to a criticism of both, with a large contingent of their chamber protesting the policies of the ministry. At the end of July, Charles's repressive six ordinances precipitated the insurgents to raise barricades, capture the Hôtel de Ville, and depose him. In August the rump parliament proclaimed Louis Philippe, duke of Orleans, king of the French. In place of a king consecrated by the grace of God, Rome was confronted by a monarch chosen by the people's will. Some delighted in the fact that the sole victim of the law of sacrilege had been the regime of Charles X.

Pius was distressed that the July revolution seemed as much directed against the church as against the legitimatist regime, but shied from sanctioning Lamennais's call for the separation of church and state. To make matters worse, at the end of August a revolution erupted in Belgium, and, to the dismay of Cardinal Albani, Catholics co-operated with liberals in overturning the regime created by the powers at Vienna. The secretary of state branded the co-operation of liberals and Catholics first in Belgium, and later in Poland, as 'monstrous'.

Rome's reliance on the restoration order made it a target for patriots in the Italian peninsula. Controversy and change troubled the sickly pope during his remaining days. In early November the frail pontiff learned of the death of Francesco of Naples and the accession of Ferdinand II, who was urged by Luigi Settembrini to seek the crown of Italy. Following these tumultuous events the Austrians requested permission to dispatch troops into the Papal States, but were thwarted by Pius VIII. Pius did not have time to fret over the implications of these developments, dying at the end of November after a short reign of a year and eight months. He was spared the pain of experiencing the tragic events of 1830. The Romans were unkind to Pius, commenting that 'he was born, cried, and died', while others sang 'the eight Pius was pope, lived and died, and no one took note'.[48]

The unexpected death of Pius VIII led to speculation that he had been poisoned, but this suspicion was not confirmed by the secret autopsy performed. It seems that the 69-year-old pontiff, who had occupied the papal see for only twenty months, died of asthma.[49] From Vienna, Metternich watched events with anxiety, appreciating that Pius had worked closely with Austria, and fearing disruption in the Papal States which were without a pontiff, as revolutionary clouds rolled over much of Europe. The July revolution had inspired the Belgians to revolt against the Dutch; in England, the Tory ministry which had sympathized with the Holy Alliance had fallen; the Poles were restive under tsarist control; while in Italy, the *carbonari* prepared for insurrection.

47 Carlen, *PP*, I, p. 23.
48 Fiorella Bartocinni, *Roma nel Ottocento* (Bologna, 1985), p. 26.
49 *Consular Relations Between the United States and the Papal States*, pp. 31–2.

Subsequently there were risings in Parma, Modena and the Papal States, overturning the legitimate regimes and pressing for the creation of an Italian republic in north-central Italy. Thus, the pontificate of Pius VIII closed in the midst of a crisis which threatened both the temporal and spiritual authority of the papacy.

CHAPTER 5

The Holy See and the first crisis of modernization: 1831–1846

The conclave at the end of 1830 proved as turbulent as conditions in the Papal States, which were stricken by political turmoil, financial crisis and nationalist agitation. Cardinal Giustiniani had been on the verge of election when his candidacy was vetoed by King Ferdinand VII of Spain, who resented that Giustiniani had advised Leo XII to appoint bishops to the republic of Colombia, which had abandoned its allegiance to the mother country. The electoral intrigues also reflected the broader schism in society between liberals and conservatives. On 2 February 1831 Bartolomeo Alberto Cappellari, prefect of the congregation of propaganda, was elected pope as Gregory XVI.[1] One of his first actions was to condemn the revolution and its perpetrators.[2] The beleaguered pope confronted an exhausted treasury and the loss of more than half his dominion.

Born in the Veneto on 18 September 1765, Gregory was in his sixties, but in vigorous health in contrast to his predecessors, Leo XII and Pius VIII. Trained in the discipline of the Camoldolese Order, which rigidly adhered to the reformed Benedictine rule, he had been a monk since his eighteenth year and remained one in spirit as he ascended the papal throne, living simply and eating frugally. Confined within the walls of his monastic cell, Gregory had been sheltered from the dislocation provoked by the economic transformation and the frustration which followed the congress of Vienna's failure to address national aspirations in Italy and Germany. A professional theologian, the new pope was unfamiliar with the industrial take-off which had originated in Great Britain, but had soon spread to Belgium, parts of France, western Germany and northern Italy, and the urbanization and increasing secularization which followed in its wake. Gregory was equally hostile to the champions of *laissez-faire* economics such as Adam Smith, Thomas Malthus and David Ricardo, and to those utopian socialists such as Charles Fourier, Count Saint-Simon and

1 *Consular Relations Between the United States and the Papal States*, ed. Leo Francis Stock (Washington, 1945), pp. 32–3.
2 *Bull Rom Cont. Gregory XVI* (Rome, 1857), XIX, pp. 1–2.

Étienne Cabet who advocated an alternative to unrestrained capitalism. Religious, rather than social or national issues remained his overriding concern.

By temperament and training hostile to innovation, Gregory was suspicious of the modern world and its philosophies. Distressed but not surprised that reform had culminated in revolution, the pope relied on Cardinal Bernetti to deal with the dilemma. Suspicious of Habsburg dominance in the peninsula, and the opprobrium attached to reliance on their forces, Bernetti hoped to avoid Austrian intervention by seeking a negotiated settlement. His efforts proved abortive. Subsequently, he petitioned France and Naples for assistance, but was disappointed by their reluctance to act. The attempt to create a popular counter-revolutionary force, drawn from the devout peasantry,[3] proved no more successful. Meanwhile, the situation became critical as papal forces either deserted or joined the revolutionaries; a provisional government was established in Bologna, and a declaration announced the end of the temporal power.

From Terni the 22-year-old Prince Louis Napoleon, the future French emperor, warned the pope that the forces marching on Rome were invincible.[4] To Gregory's dismay, appeals were made to the inhabitants of Macerata and Spoleto to join the insurgency, while the garrison of Ancona capitulated to the revolutionaries. By the end of February, the pope retained little more than the Roman Campagna. There were those who feared that the gates of Rome might be stormed. Faced with these prospects, Bernetti, who had sought to avoid an overt dependency on Austria, reluctantly appealed to Vienna to liberate Bologna.

At the end of February, Gregory's plea for assistance reached Metternich, who shared the pontiff's fear of political and social instability and dreaded the insolence of the secret societies. Despite the pronouncement of non-intervention proclaimed by the recently installed Sebastiani government of Louis Philippe, the Austrians responded promptly to the papal request to suppress the revolutionary tempest which menaced the Papal States, the quiet of the entire peninsula, and the well-being of their multi-national empire. Metternich secured French approval for military intervention by convincing Louis Philippe that the revolution was inspired by Bonapartism, which threatened his throne.[5]

As Gregory expressed gratitude for Austrian assistance,[6] liberals and nationalists in France complained that Louis Philippe had bolstered a detestable clerical administration and virtually surrendered Italy to the Austrians. Their outcry was echoed by the other powers when Bernetti issued an edict which imposed

3 T. Bernetti to Monsignor Spinola, 30 March 1831, ASV, Segreteria di Stato, *rubrica* 247.

4 Antonio Monti, *Pio IX nel Risorgimento Italiano con documenti inediti* (Bari, 1928), p. 38; Raffaele De Cesare, *The Last Days of Papal Rome*, trans. Helen Zimmern (London, 1909), p. 16.

5 Both sons of Louis Napoleon, the former king of Holland and brother of the great Napoleon, were involved in the revolutionary events of 1830–31 in the Papal States. One of these died of disease at Forli, while Louis Napoleon, accompanied by his mother, Queen Hortense, eventually fled to Spoleto where the archbishop, Mastai, who had returned, provided him with a passport to leave the country. Frank J. Coppa, *Pope Pius IX: Crusader in a Secular Age* (Boston, 1979), pp. 33–4.

6 Gregory XVI to Francis I of Austria, 5 April 1831, *Bull Rom Cont. Gregory XVI*, XIX, pp. 1–2; *TESP*, p. 185.

burdensome penalties on the revolutionaries. Indeed, the secretary of state was constrained to issue a revised and more liberal amnesty.[7] To further appease French national sentiments, Metternich agreed to a conference of the major powers (France, England, Austria, Russia and Prussia) to suggest reforms to the papal government. In May 1831 the conference of ambassadors submitted a memorandum to the pope, cataloguing reforms the powers deemed essential, including the admission of lay people to all administrative and judicial posts, the revival of a series of municipal and provincial liberties, and the public supervision of finance. The powers also endorsed the creation of a national consultative assembly to advise the pope on administrative and governmental issues. It was not welcomed at Rome.

Some believed that Louis Philippe's government wanted the Papal States transformed into a parliamentary monarchy, but Bernetti seconded the pope's determination to retain his government's ecclesiastical and absolutist character. Cardinal Bernetti rejected even the convocation of a consultative assembly, asserting that the principles inspiring it were contrary to the special nature of the papal regime, while the pope confessed that he preferred to be hounded into exile rather than accept humiliating conditions.[8] In July 1831 Gregory issued an edict promising reforms, but the memorandum of the powers remained a dead letter.

In the summer of 1831, when the Austrians, responding to French pressure, withdrew from the Papal States, a rash of convulsions followed their withdrawal.[9] Bernetti complained that concessions had brought insubordination rather than gratitude. Cardinal Albani, named special commissioner over some 5,000 troops assigned the task of restoring order in the legations, proved unable to do so. In 1832 Bernetti had no recourse but to appeal to General Radetzky and the Austrians, who returned to the legations, but this prompted a French occupation of Ancona to preserve some balance in the peninsula. This dual occupation persisted until 1838, compromising the sovereignty of the Papal States and calling into question the Holy See's ability to govern.

Gregory had problems as pope as well as sovereign. The revolutions of 1830 witnessed Catholic complicity, if not active co-operation in Poland and Belgium, inspiring a liberal Catholic movement which sought to ally the church with liberal action in Europe. The Belgian constitution, which the papal nuncio in Belgium had described as atheistic,[10] witnessed the spectacle of more than a dozen priests sitting in their new parliament. The introduction of a separation of church and state there, as well as France, inspired Félicité de Lamennais, who envisioned a regenerated church within a changing society. Born of an ennobled middle class in 1782, his first work, *Réflexions sur l'Église*

7 Alan J. Reinerman, *Austria and the Papacy in the Age of Metternich. II: Revolution and Reaction, 1830–1838* (Washington, DC, 1989), pp. 49–53.

8 Carlo Ghisalberti, 'Il Consiglio di Stato di Pio IX. *Nota storica* giuridica', *Studi Romani*, II (1954), p. 56; Reinerman, *Austria*, II, p. 70.

9 *Bull Rom Cont. Gregory XVI*, XIX, p. 32.

10 Anna Morelli, 'Cattolici liberali belgi e gli ideali mennaissiani', in *Gioacchino Ventura e il pensiero politico d'inspirazione cristiana dell' ottocento*, ed. Eugenio Gucione (Florence, 1991) I, p. 566.

en France (1808), represented an appeal for the reform of Christianity. The publication of the first volume of his four-volume *Essai sur l'indifférence* in 1817 warned that religion alone would enable a people to regain their splendour.

The basic ideas of Lamennais's theological system were revealed in his *Défense de l'Essai* (1818), a response to his enemies. He further elaborated his thought in *Le Religion considéré dans ses rapports avec l'ordre politique*, insisting that the church wrench herself from the clutches of the state. Deeming the pope the expression of humanity's universal will, Lamennais cited his need to wield absolute power, regaining the right to intervene in the affairs of the world, and acting as the supreme champion of liberty. His vitriolic outpourings against the French hierarchy led to a barage of complaints to Rome, but did not stop Lamennais from continuing his crusade.

Following the revolution of 1830–31, Lamennais focused on the advantages of constitutionalism and republicanism, which allowed Catholics the liberty to defend their rights in the political arena. With a circle of friends he founded the daily *L'Avenir*, whose motto was 'God and Liberty', and championed a separation of church and state. His support of revolutions in Poland and Belgium, and his attempt to modernize the church by building a bridge between Catholicism and liberalism, aroused the bishops and conservative Catholics who appealed to Rome. As ultramontanes and liberals petitioned the pope against the pretensions of their bishops, Gregory retorted that he never realized that the French hierarchy contained so many 'little popes'.[11]

The *Avenir* group argued that the church was influenced by political and social institutions and therefore had to respond to the emerging European civilization. Lamennais maintained the church should reject the strangle-hold of the *ancien régime*, embrace freedom, and reshape society. Labelling the monarchy the common oppressor of the church and the masses, he envisioned a natural alliance between the papacy and the people in the modern age of economic transformation, rejecting the conservative alliance and the state's imposition of a secular ideology. This priest and his allies considered freedom the best guarantee of the future prosperity of the church. The conservative hierarchy in France did not concur, banning the liberal paper in a number of dioceses, refusing ordination to seminarians who read *L'Avenir*, and appealing to Pope Gregory and the curia. They sought to convince Gregory that Lamennais's beliefs contained grave errors bordering on heresy, claiming his organization led to unrestrained anarchy and revolutionary subversion which undermined the traditional order and the church's place therein. *L'Ami del la réligion et du roi*, the foremost Catholic paper in France, found the programme and motto of *L'Avenir* contradictory, claiming one could not be both Christian and liberal.[12] The dichotomy between the two would haunt the papacy throughout the nineteenth and into the twentieth century.

11 Norman Ravitch, *The Catholic Church and the French Nation* (London, 1991), p. 91.
12 M. Patricia Dougherty, 'The Rise and Fall of *L'Ami de la Réligion*: History, Purpose, and Readership of a French Catholic Newspaper', *Catholic Historical Review*, LXXXVII, 2 (January 1991), p. 31.

In December 1831 Lamennais decided to take his case to Rome, which remained largely oblivious to the winds of change shaking the economic, social and political structure of Western Europe. Sheltered from the economic dislocation and industrialization transforming Western Europe, neither the Roman curia nor the pope comprehended the forces provoking change. The Camoldolese monk and former prefect of the office of propaganda, who sat as pope, was a traditionalist who believed in hierarchy, order and the virtue of obedience. He suspected that concessions and toleration only emboldened the revolutionaries, encouraging them to persist in their dangerous designs.

Gregory identified the interests of the church with the existing regimes, rather than relying on the faithful as Lamennais preached. Furthermore, he had serious reservations about Lamennais's theology which linked the truths of Christianity to the collective judgement of humanity rather than the traditional theology. From the first the pope remained sceptical of the Breton priest's adoration of the masses, which was subsequently echoed in Mazzini's revolutionary programme and new world order. Rather than appreciating the role of the people, the pontiff was grateful to the Austrians for the assistance they provided in restoring his revolutionary provinces.[13] Gregory's thoughts were expressed in the *Cathecism on Revolution*, published that same year. 'Does the holy law of God permit rebellion against the legitimate temporal sovereign?', the *Cathecism* asked, and answered 'No, never, because the temporal powers comes from God.' The *Catechism* proclaimed that just as the Christian had to submit to God, he had to remain subject to the prince, who was God's agent.[14]

Gregory discouraged Catholic Poles from resisting the persecution of their Russian oppressors, as Nicholas I systematically undermined those articles of the treaties of 1815 which assured Poland an independent existence. In the Russian reaction against the revolution of 1830, the tsarist regime exiled countless patriots and stripped suspects of their property. Roman Catholicism, the religion of the land, shared the burden of the persecution. Its activity was sharply curtailed, many of its church buildings seized and transferred to the Orthodox faith, while communication with Rome was hindered. Despite this persecution, Gregory castigated those who exploited religion to defy their princes, repeating this message in his encyclical of 9 June 1832 to the bishops of Poland. In this letter, he cited the need for civil obedience, condemning the revolutionary movements and insurrection in Poland, while cautioning Catholic Poles to remain submissive to the legitimately constituted authority.[15] Gregory meanwhile excommunicated those who incited rebellion in Ancona.[16]

The editors of *L'Avenir*, influenced by a society in transition, were not readily understood by the Mediterranean world of Gregory XVI, which remained largely unchanged. Not surprisingly, the 'pilgrims of God and liberty'

13 *TESP*, p. 185.
14 *Catechismo Sulle Rivoluzioni* (1832), ASV, Fondo Particolare Pio IX, *cassetta* 5, *busta* 4.
15 *Cum primum*, in Carlen, *PE*, I, pp. 233–4.
16 *Bull Rom Cont. Gregory XVI*, XIX, pp. 117–19.

received a frosty reception in the Eternal City, where they were all but ignored. Lamennais, seeking vindication, persisted, remaining in Rome for more than two months before being received by the pontiff. When he finally obtained his interview, Lamennais was dismayed that the pope did not discuss his liberal Catholicism or the controversy it engendered, dismissing him and his colleagues graciously. Nonetheless, a congregation was appointed to examine the movement and the newspaper which popularized its position.[17] Their work was reflected in Gregory's encyclical of 15 August 1832, which condemned both the ideas of *L'Avenir* as well as the general agency for the defence of religious liberty, the international organization which Lamennais had founded.[18] The encyclical had crucial repercussions for the church, the papacy, and church–state relations. It widened the rift between the church and the modern world which prevailed throughout most of the century.

Expressing an almost Manichean vision of the world, in which the forces of good and evil were in constant struggle, Pope Gregory implicitly censured the principles of the *Avenir* movement. He denounced the spirit of a false enlightenment and blind innovation, as well as the 'pestilence of indifferentism' and the 'pretensions of unrestrained religious liberty'. Rejecting the notion that salvation could be attained through the profession of any belief as the 'modernizers' preached, Gregory posited one God and one faith. In essence, the pope returned to the themes elaborated in his *Triumph of the Holy See and the Church against the Assaults of Innovators* (1799), decrying the 'insolence of science' which sought to discredit the sacred and demolish the divine faith. The pope resented the caustic criticism of the champions of change who longed to humble the divinely instituted church and curtail its rights.[19]

One of the intolerable innovations was the separation of church and state, which *L'Avenir* had advocated. Gregory considered it dangerous for the well-being of a Christian people, whose needs he propounded were best served by an integral unity. He likewise denounced the notion that Catholics should collaborate with liberals and revolutionaries to achieve their aims, insisting on obedience to the legitimately constituted authority. The union with liberal revolutionaries was explicitly denounced as a grave error. Gregory reminded the faithful that authority flowed from God, and those who resisted it, challenged His ordinances. The pope felt bound to anathematize the revolutions of the modern world and other liberal notions. Rejecting secularization and the liberation of culture and society from religious control, Gregory XVI harped on their necessary subordination to the church and the papacy.

Gregory catalogued the problems posed by the enemies of God, who camouflaged their 'evil' aims under the guise of liberty of conscience and freedom of the press. He lamented the veritable flood of errors flowing from liberalism,

17 Francesco Andreu, *Un aspetto inedito nel raporto Ventura-Lamennais*, ed. Eugenio Guccione (Florence, 1991), II, pp. 635–6.
18 *Mirari Vos*, 15 August 1832, *Bull Rom Cont. Gregory XVI*, XIX, pp. 126–32.
19 *Mirari Vos*, 15 August 1832, *Acta Sanctae Sedis* (Rome, 1865–1908) (hereafter cited as *ASS*), III, pp. 336–45.

including the impudence of science, the dissolution created in the name of liberty, and the perversions that were openly preached, to the detriment of truth and sound doctrine. Charging that the authority of the church and the papacy were opposed and their rights curtailed, he complained that the academies and schools, and their publications, brought forward 'monstrous opinions', openly undermining the Catholic faith. If the present evils continued, Gregory foresaw the destruction of public order and the overturning of all legitimate societies. He therefore invoked a crusade against the common enemies of the church and religion.[20] Gregory's *Mirari vos* was a condemnation of the entire liberal programme and a forerunner of Pius IX's *Quanta cura* and his 'Syllabus of Errors', which placed the church in conflict with modern civilization for almost a century.

Although *L'Avenir* was prohibited in all dioceses and its three editors submitted to Rome, Gregory's difficulties remained. Lamennais, like others in the movement, submitted but resented recanting his beliefs. Ruminating on his grievances, Lamennais revealed that while he accepted papal authority on religious issues, he questioned its pronouncements on temporal matters and its condemnation of collaboration between Catholics and liberals. Subsequently, Lamennais protested the papal position in *Words of a Believer* (1834), contesting Gregory's conservative position and his criticism of the Catholic campaign for liberty in such places as Ireland, Belgium and Poland. Gregory reacted quickly, issuing the *Singulari nos* of 25 June 1834, one of the few encyclicals focusing on one person's errors.[21] Gregory charged that Lamennais's attack on the princes in the name of absolute liberty represented a corruption of the gospels, reviving earlier heresies. He thus denounced the *Paroles d'un croyant* as a threat to the civil structure, exhorting the bishops to uphold the prevailing order as necessary for the welfare of both civil and sacred affairs. In October 1832 Gregory denounced the conspiracy of secret societies and the false idols worshipped by a 'modern civilization' which he neither understood nor appreciated.

The pope proved himself sufficiently pragmatic to open diplomatic relations with *de facto* governments when there were changes of regime. However, Gregory insisted this recognition represented no concession to the right of revolution. In the pope's view this arrangement conferred neither authority nor moral significance but simply represented a recognition of the existing reality. This policy, Gregory continued, had allowed the Holy See to settle the difficult issue of appointments in Latin America and India, despite the protests of Spain and Portugal. Nonetheless, he responded to the complaints of Tsar Nicholas on the part played by Catholics in the Polish revolt, by issuing *Cum primum* to the bishops of Poland (9 June 1832), which condemned the revolutionary movement in that Catholic country, urging the faithful to remain submissive to legitimate authority.[22]

20 Carlen, *PE*, I, pp. 235–8.
21 *Singulari Nos*, 23 June 1834, *Bull Rom Cont. Gregory XVI*, XIX, pp. 379–81; *TESP*, pp. 198–202.
22 Carlen, *PP*, I, pp. 25–6.

In Italy, Gregory was scandalized by the programme of Mazzini's Young Italy which emerged during the course of 1831. Like Lamennais, the Italian nationalist believed in the emergence of a new faith which stressed the progress of a united humanity towards God. 'The time has come to convince ourselves that we can rise to God through the souls of our fellow man', Mazzini wrote. 'We improve with the improvement of Humanity, nor without the improvement of the whole can you hope that your own moral and material conditions will improve.'[23] Pope Gregory found neither his theology nor his political programme any better than that of Lamennais, and did not hesitate to denounce it.

While Gregory veered along a conservative course, discouraging the faithful in Italy from resisting their princes, and prohibiting those in Ireland and Poland from battling their non-Catholic oppressors, others in the church had a different vision. The priest Antonio Rosmini hoped that the pope would assume the role of a moral arbiter, introducing the regeneration required by both society and the church. He collected his thoughts in a work entitled *On the Five Wounds of the Holy Church*. Within the pages of his unpublished manuscript, Rosmini cited the need for ending the division between clergy and people, the imperfect education of the clergy, the unfortunate mechanism of appointing bishops, and the problems created by the church's wealth. If the church was allegedly burdened by excessive wealth, the government of the Papal States faced financial crisis and found reprieve only through a burdensome loan from the Rothschilds in 1831.

Throughout the 1830s, the pope ignored the social and economic dislocation provoked by the industrial revolution while focusing on the political and religious consequences which it provoked. The pope and his successors expected the church to continue to function under the old regime which was progressively undermined. Rejecting innovations, the papacy insisted on confronting new problems with past solutions. Gregory remained preoccupied by financial exigencies at home, and church–state relations abroad, particularly the issue of mixed marriages, rejecting the liberal contention that marriage was primarily a contractual arrangement rather than a sacrament.

In May 1831 Gregory upheld the canons forbidding the marriage of Catholics with heretics, though recognizing that such marriages had sometimes been tolerated to avoid greater scandal. However, Gregory insisted that in such instances the Catholic party had to draw his or her non-Catholic partner to Catholicism and assure their offspring be educated in the faith.[24] Gregory's conservative-clerical thought was disseminated in Germany by the 1833 publication of Italian and German editions of his 1799 work *The Triumph of the Holy See*. Directed against Jansenist tendencies, it rejected the notion that the state had the right to oversee religious affairs, proclaiming the church independent of the civil authority and its earthly head infallible on matters of faith.

23 Giuseppe Mazzini, 'The Duties of Man', in *The Duties of Man and other Essays*, ed. Ernest Rhys (London, 1936), p. 47.
24 Carlen, *PE*, I, pp. 229–31.

Throughout these years, Gregory deplored the ecclesiastical legislation of the Swiss, Bavarian and Austrian governments almost as much as that stemming from Berlin and St Petersburg. Gregory perceived this legislation inspired by a 'satanic' desire to undermine the faith, virtually ignoring the changed societal relations accompanying industrialization, urbanization and political modernization. The pontiff regretted the campaign against the church by journals, periodicals, as well as some of the cantons of the Swiss federation, whose revised constitution suppressed the guarantees enjoyed by the monasteries and other ecclesiastical institutions. Supported by Rome, the new constitution was rejected by the assembly of Lucerne in 1833, whose example was followed by a number of Catholic cantons and some that were mixed.

Swiss liberals and nationalists responded with the conference of Baden in 1834, whose fourteen articles emulated the civil constitution of the clergy. Together these articles subordinated the church to the state, restricted ecclesiastical influence on matrimony, while undermining the rights of the primate and threatening the property and future of the monasteries. Not surprisingly they were denounced by Gregory. In May 1835 the pope rejected the articles which practically eliminated papal authority over Swiss Catholics. 'It is church dogma that the pope, the successor of St Peter, possesses not only the primacy of honour but also primacy of authority and jurisdiction over the whole church', he wrote, foreshadowing Pio Nono's dogma of papal infallibility.[25] Part of the Swiss Catholic community concurred, and eventually the seven Catholic regions united in the Sonderbund to protect their interests. The league, which Rome applauded for defending the faith, was denounced by liberals for undermining Swiss unity.

Relations with Vienna also remained strained, despite the fact that Rome relied on the Austrian presence to preserve order in the legations. The pope complained that Austrian marriage laws diverged from canon law, and resented the restrictions placed on communications between the Austrian hierarchy and the Holy See by the *placet regio* and other impediments. Gregory denounced the ceremonial oath for new bishops, which stressed their duties to the state rather than the church, the anti-papal tone of the curriculum of their schools, and the fact that the administration of pious foundations remained in the hands of the state rather than the church.

Metternich, desirous of preserving a harmonious relationship with Rome, sought to resolve these complaints, and urged Emperor Francis to reconcile Austrian ecclesiastical legislation and canon law. Monsignor Pietro Ostini, who had been internuncio at Vienna in the 1820s, was commissioned to draft a proposal for revising church–state relations in Austria. Presented in May 1833, it called for: (1) free communication of the Austrian clergy and laity with Rome; (2) use of the Roman ceremonial when bishops assumed possession of their Sees; (3) full episcopal jurisdiction over diocesan seminaries; (4) clerical rather than state supervision of religious instruction in the schools;

25 Ibid., I, p. 255.

(5) religious orders released from governmental interference in their internal affairs and left free to communicate with their superiors in Rome; (6) bishops to play some part in the supervision of the property of parishes, seminaries, and other diocesan religious establishments; (7) clergy accused of religious offences to be tried before the bishop's tribunal; and (8) bishops be permitted to baptize Jews who requested it, without governmental consent, as previously required.[26]

Rome found the Ostini proposal a step in the right direction, but complained it left too many aspects of Josephism in place and invoked major revisions. The death of Emperor Francis early in 1835, and the incompetence of his successor, Ferdinand, doomed the religious legislation desired by both Gregory and Metternich. Meanwhile Rome faced a host of other pressing problems in Germany, stemming from the question of church rights in general, and the question of mixed marriages in particular. In Prussia, the king had issued a royal decree on mixed marriages early in the century (1803), positing that all children from such marriages be raised in the religion of the father, who in most cases was Protestant, and deeming any promises or prenuptial agreements to the contrary invalid. Following the congress of Vienna (1815), Prussia absorbed the Catholic territories of Westphalia and the Rhineland, and in 1825 the Prussian cabinet extended the provisions of 1803 to these western provinces, creating consternation in the Catholic community. These complaints reached Leo XII in Rome, but before he could address them he was succeeded by Pius VIII, who in March 1830 issued a brief *Litteris* on the issue.

Pius, seeking to avoid confrontation with the Prussian government, provided a series of concessions including the participation of the Catholic clergy in marriages performed by non-Catholic ministers, but making it clear that their assistance was 'passive' rather than 'active', while reminding the Catholic parents of their obligations regarding the education of all ensuing children. The Prussian minister in Rome, Josias von Bunsen, sought a revision of the brief, but found Gregory obstinate. Indeed, while Bunsen intrigued for its revision in Rome, Gregory expressed his sentiments in an encyclical to the bishops of Bavaria, stressing the dangers posed by mixed marriages, reiterating the church's position on these unions, and repeating the responsibilities of the clergy in the matter.[27]

In June 1834 the archbishop of Cologne was summoned to Berlin and pressed for a compromise, and the latter consented shortly thereafter to a meeting at Coblenz, where part of the hierarchy agreed to a reinterpretation of the papal brief. By their interpretation, the Catholic clergyman was no longer a spectator at the mixed marriages, but encouraged to bless the union, while nothing was said of the Catholic partner's obligation to raise their offspring in the faith. Others in the German hierarchy were scandalized by the attempt to outskirt the papal position, and their voice strengthened following

26 Reinerman, *Austria and the Papacy*, pp. 272–84.
27 Carlen, *PP*, I, pp. 25, 27.

the election of the elderly Clemens Auguste von Droste-Vischering as archbishop of Cologne. Rejecting the compromise of Coblenz, the new archbishop insisted on the terms of *Litteris*, firming Gregory's resolve to preserve his stand.

In September 1835 Gregory condemned the errors and rationalistic tendencies of George Hermes and his disciples, which Frederick William II had sought to use as a means of reconciling Catholicism with Protestantism. Insult was added to injury when Clemens Auguste in Cologne published the papal condemnation of Hermesian doctrines without a governmental *placet*, provoking state authorities. Tensions increased in Prussia in November 1837, when the archbishop of Cologne was imprisoned in the fortress at Minden in Westphalia. Early in December, Gregory protested the persecution by the Prussian government of its Catholic subjects, who constituted some two-fifths of the population, while condemning the unjust imprisonment of the archbishop who had merely followed papal directives regarding the children of mixed marriages.

Gregory faced difficulties with a number of Catholic countries as well as Protestant ones. While not entirely happy with the policies of the Protestant minister Guizot in Paris, he appreciated the educational legislation of 1833 which provided full freedom of education for primary education throughout the 1830s. Rome failed in its efforts to secure the same privilege for the secondary schools. Difficulties also ensued in Poland, where the marriage laws of 1836 violated Catholic principles and the pope repeatedly refused to sanction them. At the same time, problems arose in the Iberian peninsula. In Spain, Gregory was confronted with conflicting claimants to the throne upon the death of Ferdinand VII in 1833, with the king's brother, Don Carlos, basing his claim on the Salic law of the Bourbons while Queen Maria Christina claimed the throne for her young daughter, Isabella, on the older Spanish law of succession. Don Carlos, sword in hand, prepared to seize the throne, encouraging the northern provinces to insurrection and finding support in the Basque provinces which resented Madrid's centralization. A bitter civil war endured for seven years.

When the government of the regent asked the Holy See for formal recognition, Gregory, whose sympathies rested with the conservative Catholic claimant Don Carlos, refused. Gregory's hesitation created ill-will in the court of Madrid, encouraging an outburst of anticlericalism. A spate of decrees were unleashed against the clergy and the hierarchy, the Jesuits were suppressed, and the property of the Inquisition was confiscated and put at the disposal of the fund to diminish the public debt. The dismissal of the papal secretary of state, Tommaso Bernetti, early in 1836, at Metternich's insistence, and his replacement by Luigi Lambruschini, who had been the nuncio at Paris, did not improve Vatican-Spanish relations. The new secretary of state was intransigent in his devotion to papal prerogatives, the rights of the church, and the Society of Jesus. As the Spanish government proceeded with its modernization, papal protests proved counter-productive, with the Cortes dissolving the remaining religious orders while nationalizing the property of the Spanish church. By the end of October 1836, all official relations between Spain and the Holy See were ended, to be resumed only in 1845.

In Portugal, as in Spain, Gregory confronted a contested succession as well as a conflict between constitutionalists and ultra-conservative Catholics. Rome had recognized the reactionary regime of Don Miguel, which restored all the privileges previously enjoyed by the church, readmitted the Jesuits, and established tribunals modelled on the Inquisition. When Don Pedro lost power in Brazil in the early 1830s, and returned to Portugal to reclaim the throne with English and French support, Don Miguel fled and found his way to Rome, where he received a warm welcome. The church paid for its flirtation with the dictator and the reactionary coterie, as the Jesuits were expelled, the regular clergy stoned in the streets of Lisbon, and Catholic institutions including schools and hospitals slammed shut. Gregory responded through a series of protests in 1833 and 1834, threatening canonical censure, but proved unable to stop the persecution.[28] Only after the accession of the fervently Catholic Queen Maria da Gloria in 1840 were relations between the Holy See and Portugal restored, and negotiations commenced for the conclusion of a concordat.

Gregory's domestic and international problems persisted, contributing to his conviction that the papacy and the church were under siege in the modern world. Gregory's reform of the administration and judicial system of his states was decidedly conservative and notoriously ineffectual.[29] Even nature seemed to work against the pope as an outbreak of cholera struck Rome and its environs despite the precautions taken by the papal authorities, sparking disturbances and disorders.[30] Other calamities followed, including floods and earthquakes, which bedevilled the Papal States, while the government's response, which further drained the papal treasury, was judged too little, too late, failing to restore public confidence. Abroad Josephism remained in place in Austria, the Prussian government continued to persecute the clergy and imprisoned the archbishop of Cologne, and in France an unrepentent Lamennais wrote yet another book, *Le Livre du Peuple* (1837), which Gregory found offensive. Meanwhile in Switzerland the government decreed that ecclesiastics who did not swear allegiance to the new constitution would be deprived of their office, and the clergy were subjected to abuse and derision in a number of cantons of the federation.

Gregory was happy to see 1837 end; the new year brought some reprieve for both the Roman church and the Papal States. After persistent procrastination, the Austrians finally withdrew from Bologna and the Romagna in November 1838, followed by the French evacuation of Ancona in December. Rome remained aloof from the annual scientific congresses which commenced in 1839, bringing together representatives from the various Italian states to

28 *Bull Rom Cont. Gregory XVI*, XIX, pp. 276–7.

29 Ibid., XIX, pp. 390–563.

30 Giacomo Antonelli to Filippo Antonelli, 28 June 1837 and 13 August 1837, Archivio di Stato di Roma (ASR). Fondo Famiglia Antonelli, *busta* I, n. 1, n. 116.

'increase the glory to the Italian nation'. Gregory was likewise suspicious of the railway projects that were being proposed to 'stitch up the boot', while remaining critical of the attempts of the various governments to restrict the rights of the church, showing himself determined to defend the traditional rights of religion.[31]

Gregory found some consolation abroad and believed that the future of the church would depend on the work of the missions which carried Catholicism beyond Europe. The pope dispatched an apostolic visitor to Peru, while apostolic vicariates were established in Korea, Ceylon and Calcutta. New dioceses were erected in New Granada.[32] While his denunciation of nationalism proved counter-productive in Italy and Europe, it had positive consequences abroad as he pleaded to purge colonialism and nationalism from the missionary crusade. To the surprise of some, the pope who denounced the 'excesses' of liberty at home insisted that the faith had to be transmitted to free men. In an apostolic letter at the end of 1839, he condemned the slave trade as unworthy of Christians.[33] The pope praised the martyrs in China (1835–40), who surrendered their lives so that the faith might live, especially praising the fortitude of Chinese women, citing their perseverance in the profession of the gospels under grievous afflictions and torments.[34]

In 1840 Gregory catalogued the contemporary tribulations of the church, the onslaught and pollution of errors, the unbridled rashness of renegades, as well as the deceitful attempts to pervert the hearts and minds of the faithful. In these difficult circumstances, Gregory was 'thankful for the success of the apostolic missions in America, the Indies, and other faithless lands'. The pope praised the missionaries who brought salvation to those still in darkness, as well as the efforts of pious organizations dedicated to the welfare of Christian society worldwide. There were words of praise for the Society for the Propagation of the Faith, organized in Lyons in 1822, spreading with speed and promoting the faith. The pope believed the time had arrived 'when the Christian battle line should smash the devil as he rages all over the world'.[35] Gregory rejected the liberal alternative to conservatism, perceiving it as a threat to his political power and spiritual authority.

The pope's siege mentality contributed to his acerbic reaction to whoever or whatever challenged the church's authority. Gregory was scandalized that in the United States, whose Catholic population approached a million, the trustees of the dioceses of New Orleans sought to undermine the authority of their bishop. He reprimanded them for their arrogance, threatening ecclesiastical censure unless they repented, while insisting that they desist from such actions in the future. At the same time, he wrote to bishops worldwide, instructing them on the pernicious programme of the burgeoning non-Catholic

31 See *Officii memores*, 5 July 1839 in Carlen, *PP*, I, p. 27.
32 *Bull Rom Cont. Gregory XVI*, XIX, pp. 149–54, 568, 577–8, 617–18.
33 See *In supremo apostolatus*, 3 December 1839, in Carlen, *PP*, I, p. 27.
34 See *Afflictas in Tunquino*, in Carlen, *PP*, I, p. 27.
35 Carlen, *PP*, I, pp. 260–1.

bible societies, which deceived the faithful.[36] He specifically condemned the recently formed Christian League of New York, warning that whosoever joined, or even aided it, was guilty of a grievous crime.

In the remaining years of his pontificate from 1840 to 1846, Gregory continued his crusade against the 'forces of evil' and those who sought to diminish the influence of the Roman church. In his mind, the two were hardly distinguishable as he denounced those who proposed reconciliation between the church and this 'modern world'. Gregory took solace in the accession of Frederick William IV in Prussia in 1840, whose government allowed the clergy to communicate directly with Rome, and the Catholic restoration in Bavaria after 1837 witnessed the termination of many of the clauses of the edict of religion. However, he was saddened by the Swiss attacks on a number of monasteries in 1841, whose spoliation he denounced. In April 1841 he protested against the Hungarian bishops' sanctioning 'mixed marriages' without the dispensation of Rome. He also denounced the attacks on the church in Spain, while praising the zeal of the episcopacy and the faithful in that Catholic country.[37]

In February 1842 Gregory urged the faithful to pray for Spain, and their appeal was apparently heard. In the following year, the Spanish moderate liberals or *moderados* launched a successful *pronunciamiento* against the progressive liberal government of General Baldmero Espartero. Isabella returned home, and General Espartero fled to England. The *moderado* government of General Ramon Narvaez and the new Cortes in 1843–44 permitted exiled ecclesiastics to return, gave bishops considerable freedom, and removed restrictions for the filling of vacant sees. Other conciliatory measures followed as president of the council Narvaez appointed a special representative to the Vatican.

Pope Gregory hoped to achieve further conciliation by proposing a new concordat. Preliminary negotiations between the Spanish government and the Holy See opened in January 1845, and in April a tentative agreement was signed in Rome. Among other things, the draft provided that Catholicism would be professed in all the dominions of the Spanish monarchy, and seminaries would be established in each diocese for clerical education and would remain under the control of the local bishops who would also enjoy the right to oversee religious instruction in the public schools. Provision was also made to return unsold clerical lands to the church and for the Spanish government to fund the maintenance of the cult and clergy. In turn, the pope would issue a bull recognizing the loss of church property prior to January 1845.[38]

The Vatican wanted more. Among other things, Gregory sought a declaration that the oath sworn to the constitution rendered no obligation to provide allegiance to anything that might violate the laws of God and the church. The pope also demanded a clause enabling him to assume direction of a number of

36 *ASS*, XII, p. 545; Carlen, *PE*, I, pp. 267–71; Carlen, *PP*, I, pp. 28–9.
37 Carlen, *PP*, I, p. 28.
38 Nancy A. Rosenblatt, 'Church and State in Spain: A Study of Moderate Liberal Politics in 1845', *Catholic Historical Review* LXII, 4 (October 1976), pp. 592–4.

vacant sees, while invoking recognition of the church's right to own property. To compensate the church for its losses, the Holy See called for a sufficient subsidy for the Spanish church and its clergy, as well as exclusion from the bishops of persons known to be hostile to Rome. Finally, Gregory insisted on a recognition of the religious and ecclesiastic liberty of the Spanish bishops as well as the reconstitution of the disbanded religious orders. While the queen was amenable, her government refused to ratify the proposed concordat.

Relations with Russia remained strained as Nicholas I (1825–55), seeking religious unity in his empire, persecuted the church. In the summer of 1842 a frustrated Gregory revealed the efforts made by Rome to reach an understanding with St Petersburg to terminate the persecution of the church within the empire. During the tsar's visit to Rome in December 1845, the pope decried his persecution of the church, warning Nicholas that he would eventually have to answer his Maker for pursuing this unfortunate policy. Closer to home, Gregory deplored violations of the concordat with the court of Turin,[39] and the outbreak of disorders in the Papal States which were suppressed by papal forces without Austrian intervention.

In Italy, Gregory continued to oppose the programme of *Giovane Italia* which the patriot Giuseppe Mazzini formed in 1831, the year that Gregory had donned the papal tiara. Gregory found Mazzini's nationalism, which stressed unitary republicanism and a deistic religious regeneration, anathema. The papacy, Mazzini contended, sought to excommunicate liberty from the world. He predicted it would not succeed, announcing that it would eventually be replaced by liberty.[40] Paradoxically, Mazzini blamed Rome for the atheism that dominated revolutionary circles, noting that patriots were inclined to accept the church and the clergy, only recoiling from them when they found priests and the papacy hostile to their national aspirations. Small wonder, Mazzini concluded, that patriots turned from the church, having seen the clergy praise the wicked and condemn the just.[41] Mazzini's analysis led the pope to condemn the entire nationalist programme.

Some argued that a form of Italian liberty and national consolidation was compatible with the church, reconciling the movement for Italian independence with the temporal power of the papacy. Dubbed neo-Guelphs, their programme sought to provide an alternative to the radicals, looking to the papacy to provide the leadership for unification. They began by re-examining and revising the assessment of the role of the papacy in Italy's history. Alessandro Manzoni, grandson of Cesare Beccaria and author of *I promessi sposi* (1827), in his *Discorso sopra alcuni punti della storia longobardica in Italia* (1822), denied that the popes were the chief obstacles to Italian unity, defending

39 Archbishop of Turin to the Secretary of State, ASV, Archivio della Segreteria di Stato, *rubrica* 257, *fasciocolo* 15, *protocollo* 39240.

40 Giuseppe Mazzini, *Note autobiografiche*, ed. Mario Menghini, 2nd edn (Florence, 1944), pp. 196–7.

41 *Mazzini's Letters*, trans. Alice de Rosen Jervis (London, 1930), p. 70.

Pope Adrian I for calling the Franks into the peninsula. According to Manzoni, this worked to preserve the Italian nation and Christian civilization against the invading Germanic hordes.

In 1828 Cesare Cantù published his novella *L'Algisio*, which focused on the positive role played by the church in reawakening the Italian spirit. Cesare Balbo, the Piedmontese writer, historian and statesman, in a series of works concurred that the papacy, with its temporal power which assured the independence of the church, was essential to the mission of Italy. Similar thoughts pervaded Niccolò Tommaseo's *Dell' Italia* (1835), which called for a unification of Italy and the marriage of Christianity and liberty. Leopoldo Galeotti, author of *Della sovranità e del governo temporale dei Papi* (1847), claimed that Italian culture was in large measure the work of the papacy. He beseeched the pope to resume a leading role in the peninsula.[42] The theologian, philosopher, priest and political figure, Vincenzo Gioberti, did the most to advance the neo-Guelph programme in Italy. His enthusiasm for Mazzini and the Polish cause led to his arrest and confinement in 1833, followed by exile, first in Paris, and later in Brussels, were he published *Del primato morale e civile degli Italiani* (1843).

Like others in the neo-Guelph movement, Gioberti considered the papacy 'the ancient protector of the nation' and 'the generous refuge of tolerance', stressing the need for its primacy in a united Italy. Gioberti believed that the glory of the peninsula could be restored by a confederation of Italian princes under the pontiff, whose moral regime would be upheld by the military might of Piedmont. The programme, he insisted, would not only improve the plight of the Italian people, but would prove advantageous to the faith. Gioberti concluded that every design of the Risorgimento would prove futile unless it had the papacy at its foundation.[43] Apparently reconciling the rift between religion and the Risorgimento, Catholic theology and the national programme, the *Primato* enjoyed a widespread popularity in Italy. It even found adherents in the Papal States, winning part of the clergy to the national cause. The illusion that the pope might achieve unification peacefully proved seductive.

Pope Gregory was not seduced. To unmask the deceptive national programme of the sects, he commissioned the conservative Catholic Cretineau-Joly to write a polemical history of the secret societies which exposed their dire political consequences. At home, he resisted reform, despite the impending revolutionary agitation which led to the fall of Rimini in 1843, before it was forcefully returned to papal control by the pope's Swiss troops. Subsequently, a rash of disturbances erupted throughout the legations in 1845, even as Gregory hosted Tsar Nicholas in Rome. In his *Recent Events in the Romagna* (1845), Massimo d'Azeglio pinpointed the abuses in the Papal States which provoked the popular explosion and the consequent papal repression. The bishop of

42 Gabriele De Rosa, *Storia del movimento cattolico in Italia. Dalla restaurazione all'età giolittiana* (Bari, 1966), pp. 42–4.
43 Vincenzo Gioberti, *Del primato morale e civile degli Italiani* (Turin, 1932), I, pp. 70, 120.

Imola, Giovanni Mastai-Ferretti, was critical of the ponderous Roman administration. Scandalized by the round of conspiracy, revolt and repression, he acknowledged that the states of the church were not well governed. During the second half of 1845, when the four cardinal legates met to ponder means to avoid further disorders, Mastai placed little hope in governmental measures. 'If God does not help us', he wrote, 'then certainly the meeting of cardinals will not provide for our salvation.'[44] Gregory seemed to prefer piety to progress, obedience to liberty.

Personally disinterested in political problems, the pope tended to ignore the increasing intellectual discontent, preferring to dwell on having Mary acclaimed Immaculate.[45] He readily confirmed the constitution of the Society of the Immaculate Conception.[46] In 1844 he again denounced bible societies and the association of Catholics with other Christians in the alliance of Christians.[47] He rejected both the liberalism flowing from the French Revolution and that emerging from the industrial revolution without discerning any difference between the two. Gregory refused to seek an accommodation with modern movements and liberal thought which he perceived violated the spirit and the laws of Catholicism. Convinced that concessions to the modern world would inevitably undermine the foundation of the faith, the pope shied from accepting even political and social innovations. Paradoxically, this intransigent opposition, meant to secure the church, worked to isolate Rome, rendering its reconciliation with the modern world difficult. As his health deteriorated in 1846, and his facial cancer spread, it is not surprising that Gregory wished to die as he had lived, as a monk rather than a prince. Gregory's recourse to prayer had not healed the rift between the church and the modern world, nor ended the threat to the temporal and spiritual power of the papacy.

44 Giovanni Maioli, *Pio IX da vescovo a Pontefice. Lettere al Card. Luigi Amat. Agosto 1839–Luglio 1848* (Modena, 1943), p. 42.
45 Carlen, *PP*, I, p. 29.
46 *Bull Rom Cont. Gregory XVI*, XIX, pp. 308–57.
47 *TESP*, p. 202.

CHAPTER 6

The Holy See in a turbulent decade: 1846–1856

The death of Gregory XVI in the sixteenth year of his pontificate appeared to mark a turning point in the course of the papacy and the Papal States as contemporaries deemed the selection of his successor of crucial importance for both church and society. As factories mushroomed in Europe and railroads tied its cities, great wealth arose side by side with wretched poverty. The application of steam to various trades and the introduction of machinery led to a revolution in the mode of manufacturing and the constitution of labour. As social ills troubled society and confronted the church, the rift between the two seemed senseless and counter-productive. The chasm opened between the church and the modern world appeared insurmountable, with dire consequences for both. Gregory's pontificate had aggravated the division, rendering reconciliation difficult. The conclave, which opened on 14 June 1846, sought a middle ground between reform and reaction, avoiding the threat of impending revolution by limited concessions while preserving the faith from liberal subversion. As in all papal elections following the upheaval of the French Revolution, the cardinals were grouped on the basis of their attitude toward reconciliation with the modern world.

Cardinal Luigi Lambruschini, Gregory's secretary of state and Metternich's choice, was the darling of the conservatives. The Capuchin Cardinal Luigi Micara was favoured by the party of progress, which sought some accommodation with contemporary developments, with Cardinal Pasquale Gizzi, lionized by Massimo d'Azeglio in his *Degli ultimi casi di Romagna*, a close second. Early on, Giovanni Maria Mastai-Ferretti, bishop of Imola, emerged as a compromise candidate. Although Lambruschini led in the first ballot, his intransigent opposition to change was deemed detrimental to the temporal power. Consequently Lambruschini's vote declined in subsequent tallies, while that of the more moderate Mastai increased, and on 16 June 1846, during the course of the fourth tally, he was elected pope. He assumed the name Pius IX, in memory of Pius VII who had rendered possible his ordination.

The new pope was relatively young at fifty-four and destined to sit in the chair of Peter for thirty-two crucial years. He was not well known in Rome, having spent little time in the capital during the last two decades. Born on 13 May 1792, during the turmoil of the revolution, his earliest education was provided by his mother. In October 1809 he suffered an epileptic seizure, and attributed his subsequent improvement to the intervention of the Blessed Virgin, to whom his mother had consecrated him as an infant.[1] At the end of 1815, determined to enter the priesthood, he enrolled in the Roman college. Ordained in 1819, by the special dispensation of Pius VII because of his malady, his first assignment as a priest was at the Roman orphanage of 'Tata Giovanni' where he remained until 1823. From 1823 to 1825, he accompanied the apostolic delegate to Chile and Peru on his visit to Latin America. Following his return to Italy, Giovanni was appointed director of the hospice of San Michele in Rome. Named archbishop of Spoleto in 1827, he remained there until 1832, when he became bishop of Imola. In 1840 Pope Gregory named him to the college of cardinals.

Although ultraorthodox in religious matters, during his years in Imola Mastai had maintained contacts with liberals and envisioned some conciliation between religion and progress, liberalism and Catholicism.[2] While some quipped that even the cat in the Mastai household was a *carbonaro*, the bishop's stress on Christian virtue, obedience, charity and devotion to Mary rendered him attractive to the traditionalists, who found him a good pastor and administrator.[3] Thus in June 1846, when he was crowned with the triple tiara, Catholics questioned the policies he would pursue. Within the next month, he convinced sceptics that he was committed to reform, promising railways, amnesties and public audiences. It appeared that Rome had finally produced a pontiff capable of healing the rift between the faith and contemporary developments. Some hoped that the new pope would baptize liberalism and nationalism.

As bishop, he liked to discuss the prospects of a conciliation between religion and progress, between the Catholic faith and liberal principles. Although not a revolutionary or even a liberal, Mastai was critical of the Roman administration which provoked revolt and repression. He suggested that the condition of the Papal States could be improved by infusing its government with Christian justice, calling for it to be better attuned to the aspirations of its people. He did not understand the attitude of the government, which persecuted the young generation and opposed the introduction of railways. Theology, Pius IX observed, was not against the development of science and technology.[4] He elaborated his position and programme in a work called *Thoughts on the Public Administration of the Papal States* (1845) in which he invoked a collegiate body to advise and co-ordinate their administration.[5]

1 Antonio Monti, *Pio IX nel Risorgimento Italiano con documenti inediti* (Bari, 1928), pp. 23–4.
2 Giovanni Maioli, ed., *Pio IX da Vescovo a pontefice. Lettere al Card. Luigi Amat, Agosto 1839–Luglio 1848* (Modena, 1943), pp. 44–5.
3 ASV, Fondo Particolare Pio IX, *cassetta* x, *busta* 2.
4 Giuseppe Pasolini, *Memorie, 1815–1876* (Turin, 1887), p. 57.
5 'Pensieri relativi alla Amministrazione pubblica dello Stato Pontificio', in Alberto Serafini, *Pio Nono. Giovanni Maria Mastai Ferretti dalla giovinezza alla morte nei suoi scritti e discorsi editi e inediti* (Vatican City, 1958), I, pp. 1397–406.

Pius seconded many of the reform proposals put forward by the memorandum of the powers of 1831. To co-ordinate the transition, he relied on the advice of Monsignor Giovanni Corboli Bussi, secretary of the congregation of state, and Cardinal Pasquale Gizzi, whom he selected as his secretary of state. Together they elaborated the general amnesty which was signed on 16 July 1846 and announced the following day.[6] Although some were excluded from its provisions,[7] the amnesty, which released hundreds of inmates while allowing scores of exiles to return to the Papal States, earned Pius a liberal image at home and abroad.[8] The pope aroused Italy from her torpor. His pontificate was considered the beginning of a new age for the church, celebrated by massive demonstrations.[9] Liberals were enchanted and nationalists gratified, convinced that Pius IX was the figure who would bring the church into harmony with the new age, ending the conflict that had developed during the revolutionary period. At home and abroad, Pius was hailed as the 'liberator pope' who would modernize the papal regime while freeing Italy from her shackles.

The pope fulfilled the expectations of progressives by removing some of the restrictions imposed on the Jews, dismantling extraordinary tribunals, and initiating a reform of the criminal justice system of his state. Concommitantly, agrarian reform was projected, railway lines planned, and telegraph companies charted. For the first time, pontifical subjects were permitted to participate in the annual scientific congresses convoked in the peninsula, while a new press law liberalized censorship. Finally plans were made for the creation of a council of ministers.[10] These innovations were greeted with frenzied enthusiasm. Praise of the pope transcended the Alps and the Atlantic. His merits were applauded not only in the Italian capitals, but Paris, London, Madrid, and even Constantinople and New York. Following a spate of glowing reports transmitted by United States consuls in the Papal States, President James Polk, in his message to congress in December 1847, recommended the establishment of diplomatic relations with Rome.[11]

From the first, neither the personality nor the performance of Pius was dispassionately examined. Observing his smiling countenance and jovial manner, an admitted departure from the austere attitude of Gregory XVI, it was assumed that Pius was an optimist. In fact, the young Mastai suffered

6 Reports of Monsignor Corboli Bussi to Pius on the first and second sessions of the Congregation of State, 1 July 1846 and 8 July 1846, ASV, Archivio Particolare Pio IX, Stato Pontificio, nn. 1 and 2.

7 For a list of those excluded from its provisions see ASR, Miscellanea di Carte Politiche o Riservate, 1846, *busta* 154, *fascicolo* 1.

8 Amnistia accordata dalla Santità di nostro Signore Pio IX nella Sua exaltazione al Ponificato, 16 July 1846, in *Atti del Sommo Pontefice Pio IX, Felicemente Regnante. Parte seconda che comprende I Motu-proprii, chirografi editti, notificazioni, ec. per lo stato pontificio* (Rome, 1857), I, pp. 4–6.

9 *Breve racconti degli avvenimenti successi in Roma*, ASV, Archivio Particolare Pio IX, Oggetti Vari, n. 515.

10 *Rapporto a Sua Santità per l'udienza del 30 settembre 1846*, ASR, Fondo Famiglia Antonelli, *busta* 3.

11 *Consular Relations Between the United States and the Papal States*, ed. Leo F. Stock (Washington, 1945), pp. 92, 114.

bouts of depression, following his epiletic seizure of 1809. Later as archbishop of Spoleto, the most common theme of his talks in the cathedral was that peace flowed not from attachment to the things of the world, but from a true love of Christ.[12] Likewise, in his years at Imola, Mastai continued to preach on these themes, and in the first speech in the cathedral there he urged his listeners to seek consolation in God rather than the material world.[13]

The new pope was neither a revolutionary nor a liberal, as can be gleaned from his first encyclical of 9 November 1846, *Qui pluribus*, on faith and religion. It foreshadowed the fundamental lines of his pontificate. Following a eulogy of Gregory XVI, whose spiritual if not his political policies Pius admired, he attacked the incredulous enemies of Christian truth, decrying the war waged against Catholic interests. His letter condemned rationalism, indifferentism and latitudinarianism, as well as other 'monstrous errors' of the age. Warning of the dangers stemming from the specious pretext of human progress, Pius repeated many of his predecessors' proscriptions of liberalism's basic principles.[14] Thus, at a time when the pontiff was in the midst of political reforms, he revealed his traditionalism in his condemnation of the errors of the day.

The *Qui pluribus* represents not only a precursor to Pio Nono's later Syllabus of Errors, but also contains the seeds of the position proclaimed in the dogma of infallibility. Criticizing those who would submit divine revelation to their own judgement, Pius proclaimed that God had established a living authority to teach and maintain the true meaning of the faith. Asserting that this 'living and infallible authority resides in the church', he further observed that 'where Peter is, there is the Church, since Peter speaks by the mouth of the Roman Pontiff'.[15] The philosophy, religious outlook and assessment of the *Qui pluribus* is entirely consistent with the pope's later position. Through his long life, he remained remarkably consistent in his religious and philosophical outlook. The change occurred primarily in the political realm.

Nonetheless, the fact that a pope revealed his preference for reform over reaction had a tremendous impact in Italy and abroad. His religious traditionalism was overshadowed by his political reformism. Pius aroused national expectations by answering the petitions of his subjects for change, and criticizing the legate in Ravenna who had arrested demonstrators for shouting anti-Austrian slogans. Some perceived Pio Nono as the liberator-pope prophesied by Vincenzo Gioberti, who would assume the burden of uniting Italy. From his exile, even the founder of Young Italy, Giuseppe Mazzini, applauded the holy father's innovations.[16] In Vienna, Metternich understood that despite the expectations of the radicals, the pope had neither the means nor the desire to

12 Sermon of 25 December 1828, ASV, Fondo Particolare Pio IX, *cassetta* ix, *busta* 1, *fascicolo* 43.
13 Ibid, *cassetta* ix, *busta* 2, n. 76.
14 Carlen, *PE*, I, pp. 277–84; *Acta Pio IX. Pontificis Maximi. Pars prima acta exhibens quae ad Ecclesiam universam spectant (1846–1854)* (Rome, 1855), I, pp. 4–24.
15 Mother E. O'Gorman, ed., *Papal Teachings: The Church* (Boston, 1962), pp. 143–4.
16 Pasolini, *Memorie*, p. 57; ASV, Archivio Particolare Pio IX, Oggetti Vari, n. 412; Alexandre de Saint-Albin, *Pie IX* (Paris, 1860), p. 47.

fulfil their aims.[17] The Austrian minister warned of the grave consequences of the pope's being led astray.

Pius sought to serve as a spiritual guide for his people, unaware of the impact of his gestures on the imagination of his subjects and other Italians. Unquestionably, Pius loved Italy and wished to see it prosper, but thought primarily in terms of its spiritual rather than its national regeneration. He was alarmed by violence, such as marked the demonstration of 17 June 1847 in Rome. On that occasion, it appeared that the city's residents were devoted to the vicar of Christ, but distrusted his government. Suspicion increased following the edict of 22 June 1847, which called for an end to the extraordinary demonstations. Although inspired by Pius, the Romans attributed the call for order to the conservative circle surrounding him.[18]

After the first hectic year of his pontificate, Pius was dismayed by the stream of demands. Prepared to increase lay participation in his ministry, he balked at the notion of the secularization of his administration. Pius IX accepted the idea of lay input into state affairs, but not those of the church, resisting constitutionalism for either. He opposed placing arms in the hands of the people by creating a civic guard, confiding that this concession would make those outside the state laugh, and those inside cry.[19] Resolved to execute the concessions he had granted, Pius IX insisted on the preservation of all of his prerogatives, unprepared to pursue the path extremists had outlined for him. 'I do not want to do what Mazzini wishes', he admonished, adding, 'I cannot do what Gioberti wants.' The pope related as much to Father Luigi Taparelli d'Azeglio, the Jesuit brother of Massimo. 'We know where they want to lead us', Pius observed. 'We will cede as long as our conscience permits us, but having arrived at the limits pre-established, we will not, with the help of God, go beyond it by one step, even if they tore us to pieces.'[20]

To please the middle classes, the pope announced his intention of calling a number of persons to the capital to form an advisory council. Pio Nono's secretary of state, Cardinal Gizzi, whose liberal reputation did not reflect his centrist beliefs, only accepted the proposal following assurances it would not evolve into a representative chamber. In April 1847 Gizzi published the edict on the Consulta di Stato.[21] The pope and his secretary of state considered this innovation the capstone of their reformist programme, beyond which they could not go without infringing upon, and threatening, the rights of the church. Reformers and radicals demanded more.

Confronted with demands he was loath to concede, Pius threatened to abdicate. Pressured by a number of cardinals and Roman princes, who claimed that permitting the civic guard was the sole means of averting revolution,

17 M.A. Klinkowstroem, ed., *Mémoires, Documents et Écrits Divers laissés par le Prince de Metternich* (Paris, 1883), VII, pp. 572, 413–16.

18 *Atti del Sommo Pontefice Pio IX, Felicemente Regnante. Parte seconda che comprende I Motu-proprii, chirografi editti, notificazioni, ec. per lo stato pontificio*, I, pp. 70, 122.

19 Maioli, *Pio IX*, p. 111.

20 Giacomo Martina, *Pio IX (1846–1850)* (Rome, 1974), I, p. 118.

21 *Atti del Sommo Pontefice Pio IX, Felicemente Regnante*, I, pp. 47–8.

Pius relented. Gizzi continued to oppose the measure. When the guard was instituted, Gizzi concurred with Metternich that Pius had sealed his fate. Alarmed and disgusted, the papal secretary of state reluctantly signed the proclamation authorizing it on the anniversary of the amnesty, resigning shortly thereafter. The cardinal predicted that if he had remained by the pope's side for a year, those who followed would not last six months, because it was impossible for a thoughtful minister to co-operate with the vacillating pontiff.[22] His prediction proved accurate.

The pope's cousin, Cardinal Gabriele Ferretti, who succeeded as secretary of state, found his task impossible. The authorities had clearly lost control of events, charged an English observer in Rome, who added that Angelo Brunetti, known by the nickname of *Ciceruacchio* or 'big-boy', more than anyone else preserved the fragile peace in the capital.[23] Unfortunately, this horse and wine dealer from the Trastevere region who orchestrated the popular demonstrations and virtually controlled the newly instituted civic guard, was a follower of Mazzini and an instrument of the radical party. The impotence of the papal regime frightened the Austrians, who responded in July 1847 by reinforcing their garrison in Ferrara. Following the attack on an Austrian official in August, they occupied the area surrounding their barracks. There was an outcry by patriots, prompting a spirited protest from the apostolic legate of the city as well as by the secretary of state, Ferretti. The papal reaction, which included letters to the emperor and empress, persuaded the Austrians to withdraw to the citadel.[24] The victory proved costly, for the protests further aroused national expectations the pope could not fulfil.

Monsignor Giovanni Corboli Bussi advised Pius that it was impossible to disarm the factions without plucking the banner of Italian nationalism from their hands, citing two means to achieve the objective. The first called for the pope to declare war against the Germans, pushing them out of Italy. The second, less dangerous course involved the formation of an Italian league that would unite the peninsula. Pius perceived the latter option more in keeping with his spiritual mission, and in the autumn of 1847 entrusted Corboli Bussi with the responsibility of securing a customs union between the Papal States, the kingdom of Sardinia and the grand duchy of Tuscany. Carlo Alberto agreed to join under certain conditions, but negotiations for the confederation moved slowly, outpaced by the growing nationalist expectation and agitation.[25]

Early in January 1848 the people of Palermo rose in rebellion against the government of Naples, prompting Ferdinand II to grant a constitution, and unleashing a wave of revolutionary agitation throughout the peninsula. Cardinal Ferretti, overwhelmed by the turn of events and in conflict with Pius,

22 Martina, *Pio IX*, I, pp. 141–3; Klinkowstroem, ed., *Mémoires*, VII, pp. 418–20; Romolo Quazza, *Pio IX e Massimo D'Azeglio nelle vicende romane del 1847*, 2 vols (Modena, 1954), II, 3–5.

23 Great Britain, *British and Foreign State Papers*, XXXVI (1847–48), p. 1226.

24 Pius to the Emperor Ferdinand, 12 September 1847, and to the Empress Maria Anna, 12 September 1847, ASV, Archivio Particolare Pio IX, Sovrani, Austria, nn. 1–2.

25 Carboli Bussi to Pio Nono, 17 October 1847, ASV, Archivio Particolare Pio Nono, Stato Pontificio.

whom he found too prone to make concessions, fled Rome by night, like a fugitive. In February he was replaced by Cardinal Giuseppe Bofondi, who likewise proved incapable of coping with the explosive circumstances.[26]

On 10 February 1848 Pius revealed his desire to develop the political institutions of his state, without violating his obligations as head of the church. The pope highlighted the unique nature of the papal state, which he proclaimed beneficial for the whole of Italy. Claiming that the Romans had 200 million brothers abroad prepared to protect the centre of Catholic unity, Pius predicted Italy would remain secure and safe so long as it contained the apostolic chair. These words were pulled out of context to give his essentially religious invocation a political and national dimension. Pressured by the course of events, Pius changed his stance on the formation of the Italian league, transcending his original vision of a commercial union to accept the political organization he had earlier deemed inadmissible.[27]

Conscious of the transcendence of his spiritual obligations over his political responsibilities, in mid-February 1848 Pius convoked a committee of ecclesiastics to determine whether the concession of the constitution violated the special nature of papal authority. The committee found no theological hindrances to the introduction of constitutionalism in the temporal realm.[28] There was no thought of extending this constitutionalism to the church or curtailing the primacy of the pope therein. Their determination, plus news of the February revolution in Paris and the turmoil throughout Europe, hastened the pope's adoption of constitutionalism. Two prelates were instrumental in drafting the basic law of the Papal States: Giovanni Corboli Bussi, the young and liberal priest who had the pope's ear at the time, and Cardinal Giacomo Antonelli, minister of the treasury and president of the newly instituted Consulta. Laymen played no role.

On 10 March 1848 Pius announced the formation of a constitutional ministry under the leadership of Antonelli, who had close ties with liberals and reformers in the state. Four days later, the Roman constitution appeared, providing for two deliberative councils for the formation of law: a high council and a council of deputies. Both were prohibited from discussing the diplomatic-religious relations of the Holy See, with the *Statuto* specifying that the new governmental form must in no way infringe upon the rights of the church or the Holy See.[29] Some disliked the provision whereby the college of cardinals was invested with the authority of a political senate. To make matters worse, its deliberations were to remain secret, providing it with political immunity while it exercised a crucial veto power. There was also opposition to the prohibition which prevented the chambers from dealing with 'mixed matters',

26 Martina, *Pio IX*, I, pp. 142–3; Klinkowstroem, ed., *Mémoires*, VII, p. 592.
27 Memorial containing considerations on the project of a confederation among the Italian states, ASV, Archivio Particolare Pio IX, Oggetti Vari, n. 368.
28 Martina, *Pio IX*, I, pp. 209–12; Luigi Rodelli, *La Repubblica Romana del 1849* (Pisa, 1955), p. 44.
29 Statuto fondamentale del governo temporale degli Stati di S. Chiesa, *Atti del Sommo Pontefice Pio IX*, I, pp. 223–4, 229–32.

including political and administrative issues that touched upon the moral and religious mission of the church.

The theoretical opposition soon found practical application in the call for disbanding the Society of Jesus in Rome. Pius considered this a scandalous attack against the church and the Holy See. Eventually Antonelli negotiated a compromise, persuading the Jesuits to leave Rome voluntarily for their safety, thus satisfying the clamour of the radicals without violating the scruples of his sovereign.[30] The pope was horrified by the prospect that the political reformism he championed might degenerate into an attack upon the faith he had pledged to safeguard. The alleged compatibility between Rome's temporal and spiritual powers, which Pius and his predecessors had long proclaimed, was rapidly unravelling.

Following the anti-Austrian insurrection in Milan of 18–22 March 1848 (the Five Days of Milan), and the Piedmontese decision of 23 March to help their brethren across the Ticino river, the clamour increased for a national crusade to expel the foreigner, and the pope was pressed to participate. As an Italian, Pius welcomed the extraordinary events of 1848, but as head of the church, he recognized his first responsibility was to preserve its integrity and independence. Thus while he allowed papal military forces to march northward, he issued instructions that their mission was purely defensive, prohibiting them from crossing the frontier or assuming an aggressive stance.

The 7 April 1848 despatch of the nuncio in Vienna, Monsignor Viale Prela, reaching the pope in mid month, proved decisive, as the emotional Pius was stunned by the report that the people of Austria held him responsible for the war waged against them. 'Italian nationalism is overrunning the whole of Italy', he wrote, 'but my position is such that I cannot declare war against anyone.'[31] Days later he wrote to Monsignor Corboli Bussi explaining that despite the reservations of his ministers, he intended to make his position public.[32] He did so in a controversial allocution of 29 April 1848, which asserted that as father of all, he was not prepared to wage war against Catholic Austria.

The Holy Father's refusal to enter the war led to the resignation of the Antonelli ministry, which was replaced by that of Terenzio Mamiani. The war issue remained, to the pope's discomfort, who found the new ministry insistent in the call for war and less to his liking than its predecessor. Pius feared the temporal power would not survive if he acceded to the demands of the Mamiani ministry. The pope's minister recognized what Pius refused to acknowledge: the incompatibility between the spiritual and temporal power of the papacy, which was highlighted during the first war of national liberation. Mamiani sought to resolve the dilemma by separating the temporal from the spiritual power and having the ministry declare war for the pontiff. The pope rejected this solution.

30 Gregorio to Filippo Antonelli, 27 March 1848, ASR, Fondo Famiglia Antonelli, *busta* 7, *fascicolo* 9; Great Britain, *British and Foreign State Papers*, XXXVIII (1848–1849), p. 918.
31 Maioli, *Pio IX*, p. 117.
32 Pius to Corboli Bussi, 27 April 1848, ASV, Archivio Particolare Pio IX, Stato Pontificio.

Pius consulted a number of theologians to clarify the issue. Pointing to the agitation which arose in his states after his April allocation, and the prospect of additional anarchy, he inquired if it would be legitimate to avoid these evils by assuming an active part in the war against Austria for Italian independence. Only two of the twelve questioned responded affirmatively, with the others advising the pope to avoid such a war, citing the relativity of the principle of nationality, and Austria's legitimate rights.[33] Whatever Pio Nono's personal feelings for the Italian cause, he was guided by the ecclesiastics' decision as theology once again prevailed over politics. In light of the conflicting position assumed by the sovereign and his minister, collaboration proved difficult, if not impossible.

In mid-September Pius appointed Pellegrino Rossi, a former radical and later Louis Philippe's ambassador to Rome, head of the papal government. He was one of the few patriots willing to defend the pope's stand against the war, considering it unseemly that those who had earlier deified the pope now demonized him. The new minister championed a confederated Italy which could presumably assume responsibility for measures which the pope, as head of the faith, would find difficult to sanction. As before, the Roman initiative received little encouragement from Turin, and failed. There were those who held Pius responsible for the impasse, but Rossi countered that the Turin government was to blame,[34] and curtailed the demonstrations which troubled the Eternal City.

On 15 November 1848, when Rossi appeared for the opening of the chamber, a dagger was thrust into his throat, and within five minutes he bled to death. Following the assassination of perhaps the last figure willing and able to uphold the Holy See's position against popular pressure, Pius found himself abandoned by the political establishment. On the morning of 16 November there were demonstrations which degenerated into rebellion as a large crowd, with the deputies of the chamber at its head, marched upon the pope's residence, demanding a democratic ministry and a declaration of war against Austria. Pius promised to consider their demands, urging the crowds to disband before naming a new ministry, but this provoked an attack upon his palace which resulted in injury to some of the Swiss guards and the death of his secretary, Monsignor Palma.[35]

Pius was warned that unless he satisfied the will of his people, the palace would be stormed, and all would be destroyed save the pope. Confronted with this prospect, the holy father reluctantly accepted the ministry imposed by the people. The popular club insisted that the Swiss guard be disbanded, and Pius again submitted. When on 17 November 1848 the civic guard occupied all of the places earlier kept by the Swiss, Pius considered himself a prisoner of the revolution. To make matters worse, he feared that toleration of this radical,

33 ASV, Archivio Particolare Pio IX, Oggetti Vari, *n.* 415; Martina, *Pio IX*, I, p. 248.

34 *Gazzetta di Roma*, 4 November 1848.

35 ASV, Archivio Particolare Pio IX, Oggetti Vari, *n.* 515; ASR, Miscellanea di carte politiche o riservate, *busta* 124, *fascicolo* 4345; *Il Risorgimento*, 22 November 1848.

anti-Austrian government would provoke a schism in the church.[36] With the assistance of the French, Bavarian and Spanish ambassadors, and his former minister Antonelli, he fled his capital the evening of 24 November 1848. Thus Pius IX, like Pius VI and Pius VII before him, was forced out of Rome. Some days later, Pius IX issued a statement from Gaeta, in the kingdom of Naples, describing the motivation for his departure. In retrospect, it proved to be a flight from reformism as well as the revolution.

The events of 1848 led Pius to question his earlier concessions. He informed Father Antonio Rosmini, who still sought some accommodation with constitutionalism, that, after long prayer, he appreciated its incompatibility with the government of the states of the church, while endangering its spiritual mission. Furthermore, he had come to assess freedom of the press and liberty of association as subversive, arguing his conscience could accept neither. Liberalism he branded a dangerous delusion.[37] Subconsciously, the pope deemed his earlier flirtation with liberalism partly responsible for the outbreak of revolution in Italy. They were living in dangerous times, he wrote to the archbishop of Paris, warning of the grave consequences risked by ecclesiastics who courted the popularity of the masses. Pius continued to defend his decision not to assume leadership of the national movement while lamenting that his political programme had jeopardized his spiritual mission. 'Who can doubt that the pope must follow a path which extols the honour of God and never that sought by the major demagogues of Europe?', he asked, adding, 'And with what conscience could the pope have supported such a national movement, knowing for certain that it would only lead to the profound abyss of religious incredulity and social dissolution?'[38] The events of 1848 exposed the obvious conflict between the exercise of the pope's political power and national self-determination, marking the beginning of the end of the temporal power.

During the course of the conference at Gaeta, which opened in March, Spain, Austria, Naples and France agreed on a joint intervention to restore Pius IX to Rome. In the interim, the Austrians, having defeated the Piedmontese at the battle of Novara on 23 March 1849, opened their way to central Italy. The French republic, fearful of a unilateral Habsburg intrusion into the peninsula, provided funding for a Gallic intervention. Paris and Vienna proceeded to co-ordinate their actions, with the French focusing on Rome, leaving the Austrians free to secure the legations and Tuscany. As Habsburg forces marched towards Rome, a French expedition landed in Civitavecchia on 24 April, while Spanish and Neapolitan forces pushed north from Gaeta. Towards the end of June, Rome fell, and shortly thereafter Pius received the keys of the capital from the French.

36 Narration of events of 16 November 1948, ASV, Archivio Particolare Pio IX, Stato Pontificio, n. 19.

37 Antonio Rosmini, *Della missione a Roma* (Turin, 1854), pp. 143–4; Pius to Archbishop Dupont, 10 June 1849, ASV, Archivio Particolare Pio IX, Francia, Particolari, n. 18; Segreteria di Stato Esteri, corrispondenza da Gaeta e Portici, 1848–50, *rubrica* 248, *fascicolo* 2, *sottofascicolo* 4.

38 Pius to Archbishop of Paris, 17 September 1849, ASV, Archivio Particolare Pio IX, Francia, Particolari, n. 30.

Louis Napoleon, committing his government not only to restore peace to Italy, but to re-establish constitutional government in Rome, pressed the pope to preserve the *statuto*.[39] The French foreign minister catalogued the reforms he deemed essential, including an amnesty, a law code patterned on that of France, abolition of the tribunal of the Holy Office, substantial curtailment of the rights of ecclesiastical tribunals in civilian jurisdiction, and granting the *Consulta* a veto on financial issues.[40] These suggestions were rejected by Antonelli, who noted that the holy father would resist any concession which might compromise his temporal power.

To prevent the French from introducing liberal reforms, Pius nominated a conservative commission of cardinals to govern in his absence. By August, the 'red triumvirate', in their first decree, annulled all the measures that had been passed in the capital since 16 November 1848. The French, while transferring part of the powers exercised by their military to the cardinals of the governing commission, urged the pope to return to Rome. Pius hesitated, awaiting the restoration of order in his capital. Dissatisfied with the progress to date, Napoleon wrote a letter to his friend, Colonel Edouard Ney of the expeditionary force, in mid-August 1849, reminding the public that the French republic had not sent an army to snuff-out Italian liberty, but to regulate and preserve it, insisting on reformism in Rome. Pius and Antonelli relied on Vienna to offset the pressure from Paris.[41]

In the face of mounting French demands, Pius proclaimed a general amnesty out of the question, refused to base his laws on the Code Napoléon, and resisted a rapid secularization of his administration. In July the Jews were again restricted in their movement, with the pontifical government stipulating that Israelites should not be permitted to leave their usual residence without a permit from the Holy Office.[42] Early in September 1849 the pope revealed the institutions he would grant his people in a decree of 1849. Reflecting Pio Nono's original moderate reformism, it provided for administrative autonomy and judicial reforms, a council of state for administrative matters, and a *Consulta* for finances. The pope's retreat from his earlier constitutionalism, his procrastination in returning to Rome, and the curia's intransigence on church–state issues, antagonized the Piedmontese as well as the French, and led Count Camillo di Cavour to preach the separation of church and state.

Pius, for his part, antagonized liberals by challenging their basic beliefs, including the equality of citizens under the law. He warned the grand duke Leopold of Tuscany that certain limited concessions might be granted non-Catholics and Jews, but denounced granting equality to all sects in a Catholic country. He condemned constitutional Piedmont, which restricted ecclesiastical

39 Great Britain, *Hansard's Parliamentary Debates*, CV (1849), p. 376.

40 ASV, Segreteria di Stato Esteri, corrispondenza da Gaeta e Portici, 1849, *rubrica* 242, *sottofascicolo* 76.

41 Antonelli to Archbishop of Cartagina, 16 January 1849, ASV, Corrispondenza di Gaeta e Portici, *rubrica* 247, *sotto fascicoli* 87–8.

42 Despatch of the Holy Office on the movement of Jews in the Papal States, 29 July 1849, ASV, Archivio Nunziatura Parigi, 1849, n. 77.

control over education and placed supervision of the curriculum in state hands. He concluded that the Savoyard state was dominated by anti-religious sentiments, and its expansionism posed a threat to the pope's temporal and therefore his spiritual power. Furthermore, he sympathized with the archbishop of Turin, Luigi Fransoni, and the bishop of Asti, Filippo Artici, who had been compelled by popular pressure to withdraw from their dioceses for their conservative and anti-nationalist stands.[43] Antonelli protested against the violations of the concordat to the chargé d'affaires of the Sardinian king.[44]

The Piedmontese minister, Count Giuseppe Siccardi, who met with Antonelli and Pius at Portici outside of Naples in 1849, found the holy father suspicious of his country's projected ecclesiastical modernization, which he denounced as a vicious attack upon the rights of the church and religion. The pope was also scandalized by articles in *L'Ami de la Réligion* in France which referred to the gospel as nothing else than human reason restored and extended. It was not Rome's position, and Pius IX demanded to know what steps the French hierarchy intended to take in retaliation.[45] The pope and his secretary of state were somewhat mollified by the Falloux law passed in Paris which assured the religious orders the right to teach, which in Rome's view worked to the advantage of both the religious and the social order in France.[46] On 12 April 1850 the pontiff, whose hair had grown grey during his seventeen months in exile, returned to Rome.

Once Pius returned to his capital, the commission of cardinals was dissolved, French troops diminished, and the locus of political power placed in the hands of Cardinal Giacomo Antonelli. Pius, who shunned the Quirinale where he had been a monarch more than a pope, preferred to live in the Vatican where he could better exercise his spiritual duties. Following the restoration of 1849, and his return to Rome in 1850, Pius increasingly turned his attention to religious matters, addressing the spiritual needs of the universal church, while placing the major responsibility for the governance of his state in the hands of Antonelli, who was confirmed as secretary of state. Under Pio Nono's guidance, the curia, responsible for the governance of the church, was transformed as non-priests and the more worldly clergy were systematically removed.

As Antonelli busied himself in designing the governmental framework for the restored regime, Pius concerned himself with dogma and discipline in the church. Following his experiment with liberalism, Pius proceeded to condemn those clergymen who had shown themselves receptive to liberal ideas, including Vincenzo Gioberti for his book *The Modern Jesuit* and Father Rosmini for his *Five Wounds of the Church*. In April 1849 Pius deplored the evils facing

43 Pius to Victor Emmanuel, 9 November 1849, ASV, Archivio Particolare Pio IX, Sovrani, Sardegna, 22; Pasolini, *Memorie*, p. 213.
44 ASV, Archivio Nunziatura Sardegna, 1850, n. 78.
45 ASV, Corrispondenza di Gaeta e Portici, 1848–1850, *rubrica* 248, *fascicolo* 1, *sottofascicolo* 162.
46 Antonelli to the Nuncio in Paris, 25 July 1849, ASV, Corrispondenza di Gaeta e Portici, *rubrica* 248, *fascicolo* 1, *sottofascicoli* 154–5.

the church and society, alluding to the danger posed to the temporal power of the Holy See, which he perceived as vital for the protection of its spiritual authority. He repeated these warnings in his encyclical of 8 December 1849 to the archbishops and bishops of Italy.[47] Pius also called for veneration for the supreme See of Peter, noting that 'the successor of Peter, the Roman pontiff, holds a primacy over the whole world and is the true Vicar of Christ'. It represented a precursor to the doctrine of papal infallibility.

At the same time, Pius paved the ground for the proclamation of another dogma. Devoted to Mary, to whom he had frequent recourse in prayer, he believed that though naturally conceived, she was from the moment of her conception free from original sin. Indeed, during the turmoil of revolutionary 1848, Pius had appointed a commission of twenty theologians to study the matter, and dwelled upon it during his exile. On 2 February 1849 Pius addressed an encyclical to the patriarchs, primates, archbishops and bishops of the church to assess their opinions.[48] Following the approval expressed by the majority polled, the pope had fathers Passaglia and Perrone of the Society of Jesus prepare a draft of the dogma, which was later modified by the bishops, and solemnly proclaimed in Rome on 8 December 1854. The belief in *Maria Immaculata* was henceforth a dogma of the Catholic church.

In 1850 Pius preoccupied himself with a series of beatifications, commencing with that of the Jesuit missionary Peter Claver who had converted countless Negroes in Latin America, and in the autumn he re-established the hierarchy in England. Queen Victoria, who was well disposed towards the pope, apparently wanted an English ambassador attached to the Holy See. This did not materialize at the time. However, by the brief *Universalis ecclesiae* of 1850, a metropolitan with twelve suffragan bishops was appointed in place of the system of vicars apostolic by which the affairs of English Catholics had been managed since the reign of James II.[49] English Catholics now numbered almost a million. Nicholas Wiseman, for whom Pio Nono had affection and respect, was called to Rome to receive a cardinal's hat, and shortly thereafter was named archbishop of Westminster. He was one of the ten foreign cardinals created that year, in which Pius IX created only four Italian cardinals, thus commencing the process of de-Italianizing the sacred college.

The restoration of the hierarchy stirred up considerable controversy in England with the resurgence of cries of 'no popery', the Ecclesiastical Titles bill of Lord John Russell (1851), which made the new titles illegal, and protests from the press and Protestant pulpits. Fanned by the rage of the press and especially *The Times*, much of parliamentary life in 1851 was consumed by the alleged papal aggression. By 1852, public processions and wearing ecclesiastical habits

47 *Nobis et nobiscum*, December 1849, in Carlen, *PE*, I, pp. 295, 298.

48 *Ubi Primum*, 2 February 1849, in Carlen, *PE*, I, pp. 291–3.

49 James Flint, 'The Attempt of the British Government to Influence the Choice of the Second Archbishop of Westminister', *Catholic Historical Review*, LXXVII, 1 (January 1991), pp. 42–3; Wilfrid Ward, *The Life and Times of Cardinal Wiseman* (London, 1897). The first volume of this two-volume work examines developments up to the restoration of the English hierarchy in 1850.

in public were prohibited the Catholic clergy in Great Britain. The reaction provoked by the restoration in England led Pius to move cautiously in the restoration of the hierarchy in Holland, but did not prevent his pressing forward. Dutch Catholics, like the English, numbered some one million, but in Holland they totalled one-third of the population whereas in England they represented only one-eighteenth. Furthermore, under the leadership of monsignor Jan Zwijsen, the country witnessed a remarkable Catholic revival. This enabled Pius, in 1853, to establish five dioceses under Monsignor Zwijsen as archbishop of Utrecht. The restoration, here too, was not without opposition, provoking a popular outcry known as the 'April Agitation' which precipitated the fall of the Dutch cabinet. In Holland, as in England, the pope's spiritual crusade was achieved at the cost of diminished support for the Papal States and the temporal power.

In the United States, the pope elevated the sees of New York, New Orleans, St Louis and Cincinnati to the rank of archbishoprics. In 1853 the diocese of Brooklyn was created, while San Fransisco was made an archdiocese and bishop Alemay appointed its first archbishop. In 1853 Monsignor Gaetano Bedini visited the United States and raised the prospect of Rome appointing a papal nuncio to that country. He was not encouraged by the American government or people. Anti-papal demonstrations erupted in a number of American cities, fuelled by anti-Catholicism and by the disapproval of the conservative policies pursued by Rome following the collapse of the Roman republic and the papal restoration of 1849. Hanged in effigy in Baltimore, Bedini prudently slipped out of the country. Following his departure, he noted the problems of the church in the United States: the enormous diocesan and parochial debts and the 'excessive' independence of the clergy, and the American annexation of Texas, New Mexico, Arizona and California, which contained large numbers of Catholics. Bedini called for the establishment of a nunciature in the United States. He also proposed the establishment of a national college for training the American clergy in Rome. In Mexico and much of Latin America, Rome confronted a liberalism which pursued a vigorously anticlerical policy.

Following the papal restoration in Rome, Pius returned to the theme of the education and moral life of the clergy. He especially encouraged seminarians to venture to Rome, reorganizing the older national colleges and seminaries and adding to their number, including a Belgian seminary, a French one, a Latin American college, a Polish seminary, as well as a new Irish college. In 1855 Pius, in conjunction with Cardinal Barnafo, prefect of propaganda fide, and Monsignor Bedini, laid the plans for the North American College. Pius selected the seventeenth-century palace on the Via della Umiltà for its quarters, providing the 42,000 *scudi* for its acquisition. Pius generously rewarded priests he deemed loyal to Rome, creating more *monsignori* in his pontificate than his predecessors had produced in the last two centuries. At the same time, his apostolic nuncios, whose function had been largely diplomatic and political, representing the interests of the Papal States, increasingly served as intermediaries between the pope and bishops in the governance of the church.

Pius called for the veneration of, and complete obedience to, the Holy See, insisting that the national episcopies execute whatever the Holy See teaches, determines and decrees. The pope encouraged the bishops to visit Rome regularly and periodically called large episcopal assemblies such as that of 1854. Likewise in the liturgy, Pius favoured centralization, letting it be known that he deplored disparity, calling for the adoption of the Roman liturgy in every diocese. At the same time, Rome favoured the conclusion of a series of concordats to protect the interests of the church in a number of countries. In 1851 Madrid's *moderado* government of Isabella II concluded an accord which pronounced Catholicism the religion of state, while the clergy was invested with broad powers and rights, including the supervision of education and settling matrimonial disputes without civil intervention. It proved to be short-lived, set aside by the revolution of 1854.

Negotiations were also opened with the Vienna government, which in 1855 resulted in a concordat which made broad concessions to the church, as Franz Josef proclaimed his loyalty and devotion to the Holy See.[50] Under the terms of the agreement, the clergy was entrusted with the censorship of literature and supervision of the schools, while the state promised to repeal all legislation in conflict with canon law. Bishops were accorded a say not only in religious education, but in the overall educational system of the empire. At the same time, the monarchy promised to introduce no measure detrimental to Catholic principles in the curriculum. Finally, the bishops were authorized to select members of the teaching staff, guaranteeing that only Catholic teachers would staff the Catholic schools. Pius also secured favourable agreement from Hesse (1854) and Württemberg (1857).

The deference shown Rome by Madrid and Vienna highlighted the ecclesiastical policies of the Turin government which Pius found deplorable. A papal allocution towards the end of 1850 condemned Piedmontese actions.[51] To further widen the rift, in 1852 the *connubio*, or marriage of the centre-right led by Cavour and the centre-left led by Urbano Rattazzi, provided the parliamentary basis for additional ecclesiastical legislation and the downfall of the d'Azeglio government. Rome denounced Turin's modernization programme as dangerous and destructive. When the Cavour–Rattazzi bloc pressed for the passage of civil matrimony, the king hesitated approving the measure because of the opposition of the pope. Unable to secure its passage, d'Azeglio resigned. At the end of 1852, Cavour assumed the presidency of the council of ministers with freedom of action on religious legislation, although he promised not to make a cabinet issue of the civil matrimony law.

Cavour's ministry, to the Holy See's displeasure, assumed a more radical position on ecclesiastical issues as it sought to transform Piedmont into a progressive, European country. Turin revealed its determination in 1854 by presenting a project which envisioned the suppression of a number of the

50 Franz Josef to Pius IX, ASV, Archivio Particolare Pio IX, Sovrani, Austria.
51 Allocution of 1 November 1850, *ASS*, VI, pp. 146–54.

country's ecclesiastical orders and the repression of over 300 religious houses. Pio Nono responded by deploring the grave damage done to the church by the Piedmontese government in general, and specifically attacked the pending law of convents. Denouncing the measure as illegal, he repeated the canonical censure prescribed for those who were responsible for the measure. Convinced that a virtual war was being waged against the church and the temporal power by the Piedmontese, Pius commenced his counter-offensive. At the end of 1854, Pius attacked the indifferentism which glossed over the distinction between truth and error, the rationalism that dragged religion down to a purely material plane, and the progress which refused to recognize the limits imposed on purely human aspirations. Pius repeated his denunciation of the Turin government the following year.[52] The promise of a reconciliation between the church and the modern world during the first two years of the pontificate had disappeared by the 1850s, degenerating into open warfare between the two with far-reaching consequences for both.

52 *Cum Saepe*, 26 July 1855, *ASS*, VI, pp. 154–6.

CHAPTER 7

Papal intransigence and infallibility in an age of liberalism and nationalism

Throughout the turbulent decade following Pio Nono's return to Rome, the pope sought to safeguard the rights of the church in Italy, Europe and the world beyond, threatened by the 'spasm of revolution' and the 'mania for modernization'. News from abroad provided little consolation for the beleaguered pontiff, who challenged the 'utopian pretensions' of the liberals whose preoccupation with progress challenged Christian values. At the close of 1851, he deplored the sad state of the times, decrying the tendency to submit to unbridled desires which threatened religion as well as the established order worldwide.[1] Even in Colombia, the first Spanish republic officially recognized by the Holy See (1835), difficulties emerged. Despite the 1843 constitution's recognition of Catholicism as the official state religion, the Liberal Party's victory in 1849 ushered in a programme aimed at curtailing the prerogatives of the church and the clergy.

During the course of 1851 Pius, repelled by the 'ostentatious indifference to the rights of religion', received word of a spate of anticlerical measures in Colombia, including the annulling of tithes, the abolition of the ancient right of asylum in churches, the empowering of city councils to nominate parish priests, and the elimination of the clergy's ecclesiastical courts. Much of the programme mirrored developments in Piedmont which aroused the pope. Rome rejected the main provisions of Colombia's legislation, considering it a part of the universal, liberal conspiracy. Pius denied that matrimony could be judged a civil contract, divorce sanctioned by the state, or that matrimonial disputes should be adjudicated by the civil courts. The Vatican insisted that a consumated marriage, based on divine and natural law, could not be dissolved for any reason, not even by the pope.[2] Pius charged this 'oppressive' legislation deprived humanity of the consolation of religion.[3]

1 *Exultavit cor Nostrum*, 21 November 1851, Carlen, *PP*, I, p. 32.

2 *Papal Teachings on Matrimony compiled by the Monks of Solesmes*, trans. Michael J. Byrnes (Boston, 1963), pp. 110–13; J. Lloyd Mecham, *Church and State in Latin America: A History of Politico-Ecclesiastical Relations* (Chapel Hill, 1966), pp. 115–20.

3 *Acerbissimum vobiscum*, 27 Septemer 1852, in Carlen, *PP*, I, p. 33.

The victory of general José Maria Obando in the election of April 1853 accelerated the anticlerical campaign. The new constitution guaranteed all Colombians freedom of religion, providing for the complete separation of church and state that liberals invoked. Pius was scandalized by this first separation act in Latin America, and the transfer of church property from the clergy to the resident Catholics of the parishes. Throughout the year of Obando's administration hostile measures continued: civil marriage was made mandatory, cemeteries were secularized and placed under municipal control, and Colombia's representatives in Rome were recalled.[4] Pius also complained about Paraguay, where he perceived the Catholic church burdened by oppression during much of the nineteenth century, while a series of Bolivian governments steadfastly refused to sanction a concordat with Rome. In the late 1850s, elements antagonistic to the church secured control of the government of Uruguay, while special ecclesiastical tribunals were eliminated in Peru. Rome perceived these measures as a manifestation of liberalism's universal design to lead the unwary astray.

The pope found little comfort at home where Italian nationalists posed a threat to his spiritual and temporary power. In the pontiff's mind the two were inextricably intertwined, for he regarded the sovereignty of the Papal States as a crucial guarantee of his spiritual independence. Consequently, he perceived the Risorgimento, which threatened the stability of his state, as doubly damnable. It explains his preference for Catholic Austria, which sought to preserve the traditional order, to revisionist Piedmont, which aimed to unite the peninsula under its banner. The twists and turns of Louis Napoleon were difficult to chart, and remained an enigma to the Vatican. Both the pope and his secretary of state, Giacomo Cardinal Antonelli, resented the pressure from Paris and Turin to introduce liberal reforms in Rome or admit 'the enemy' within its gates.

Pius claimed that much of Piedmont's programme was contrary to the rights of the church, accusing that state of interfering in the administration of the sacraments.[5] To make matters worse, the pope feared that the Turin government would export its power and policies to the other states of the peninsula, threatening to pollute even the Papal States. Although rumour spread that Napoleon III had promised General Collegno, the Piedmontese minister in Paris, that he would champion their cause, a commitment confirmed to his successor the Marquis Villamarina,[6] Antonelli remained confident that Austria could check their designs. The astute secretary of state concurred with the nuncio at Vienna, Michele Viala Prela, that so long as things remained quiet in

4 Mecham, *Church and State*, pp. 121–2.
5 Report of 20 January 1852, ASR, Miscellanea di Carte Politiche o Riservate, *busta* 121, *fascicolo* 4214; Memorandum of 23 June 1852, ibid., *fascicolo* 4213; *L'Osservatore Ligure-Subalpino*, 25 June 1852; Consistorial Allocution of 1 November 1850, in *Papal Teachings on Education compiled by the Monks of Solesmes*, trans. Rev. Aldo Rebeschini (Boston, 1960), pp. 43–4.
6 Michelangelo Castelli, *Ricordi di Michelangelo Castelli*, ed. Luigi Chiala (Turin, 1888), pp. 176–7; Marco Minghetti, *Miei Ricordi*, 3rd edn (Turin, 1888), III, p. 84.

Europe, Austrian arms could preserve the peace.[7] Much depended on the attitude of Napoleon III, the key to Gallic policy and the European equilibrium. Having failed in his attempt to convoke a European congress to revise the treaties of 1815, the impenetrable emperor envisioned a war against Russia as his best means of disrupting the Holy Alliance and reorganizing Europe along national lines. By the spring of 1854, the British and French were ranged in a war against the Russians.

Pio Nono and Antonelli feared that Austrian involvement in the war would lead to a relaxation of her efforts in Italy, encouraging revolutionaries to unleash another wave of terror. Rome was likewise troubled by Piedmont's efforts to ingratiate herself with the English by denouncing the temporal power.[8] In August the pope urged the faithful to pray for peace, lamenting the injuries endured by a Christian people from bellicose afflictions.[9] His words were wasted on the Piedmontese Machiavelli. Initially Cavour had reservations about Rattazzi's law of convents which envisioned the suppression of a number of the country's religious orders and the closing of over 300 of their houses, fearing it might be construed as an all-out war on the church. As Cavour predicted, the Catholic party in Piedmont commenced a bitter opposition to the legislation, and the pope echoed their criticism. While the count did not wish to provoke a religious crisis, his need for Rattazzi's votes for Piedmontese participation in the Crimean War overcame his hesitation. He supported the suppression of the orders, in return for Rattazzi's unconditional commitment to bring Piedmont into the Crimean War on the side of England and France. Predictably, in July 1855, following approval of the law of convents, the pope excommunicated all those who had approved, sanctioned or executed this 'odious' measure.[10]

During the course of 1855, Pius had to confront a series of personal as well as religious and political crises. In April, following the news that the tomb of Pope Alexander and a number of martyrs had been excavated, a curious pope, followed by his entourage, ventured to inspect the findings. On the return to Rome, they stopped at the convent of Sant' Agnese for lunch, where a crowd gathered to greet him. Unfortunately, as the students surged into the room, they were startled by the sound of sagging beams, and the entire group, including the pope and his minister, were hurled into the lower story with a deafening crash and a cloud of dust. Those on the outside feared the worst, but not one of the 130 to take the plunge suffered any harm. Some considered it miraculous, while others saw it as symbolic of the impending collapse of the papacy.[11]

7 Viala Prela to Antonelli, 31 January 1850, ASV, Segreteria di Stato Esteri, Corrispondenza da Gaeta e Portici, *rubrica* 247, *sottofascicolo* 222, ASV, SSE.

8 Michele Viala Prela to Antonelli, 9 June, 14 June, 1853, ASV, SSE, 1853, *rubrica* 242, *fascicolo* 3, *sottofascicoli* 19 and 24; Minghetti, *Miei Ricordi*, III, p. 26.

9 Apostolicae nostrae caritatis, 1 August 1854, Carlen, *PE*, I, pp. 331–3.

10 Allocution *Cum Saepe* of 26 July 1855, *ASS*, VI, pp. 154–6.

11 Franz Josef to Pius, 24 April 1855, ASV, Archivio Particolare Pio IX, Austria, Sovrani, n. 13; General Rostolan to Pius, 24 April 1855, ASV, Archivio Particolare Pio IX, Francia, Particolari,

To cement his relations with England and France, in 1855 Cavour accompanied King Victor Emmanuel to the allied capitals. The English showed themselves sympathetic to the plight of the peninsula, while the French emperor invited them to transmit a memorandum, indicating what he could do for Italy. Pius also sought to win the goodwill of the French emperor, thanking him for retaining a contingent of 3,500 men in his dominions, despite the exigencies of the war, and applauding the protection provided the faith in France.[12] In February 1856, as the congress ending the Crimean War was about to convene, Pius implored Napoleon's protection for the church. He asked the French ruler to prevent the congress from discussing papal affairs.[13] The papal pleas were thwarted by Cavour.

In April, when the official work of the congress had been completed and the terms of peace accepted, Walewski, at Napoleon's bidding, proposed discussing problems that might trouble the peace of Europe. While the Austrians and Russians complained they lacked instructions on Italian issues, Cavour denounced the irregular state of affairs in the Papal States, suggesting that its troubles disturbed the entire peninsula. Pius was exasperated by Cavour's tactics, lamenting that he had even charmed the Russians, who did not resent the war he had waged against them. Some seemed oblivious to the danger Cavour's Piedmont posed. Perhaps it was because a big dog does not notice the barking of a small one, he confided to his brother, adding that he had certainly followed the Piedmontese antics.[14]

1856 Cong.

Rome wondered why the report Napoleon had commissioned on the papal government, finances and administration had not been released in 1856. Pius suspected the Rayneval report was buried because it proved positive in its evaluation, combatting English and Piedmontese criticism of the papal regime. The 'abuses' of the regime, and the 'corruption' found therein, the report revealed, were neither qualitatively nor quantitatively greater than those found elsewhere.[15] However, the best efforts of the French ambassador, Rayneval, to alter Napoleon's negative evaluation of the papal regime failed. The conservative, clerical and anti-national pontifical regime offended liberal Europe which denounced the temporal power as an anachronism.

During a secular age when modernization inspired the major capitals, Pius revealed his mission was more religious than political, explaining to Napoleon that his aims remained the glory of God and the propagation of the faith. He

n. 77; Pius to the Youth Club of St Peter's, 12 April 1875, Pasquale De Franciscis, ed., *Discorsi del Sommo Pontefice Pio IX Pronunziati in Vaticano ai fedeli di Roma e dell'orbe dal principio della sua prigionia fino al presente* (Rome, 1875), III, pp. 466–7.

12 Pius IX to Louis Napoleon, 24 January 1855, ASV, Archivio Particolare Pio IX, Francia, Sovrani, n. 26.

13 Pius IX to Napoleon III, 19 December 1855, Pius to Napoleon III, 8 February 1856, ASV, Archivio Particolare Pio IX, Francia, Sovrani, nn. 30 and 32.

14 Antonio Monti, *Pio IX nel Risorgimento Italiano con documenti inediti* (Bari, 1928), p. 260.

15 Report from the Count de Rayneval, the French envoy at Rome, to the French minister of foreign affairs, 14 May 1856, in John Francis Maguire, *Rome: Its Rulers and its Institutions* (London, 1857), pp. 579–603.

could not permit the radicals to poison society with their liberal ideology. Nonetheless, he sought to preserve the goodwill of the French. When Pius heard of the birth of the prince imperial, the pope sent the golden rose to Empress Eugenie, who favoured the papal cause. To strengthen the ties between Rome and Paris, Pius agreed to serve as godfather of the child.

The cardinal secretary of state sought to capitalize on the pope's personal popularity by having Pius tour his dominions and provinces, negating the impression that only foreign bayonets upheld the regime. While Antonelli stressed the political advantages to be gained, the pontiff was primarily moved by religious sentiments. Convinced that the Virgin had shielded all from certain death at Sant' Agnese, Pius had vowed to make a pilgrimage to the shrine in Loreto in appreciation. The Crimean War forced its postponement. When Pius finally visited Imola in the spring of 1857, he met with his former minister, Giuseppe Pasolini, revealing his disenchantment with liberal government. The pope feared that all liberal regimes would inevitably follow Piedmont's pattern and prove anti-Christian. In Bologna, he told Marco Minghetti the same thing. The pope concurred with his secretary of state that these 'notable progressives' sought to substitute reform and reason for God's harmonious society, and ultimately to undermine the pontifical government.[16]

Much of the goodwill generated by the pope's visit to the provinces was squandered by Pio Nono's stance during the Mortara affair of 1858. The Hebrew child, Edgardo Levi Mortara, secretly baptized by a Christian servant of the household during a life-threatening childhood illness, was seized from his parents in June 1858 to assure the salvation of his soul. There were protests from his family, the Jews of Italy and Europe, and the various courts, but Pius would not relent. Rather than soothe public opinion, he preferred to preserve his principles. He knew his responsibility, he confided to the Neapolitan ambassador, and would rather have his hands cut off than shirk his duty. When the French ambassador revealed the universal depth of public outrage over the action, Pius pointed to the Crucifix and confidently announced, 'He will defend me'.[17]

Cavour utilized the Mortara affair to discredit Rome as medieval and retrograde, secretly scheming with Napoleon to reorganize Italy. At Plombières in late July 1858, the two plotted war against Austria and a diminution of the Papal States. Favouring a reconstruction of northern Italy under Piedmont, Napoleon insisted that the pope, deprived of the legations, be treated with circumspection. The nuncio in Paris, Sacconi, reported that the French government said

16 Rafaelle De Cesare, *Roma e lo Stato del Papa dal ritorno di Pio IX al XX Settembre* (Rome, 1907), I, p. 261; Marco Minghetti, *Miei Ricordi*, 3rd edn (Turin, 1888), III, pp. 177, 181; Cardinal Antonelli to Pius IX, 17 June 1857, ASV, Archivio Particolare Pio IX, Sovrani, Stato Pontificio, nn. 19, 22.

17 Mariano Gabriele, ed., *Il Carteggio Antonelli-Sacconi (1850–1860)* (Rome, 1962), I, p. xiii; Giuseppe Massari, *Diario delle cento voci* (Bologna, 1959), p. 67; Salomone Mortara to Pius IX, 19 September 1858, ASV, Archivio Particolare Pio IX, Oggetti Vari, n. 1433; Prussian and German Rabbis to Pius IX, ibid., *fascicoli* 109–16; 'Breve cenni e riflessione . . . relative al Battesimo conferito in Bologna al fanciullo Edgaro, figlio degli Ebrei Salomone e Mariana Mortara', ibid.

little good about the papal government, proposing the pope have a smaller state so he would be less embarrassed by the burdens of power.[18]

Pius deplored the prospect of war, exhorting the faithful to turn to prayer to avoid the catastrophe.[19] Fearing a Franco-Austrian conflict, and worrying that their occupying forces would turn his state into a battlefield, he sought their removal. Meanwhile, Vienna dispatched an ultimatum to Turin on 23 April 1859, and on 29 April 1859 the Austrians declared war. Napoleon, who cast his lot with Piedmont, promised to protect Rome, publicly proclaiming he would uphold the cause of the Holy See. The pledge was violated under the pressure of events, as was that of King Victor Emmanuel, who promised to remedy the problems confronted by the church in his state at the war's end.[20]

Following the battle of Magenta on 4 June 1859, the Austrian garrisons were withdrawn from Pavia, Piacenza, Ancona and Ferrara, encouraging revolutionaries in Bologna to move against the legate who fled to Ferrara. It proved less than a safe haven as insurrections exploded in Ferrara, Ravenna and Forli, while the papal regime in the legations collapsed. With the entire region on the verge of falling into Piedmontese control, and Catholics in France petitioning Napoleon to protect the temporal power, the emperor blocked Piedmontese annexation of the area. At the same time, Pius warned Victor Emmanuel that he would fall under censure should new attacks be launched against the church. Antonelli, in turn, ordered the Swiss troops to retake Perugia and restore the marches to papal sovereignty. There was a call for the papal government to mediate the Franco-Austrian dispute and restore peace, but Pius realized that Vienna's call for a return to the status quo would be unacceptable in Paris.[21] In June 1859 Pius sounded the alarm that the Papal State was in danger, charging that an insatiable revolutionary movement menaced the sovereignty essential for the Holy See's exercise of its spiritual mission.[22] Pius IX excommunicated all those involved in the rebellion.[23] He unequivocally rejected Napoleon III's suggestion that the Romagna be placed under Piedmontese protection, and all other solutions which compromised the temporal power.[24]

The second war of Italian liberation (1859) and Sardinia's occupation of more than 80 per cent of papal territory hardened Pio Nono's heart against

18 Gabriele, ed., *Il Carteggio Antonelli-Sacconi*, I, p. 5; Massari, *Diario*, pp. 84, 93; Castelli, *Ricordi*, pp. 75–7; Minghetti, *Miei Ricordi*, III, p. 219.
19 *Cum sancta mater ecclesia*, in Carlen, *PP*, I, p. 35.
20 Napoleon III to Pius IX, 1 May 1859, ASV, Archivio Particolare Pio IX, Sovrani, Francia, n. 42; 'Proclamation L'Empereur au Peuple Français', *Le Moniteur Universel. Journal Officiel de L'Empire Français*, 3 May 1859; Victor Emmanuel to Pius IX, 25 May 1859, ASV, Archivio Particolare Pio IX, Sovrani, Sardegna, n. 52.
21 Pius IX to Victor Emmanuel, 6 June 1859, ASV, Archivio Particolare Pio IX, Sovrani, Sardegna, n. 53; Gabriele, ed., *Il Carteggio Antonelli-Sacconi*, I, pp. 136–8; Federico Sclopis di Salerano, *Diario Segreto (1859–1878)*, ed. P. Pietro Pirri (Turin, 1959), p. 134; P. Pietro Pirri, ed., *La Questione Romana* (Rome, 1951), II, p. 80.
22 Encyclical *Qui Nuper* of 18 June 1859, *ASS*, VI, pp. 157–8.
23 Allocution *Ad gravissimum* of 20 June 1859, ibid., VI, pp. 158–61.
24 Encyclical *Nullis Certe* of 19 January 1860, ibid., VI, pp. 161–5.

the Piedmontese and the liberal and nationalist ideologies by which they were inspired. Convinced that a brutal campaign had been unleashed against the church and the papacy, in the decade between the restoration and the proclamation of the Italian kingdom in 1861, Pio Nono issued more than a dozen condemnations of Cavour and his colleagues responsible for unification. In March 1861 he noted that the adherents of 'modern civilization' demanded that he reconcile himself with 'progress', 'liberalism' and 'modern civilization', while those who defended the rights of justice and religion understood his need to preserve the 'immovable and indestructible principles of eternal justice' intact.[25]

The embattled pontiff refused to compromise the church with 'modern civilization', repeating he could not consent to the 'vandalous aggression' without violating his principles. He did more than denounce the Piedmontese expansion and extension of their anticlerical legislation to other parts of the peninsula, assailing the modern doctrines which promoted non-Catholic cults, while encouraging the press to subvert the faith and undermine the church.[26] Pius would not forsake his solemn oath to uphold the apostolic constitutions which forbade the alienation of the territories of the Roman church. Nonetheless, Cavour continued his challenge, and in March 1861 he had Rome proclaimed the capital of the newly formed kingdom. Trusting in divine providence, the diplomacy of Antonelli and the troops of Napoleon III, Pio Nono remained in the Eternal City while the greater part of his state was merged into the kingdom of Italy.

The spoliation of his temporal power took a toll on the pope's health, weakening his resistance, and in April 1861, fever-stricken, he collapsed in the Sistine Chapel. However, in 1861 the angel of death, bypassing the aged and ailing pontiff who would live to 1878, removed the 51-year-old Cavour, who had just become Italy's first prime minister. Although Pius prayed for his rival, he refused to recognize his *fait accompli*, exacting the return of the entire papal dominion. The pope was scandalized by the extension of the Piedmontese Casati education law of 1859 to the other provinces in the quest to create a national consciousness and restrict the influence of the church on the young. Various provisions of the measure alarmed Pius, especially the stipulation that the state supervise all schools, including religious ones. The Italian scholastic policy challenged the clergy's role in education, seeking to introduce by means of lay teachers and a secular curricula a non-confessional culture.[27] The pope judged these measures an insidious attack upon the faith, which he contrasted to the more open but abortive assault on Rome by Garibaldi and his supporters in the summer of 1862.

25 *Iamdudum* of 18 March 1861 in ibid., VI, pp. 175–6.

26 Pius IX to Archduke Ferdinand Maximilian, 7 August 1860, ASV, Archivio Particolare Pio IX, Sovrani, Austria, n. 35.

27 Italia, Ministero della Pubblica Istruzione, *Testo Unico delle Leggi sull' Istruzione Superiore* (Rome, 1919), pp. 73, 140; ibid., *Relazione presentata a S.E. Il Ministro della Pubblica Istruzione Prof. Comm. Nicolo Gallo sugli Istituti Femminili di Educazione e di Istruzione in Italia* (Rome, 1900), p. 92.

Pius sought solace in the universal church. Whereas some 200 bishops ventured to Rome for the proclamation of the Immaculate Conception in 1854, over 300 presented themselves for the canonization of the twenty-six Japanese martyrs in 1862, and the vast majority concurred on the need for the temporal power to assure the independence of the pontiff. While Pius rejoiced at the loyalty of the assembled bishops, he was distressed by the congress of Malines (Belgium) called the summer of 1863, seeking to Christianize democracy and reconcile the church with the modern world. He feared the interaction would lead to the contamination of the church by the 'totally degenerate' secular society. He likewise opposed the Munich congress, called in September 1863. Theologians at both proposed a more liberal approach to contemporary developments than envisioned at Rome. The pope remained suspicious of the presentation of Christianity as a product of history and philosophy.[28] Rome was also agitated by the rumour of secret Franco-Italian negotiations to end the French occupation of Rome, entrusting the Italians with the pontiff's security. This materialized on 15 September 1864 when the Minghetti government signed an accord with the French empire to regulate the Roman Question, shocking Pius and upsetting Antonelli, neither of whom had been consulted.

The terms of the September Convention, providing that Napoleon would withdraw his forces from the Eternal City within two years, while the Italian government promised not to attack the patrimony of St Peter and to prevent others from launching an attack from its territory, upset the Holy See. Pius did not trust the 'wolves' to guard the 'lamb' and suspected they would stoop to devouring their ward. Suspicious of Piedmontese motives, the pope also smarted from the Turin government's insistence, in 1863, on its right to exercise the *exequatur*, requiring its consent to have papal bulls or other documents applied in the kingdom, as well as the *placet*, requiring approval for ecclesiastical enactments. The pontiff was anxious to condemn these abuses. There had been talk earlier of tying the condemnation of modern errors, and the moral gap between the church of God and contemporary society, to the proclamation of the Immaculate Conception in 1854, but this was deemed inappropriate. The pope returned to the need for a forthright condemnation of the mundane values of the age which generated the indifference to religion, following the seizure of the greater part of the Papal States, which he perceived as flowing from these 'pernicious' doctrines. In June 1862 he catalogued many of the errors later listed in the Syllabus.[29]

The September Convention encouraged Pius to unleash the spiritual weapons in his arsenal against a 'deluded generation'. On 8 December 1864 he issued the encyclical *Quanta cura*, to which he appended the Syllabus of Errors, listing eighty errors drawn from over thirty previous papal documents condemning

28 *Tuas libenter*, 31 December 1863, and *Non deve maravigliare*, 22 April 1863, Carlen, *PP*, I, p. 37; Donald J. Dietrich, 'Priests and Political Thought: Theology and Reform in Central Europe, 1845–1855', *Catholic Historical Review* LXXI, 4 (October 1985), p. 520.

29 Report of the supreme sacred congregation of the Holy Office on the propositions containing the 70 principal errors of the time, ASV, Archivio Particolare Pio IX, Oggetti Vari, n. 1779.

various movements and beliefs.[30] Sweeping in scope and harsh in tone, under ten headings Pius proscribed pantheism, naturalism, materialism, absolute as well as moderate rationalism, indifferentism, and false tolerance in religious matters, finding most of the liberal agenda incompatible with the Catholic faith. Articles 37 and 54, respectively, stipulated that no national church could exist beyond the authority of the Roman pontiff and that neither princes, kings nor other sovereigns were exempt from the church's jurisdiction. In addition, socialism, communism, secret and bible societies, and liberal clerical associations were denounced. Likewise condemned were errors regarding marriage as well as those on the temporal power of the pope. The critique of the 'distorted values' and 'errors' of the liberalism of the day caused the greatest controversy in the progressive camp, which denounced the Syllabus as hopelessly reactionary. Reformers were especially offended by the condemnation of the eightieth and final error, which called for the Roman pontiff to reconcile himself with progress, liberalism and recent civilization. In Rome, works critical of the Syllabus were placed on the Index.[31]

Pius perceived liberalism's principles in conflict with the traditional moral order, invoking unity against the creeping incredulity of the times, revolutionary convulsions, and the disposition to wage war openly against the church. The Holy See appealed for the episcopacy's support against the enemies of the faith, decrying that time-honoured laws and convictions were ridiculed while the Christian heritage was derided as obsolete and outworn. He condemned and damned the masonic sects,[32] blasting their lodges as 'synagogues of Satan'. The pope complained that the line between truth and error was progressively obliterated.[33] He also resisted the attempts on the part of the British government to influence his selection of the second archbishop of Westminister following the death of Cardinal Wiseman in 1865.[34]

Pius considered convoking a council to confront comprehensively the contemporary dilemma and hoped to have the council open shortly, but difficulties at home and abroad conspired against an early convocation. In 1866 Europe was troubled by the war waged by Prussia and Italy against Austria, while Rome was distressed by the continuing call to cede the rest of its temporal power. Even events in Catholic Austria generated anxiety in Rome. Pius judged Vienna's measures against the church's role in education no less reprehensible than those of the Italian government, which had been transferred to Florence following the September Convention.[35] Responding to the rumour that the pope intended to close the American Protestant church in Rome, in 1867 the United States congress discontinued funding for their legation in Rome,

30 *Quanta cura* and the Syllabus of Errors, 8 December 1864, *ASS*, III, pp. 160–7, 167–76.
31 Congregation of the Index, 26 September 1865, ibid., I, p. 250.
32 Allocution of 25 September 1865, ibid., I, p. 193.
33 Pius IX to Archbishop of Paris, 24 November 1864, ASV, Archivio Particolare, Particolari, Francia, n. 168.
34 James Flint, 'The Attempt of the British Government to Influence the Choice of the Second Archbishop of Westminister', *Catholic Historical Review* LXXVII, 1 (January 1991), pp. 42–55.
35 Allocution of 22 June 1868, *ASS*, IV, p. 10.

ending diplomatic relations between Washington and the Holy See. Finally, there was the trauma of yet another of Garibaldi's incursions into the Papal States in 1867, before it was halted by a Franco-Papal military force at Mentana, outside of Rome. As a result, French forces returned to Rome.

On 29 June 1868 the papal bull of convocation, *Aeterni patris*, appeared, explaining the general aims of the twentieth church council: the combatting of error, defining and developing doctrine, while upholding ecclesiastical discipline and fighting corruption.[36] The council opened on 8 December 1869, the feast of the Immaculate Conception, 300 years after the council of Trent, the last church council. More than half the prelates from Europe hailed from Italy. That very day, the masons convoked an anti-council in Naples to counter the oppression expected from Rome. It lasted three days. In an apostolic letter which followed in September, the pope cited the concurrence of calamaties which moved him to repair the damage to the church of God and its flock. Pius resolved to unmask the enemies of Christian society and free it from the grasp of 'Satanic forces' and 'pernicious pretensions'.

The powers were less than pleased by the prospect of the council, fearing that the pope would have himself declared infallible, and the strictures of the Syllabus, with its condemnation of modern civilization and liberalism, assured a form of divine sanction. The fears were not without foundation, for in February 1869 an article in the *Civiltà Cattolica* suggested that the church fathers would unanimously proclaim papal infallibility, approving by acclamation the censures of the Syllabus. Though the cardinal secretary of state sought to calm the fears provoked, dismissing them as founded on phantoms,[37] concern continued. The Bavarian prime minister Hohenlohe, very likely advised by Doellinger, despatched a note to the cabinets of Europe, urging their cooperation in preventing the proclamation of papal infallibility, which he deemed injurious to all.

Johann Josef Ignaz von Doellinger, head of the 'Munich school of theologians', in September 1863, during the first congress of Munich, harped upon his favourite project of reconciling the three great churches – the Roman, Greek and Anglican – by suppressing all that separated them all. In his desire for unity, he sought to purge from Catholicism all that repelled Protestants, without injury to their common faith. Papal infallibility worked to undermine his scheme. These views were shared by the redemptorist Father Isaac Hecker, who envisioned a conversion of the Protestant United States to Catholicism, and therefore opposed the proclamation of infallibility as inopportune.[38] Pius, who also sought a restoration of Christian unity, from the first indicated it would have to be achieved on Rome's terms.

Desirous of re-establishing relations with the church of the east, on 8 September 1869 Pius despatched invitations to those eastern bishops not in

36 Ibid., IV, pp. 3–9.
37 'Correspondance de France', *Civiltà Cattolica*, 6 February 1869; Baron John Acton, *The History of Freedom and Other Essays* (London, 1922), p. 518.
38 In this regard see William L. Portier, *Isaac Hecker and the First Vatican Council* (New York, 1985).

communion with the church of Rome, beseeching and admonishing them to attend the council to resolve the long dissension.[39] He even offered to assume all their expenses. Nonetheless, all the responses were negative. His missives exhorting Protestants and other non-Catholics to return to the fold were likewise rejected.[40] In 1869 the *Allgemeine Zeitung* published a series of unsigned, anti-papal articles, written by Doellinger, who included them in the volume *The Pope and the Council by Janus*, which rejected not only the infallibility of the pontiff but that of councils.

Pius, who invoked traditionalism and centralization in the church against the evils of secularism, liberalism and nationalism, addressed the bishops in the first public session.[41] In his subsequent meetings with the English, Italian and other hierarchies, Pius revealed his resolve to play a key role in the proceedings. This could also be gleaned from the bull, *Multiplices inter*, of 27 November 1869, providing the guidelines and official machinery for the Vatican council. It reserved to the pope the right to propose questions for discussion, while allowing a special committee to entertain proposals from the fathers. Pius nominated the five cardinals, who in his name were to preside over the five congregations of the council as well as its secretary.[42]

The committees devised fifty-one categories, or schemata, for consideration, but eventually only two were discussed: (1) *Dei filius*, divided into four chapters, on God, creator of all things, Revelation, Faith, and Reason; and (2) *De ecclesia*, on the church. The former, adopted by a unanimous vote on 24 April 1870, not only condemned rationalism, modern naturalism, pantheism, materialism and atheism, but elaborated the positive doctrines which these 'errors' violated. Reason was not rejected, but its limitations exposed in the natural order, and more so in the spiritual sphere. Revelation was seen to supplement rather than substitute for reason, with the fathers insisting that while natural reason and divine faith may differ as sources of knowledge, they were never in conflict. The dogmatic constitution on the faith was intensely debated and approved only following some 500 amendments.

De ecclesia, which contained three chapters on the pope's primacy, and one on his infallibility, generated even greater controversy. Pius had strong opinions on both issues, reported the bishop of Birmingham, who claimed that Pius constantly supported the majority in favour of infallibility. Thus not many were surprised, at the end of April, when he gave precedence to the schema on the powers of the pope, removing it from its proper order despite the opposition of the minority and the reservations of part of the majority.[43]

The primary issues debated during the course of the council were ecclesiastic. In mid-May the chapters on the papacy of the schema *De ecclesia* were

39 *Arcano Divinae Providentiae*, 8 September 1869, in *ASS*, IV, pp. 129–31, and in Carlen, *PP*, I, p. 40.
40 *ASS*, IV, pp. 131–5.
41 Ibid., V, pp. 273–7.
42 *Multiplices Inter*, 27 November 1869, ibid., V, pp. 231–42.
43 Cuthbert Butler, *The Vatican Council: The Story Told from Inside in Bishop Ullathorne's Letters* (New York, 1930), II, p. 33.

placed before the general assembly. Major differences remained between the infallibilists, the anti-infallibilists, and the inopportunists, who questioned not the doctrine but the wisdom of its proclamation. More than fifty of those who could not bring themselves to grant approval left Rome rather than publicly vote against it on 18 July 1870.[44] On the final vote, 535 assented to infallibility while only two opposed: the bishop of Little Rock, Edward Fitzgerald, and the bishop of Caizzo, Luigi Riccio. The dogma, defined and declared divinely revealed, read, 'that the Roman Pontiff, when he speaks ex cathedra, that is, when in discharge of the office and doctor of all Christians, by virtue of his supreme Apostolic authority, he defines a doctrine regarding faith or morals to be held by the universal Church . . . is possessed of that infallibility with which the divine Redeemer willed that his Church should be endowed for defining doctrine regarding faith and moral'.[45]

Many in the chancellories of Europe warned that infallibility was a 'Pandora's box' that would haunt the Catholic world. Although most of the German bishops has been 'inopportunists', none of them rejected the decisions of the council. Doellinger did, and in March 1871 the *Allgemeine Zeitung* published his declaration that as a Christian, theologian, historian and citizen he could not accept the infallibility of the Roman pontiff. Very few followed his lead and broke with the church, or joined the Old Catholic movement that rejected the innovations introduced by the council.

The controversy continued. Even the outbreak of the Franco-Prussian War, the day after the proclamation, did not curtail the opposition. Pius understood that the European conflict and the instability in its wake did not bode well for the remnant of the temporal power, and sought to mediate between the French and Prussians. His efforts proved abortive,[46] rendering Rome vulnerable to the vagaries of war. As the situation deteriorated for the French, they were obliged to evacuate their remaining troops from Civitavecchia at the end of July and early August, trusting that the Italian government would honour the commitment made in the September Convention. The pope and Antonelli predicted they would not, and events proved them correct.

Pius hoped that some other power would step into the breach left by the departure of the French from Rome, but found no volunteers. Bismarck adhered to a policy of non-intervention. The Austrians, pushed out of Italy, had broken their concordat with the church,[47] and were adjusting to the recent reconstitution of their state by the *Ausgleich* which created the dual monarchy of Austria-Hungary. Bavaria, sympathetic to the opposition of Doellinger to papal infallibility, was preoccupied with the war with France and the reorganization of Germany. London and St Petersburg were hostile to the papacy,

44 *De Ecclesia Christi, Pastor aeternus, ASS*, V, pp. 45–8.
45 G.A. Kertesz, ed., *Documents in the Political History of the European Continent, 1815–1939* (Oxford, 1968), 242.
46 Louis Napoleon to Pius IX, 27 July 1870, ASV, Archivio Particolare Pio IX, Sovrani, Francia, n. 86.
47 Allocution of 22 June 1868 in *ASS*, IV, pp. 10–13.

while Spain foundered in the throes of internal conflict. Meanwhile, the Italians fielded an 'army of observation' in central Italy under the command of General Rafaelle Cadorna, informing their representatives abroad of their decision to make Rome the capital.

The intransigent element in the Eternal City urged Pius to flee Rome, and the Empress Eugenie, acting as regent, sent the man-of-war *Orenoque* to Civitavecchia to evacuate the holy father to France. However, the old pope opposed a second flight; at the age of seventy-eight he wanted to die at home. The fall of the empire made the September Convention a dead letter, prompting the Italians to move quickly against Rome; on 6 September 1870 the Italian army crossed the frontier. Shortly thereafter, on 8 September, Victor Emmanuel sent his envoy, Count Ponza di San Martino, to the pope, justifying the necessity of occupying what remained of the Papal State, for the security of Italy and the Holy See. 'Nice words, but ugly deeds', Pius muttered as he read the king's letter, responding with a firm refusal. 'I bless God, who has permitted that your Majesty should fill the last years of my life with bitterness', he wrote, adding, 'I cannot admit the requests contained in your letter nor support the principles contained therein.'[48]

On 20 September 1870, as the Italians bombarded the three gates of the city, the pontiff denounced the 'sacriligious' action to the ministers of the powers who surrounded him.[49] Early in October the occupiers engineered an 'election' on whether the citizens of Rome and its environs wished union with the constitutional monarchy of Victor Emmanuel. The vote was overwhelmingly in favour of inclusion in the Italian kingdom. On 9 October 1870, by royal decree, Rome and its provinces were incorporated into the kingdom of Italy. Questioning the legality of the vote, Pius withdrew into the Vatican, proclaiming himself a prisoner of Victor Emmanuel. On 20 October 1870 he suspended the meeting of the Vatican council until a more propitious time.[50] Rejecting the numerous offers of asylum, he remained in Rome to defend his rights.[51] In November 1870 Pius invoked the major excommunication for all those who had perpetrated the invasion, the usurpation, and the occupation of the papal domain, as well as those who had aided or counselled the 'pernicious' action.[52]

In order to calm and reassure Catholics, as well as the powers, in December 1870, president of the council, Lanza, introduced a law of guarantees which recognized the inviolability of the pope, while investing him with the attributes of a sovereign. As financial compensation for the loss of his territory, he was pledged annually, and in perpetuity, the sum of 3,225,000 *lire*, not subject

48 Pius to Victor Emmanuel, 11 September 1870, ASV, Archivio Particolare Pio IX, Sovrani, Sardegna, n. 82; *ASS*, VI, p. 64.

49 Letter of Cardinal Giacomo Antonelli to diplomatic community, 20 September 1870, *ASS*, VI, pp. 56–60.

50 Ibid., VI, pp. 65–7.

51 Monsignor Mermilliod to Pius IX, 12 October 1870, ASV, Archivio Particolare Pio IX, Stato Pontificio, n. 181.

52 *Respicientes*, 1 November 1870, in *ASS*, VI, pp. 136–45 and in Carlen, *PE*, I, pp. 393–7.

to taxation. Regarding church–state relations the *exequatur* and *placet* were abolished, along with other government mechanisms for controlling the publication and execution of ecclesiastical acts, in accordance with Cavour's notion of a separation of church and state. The law of papal guarantees was approved by the Italian chambers, becoming effective in May 1871. Pius quickly repudiated it and rejected reconciliation.

Following the loss of Rome and the 'Italian persecution', Pius had to confront grave problems in Germany at the hands of the 'iron chancellor' and the National Liberals in the so-called *Kulturkampf*, or struggle for culture. Authoritarian by inclination, Bismarck had earlier proclaimed that one day 'the open fight' against Catholics must 'commence in Germany'.[53] In a diplomatic circular to German representatives abroad, Bismarck warned that the power of the pope, cloaked with the mantle of infallibility, was more absolute than that of any monarch. The iron chancellor derided the contention that the triple tiara represented papal authority over heaven, hell and earth. Prepared to concede the first two realms to Rome, Bismarck claimed the third for his state. Pius, in turn, recalled that the German government had shown itself sympathetic to Doellinger, who refused to submit to the declaration of infallibility, while supportive of the Old Catholic movement, which also broke with Rome over the issue of infallibility. Addressing a delegation from Alsace in June 1871, he expressed his hope that their new masters would leave them alone, especially as regards religious matters.[54] Such was not to be the case.

In July 1871 the Catholic section of the Prussian ministry of worship, in place since the ordinance of Frederick William IV in 1841, was eliminated. In September the 'Old Catholics', who met in congress in Munich, called for the expulsion of the Jesuits for the good of the state as well as the faith. At the end of the year, in December 1871, the 'pulpit law' was passed, imposing penalties, including imprisonment, upon the clergy for criticism of the Reich and its constitution, from the pulpit. The campaign against the church continued the following year with the secularization of education, terminating all ecclesiastical supervision in the primary schools, followed by the imperial law against the Jesuits, which excluded the Society of Jesus and other 'related orders': the Redemptorists, the Congregation of the Holy Ghost, the Vincentians, and the Religious of the Sacred Heart. The legislation was approved by the Reichstag and sanctioned by the emperor in July 1872.

To make matters worse, Prince Chlodwig zu Hohenlohe, hostile to the court of Rome, was elected president of the Reichstag. He adhered to his earlier conviction that papal infallibility elevated the power of the pontiff above princes and people, to the detriment of both. Subsequently, his brother Cardinal Gustav Adolf zu Hohenlohe, who had likewise questioned the wisdom of proclaiming papal infallibility, was selected to represent the German

53 'The Impregnable Fortress: Prince Bismarck and the Centre Party', *American Catholic Quarterly Review*, XV (July 1890), p. 401.
54 Speech of Pius IX to a deputation from Alsace, 20 June 1871, De Franciscis, *Discorsi del Sommo Pontefice Pio IX*, I, p. 146.

empire at the Holy See. Pius found the appointment unacceptable, arousing Bismarck, who determined to wage war against the ultramontanes and even the church in earnest.[55] At the end of 1872, Pius protested against the persecution of the church in Germany, denouncing the 'secret machinations', 'brute force', and other abusive means to eliminate Catholicism in the new German empire.

With the assistance of Adalbert Falk, the minister of ecclesiastical affairs and education, a series of laws were passed in Prussia known as the May or Falk laws. The first of these on the education and appointment of priests (11 May 1873) and on the limitation of the ecclesiastical power of discipline and punishment (13 May 1873) ostensibly aimed at securing liberty to the laity, a German rather than an ultramontane training for the clergy, and protection for the lower clergy against their superiors. Together they provided that the state should control the education of the clergy, with the right to approve or reject all candidates for the priesthood, and that Catholics could not acknowledge any ecclesiastical disciplinary power outside of Prussia. Thus, they placed the administration of the church under state control, while attempting to break the authority of the bishops and the power of the papacy in Prussia. Pius protested to the Emperor William I about the recent legislation against the church, noting his responsibility in 'telling the truth to all, even to those who are not Catholics – for everyone who has been baptized belongs in some way or other . . . to the Pope'. He warned the emperor that the legislation which aimed 'more and more at the destruction of Catholicism' would ultimately prove detrimental to the emperor's throne.[56]

Neither Bismarck nor his liberal allies in the war against the church were prepared to go to Canossa and they refused to gratify the 'arrogance' of the 'autocratic' pontiff. Early in 1874, Falk asked the Prussian Landtag to approve additional measures against the church, particularly regarding vacant sees. Subsequent legislation provided harsh penalties for the clergy who violated the state's ecclesiastical laws, including internment, imprisonment and banishment. Under its provisions, and the previous punitive measures which it supplemented, scores in Germany's Catholic hierarchy were penalized, and in the first months of 1875 over one hundred priests were imprisoned or expelled.

In the summer of 1875 a Prussian bill provided an endowment for the 'Old Catholics' who had broken with the church, assuring them the use of Catholic churches as well as the right to bury their dead in Catholic cemeteries. It formed part of a package of five laws enacted against the church that year. Among other things, the 1875 legislation regulated the administration of ecclesiastical revenues, suppressed all the allowances made by the state to bishops, assigned part of the Catholic churches' revenues to the 'Old Catholics', imposed

55 Pius IX to Cardinal Hohenlohe, 26 April 1872, ASV, Archivio Particolare Pio IX, Stato Pontificio, n. 203; Bruno Gheradine, 'Pio IX, episcopato e Kulturkampf', *Pio IX*, 1, VI (January–April 1977), pp. 35–6.
56 Pius IX to William I, 7 August 1873, Kertesz, ed., *Documents*, p. 248.

additional burdens upon the convents and religious congregations, and suppressed the paragraphs in the Prussian constitution which guaranteed religious liberty to Catholics. Catholic resistance continued and by 1876 all the Prussian bishops had been imprisoned or forced to take refuge abroad, and one-third of all parishes were without priests.

The aged pontiff encouraged the resistance to the persecution of the church in Germany, finding it no less dangerous and destructive than developments in Italy and Switzerland. He deplored the Austrian attempt to imitate developments in the Reich and Prussia, protesting against their laws which sought to subjugate the Catholic church to the civil authority.[57] He again denounced the Prussian legislation which undermined the rights of the bishops, excommunicating those who accepted these obnoxious laws.

Distressed by developments in Germany, Italy, Switzerland, Russia, Austria, the Ottoman empire and the Americas, Pius galvanized the church to fight the 'false principles' and 'poison' of the liberal revolution in the new world as well as the old. In Venezuela, Antonio Guzman Blanco, the liberal leader, sought to curb the power of the church by depriving the clergy of control of the civil registry and cemeteries, and in the early 1870s confiscating monastic and church property. Subsequently, seminaries were suppressed and priests were educated at the national university where the doctrine of infallibility was repudiated. In Colombia, General Tomas Mosquera, who gained control of the government in 1861, declared a 'kulturkampf' which ordered the Jesuits out of the country, while the property held in the hands of religious corporations reverted to the state. In Ecuador, President Borrero suspended the concordat as contrary to national sovereignty. Likewise in Chile, the administration of President Federico Errazuriz (1871–76) opposed the pretensions of the church and the papacy. In the Brazil of Pedro II, where a form of regalism prevailed, the emperor's government refused to accord the *exequatur* to the encyclical *Quanta cura* and the appended Syllabus of Errors.[58]

Pius found the course of public affairs unfortunate, and threatening to become worse, but abandoned himself to the hands of God, certain He would ultimately resolve matters in favour of the faithful.[59] The prevailing climate confirmed the pope's conviction that the faith everywhere confronted a brutal persecution. The pope saw the need to strengthen Catholic ideology and safeguard the pontifical magistracy, which was threatened by the revisionist, heretical and liberal current which had spread worldwide. Small wonder that Pius was prepared to resist to the end, openly condemning whatever and whomever he deemed in error, regardless of rank, popularity or power. He perceived himself the agent of truth and justice, which had been outraged and

57 *Esti multa*, 21 November 1873, and *Vix dum a Nobis*, 7 March 1874, in Carlen, *PP*, I, p. 41; *Quod nunquam*, Encyclical of Pope Pius IX on the Church in Prussia, 5 February 1875, in Carlen, *PE*, I, pp. 447–9; De Franciscis, *Discorsi del Sommo Pontefice Pio IX*, III, pp. 562–5.
58 Mecham, *Church and State in Latin America*, pp. 105–8, 123–5, 152–3, 210, 270–2.
59 Pius IX to De Corcelles, 17 December 1876, ASV, Archivio Particolare Pio IX, Francia Particolari.

offended, believing that without the pope there was no church, and without the Holy See there was no Catholic society.[60]

Pio Nono's claim to be God's representative on earth, and his assertion that the church had to instruct, direct and govern the Christian world, clashed with the liberal demand for popular sovereignty and the nationalist call for the omnipotence of the state. He judged the triumph of liberalism and nationalism attained at the expense of the faith and the enslavement of the church. The pope's abhorrence of nineteenth-century liberal thought was intense, propelling his crusade against their 'unbridled reason', which deprived humanity of the consolation of the faith. He likewise disdained the liberal call for individual self-maximization, in place of God's harmonious society.

There was little room for compromise between Pius's traditionalism and ultramontanism and the liberal parliamentary notions which prevailed in Western Europe. Rome reproached the love of political innovation as a snare devised to divide the faithful. Liberal Catholics came in for a special condemnation from the pope, who charged they undermined the spiritual unity of the church while championing a false liberty. In their efforts to reconcile 'human progress' with the gospel, the claims of science with the dogmas of religion, light with darkness, Christ with Satan, they did more harm than good.[61] The gap between contemporary civilization and the papacy, the church and the modern world had grown throughout the last two decades of Pio Nono's 32-year pontificate, and represented one of the major challenges facing his predecessor following this pope's death in 1878.

60 Speech of Pius IX to former employees, 2 July 1873, De Franciscis, *Discorsi del Sommo Pontefice Pio IX*, II, 366.
61 Pius to a delegation from the Federation of Catholic Clubs of Belgium, 8 May 1873, *Dublin Review*, new series XXVI (1876), p. 489.

CHAPTER 8

Rome's attempt at accommodation with the modern world, 1878–1903

At the death of Pius IX, the papacy, if not the church, found itself estranged from 'modern civilization' and in conflict with a series of European powers. Two of the continent's most powerful empires, Russia and Germany, had severed their diplomatic intercourse with the Roman pontiff, while the American republic had suppressed its legation at the Vatican.[1] The Vatican was opposed or abandoned by many of the courts of Europe, ignored by the universities, and ridiculed as hopelessly out of touch with the times by critics who claimed to speak for the masses. Consequently the task of the 61-member conclave of 1878 did not prove easy. The long and stormy pontificate of Pio Nono (1846–78) had not only seen the church shorn of its temporal power, but had witnessed conflicts with the kingdom of Italy over the Roman Question, and with the German empire in the *Kulturkampf*, with ramifications in Austria and Switzerland. Relations with the French republic were little better as the French hierarchy openly cavorted with the monarchical pretenders, provoking retaliation by the republicans as Leon Gambetta proclaimed clericalism the mortal enemy!

The church also continued to confront problems in the world beyond Europe in the last quarter of the nineteenth century, upsetting the officials at the propaganda fide, the congregation to which much of the Americas remained subject. Propaganda was bombarded with warnings of the enormous diocesan and parochial debts in the United States, and the 'selfishness and exaggerated independence' displayed by part of its clergy.[2] The Vatican also worried about developments to the north, where the French-Canadian clergy flagrantly interfered in the political life of Canada, threatening the constitutional and religious stability in that vast territory. Meanwhile, tensions continued with a number of the Latin American states whose anticlerical measures led the curia to fear for the future of the church there. Finally, the papacy sought to regain for the

1 Bernard O'Reilly, *Life of Leo XIII. From An Authentic Memoir Furnished by His Order* (New York, 1903), pp. 33–4.
2 Relazione sul progetto di stabilire una Delegazione Apostolica nell'America del Nord, Archivio di Propaganda Fide, Rome, *Acta* 1877, v. 245, f. 39.

Cross peoples in the western portion of Asia and the northern half of Africa who had succumbed to the ascendent Crescent.

Serious ideological dissension complicated the picture, with residual resentment of papal policy within the church, but much more outside. Critics questioned the measures of the 'unmoved and immovable' Pio Nono. There was censure of this pope's reluctance to concede the loss of the temporal power and resentment of his 'ultramontane pronouncements': the dogma of the Immaculate Conception (1854), the Syllabus of Errors (1864), and the decree of papal infallibility (1870). While some hoped that the new pontiff would liberate the papacy from the 'reactionary shadow' of his predecessor, others praised the saintly Pius, who had stood firm in the face of the insidious political and moral revolution. Under these circumstances, the burdens of the tiara were heavy and the course of the new pope would prove difficult.[3]

Surprisingly, the conclave which opened ten days after the death of Pius proved to be one of the shortest in church history, requiring only two days and three votes to select 68-year-old Gioacchino Vincenzo Rafaelle Pecci, the cardinal bishop of Perugia, on 20 February 1878. Some prayed that the new pope, who assumed the name Leo XIII, after Leo XII whom he had met while a student, would adopt a more flexible policy than his predecessor, easing tensions with the contemporary world. The course he would pursue remained problematic because outside of Benevento, Perugia and Belgium, contemporaries know little about Pecci.

Pecci, the sixth child and fourth son of Count Luigi Domenico Pecci and his wife, Anna Prosperi Buzi, was born on 2 March 1810 in Carpineto (Frosinone), in the diocese of Anagni, where this family of the lower nobility had emigrated from Sienna. Like his brother Joseph, who later joined the Society of Jesus, he studied at the Jesuit College of Viterbo (1818–24), followed by the Roman College (1824–32), where he received a degree in sacred theology (1832) and entered the academy of noble ecclesiastics, preparing for a future in the Roman diplomatic service. In 1837 Pecci was ordained a priest and appointed apostolic delegate at Benevento, a principality of some forty-six square miles in the kingdom of Naples, and in 1841 transferred to Perugia where he served as papal governor. In both places, he proved a competent administrator, prompting Gregory, in 1843, to dispatch the 33-year-old prelate as nuncio to Belgium (1843–46). In Brussels, his support of the episcopacy against the government's educational measures led Leopold to request his recall. In 1846 Gregory XVI named him bishop of Perugia (1846–77), where he presided in relative obscurity for more than thirty years. Created a cardinal in 1853, he remained in Perugia.

Some believed that Pecci's exile from Rome was provoked by Cardinal Giacomo Antonelli, a notion fuelled by the fact that following the cardinal

3 Foreign Correspondent, 'The Death of Pius IX: The Conclave and the Election', *Catholic World*, XXVII (April 1878), p. 129; Harry C. Koenig, ed., *Principles for Peace: Selections from Papal Documents from Leo XIII to Pius XII* (Washington, DC, 1943), pp. 1–2; Reuben Parsons, *Studies in Church History* (New York, 1900), VI, pp. 139–51.

secretary of state's death in 1876, Pius invited Pecci to Rome in 1877 to head the apostolic chamber. In fact, Pius, rather than Antonelli, had kept Pecci at bay because he had expressed reservations about the proclamation of the dogma of the Immaculate Conception, dear to the heart of the pope. Furthermore, Pecci's support of the Syllabus was rumoured to be lukewarm.[4] However, he redeemed himself at the Vatican council where he voted with the majority in favour of infallibility and supported Pio Nono's condemnations, adding that these did not necessarily anathematize the modern world and the church was not against progress, properly understood. Such assertions encouraged moderates and even some liberals.

Clearly Leo proved more pragmatic than Pius IX and took immediate action to end the diplomatic isolation of the papacy. On his first day in office, he wrote to President MacMahon of France, one in a series of steps to seek rapprochement with the republic. Relations between Paris and the Vatican had been less than cordial during the last years of his predecessor's pontificate, as the church aligned itself with the monarchists against the third republic. The new pope regretted this development, believing that improved relations would prove beneficial for both. The pontiff also considered the conflict with Germany counter-productive. He therefore dispatched a letter to the German emperor, calling for the restoration of amicable relations between Rome and the Reich. On 4 March 1878, the day following his coronation, Leo completed Pius IX's effort to reconstitute the Catholic hierarchy in Scotland.[5] Other encouraging developments followed.

Cardinal Alessandro Franchi, the newly appointed secretary of state, was far from an intransigent. Indeed, Franchi deplored the reactionary course of the Quebec hierarchy and their rabid support of the conservative party against the governing liberals in Canada. The secretary of state sent George Conroy, bishop of Ardagh, to Canada as apostolic delegate, with instructions to remind the conservative clergy that in condemning liberalism the Holy See did not intend to attack all parties bearing that label. The mission proved delicate.[6] Meanwhile Leo personally appealed to Belgium's Catholics to sustain their constitution, concluding that the system of liberty established in their country proved beneficial to the church.

Those seeking reconciliation between Rome and the revolution, the papacy and the Risorgimento, were to be disappointed. In his first encyclical of April 1878 which explored God's inscrutable design, Leo bewailed the evils of the day, renewing most of the condemnations of his predecessor.[7] His message, if softer in tone than that of Pius IX, proved no more conciliatory. Cardinal

4 Paolo dalla Torre, 'Il Cardinale Giacomo Antonelli fra carte di archvio ed atti processuali', *Pio Nono*, VIII (1979), pp. 168–71.

5 *ASS*, XI, p. 3.

6 Archivio di Propaganda Fide, Rome, *Acta* 1879, Sulla nomina di un nuovo delegato apostolico per Canada e sulle specializi istruzioni da darsi al medesimo, v. 247, *fascicoli* 351–79.

7 Allocution of 28 March 1878, *ASS*, X, pp. 577–9; *Inscrutabili Dei Consilio*, in *ASS*, X, p. 585, also in Carlen, *PE*, II, pp. 5–10; Koenig, ed., *Principles for Peace*, pp. 3–6.

Franchi remained secretary of state for less than half a year, succeeded by Cardinal Lorenzo Nina. Leo continued to seek reconciliation, promising the archbishop of Cologne that he was working to obtain the blessing of a lasting peace for the German people. Perceiving the menace of Marxism, Leo insisted that the church of Christ had the power 'to ward off the plague of socialism', and urged the restoration of the church to a condition of liberty so she could 'exert her healing force for the benefit of all society'.[8]

Within his early messages, Leo echoed the traditionalism of Pius IX on religious issues and the Roman Question, revealed a transitional stance on political and diplomatic developments, while hinting at a new approach to the social question. In *Aeterni patris* of 4 August 1879, Leo suggested that a reinvigorated scholasticism could help harmonize faith and reason, providing a metaphysical base for the Christian social programme he eventually evolved.[9] He denied the notion that the church sought to usurp civil power, recognizing the right of a people to choose their form of government. Neither rulers nor the ruled, Leo reported, had reason to fear papal interference in the temporal order. Even in the grey area where political and spiritual interests mingled, Leo called for harmony.

Nonetheless, Leo was disturbed by developments in France as well as Italy, where the rights of the church in education were curtailed. The January 1879 elections in France assured the republicans a majority in the senate, forcing the monarchist President MacMahon to resign. The republicans showed themselves anticlerical for ideological as well as political reasons, urging a crusade against the church and a programme of laicization as a means of forging unity among the disparate elements in the coalition government. In the spring of 1879, minister of education Jules Ferry presented two bills: one on secondary education and the other on higher education, both restricting the role of the church. Among their hostile provisions was one forbidding members of non-authorized religious congregations from teaching in the public or private schools or directing any educational establishment.

The papal response to the French ecclesiastical legislation proved measured. Leo hoped to mitigate the anticlericalism of the republic by recalling Monsignor Meglia as nuncio to France, replacing him with Monsignor Wladmir Czacki, who proved more tactful. The new nuncio revealed to Gambetta and the other republicans that the church was not bound to any particular party, nor was she biased against any constituted authority that did not infringe upon her freedom of action.[10] The pope's representative explained that while the church believed in social order and obedience to legitimately constituted authority, the Vatican was neutral *vis-à-vis* the various forms of government. The pope remained less tolerant towards Italy than France because the seizure of Rome rendered the papacy vulnerable. Leo vehemently opposed the

8 *Quod Apostolici Muneris*, 28 December 1878, in Carlen, *PE*, II, p. 15.
9 Carlen, *PP*, I, pp. 43–4.
10 Eduardo Soderini, *Leo XIII, Italy and France* (London, 1935), p. 143.

compulsory civil marriage law introduced in Italy as well as the attempts to further secularize education, and the strong opposition of the Vatican and the church played a part in blocking their passage, much to the annoyance of Garibaldi.[11]

Some Italians were alarmed by the Vatican's courtship of Paris, St Petersburg, Berlin and even powers beyond the shores of Europe to champion its cause against the Rome government. In 1880 Leo wrote to the archbishop of Paris, decrying Catholic support for the various demonstrations in favour of 'Henry V' or other pretenders to the throne, explaining that in its dealings with governments, the church has as its main objective to preserve Christianity. He reassured Alexander of Russia that the Catholic religion strove to promote peace and harmony between subjects and rulers in all countries.[12] In 1882 the Russian Chancellor Giers visited the Vatican, leading Leo to hope for improvements in relations with Russia, especially with respect to Poland. An 1882 agreement between the Vatican and St Petersburg provided greater freedom to Catholic seminaries in the empire, and the Russian chargé d'affaires promised that the prosecutorial degree of 1865 would be suppressed. That same year diplomatic relations between the Vatican and Prussia, which had been broken since 1872, were re-established.

When the pope had to choose a new secretary of state following Cardinal Nina's resignation, Leo appointed Cardinal Jacobini, who had aided him in Austrian and German affairs. This bore some fruit, for that same year, 1880, Bismarck took his first steps towards Canossa, introducing legislation in the Landtag renouncing the government's right to depose ecclesiastics. Subsequently, the Prussian Landtag voted funds for reopening diplomatic relations and nominated a minister plenipotentiary to the Vatican. The six clauses of the church bill of 5 June 1883 modified the most oppressive features of Prussia's ecclesiastical legislation. The pope continued his diplomatic 'campaign' at the end of 1880, commending French societies devoted to spreading the faith abroad, praising the French for providing both money and religious for this crucial missionary work.[13]

The results of the pope's diplomatic initiative proved mixed. While papal relations with Germany and Russia improved, there was a deterioration in relations with Italy. Relations between Rome and the Vatican reached a low point in July 1881 when a violent demonstration was orchestrated against the papacy as the body of Pio Nono was transported from St Peter's to its final resting place in San Lorenzo outside the walls. The attempt to dump the casket of the pope who had opposed unification into the Tiber, moved Leo to action. His appeal to the powers in August 1881 appraised the world of the perilous position of the papacy in the Eternal City and invoked intervention.

11 Garibaldi to Depretis, 20 April 1879, Archivio Centrale dello Stato di Roma, Archivio Depretis, *busta* 4, *fascicolo* 11, *sottofascicolo* 21.
12 Koenig, ed., *Principles for Peace*, pp. 11–12.
13 *Sancta Dei civitas*, 3 December 1880, in Carlen, *PE*, II, p. 44.

Leo deplored the plans of the Italian masonic movement to convoke a congress in the Holy City during the course of the following year, appealing to the powers to no avail.[14]

In France, Gambetta's ministry mimicked many of the actions of Agostino Depretis's liberal regime by confiscating the property of the religious orders, seeking to restrict the influence of the church in society and the schools. The archbishop of Paris proved unable to curtail these measures. In June 1881 Leo decried the bitter campaign launched against the faith, claiming it endangered society as well as the civil power on which public safety relied. He offered an olive branch to the French republic by asserting that the church did not prefer one form of government over another, adding that a people should be free to select that form of government which best suited their disposition, institutions and customs.[15]

The pope returned to these themes in an encyclical to the bishops of Belgium on the question of forms of government and their conformity to Catholic doctrine. Acknowledging the papacy's preference that human society be governed 'in a Christian manner', Leo added that the church from the first showed herself prudent in matters of this nature. Restraining those who were quick to advocate revolution against regimes hostile to ecclesiastical interests, the pope explained that it 'commonly happens in human affairs she [the church] is often constrained to tolerate at times evils that it would be almost impossible to prevent, without exposing herself to calamities and troubles still more disastrous'.[16] This was a position later assumed by other pontiffs, above all Pius XII, contributing to his 'silence'.

In his campaign to win the support of the powers, Leo did not neglect Great Britain and Spain. In August 1882 he cautioned the Irish bishops to educate the faithful to shun secret societies and preserve the peace. Saddened by Ireland's unfortunate condition, he praised its people for their long-suffering, and unshaken constancy in the faith. Understanding that men have a right to a legitimate redress of their grievances, he admonished that a nation's welfare could not be procured by revolutionary agitation tinged by dishonour and crime.[17] Just ends could not be achieved by inherently evil means. His position pleased the British. Rejecting the separation of church and state, Leo dismissed the tendency to identify their religion with one particular party or group, warning his flock not to mix religion and politics as had occurred in France and Canada. Indeed, the pope invoked the Spanish clergy to display moderation, cautioning them not to fall prey to the rivalry of parties. In Spain, as in Italy, Leo relied upon the activities of Catholic associations, under the leadership of their bishops, to uphold the interests of the faith. Since the members of such associations might differ on political questions, Leo

14 Reuben Parsons, *Studies in Church History* (New York, 1900), VI, pp. 157–60, 184; Soderini, *Leo XIII*, pp. 24–35.
15 *Diuturnum*, 29 June 1881, in Carlen, *PE*, II, pp. 51–8.
16 *Licet Multa*, 3 August 1881, ibid., II, pp. 59–61.
17 Koenig, ed., *Principles for Peace*, pp. 17–18; Carlen, *PP*, I, p. 45.

removed politics from Catholic action, whose primary purpose was to promote Catholic unity.[18]

Concluding that anticlericalism in Spain was fed by the clergy's interference in the country's political life and widespread support of Carlism, Leo cautioned them to curb this intervention. A similar situation existed in France where the death of the count of Chambord in 1883 united royalists and clericals behind the banner of the count of Paris, and a programme proposing the full restoration of religious liberty. The pope feared the clerical-conservative alliance would provoke renewed tension between the republic and the church, to the detriment of both. The French clergy in Quebec created the same sort of problem in Canada, interfering in the political process and antagonizing the central government. To cope with this dilemma, in the summer of 1883 propaganda fide appointed Henri Smeulders, a Belgian Cistercian resident in Rome, apostolic commissioner to Canada. Smeulders transmitted the Vatican's orders to the clergy to cease their interference in the political arena.[19] Leo was also upset by the reports he received from the propaganda's agent on church conditions in the United States, reflecting earlier criticism of both the quality and independence assumed by their higher clergy.[20]

Confident that truth as well as justice was on the side of the church, Leo implemented his promise to open the Vatican archives for the scrutiny of scholars and historical research. In a letter to Cardinals De Luca, Pitra and Hergenroether, the pope reviewed past attempts to cast suspicion on the actions of the church and the papacy, claiming that such rash assertions lacked reliability, laborious investigations, maturity of judgement, and the critical analysis required of historical objectivity. The pope derided those who feared opening the archives as *piccole teste* or small-minded, confident that an exploration of the past would provide a stronger foundation for the future. The pope urged Catholics to pursue historical studies, urging the publication of facts 'to correct fancies'. 'If the Gospels had been written in our days', he confided to Cardinal Manning, 'the history of the fall of St Peter and of the treachery of Judas would have probably been left out as not edifying.'[21]

The holy father resented the continuing confiscation of ecclesiastical property in France. To stem this course, Leo advised the French faithful to exercise greater vigilance over the education of the young and the defence of religious groups and organizations. Ideally, church and state would work in harmony for their common well-being.[22] Leo remained critical of the freemasons, whom

18 *Cum Multa*, in Carlen, *PE*, II, pp. 75–9; William J. Kiefer, *Leo XIII: A Light from Heaven* (Milwaukee, 1960), p. 127.

19 Roberto Perin, 'Una furia piu "che francese": The Quebec Church and Vatican Diplomacy in the Age of Anglo-Canadian Protestant Domination', in Peter C. Kent and John F. Pollard, eds, *Papal Diplomacy in the Modern Age* (Westport, CT, 1994), pp. 50–1.

20 Bishop Johann Franzelin, Relazione con sommario e nota del Archivio circa le presente condizioni della chiesa Cattolica negli Stati Uniti d'America . . . , Archivio di Propaganda Fide, Rome, *Acta* 1883, pp. 1080–108.

21 Cardinal Gasquet, *A Memoir*, ed. Shane Leslie (New York, 1953), pp. 34–5.

22 *Nobilissima Gallorum Gens*, 8 February 1884, in Carlen, *PE*, II, pp. 85–9.

he denounced in April 1884 as a danger to the church, state and society, cataloguing the condemnations of some nine predecessors during the course of more than a century. The pontiff believed that the state and church, working together, had to overcome the evil designs and pernicious programme of the sects, preserving public order and tranquillity.[23]

Leo further explored church–state relations in his 1885 encyclical on the Christian constitution of states. Acknowledging the immediate and natural aim of the church consisted in saving souls, he never denied its impact on, or its interest in, the temporal world. Leo repeated the church dictum that the right to rule was not bound to any specific form of government, one being as legitimate as another. To illustrate this longstanding position, the pope cited the example of the early Christians who did not attempt to overthrow the pagan ruling power. When his immediate predecessors, Gregory XVI and Pius IX, condemned certain governmental theories, the pontifical reproach was not vented against any form of government, considered in itself. Nor did the pope's comment on the greater or lesser share of popular participation desirable in governmental matters, a role that is often useful and sometimes obligatory. Nor should one deduce from these pontifical condemnations that the church opposed real liberty or scientific and intellectual inquiry.

Pope Leo claimed that the church favoured most things which fostered the development of science, progress, art and handicraft. He rejected the charge that either the church or papacy opposed progress. What both could not accept was 'naturalism or rationalism, the essence of which is utterly to do away with Christian institutions and to install in society the supremacy of man to the exclusion of God'.[24] Leo repeated that the church would recognize any form of government that respected its rights, adding that it is not wrong to prefer a democratic form of government, so long as it respected the Catholic doctrine regarding the origin and exercise of power.[25] He thus proved more diplomatic and discriminating than Pius IX in his rejection of progress, separating legitimate from impermissible developments. This pope sought an accommodation of sorts with the modern world, but on Christian, Catholic and papal terms.

Despite his critique of liberal excesses, Leo continued his campaign to bring the papacy and church into a more cordial relationship with the modern world. His reconciliation had political and diplomatic dimensions as well as economic and social ones. During the course of 1885, Leo wrote to the emperor of China and the mikado of Japan. Pope Leo sent the primate of the Coptic church in Egypt, Monsignor Marcario, to facilitate the release of the Italians imprisoned by Menelik following the battle of Adowa in 1896. Another, more successful diplomatic effort occurred when the pope accepted Bismarck's

23 *Humanus genus*, in Carlen, *PP*, I, p. 46.
24 *Immortale Dei*, in Carlen, *PE*, II, p. 117.
25 *Libertas*, 20 June 1888, in ibid., II, pp. 169–81.

invitation to mediate the dispute between Germany and Spain in the Caroline Archipelago in the South Seas, proposing an amicable arrangement between the contesting powers, which was accepted in December 1885. Subsequently, the Reichstag passed the 'fourth law for peace' which virtually brought the *Kulturkampf* to a close. In 1887 Leo dispatched Cardinal Luigi Galimberti to Berlin on a special mission to attend celebrations for William I's ninetieth birthday and the pope's emissary received a cordial welcome. In the interim, Leo named Bismarck a knight of the Order of Christ. In 1890 it was announced that a bill would be submitted to the Reichstag providing restitution to the Catholic church for the entire accumulated capital formed by the confiscation of priests' salaries during the *Kulturkampf*.[26] Following instructions, the papal representative to the United States opened a dialogue with the Mexicans to restore that country's diplomatic relations with the Holy See.[27]

Shorn of the temporal power, Pope Leo attempted to enhance the international position of the papacy and advance the interest of the universal church. He sought amicable relations with the states of the world and his success could be gauged as early as 1888, the year of his priestly jubilee, in which most monarchs of Europe and the other heads of Christian governments sent representatives and congratulations, including a number of non-Christian regimes. In 1895 a permanent representative from Russia to the Holy See was established, enabling Leo to regulate better the ecclesiastical life of the Catholics in that sprawling empire. In his first diplomatic note to the minister of Russian foreign affairs, Cardinal Rampolla, the papal secretary of state, affirmed that peace could only be established on the foundation of Christian public law.[28]

Despite Pope Leo's sustained efforts, relations did not improve dramatically with the third French republic, presided over by positivists who espoused secularism. Its chamber of deputies perceived the church and the papacy as enemies to be restricted. Among other things, its laic laws sought to secularize education, render seminarians liable to military service, and reintroduced divorce. In response, the pontiff protested against the suppression of ecclesiastical stipends, and the bills which proposed divorce and military service for seminarians. President Grevy did not deny that Leo had cause for complaint, but advised him to persuade French Catholics to abandon the royalists and thus work to disarm the republican opposition to the church. Leo accepted the suggestion, having the *Osservatore Romano* criticize the ultra legitimist trend of the *Journal de Rome*, while continuing his efforts to seek a reconciliation with the republic.[29] The coincidence of Leo's priestly jubilee with that of Queen Victoria provided the basis for a friendly interchange in 1888 between the Vatican and Windsor. This did not prevent Leo from refusing to recognize the

26 *New York Times*, 30 December 1890.
27 Francesco Satolli to Cardinal Rampolla, 29 September 1893, ASV, Segreteria di Stato, 1896, *rubrica* 280, *fascicolo* 2.
28 Koenig, ed., *Principles for Peace*, pp. 93–4.
29 *Cum de Carolinis insulis*, in Carlen, *PP*, I, p. 47; Soderini, *Leo XIII*, pp. 183–4; Koenig, ed., *Principles for Peace*, pp. 23–5, 31–2.

legitimacy of Anglican holy orders, despite the inclination of Cardinals Gasparri and Rampolla to do so.[30] He alerted the bishops of Hungary and Portugal to preserve the Christian bases of society, but warned them and the clergy elsewhere to recognize and respect the division between politics and religion.[31]

At the turn of the century, Leo was preoccupied by the problems of the church beyond Europe as well as those closer to home, establishing eight ecclesiastical provinces and a hierarchy in India at the end of 1886. At the same time, the pope opened talks for the creation of nunciatures in Peking and Tokyo, while applauding the abolition of slavery in Brazil. He urged the archbishop of Carthage to do all within his means to end the nefarious traffic in human souls in Africa. Leo appreciated that the Catholic migration from France and Italy to the shores of North Africa and the Middle East restored Christianity to an area dominated by Islam. Nonetheless, he recognized that the church's missionary efforts were frustrated by its close association with European imperialism. A similar identification prevailed in the Far East. Leo advised missionaries to respect the native culture, preserving their independence from the colonial power structure.

Rome applauded the constitution proclaimed by the mikado in 1891 which established religious liberty for his subjects. That same year, Pope Leo made Tokyo an archipiscopal see, having for suffragan dioceses those of Nagasaki, Osaka and Hokodate. In 1899 there was a national council in Rome of all the Latin American bishops. Thus, Leo continued the efforts of Pius IX to render the church less Eurocentric and more truly universal. While neither he nor his predecessors, Gregory XVI and Pius IX, accepted the separation of church and state, they worked to liberate the church from the embrace of the political structure. Thus, while Lamennais's principles remained anathema, in practice the papacy withdrew the clergy from the political arena in Italy, France, Canada and elsewhere.

As the nineteenth century drew to a close, the Vatican found developments in the United States disconcerting. Despatching Monsignor Germano Straniero to deliver the cardinal's hat to James Gibbons, Leo instructed this emissary to tour the country and report to Rome. His recommendation urged the pope to dispatch an apostolic delegate to the United States.[32] Shortly thereafter, in November 1889, 100 years after the institution of a regular hierarchy in the United States by Pius VI, a theological school opened in Washington D.C., the beginning of the Catholic University of America. Archbishop Francesco Satolli, president of the pontifical academy for noble ecclesiastics, represented Rome at its inception. Upon returning to Rome, he also called for the establishment of an apostolic delegation, which materialized in 1892–93, following

30 Gasquet, *A Memoir*, p. 67.

31 See *Quod multum*, to the bishops of Hungary, and *Pergrata*, to the bishops of Portugal, in Carlen, *PP*, I, p. 48; Koenig, ed., *Principles for Peace*, pp. 35–6.

32 Rapporto sulle condizioni della Chiesa Cattolica negli Stati Uniti d'America umiliato alla Santità di Nostro Signore Leone XIII da Monsignor Germano Straniero, ASV, Segreteria di Stato, 1902, *rubrica* 280, *fascicolo* 10.

papal participation in the Columbian Exposition of 1892 in Chicago, in honour of the 400-year anniversary of the discovery of America. In January 1893 Satolli, a close friend of the pope, was appointed apostolic delegate to the United States. Although his official function was to represent the pope to the American Catholic episcopate rather than being accredited to the United States government, from the first he unofficially assumed diplomatic and political responsibilities. This apostolic delegation was established within the broader framework of Leo's policy of seeking rapprochement with the emerging masses, particularly in the democracies.

At the opening of the 1890s, Leo continued his efforts to achieve rapprochement between the Vatican and the French republic, as well as between French Catholics and a string of anticlerical ministries. Disinclined to sanction political means to achieve ecclesiastical ends, Leo discouraged the efforts of Count Albert de Mun to establish a Catholic party. The pope showed himself more supportive of the efforts of Jacques Piou to create a constitutional bloc of the right that would accept the republic, in the hope of guiding it towards a more conservative course. Leo was seconded in his efforts to achieve a rapprochement or *ralliement* by Monsignor Ferrata, who advocated conciliation, the papal secretary of state, Cardinal Mariano Rampolla del Tindaro, who shared his vision, and the primate of Africa, Cardinal Lavigerie, who urged the pope to make some dramatic move in the matter. In October 1890 Lavigerie returned to Rome, and during the course of his visits with Leo, Rampolla and Ferrata, it was decided that he would appeal to French Catholics to adhere to the republic for the good of their faith.[33]

When the French fleet visited Algiers in early November 1890, the archbishop invited the officers of the fleet, overwhelmingly royalists, to a banquet. In his toast, Lavigerie observed that the union of all French citizens was the cherished hope of the church, her pastors, and the hierarchy, repeating Leo's assertion that the form of government remained inconsequential. Noting that the will of the people had been expressed, Lavigerie advised Frenchmen to accept the republic for the salvation of country and faith. His message found few converts in the royalist audience, provoking a storm of controversy in France. Many monarchists were conservative first and Catholic second. Rumour circulated that Lavigerie had spoken on his own, and to combat that impression Monsignor Baduel, the archbishop of Saint Flour, suggested the holy father reveal his sentiments. Responding to this request, secretary of state Rampolla repeated that the Vatican had shown no preference for any form of government, adding it would be improper to involve the church in political strife. He advised the French faithful to follow the course of the Holy See, which recognized all established governments in order to defend religious interests.

Until this juncture, Leo avoided any direct intervention in French affairs, but was urged to do so by part of the French hierarchy as well as Vatican

33 Soderini, *Leo XIII*, pp. 205–6.

supporters of the *ralliement*. In February 1892 Leo granted an audience to Ernest Judet, one of the editors of the *Petit Journal*. Acknowledging that French Catholics had a right to their own political opinions, the pope cautioned them to respect the republic as the duly constituted government of their country, considering it as legitimate a form as any other. These words, published in the *Petit Journal* of 17 February 1892, left no room for misunderstanding. They were reinforced that same month by Leo's encyclical to the bishops, clergy and faithful of France on church–state relations in their country. Observing that various political governments had succeeded one another in France during the last half century, Catholics, like other French citizens, had the right to prefer one form over another, because none of them necessarily opposed the maxims of Christianity. Probing the difference between constituted power and legislation, his letter stressed that laws were the work of men in power rather than the form of government. The former, especially the anticlerical measures, might legitimately be opposed, while one respected the republic.[34]

Monsignor Ferrata, nuncio in Paris, and Rampolla, the papal secretary of state, both believed that if the parliamentary right accepted Leo's call to rally to the republic, breaking the mischievous alliance of the French church with the royalist cause, the anticlerical policies of the radicals would lose support. Neither occurred. True enough laymen such as Albert de Mun, Étienne Lamy and Jacques Piou renewed their political effort in the direction Leo had charted, but their impact was limited. The declaration of the monarchist right pronounced that as Catholics they bowed to the holy father's infallible authority on matters of faith, but as citizens they exercised their individual political option. Despite the submission of a few, the majority of conservative Catholics refused to bow to the strictures of Leo and unite for a common defence. During the Panama canal scandal and the Dreyfus affair at the turn of the century, their alliance with the royalist right worked to undermine the position of the church in France.

The alliance between conservatives and Catholics also assumed a dangerous turn in Canada, where the higher clergy intervened in the elections of 1896 on behalf of the conservative cause, leading moderate Canadians and distressed Catholics to appeal to Rome to restore order and discipline.[35] In their collective letter of May 1896, the bishops of Quebec province had warned the faithful of the grave sin incurred by those who voted for the persecutors of their religion, namely the Liberals. When the latter emerged victorious in the federal elections of June 1896, the Liberal prime minister Wilfrid Laurier called upon the Vatican to curb the Canadian Catholic hierarchy.[36] Leo ordered the congregation for extraordinary ecclesiastical affairs to investigate the matter and moved to achieve a rapprochement between the Canadian hierarchy and

34 *Au Milieu des Sollicitudes*, 16 February 1892, in Carlen, *PE*, II, pp. 277–83.
35 Calls for an Apostolic Delegate in Canada, ASV, Delegazione Apostolica del Canada, *scatola* 76; Francesco Satolli to Cardinal Rampolla, 30 June 1896, *ASV, Segreteria di Stato, rubrica* 280.
36 Stephen T. Rusak, 'The Canadian Concordat of 1897', *Catholic Historical Review*, LXXVII, 2 (April 1991), pp. 209–12.

the Liberal Canadian regime. The 32-year-old Monsignor Rafael Merry del Val, assigned this delicate mission, submitted a report to Rome in September 1897. He believed that the higher clergy in Quebec provoked the crisis by their clumsy attempt to dictate the political policies of the flock.

Although a good part of the curia seemed to favour the Canadian bishops against the Liberals, the pope concluded that a systematic opposition to the Liberal party in power threatened Catholic interests throughout Canada. In an encyclical of December 1897 to the bishops of Canada on the school question, Leo urged moderation for the peace of the country, admonishing the Canadian hierarchy to accept the status quo. They did so grudgingly.[37] Even after 1899, when Diomede Falconio was named as Canada's first permanent apostolic delegate, part of the clergy remained recalcitrant. In many ways developments in Quebec mirrored those in France, although Leo found it easier to curb the conservative course of the hierarchy in Canada than the royalist stance of laymen in France.

Leo proved more successful in his efforts to win over the working classes, issuing a series of encyclicals on the social problem plaguing the contemporary world. Like his predecessors, Leo deplored the excesses of unrestrained capitalism and the *laissez-faire* preoccupation with the maximization of the self to the detriment of social conscience and responsibility. He also shared Gregory XVI's and Pius IX's aversion to socialist solutions. As early as December 1878, Pope Leo catalogued the Christian principles which he deemed more appropriate for a resolution of the social question than socialism or communism. This was followed by *Immortale dei* of November 1885, on the Christian orientation of society and the need for the church and state to work together for the well-being of citizens; *Libertas praestantissimum* of June 1888, on real liberty; and *Sapientiae christianae* of January 1890, on the duty of Christian citizens. In the last, Leo chastized the greed which led to the exploitation of the poor. It set the stage for his *Rerum novarum* of 15 March 1891, on the rights and duties of capital and labour, which offered a Christian solution to the social dilemma, and *Graves de communi* of 18 January 1901, on Christian democracy.

The pope proved far more understanding of the problems faced by the workers than did the archbishop of Quebec. The latter condemned the Knights of Labour, an American union, some 750,000 strong, under the presidency of Terrence Powderly, who was Catholic, as was a large part of the membership. Some felt that Rome favoured a condemnation of the Knights because of the closely connected imbroglio over the suspension of Father Edward McGlynn in New York for his support of Henry George's single tax theory.[38] Cardinal Gibbons, supported by the American bishops, urged the pope not to issue a condemnation of the union, and Leo, sensitive to the plight of labour, followed his advice in 1888. Nor did he censure Cardinal Manning two years later when he mediated the massive strike of dock workers in London. The

37 Ibid., pp. 230–4; Carlen, *PP*, I, p. 59.
38 Gerald P. Fogarty, *The Vatican and the Americanist Crisis: Denis J. O'Connell, American Agent in Rome, 1885–1903* (Rome, 1974), p. 160.

pope agreed with Karl Marx that the prevailing social order was unjust, but rejected the socialist solution.

As early as 1881, Leo had established a commission to examine economic conditions and explore the thought of Catholic social reformers. Influenced by a small but articulate group of 'social catholics' in France, Belgium, Switzerland and above all Germany, Leo was convinced that the church could function within secular society, assisting in the resolution of its difficulties. Borrowing from German social Catholicism and the programme of the German Centre Party, Leo issued his *Rerum novarum* of 1891, on the rights and duties of capital and labour. Its originality lay in its heightened awareness of the social problem and the presentation of a Christian programme for its resolution. The best known of Leo's encyclicals, it was at once a condemnation of socialism and the civilization that produced it, while introducing a Catholic solution to the social problems of the age. Tracing the vast expansion of industrial society, and the changed relations between workers and employers, which the Vatican had largely ignored, the pope stressed the need for an opportune remedy for the plight of the workers. Leo rejected the Marxist solution of eliminating private property and creating a community of goods, considering it a cure worse than the disease. Socialism could not substitute for the spiritual bond of Christianity in creating a brotherhood of humanity. Acknowledging that it was no easy matter to define the relative rights and mutual duties of rich and poor, capital and labour, Leo insisted that some remedy had to be found to end the misery pressing heavily and unjustly on the working classes.[39]

Deploring the hard-heartedness of employers and the unchecked competition, the pope considered it shameful and inhuman to treat men like chattels in the quest for profit. Leo considered self-maximization to be self-deception. The problems created by the new industrial society, and irresponsible wealth which ignored the moral order, required the co-operation of church, state, employer and employee, each doing its part. Rejecting class conflict, *Rerum novarum* proclaimed the workers' right to protection against economic exploitation and social injustice, indicating that when the mistreated workers could not defend their own rights, the state had to intervene on their behalf. Leo specifically recommended associations which could help the distressed, enumerating societies for mutual help, various benevolent foundations, as well as institutions for the welfare of the young and the aged. The papal encyclical referred to workingmen's unions, but thought in terms of guilds rather than modern industrial unions. Nonetheless, this pope recognized that workingmen's organizations should be established to better their conditions in body, soul and property.[40]

The response to the encyclical, translated into most of the world's languages, was initially mixed, with those on the left sceptical of its motivation

39 *Rerum Novarum*, 15 May 1891, in *The Great Encyclicals of Pope Leo XIII*, ed. John J. Wynne (New York, 1903), p. 209.
40 *Rerum Novarum*, 15 May 1891, in Carlen, *PE*, II, pp. 241–61.

while some capitalists resented its condemnation of entrepreneurial greed and call for regulations. Most, however, applauded its demand for justice for the oppressed worker, and its critique of lawless wealth which challenged Christian precepts. Few could argue with Leo's contention that the worker had a right to a living wage or discount the well-documented abuses of unrestrained *laissez-faire* liberalism. The discussion it provoked, followed by organized pilgrimages to Rome to thank the pope, earned Leo the title of the 'workingman's pope' and 'the enlightened pontiff', while his encyclical was dubbed the 'social Magna Carta of Catholicism'. It inspired Catholic social action in Europe and abroad, sparking the formation of Catholic associations or white syndicates to uplift the working class.

After the publication of *Rerum novarum*, the Sicilian priest Luigi Sturzo, whose priestly aspirations had earlier favoured the intellectual apostolate, developed a keen interest in the plight of the poor, especially those of southern Italy. As his social apostolate grew, Sturzo began organizing co-operative banks and parish councils for the improvement of the rural masses and became a prime mover in the organization of the Italian Popular Party, the precursor of the Christian Democratic Party of Italy. In an encyclical of 1895 on Catholicism in the United States, Leo reminded Americans that the working classes had the right to form unions for the promotion of their interests, but cautioned them to shun associations that Rome judged dangerous.[41]

During the last decade of his pontificate, from 1893 to 1903, Leo focused on the issue of peace within the various states as well as peace between nations, convinced that adherence to Catholic principles would promote both. He prompted his secretary of state, Rampolla, to write to the Seventh World Peace Conference meeting at Budapest in December, noting that the pope as head of the universal church had a special obligation to promote peace. Its president, on behalf of the congress, thanked the pope for his pacific efforts worldwide. Both the pope and Rampolla insisted that mediation and arbitration rather than force provided the best solution for international disputes. During the course of the First World War, Benedict XV would pursue this path and programme outlined by Leo.

Leo XIII and his secretary of state applauded the efforts of the International Peace Conference convoked at the Hague in May 1899, at the initiative of Tsar Nicholas of Russia. Having the limitation of armaments and the pacific settlement of international disputes on its agenda, Nicholas dispatched an invitation to Leo, and the Vatican received it favourably. The host, Queen Wilhelmina of Holland, also desired the co-operation of the pope, seeking his moral support. Leo responded positively, supportive of measures to counter the narrow, nationalist perspective, while assuring some order and security in the international community. Citing the influence of his predecessors to soften the inexorable laws of war and to vindicate the rights of the weak against the pretensions of the strong, the pope told the queen that the authority of the

41 *The Great Encyclical Letters of Pope Leo XIII*, p. 331.

supreme pontiff embraced 'all people to the end of federating them in the true peace of the Gospel'.[42] Unfortunately, the Dutch failed to consult the Italians, whose conflict with the papacy over the Roman Question remained an open wound, leading them to oppose papal participation. The Italians prevailed upon the Russians and Dutch to withdraw the invitation, to Leo's disappointment.

In his address to the college of cardinals in December 1899, the pope regretted the exclusion of the Holy See from the International Peace Conference at the Hague. Leo insisted that treaties and conferences had to be anchored in Christian principles, warning that without the acknowledgement of God's supremacy there could be security neither at home nor abroad. He predicted that as nations repudiated Christian principles, the prospect of war escalated. Prayer, he insisted, should not be discounted, as he called upon the faithful in March 1900 to invoke a speedy conclusion of the war in South Africa.[43] Leo, no less than Pius IX and Gregory XVI, rejected the secularism of the century and the attempts to marginalize the papacy. However, his defence of the Christian order proved more subtle and diplomatic than that of his two immediate predecessors.

In his encyclical on Christian democracy, *Graves de communi re* of 18 January 1901, Leo invoked co-operation rather than conflict between classes. Leo elaborated the differences between social democracy and Christian democracy, insisting they differed from each other as much as socialism from Christianity.[44] He claimed that social democracy sought to reduce all of humanity to the same level, striving for a community of goods, and abrogating the right of private property. In contrast, Christian democracy, flowing from the principles of the divine faith, also sought to provide better conditions for the masses, but with the primary aim of promoting the perfection of souls. Pope Leo viewed Christian democracy not as a political movement, but as beneficient Christian action on behalf of the masses, without favouring one type of government over another. While looking after the needs of the working classes, the movement embraced all groups, irrespective of rank or position, as members of the same family, redeemed by the same saviour. Leo elaborated these points to eliminate suspicion of Christian democracy so the movement might flourish, considering the elevation of the masses a mission of the church.[45]

Although in his nineties, the pontiff remained active on behalf of church and society, issuing nine of his sixty encyclical letters and epistles in 1902, more than in any previous year of his long reign. In 1903 Leo, who some feared would survive only a few weeks after his election, celebrated his silver anniversary, occupying the chair of Peter for twenty-five years. Angelo Roncalli, the future Pope John XXIII who was influenced by Leo, noted the twenty-fifth anniversary in his diary and prayed that God would preserve the pope,

42 Harry Koenig, 'The Popes and Peace in the Twentieth Century', in Waldemar Gurian and M.A. Fitzsimons, eds, *The Catholic Church in World Affairs* (Notre Dame, 1954), pp. 48–9.
43 Koenig, ed., *Principles for Peace*, pp. 91–100.
44 *Graves de Communi*, 18 January 1901, *The Great Encyclical Letters of Pope Leo XIII*, p. 482.
45 *Graves de Communi Re*, in Carlen, *PE*, II, pp. 479–86.

who had revealed clearer horizons of justice and evangelical charity.[46] Leo died on 20 July 1903, conferring with the curia until the end. His pontificate was momentous as he succeeded in ending the *Kulturkampf* in Germany by negotiating a compromise on the may laws against the Catholic church. His *ralliement* persuaded some French Catholics to rally to the republic and prevented the separation of church and state which ensued during the reign of his successor. Leo sought the friendship of England, made peace with Switzerland, and wrote to the emperor of China asking him to protect Catholic missionaries.[47]

The pope lent his moral and material support to the missions in Asia, Africa and Oceania and paid considerable attention to the church beyond Western Europe, using his influence with the rulers of Russia, China, Japan and Persia to secure religious freedom for Catholics. Diplomatic relations were restored with Orthodox Russia, and in 1894 Alexander Isvolsky was appointed minister plenipotentiary to the Vatican. The Catholic hierarchy expanded worldwide, while the organizational church was increased by some 300 dioceses and vicariates during his pontificate. Leo re-established the regular hierarchy in Scotland, in Bosnia-Herzegovina, in North Africa and Japan. In 1894 he supported an African pilgrimage to Rome. That same year, through the intermediary of Francesco Satolli, the apostolic delegate in the United States, Leo opened talks with the ministers of Nicaragua and Guatamala to regularize their positions with the papacy and to restore relations between the Holy See and Costa Rica.[48]

Unquestionably, Leo's diplomatic finesse worked to uplift the prestige of the papacy while improving the image of the Vatican. Mark Twain was so impressed with Pope Leo XIII's image, he decided in the late 1880s that his memoir would become a best-seller. He dispatched his nephew Charles L. Webster to the Vatican to convince the pope, who remained sceptical. 'I know you do great work in America; I know you have done a great thing, and noble work in regard to General Grant's book', Leo observed, adding, 'but that my life should have such a sale seems impossible.'[49] Although Leo had reservations, publication was agreed upon, but as the pope had predicted, *The Life of Pope Leo XIII* did not outsell the Koran and the Bible as Twain had boasted. The country's twenty million American Catholics failed to buy the book and the Protestant majority virtually boycotted it.

Despite the modest sales of the volume, Leo's popularity increased towards the close of his pontificate. In April 1903 Edward VII, the Protestant king of England and emperor of India, visited the Vatican and secured an audience with the pope. In May he was followed by William II, emperor of Germany, inspiring Roncalli to note in his diary that after centuries of hostility, a Protestant emperor ascended the stairs of the Vatican to pay homage to a pope.[50]

46 Pope John XXIII, *Journal of a Soul*, trans. Dorothy White (New York, 1965), p. 113.
47 Peter Hebblethwaite, *Pope John XXIII: Shepherd of the Modern World* (Garden City, NY, 1985), p. 41.
48 Satolli to Rampolla, 13 April 1894, ASV, Segreteria di Stato, 1897, *rubrica* 280, *fascicolo* 2.
49 *New York Times*, 4 November 1994.
50 John XXIII, *Journal of a Soul*, pp. 121–4.

Roncalli interpreted the visits as a double triumph for the papacy. For many, the crowning achievements of Leo's pontificate stemmed from his teaching on social, political and economic questions aimed at restoring the social order under the direction of the church. In *Rerum novarum*, he recognized the right of workers to form unions and laid down the broad principles underlying the rights and obligations of workers, employers and the state, placing the force of the 'revolution' at the service of the church. In *Graves de communi re*, he outlined the nature of Christian democracy, broadening the role of Catholicism in the social and political order. Under Leo's guidance, the Vatican made its first tentative efforts to bridge the gap between itself and the developments of the age, ending the alienation between church and society.

Following Leo's pontificate, the church and papacy could no longer be represented as reactionary enemies with no appreciation of modern society or role therein. Leo was acclaimed as the old man who rejuvenated the church, narrowing the gap between the faith and the contemporary world. This was his greatest legacy. To be sure problems remained: difficulties with France continued, the chasm between Italy and the Vatican was not bridged, and certain philosophical currents and practices threatened the faith. The 'pope of conciliation' addressed but did not resolve all of these 'problems', which were inherited by his less diplomatic successor, Pius X.

CHAPTER 9

The Vatican's condemnation of Americanism and modernism

Pope Leo XIII, who envisioned a Christian solution to the social question and sought reconciliation with the democracies, did not totally abandon the conservative and centralizing course of his predecessor, which was reinforced by his successor, Pius X.[1] A traditionalist in his religious convictions, Leo refused to jettison the Jesus of revelation and the Resurrection for the 'historical' Jesus sought by the revisionist historians, philosophers and theologians. Furthermore, Leo proved no more willing than Pius IX to renounce the temporal power or recognize the Italian state. Leo categorically rejected the law of guarantees (1871) converting the *non-expedit*, which deemed Catholic participation in national political life in Italy inexpedient, to the *non-licet* of 1886, which explicitly prohibited it. Scandalized by the repression initiated by the Marquis Antonio di Rudinì against the church in 1898, Leo protested against the actions of the Italian government.[2]

During these years Leo continued to denounce the contemporary evils of the age, tracing many of these evils to the rejection of church authority.[3] In 1896 Leo affirmed as the first and necessary condition for Catholic unity the acceptance of the divinely instituted jurisdiction of the pope over the entire church. His position on papal power paralleled that of Pius IX. In 1897 Leo amended, but preserved, the Index of forbidden books.[4]

Leo's condemnations were repeated in his Easter message of 1902, which represented a review of the twenty-five years of his pontificate, providing a virtual last testament. Scandalized by the 'conspiracy of hostile forces', he described the disorders in social relations and family life, the prevalence of socialism and anarchism, while citing the dangers posed by freemasonry and the snares set for the souls of believers. Distressed by the unjust warring of strong nations against the weak, he warned the faithful that liberty and peace

1 Leo's Allocution of 28 March 1878, *ASS*, X, pp. 577–9.
2 *Spesse Volte*, 5 August 1898, in Carlen, *PE*, II, pp. 439–43.
3 *Inscrutabili dei consilio*, in ibid., II, pp. 5–10.
4 Carlen, *PP*, I, pp. 43–4, 51–3, 57–8; *The Great Encyclical Letters of Pope Leo XIII*, ed. John J. Wynne (New York, 1903), pp. 407–20.

were illusory apart from religion. By refusing to acknowledge the supremacy of the Holy See, the divine structure of faith had been shaken to its foundation.[5]

Some feared the pope's conservative agenda would cross the Atlantic to the United States, antagonizing Americans and endangering the progress of an expanding church. Although liberal Catholics discouraged the pope from condemning the secret societies found in the new world, the Holy Office in August 1894 denounced the Odd Fellows, the Knights of Pythias, and the Sons of Temperance. When the American bishops, assembled in their annual meeting, voted not to publish the condemnation, they were told that Leo wanted the decree promulgated. In his letter to the archbishops and bishops of the United States in 1895, he stipulated it would be wrong to conclude their separation of church and state was either universally desirable or lawful, suggesting the church might have borne more abundant fruit in America if liberty had been bolstered by the patronage of public authority.[6] That same year he cautioned his apostolic delegate Archbishop Francesco Satolli against American Catholic participation in interfaith congresses such as had occured in Chicago in 1893.[7]

Pope Leo was concerned by news from across the Atlantic during the last decade of the nineteenth century, which indicated that the American hierarchy was divided into two opposing camps. The liberals were led by John Ireland, archbishop of St Paul, and Cardinal John Gibbons, archbishop of Baltimore, aided by Denis John O'Connell, rector of the American College in Rome and agent for the liberals in the Eternal City. The conservative cause was championed by Michael Corrigan, archbishop of New York, who warned Rome that 'a party of advanced views' sought dominion over the American church. Corrigan and the German-speaking bishops of the United States denounced the liberal party, pointing to O'Connell as their 'acknowledged agent and representative' in the Eternal City. His identification with this liberal current, subsequently known as Americanism, led many conservatives to refuse to send their students to the American College. O'Connell's partisan liberal position and his tireless efforts on behalf of progressive causes contributed to his removal from the rectorship of the North American College.[8]

Some suggested that eventually the scientific pragmatism of Roger Bacon would replace the superseded scholasticism of St Thomas, as they propagated Americanist sentiments in France.[9] The broad acceptance of new scientific discoveries in the United States during the middle decades of the nineteenth

5 *The Great Encyclicals of Pope Leo XIII*, p. 559; *Annum ingressi*, 19 March 1902, in Carlen, *PE*, II, pp. 554–80.

6 Gerald P. Fogarty, *The Vatican and the Americanist Crisis: Denis J. O'Connell, American Agent in Rome, 1885–1903* (Rome, 1974), p. 165; *Longinqua*, 6 January 1895, in *The Papal Encyclicals*, Carlen, *PE*, II, pp. 363–70; 'The Pope's American Encyclical', *Independent*, XLVII (7 February 1895), p. 10.

7 'Pope Leo XIII on Religious Congresses', *Literary Digest*, XII (9 November 1895), p. 50; 'Archbishop Keane for New Orleans', *Independent*, XLIX (20 August 1897), p. 13; 'The Conflict in the Catholic University', ibid., XLIX (28 October 1896), pp. 10–11.

8 Fogarty, *The Vatican and the Americanist Crises*, pp. 89–91, 120, 134, 254.

9 Cardinal Gasquet, *A Memoir*, ed. Shane Leslie (New York, 1953), p. 197.

century presented a challenge to its Catholics. The Paulists or the Missionary Society of St Paul the Apostle, founded in New York by Father Isaac Thomas Hecker in 1858, sought to persuade Americans that the church was open-minded about science in order to gain adherents and affect the conversion of the United States. Their programme was partly undermined by Pius IX's encyclical *Quanta cura* and the attached Syllabus of Errors in 1864. Nonetheless, the Paulist periodical, the *Catholic World*, which began publication after 1865, still sought an accommodation between science and the faith.[10]

While Pope Leo appreciated many of the ideas and values of the Americans, prizing their energy, pragmatism, resourcefulness and enthusiasm, he feared that in the new world the modern shibboleths of progress and science were widely accepted. Subsequently, the Roman pontiff was alarmed by reports of anti-European and anti-Roman sentiments prevalent in certain American theological circles. Reluctant to proceed against Catholic scholars by hurling condemnations, Pope Leo chose more courteous methods and diplomatic means than Pius IX who proceeded him, or Pius X who followed. Despite Leo's attempts at accommodation with the modern world, Rome remained wary of a theological system which preferred the 'active' over the 'passive' virtues. Pope Leo rejected the approach which focused on the natural as opposed to the supernatural, and sought to accommodate Catholic truth to the new world mentality and American ambience to facilitate conversions.

The theoretical foundations of these views were influenced by the work and thought of Isaac Thomas Hecker. Born in New York in 1819, this son of German immigrants converted to Catholicism in 1845, taking vows as a Redemptorist in 1846. Inspired by his conversion, Hecker sought to convert his fellow countrymen, with some charging that in his zeal for mass conversion he downplayed the differences between Catholicism and Protestantism. In 1854 he wrote *Questions of the Soul*, his first major work, followed in 1857 by his *Aspirations of Nature*.[11] Believing Catholicism compatible with American institutions, and best suited for the country, he founded the Paulists in 1858 to spearhead his missionary goals.

Convinced that the Holy Spirit infused him to guide the church and assure its reconciliation with the modern world, Hecker looked to the Paulists to mediate between Catholicism and Protestantism. Under the patronage of Archbishop John Hughes, his order was provided with a parish in New York City on 59th Street and 9th Avenue, where Hecker preached. Soon thereafter, Hecker called for a national conference attended by lay and clerical delegates to discuss the religious situation in the United States. In 1863 he attended the congress of Malines, and in 1869 travelled to Rome for the Vatican council, associating with those who considered a proclamation of infallibility inopportune. During

10 William J. Astore, 'Gentle Skeptics? American Catholic Encounters with Polygenism, Geology, and Evolutionary Theories from 1845 to 1875', *Catholic Historical Review*, LXXXII, 1 (January 1996), pp. 40–76.
11 Isaac T. Hecker, *The Questions of the Soul* (New York, 1855); idem., *The Aspirations of Nature* (New York, 1857).

his travels in Europe, Hecker concluded that just as the old continent was being influenced by American democracy, it might be spiritually renewed through the impact of the new world.[12]

By the mid-1870s, when he wrote his work on the church in the present age, Hecker believed the well-being of society depended on the renewal of religion, which in turn depended on the Holy Spirit, convinced that American Catholicism could serve as a model for the universal church. Influenced by a theology of history dominated by two convictions – the conversion of America to Catholicism and the subsequent triumph of the church – Hecker ascribed a providential role to the United States for the fulfilment of history's goals.[13] Hecker's death at the end of 1888 found a group of disciples on both sides of the Atlantic, nurtured by a French translation of Father Walter Elliott's *Life of Father Hecker* (1891). Translated by the Countess de Ravilliax, and abridged by the Abbé Felix Klein, who produced its preface, it presented Hecker not simply as an American priest attempting to mediate Catholicism and Protestantism, but as the ideal new priest, seeking to harmonize the church with modern scientific developments, assuring its future would be based on freedom rather than bureaucracy. Hecker's spirituality was seen to flow from the Holy Spirit rather than the external authority of the institutional church. As early as January 1870 Hecker wrote in his notebook, 'Europe may find not only her political regeneration in the civilization on the other side of the Atlantic, but also the renewal of Catholicity'. This inspired a group of liberal American Catholics soon labelled Americanists.

During the international Catholic scientific congress held at Fribourg, Switzerland, Father Denis O'Connell on 20 August 1897 delivered an address entitled 'A new idea in the life of Father Hecker', describing both political and ecclesiastical Americanism. O'Connell, who had long hosted a liberal coterie of clergymen in his apartment in Rome, dubbed 'Liberty Hall', reckoned that the people were the immediate source of power as interpreters of the natural law of God. He also believed that the separation of church and state which existed in America proved more beneficial to the church than the integralism or unity championed by traditionalists. Indeed, his Americanism concluded that the church should be reorganized along democratic lines. O'Connell and the members of his 'club', which included Cardinals Serafino and Vincenzo Vannutelli, the Abbé Louis Duchesne, rector of the École Française in Rome, and the Baron Friedrich von Hugel, among others, all favoured change within the organization of the church. O'Connell considered Americanism the will of God and humanity, confident that the victory of American over Spanish arms in the recent war (1898) had broken the monopoly of European control, exposing the inability to govern the universal church by Spanish and Italian methods.[14]

12 John Farina, *An American Experience of God: The Spirituality of Isaac Hecker* (New York, 1981), pp. 118–40.
13 William L. Portier, 'Isaac Hecker and the First Vatican Council', *Catholic Historical Review*, LXXI, 2 (April 1985), p. 219.
14 Fogarty, *The Vatican and the Americanist Crisis*, pp. 257–62, 279–81.

While Americanists applauded the victory in the Spanish-American War, this posed problems for the Holy See, which found it necessary to adjust church interests with the establishment of a 'Protestant power' in Catholic Cuba, Puerto Rico and the Philippines.[15]

O'Connell's policies and other Americanist views were deemed dangerous by traditionalists and during the summer and autumn of 1898 the Vatican investigated Americanism. Critics charged that O'Connell's convictions were strikingly similar to those of Lamennais condemned by Gregory XVI and Pius IX. In France, Father Charles Maignen of the Society of the Brothers of St Vincent de Paul commenced a critique of Hecker's doctrines. In his view, the central doctrines of Americanism had been condemned by the seventy-seventh, seventy-eighth, and seventy-ninth propositions of Pio Nono's Syllabus of Errors. Seeking to gather his articles in book form, when Maignen failed to receive the approval of cardinal François-Marie Richard to do so, he obtained the necessary imprimatur from Father Albert Lepidi, Master of the Sacred Palace, to publish them under the title *Le Pere Hecker: Est-il un Saint*? Fearing that the negative picture which emerged reflected the opinion of the curia, O'Connell decried its alleged duplicity. Charging that the curia had been in constant conflict with the church, he wrote to Ireland on 3 June 1898, 'If we are not Catholics, let them frankly say so'.[16] Although Leo did not have the Hecker biography placed on the Index, he appointed a committee to examine the issue of Americanism.

As the controversy over Americanism continued, the sides were drawn with the Dominicans allegedly joining the Jesuits in opposing it. Americanism reached Germany as well.[17] Leo determined to end the bickering by his letter of 22 January 1899 to Cardinal Gibbons, *Testem benevolentiae* or proof of affection, condemning the attempt to reconcile the church with the age or advance the Americanization of the church in the United States. Without criticizing the American system of government, the separation of church and state which prevailed in the United States, or American customs and laws, the pope pointed to the difference between the church which is of divine right, and other associations, which subsist by the free will of man. Leo announced that the pope could not sanction the existence of a church in America different from that which prevailed in the rest of the world. He likewise rejected the suggestion that there could be an elimination of external spiritual direction with total reliance on the Holy Ghost, and that liberty should be guaranteed to Catholics, without concern for the teaching of the infallible pontiff. The pope also resented the contention that religious vows cramped individual freedom, contesting the 'Americanist' vision of liberty.[18]

15 On this issue see Luigi Bruti Liberati, *La Santa Sede e le origini dell'impero americano. La guerra del 1896* (Milan, 1984).

16 Fogarty, *The Vatican and the Americanist Crisis*, p. 283.

17 Benedetto Lorenzelli to Secretary of State Cardinal Mariano del Tindaro, 21 January 1899, ASV, Segreteria di Stato, *rubrica* 255, *fascicolo* 41.

18 *Testem benevolentiae nostrae*, 22 January 1899, in *The Great Encyclical Letters of Pope Leo XIII*, p. 445.

Although American Catholics, clergy and laity promptly submitted to the pope's position, liberals did not deny that they sought to reconcile the church with democracy and science while calling for a greater de-Romanization of the American church. However they argued their programme neither jeopardized nor undermined their Catholic faith.[19] Meanwhile, conservatives such as Corrigan of New York applauded Leo for having saved the American church from heresy. Protestant periodicals criticized Rome's attempt to end the attempt of an enlightened few within the church to bring it into harmony with the age and American democracy. Liberal Catholics hoped for the election of the conciliatory Cardinal Serafino Vannutelli to succeed Leo, but doubted he would prevail. The prediction proved accurate.

In the conclave of sixty-two cardinals which opened the evening of 31 July 1903 (the first to include an American), Cardinal Rampolla, Leo's secretary of state, emerged as the leading figure. His candidacy was torpedoed when the cardinal of Krakow, Jan Puzyna, reportedly invoked the veto of the Austrian emperor, who considered him too Francophile. It proved an important factor in the search for an alternative, a less political and more pastoral candidate, leading to the election of the patriarch of Venice, Cardinal Giuseppe Melchiore Sarto, on 4 August 1903. Sarto chose the name Pius Decimus in memory of Pius IX. He asked the young and aristocratic Cardinal Rafaelle Merry del Val, of Spanish-Irish descent, and educated in England, to serve as his secretary of state, the first non-Italian to hold the post. On Sunday 9 August 1903 Pius X, who bore a striking physical similarity to Pius IX, was crowned with the triple tiara decorated with 32 rubies, 19 emeralds, 11 sapphires, 252 pearls, and 529 diamonds.[20] A simple, sincere, and holy man of prayer, Pius displayed an aversion for diplomacy and statecraft in sharp contrast to his predecessor.

Sarto was born 2 June 1835 in the north-eastern Italian hamlet of Riese, within the province of Treviso in the Veneto, then under Austrian rule. One of eight surviving children of a family of modest means, his father supplemented his farming income by serving as caretaker for the town hall, while his mother took in sewing. In 1850 Giuseppe entered the seminary at Padua, and in September 1858 was ordained a priest. In November he was appointed an assistant to the parish of Tombolo, a nearby farming village, and in 1866 was appointed parish priest of Salzano, a community of some 2,000 inhabitants. Sarto spent the first seventeen years of his life in pastoral work in these two small communities of the Veneto, a stronghold of Catholic orthodoxy. In 1875 the bishop of Treviso named him spiritual director of the major seminary, and in 1884 he was named bishop of Mantua. In 1893 he was transferred

19 Samuel J. Thomas, 'The American Periodical Press and the Apostolic Letter Testem Benevolentiae', *Catholic Historical Review*, LXIII, 3 (1976), pp. 408–9, 412.

20 Hartwell de La Garde Grissell, *Sede Vacante, Being a Diary Written During the Conclave of 1903* (London, 1903), p. 48; Amleto Giovanni Cicognani, *A Symposium on the Life and Work of Pope Pius X* (Washington, DC, 1946), pp. 13–14; Cardinal Merry del Val, *Memories of Pope Pius X* (Westminster, MD, 1951), pp. 1–8.

to Venice and made both a patriarch and cardinal. He remained there until his election as pope.

Pius X was one of the few popes not drawn from the aristocracy. Born of peasant stock, he shared with many of his people a suspicion of change and fear of the excesses that flowed from democracy and social innovation, convinced that often philosophy and science, literature and art produced corrosive consequences for church and society. He did not believe that Catholic beliefs and convictions should be reconciled with 'contemporary scholarship'. Deeply engrossed in pastoral work, Sarto, known as the 'peasant pope', found few distractions and little time for literary and artistic pursuits that might have tempered his preoccupations. He spurned art for administration, philosophy for theology, preserving an interest in seminary reform, church law and sacred music. Not surprisingly, he had long shown himself staunchly opposed to secular liberalism, and to the notion that there could be a compromise between rationalism and religion, defining himself as 'intransigent to the core'. A few days after his election, he dispatched a letter to the bishop of Orvieto deploring the publication of a weekly review which called for the foundation of a Christian democratic party independent of the Opera dei Congressi.[21]

Lamenting the widespread 'apostasy from God', Sarto expressed his ideas in his first encyclical of 4 October 1903. He concluded therein that society was suffering from a deep-rooted malady which was dragging it to destruction, hence his programme 'to restore all things in Christ'. Pius preached that the way to reach Christ was through his church. 'This is what We, in submitting Ourselves to the manifestations of the Divine will, purpose to aim at during Our Pontificate, and We will use all industry to attain it.'[22] Pius proved true to his promise.

This pope was more distressed than his predecessor by the thought and action of those who desired to modernize the church by adopting Catholicism to the climate of the time, seeking to emancipate the faithful from ecclesiastical authority, science from dogma, and the state from the church. He rejected the attempt to achieve a rationalization of Christianity and radical transformation of thought in regard to God, man, the world, and the afterlife. In the pope's mind, such modernization represented a rejection of, and revolution against, the true faith. Pius X was determined to preserve a society based on religion against the pretensions of a secular society, seeking to preserve a Christian heritage in a culture increasingly motivated by non-religious values. The 'modernist' attempt to integrate Catholicism into the modern, secular world was perceived as treason by the pope.

As early as his pastoral letter of 1887, Sarto criticized those who preached the church had to adapt to the age, rejecting the new philosophy while deriding its liberty as licence. Included in the group which aroused Pius X's concern was the historian of early Christianity, Louis Marie Duchesne. Ordained in 1871,

21 Merry del Val, *Memories of Pope Pius X*, pp. 35, 58; Ernesto Vercesi, *Il movimento cattolico in Italia (1870–1922)* (Florence, 1923), p. 99.
22 *E Supremi*, 4 October 1903, in Carlen, *PE*, III, p. 8.

Duchesne was drawn into the study of critical history, focusing his doctoral thesis on the eighth-century *Liber Pontificalis*. After teaching at the École Française de Rome, in 1877 he joined the faculty of the Institut Catholique de Paris where he founded the *Bulletin critique*, which published his critical studies as well as those of his students such as Alfred Loisy and Pierre Batiffol. In the mid-1890s he returned to Rome as director of the École Française. In 1912 his three-volume *History of the Early Church* was placed on the Index for ignoring the supernatural dimension of history. Duchesne immediately submitted to the pope who had earlier praised the first volume of his work. Duchesne's students and associates were also suspect, including Loisy whose doctoral dissertation had proved so liberal that in 1893 he had been removed from the Institut Catholique in Paris. At least five of his books were placed on the Index.

Baron Freidrich von Hugel, influenced by Alfred Loisy and the Irish-born Jesuit George Tyrrell, was at the centre of the modernist controversy, becoming in France and to a certain extent in Europe the standard-bearer of modernism. After the condemnation of the movement and his publication of additional books of higher criticism on scripture, he was excommunicated in 1908.[23] Tyrell also rejected scholastic philosophy, subjecting dogma to modern historical criticism and interpretation. In 1903 he published *The Church and the Future* under a pseudonym. For these reformist and evolutionary views, Tyrrel was suspended from his order in 1906, and from the exercise of his priesthood.[24]

In Italy, the thought of Alfred Loisy was influential in the north, especially Turin, Bergamo, Milan and Novara. The works and action of the priest, Romolo Murri, and later Salvatore Minocchi and Ernesto Buonaiutti, sought to modernize practice as much as thought. Thus, during the last decade of Leo's pontificate Romolo Murri conceived a programme and a party to achieve Christian democratic ends, hoping to use the church to convert the state. Pius opposed the plan. Criticizing the National Democratic League formed by Murri and his followers at Bologna, when Murri decided to call a convention to form this political organization, Pius forbade the faithful, both clergy and laity, from taking part. The pope condemned the League and the attempt to create a separate and non-denominational political party, accusing Murri of confusing Catholic action and the action of Catholics, the religious undertaking of believer and the social vocation of the militant, the sphere of the church and the sphere of the state. He was likewise critical of Murri's review, the *Rivista di Cultura*.[25] Eventually, Murri left the priesthood, married, and entered parliament as a radical deputy.

In a decree of December 1903, Pius restated the principles of Catholic action in Italy, providing nineteen norms for the fundamentals of such activity. They

23 Decree of 7 March 1908, *ASS*, XLI, p. 141.

24 Lawrence Barmann, 'Freidrich von Hugel as Modernist and More than Modernist', *Catholic Historical Review*, LXXV, 2 (April 1989), pp. 211–32; Igino Giordani, *Pius X: A Country Priest*, trans. Thomas J. Tobin (Milwaukee, 1954), p. 148.

25 Giovanni Spadolini, *Il Mondo di Giolitti* (Florence, 1969), p. 162; Giordani, *Pius X*, pp. 143–4; Vercesi, *Il movimento cattolico*, p. 104; Cicognani, *A Symposium*, pp. 21–2; Carlen, *PP*, I, p. 69.

included: (1) the inequality in human society created by God; (2) the equality of members of society considered in their redemption by the church; (3) the need for societal divisions such as rulers and subjects, employers and wage earners, rich and poor, aristocrats and commoners, all united by mutual service; (4) man's right to the use and ownership of the world's goods; (5) private property as an inviolable natural right; (6) that vindication was necessary in class conflict only when justice had been violated; (7–11) ennumerated the rights and duties of employers and wage earners; (12) democratic Christian action should aim for the elevation of the wage-earning class; (13) Christian democracy in Italy must never become embroiled in politics; (14–15) Christian democracy must rely on ecclesiastical authority; (16–19) Catholic writers, whether Christian democrats or not, must submit their writings of a religious or moral nature to ecclesiastical authorities, refraining from public arguments of a political or social nature. More or less, the same message was transmitted by his secretary of state.[26] Pius approved of the three Catholic organizations which replaced the suspect Opera dei Congressi. However, the pope insisted that the Unione Popolare, Unione Elettorale and the Unione Economico-Sociale which replaced the dissolved organization, all be supervised by the Italian bishops and exclude those who sought to introduce partisan ends.[27]

Pius, perceiving himself as 'shepherd of souls', returned to many of these themes and the troubled currents of Christian democracy in his encyclical of March 1904. He also catalogued the causes of the rift between the world and the faith, citing heresies, schisms, denial of the supernatural, the abandonment of true philosophy and the development of a false historical criticism. Those who made concessions to 'modern' or 'false' science under the illusion that they could thus win over those in error, did more harm than good. This pope considered the denial of the supernatural the chief error of the present age, from which many others sprang. Pius also showed himself suspicious of Christian democrats. Striving to promote the material well-being of the masses, these Christian democrats supposedly ignored their spiritual welfare. Acknowledging that the times had changed, Pius claimed that nothing had changed in the life of the church. In his view, the church 'inherited the virtue of being able to supply at all times, all that is required not only for the spiritual welfare of souls, which is the direct object of her mission, but also everything that aids progress in true civilisation'.[28]

Throughout 1906 Pius continued his crusade against the prevailing cultural currents at the turn of the century, charging that modernism in thought and practice was corrupted by 'audacious sacrilege'. He was appalled by those who preached the evolution of dogma, the call to examine the gospels stripped of theological explanations, and the need to adapt to the times. Not surprisingly, the pope proved supportive of the bishops of Turin, Vercelli, Catania,

26 Carlen, *PP*, I, p. 66; Giordani, *Pius X*, pp. 133–4; Joseph B. Collins, ed., *Chatechetical Documents of Pope Pius X* (New York, 1946), p. 140.
27 Letter of Merry del Val, 24 March 1906, *ASS*, XXXIX, p. 152.
28 Carlen, *PE*, III, p. 27.

Verona and Acerenza who decried the alleged modernist attempt to substitute knowledge for faith. At the same time, the pope criticized the spirit of independence displayed by part of the clergy, especially its younger members. He called upon the bishops to demand obedience, to exercise greater care before admitting candidates to sacred orders, urged their dismissal of candidates corrupted by the modernist programme, and demanded the careful supervision of seminaries as well as a vigilant observation of priests engaged in social work, writing or publishing. Seminarians, as well as priests, were to be discouraged from attending public universities and sheltered from the perilous snares of modernist thought and practice. Finally, the bishops were warned to censor in Catholic publications references to 'new orientations for Christian life', 'new direction for the church', 'new aspirations for modern souls', 'new Christian civilization', and the like.[29] In April 1906 Antonio Fogazzaro's novel, *Il Santo*, which called on the church to restrict legalism and authoritarianism within its ranks, was placed on the Index.[30] That same year, the pope denounced the publication in Cremona of *La Chiesa e i tempi nuovi*, which he insisted expressed a modern liberalism unacceptable to the church.[31]

In April 1907 Pius X denounced those who preached 'monstrous errors' on the evolution of dogma, on the return to the pure gospels or who advocated an emancipation of the church.[32] In the decree *Lamentabili sane exitu* of 3 July 1907, a virtual syllabus of modernist errors, the Holy Office catalogued a list of erroneous propositions being paraded as science and progress. Divided into two groups, the first dealt with the interpretation of scripture while the second category concerned the mysteries of faith. Together they contained sixty-five propositions condemned by the congregation of the Holy Office along the lines of Pio Nono's Syllabus of Errors. In *Lamentabili*, errors one to thirty-eight focused on errors of the interpretation of scripture, while the remaining thirty-seven catalogued errors in the interpretation of dogma.[33] The final error refuted was the notion that modern Catholicism could be reconciled with science only if it were transformed into a non-despotic faith, a sort of broad and liberal protestantism. In August 1907 the congregation of the Index issued instructions to lycées, seminaries and universities to shun these modernist errors.[34] In turn, the papal secretary of state, Merry del Val, cautioned the French hierarchy to discourage their clerics from attending public universities and to be especially wary of having them enrol in 'dangerous' courses such as history and philosophy in secular schools.

The encyclical *Pascendi dominici gregis* on the doctrine of the modernists (8 September 1907) listed the collection of heresies collected under the term modernism. Pius X defined this as a 'synthesis of all heresies', and a distillation

29 Encyclical letter of 28 July 1906, *ASS*, XXXIX, pp. 321–30.
30 Congregation of Index, 5 April 1906, ibid., XXXIX, p. 96.
31 Pius X to Cardinal Ferrari, Archbishop of Milan, 27 February 1906, ibid., XXXIX, pp. 26–7.
32 Ibid., XL, pp. 266–9.
33 *Lamentabili*, 3 July 1907, ibid., XL, pp. 470–8.
34 Ibid., XL, pp. 727–8, XLI, pp. 41–2.

of most of the mental and moral poison of the past century.[35] Citing his responsibility to guard the deposit of faith and reject novelties and false knowledge, he warned that the partisans of error were found not only among the church's enemies, but within her clergy. In the encyclical, Pius explored the modernist philosopher, believer, theologian, historian, critic, apologist and reformer, noting the errors of each and how they undermined the faith.

Pius reserved his greatest criticism for the modernist theologian who allegedly applied immanentism and symbolism to the dogmas of the church, presenting them as the products of the evolution of the human spirit, subordinating them to subjective criticism. Likewise, he proved critical of the historical-critical modernist who applied to persons and events a criticism that was agnostic and evolutionist. Nor could he concur with the modernist reformer who demanded a rationalistic theology, a democratization of the government of the church, and a decentralization of its administration. The pope traced the roots of modernism to idle curiosity and satanic pride, which combined to elevate human reason and devalue the supernatural. Some even charged that Cardinal Newman was the grandfather of the movement, charging he disdained scholasticism, and branding his 'development of doctrine' a variant of modernism's 'evolution of doctrine'. Cardinal Gasquet denied that *Pascendi* had denounced Cardinal Newman's theme of development, while striving to convince the pope that England was not burdened by modernism.[36]

The conservative pontiff disagreed with the modernist conclusion that faith and science were strangers to one another by reason of the diversity of their objects, or that church and state differed because of the divergence of their ends, the one being spiritual and the other temporal. He feared that just as modernists held that faith was subordinate to science, they would eventually assert that the church should be subject to the state. Rejecting such contentions, Pius proposed remedies against this 'host of grave errors' including the study of scholastic philosophy, which he ordained as the basis of the sacred sciences. Second, he prescribed that directors and professors of seminaries and Catholic universities imbued with modernism should be excluded. Third, he enunciated the duty of bishops to prevent writings infected with modernism from being read. Fourth, the bishops were encouraged to exercise censorship, using 'the utmost severity in granting permission to publish'. Citing the use made by modernists of congresses and public gatherings to propagate their opinions, Pius warned the bishops to prohibit such gatherings of priests except for rare occasions. Finally, he called for the establishment of diocesan watch committees 'to extirpate the errors already propagated and to prevent their further diffusion'.[37]

Pascendi represented a rejection of the attempt to conciliate Catholic civilization with the 'insanities' of the modern world. Those who rejected its warnings

35 *Pascendi dominici gregis*, 8 September 1907, ibid., XL, pp. 593–650.
36 Gasquet, *A Memoir*, p. 188.
37 *Pascendi dominici gregis*, 8 September 1907, in Carlen, *PE*, III, pp. 71–98; Giordani, *Pius X*, pp. 154–6.

were threatened with excommunication. A decree of the congregation of the Index in January 1908 found the Roman journal *Nova et Vetera* infected with modernist heresies. In February the French dailies *La Justice Sociale* and *La Vie Catholique* were added to the increasing list of suspect publications. The secretary of the congregation of the Index protested against the publication of the Milanese review *Il Rinnovamento*, denounced as an Italian version of the *Demain*, charging that within its columns writers such as Fogazzaro, Tyrell, von Hugel, Murri and others sought to preach to the pope. Reformist groups such as that organized by Tommaso Gallerati Scotti were dissolved. Meanwhile, a wide range of pamphlets and books was added to the list of works condemned by the Index.[38] Even priests who rode bicycles were judged suspect by some.

To ensure compliance with the strictures of *Pascendi*, 'councils of vigilance' were formed in the dioceses of Italy which were fed information by a network of informants and 'apostolic visitations', dubbed 'apostolic vexations' by Cardinal Ferrari of Milan. Pius remained preoccupied with the dangers of modernism and a decree of November 1907 condemned those who disagreed with the decisions of the Pontifical Biblical Commission or the decrees of the Roman congregations approved by the pontiffs. Reaffirming the decree *Lamentabili* and the encyclical *Pascendi*, Pius prescribed excommunication for those who contradicted them.[39]

Convinced that modernism persisted, Pius returned to it in his encyclical commemorating the eighth centenary of St Anselm. Pius condemned both the persecution of the church from without and the domestic war waged from within, carried out by 'unnatural sons' whom he claimed were hidden in her bosom. Similar condemnations were launched in his encyclical letter on St Charles Borromeo, where he railed against the 'wicked men' who uprooted everything in the name of a 'deceitful liberty'.[40] A decree of the congregation of the Index of 17 March 1908 condemned a new set of books infected by modernist sentiments including *Il programma dei modernisti. Risposta all' enciclica di Pio X, Pascendi*.[41] In 1909 Pius excommunicated the priest Murri, who had founded the Lega Democratica Nazionale, and rejected the plan of the directors of the Unione Populare in Italy to downplay its Catholic nature to increase its appeal. The pope preferred that the association be reduced in size but retain its Catholic nature. Shortly thereafter, he condemned Marc Sangnier's *Sillon* in France, citing its erroneous social theory in conflict with Catholic doctrine, and viewing it as part of the greater apostasy of the age.

A decree of September 1910 established laws for combatting modernism, reiterating the strictures of *Pascendi*. Among other things, it urged the promotion of theology and scholastic philosophy as ordained by Leo XIII. It also provided rules for Italian clerics, demanded close adherence to Leo's *Officiorum*

38 *ASS*, XL, pp. 26–7, 272; XLI, pp. 128, 141.
39 *Motu proprio* of 18 November 1907, ibid., XL, pp. 723–6.
40 *Communium rerum*, 21 April 1909; *Editae saepe*, 26 May 1910, in Carlen, *PE*, III, pp. 99–113, 115–26.
41 *ASS*, XLI, p. 211.

with reference to reading and publications, restricted congresses of priests, while entrusting to vigilance councils the supervision of social institutions. Finally, it decreed triennal reports by the bishops on these prescriptions and on the thought and action current among their clergy, and the imposition of an anti-modernist oath on both clerics, of every rank and order, and seminarians.[42] The anti-modernist oath emphasized the fixity of doctrine, demanded that all clerics and office-holders adhere to the proscriptions of *Pascendi* and *Lamentabili*, while excluding anyone tainted with modernist thought, sympathies or action. Roncalli, the future John XXIII, who appreciated the desire of some to adapt the ancient truths of Christianity to modern needs on the one hand, saw on the other many good men fall into error, perhaps unconsciously.[43]

In his obsession to eradicate the evil of modernism, Pius seconded the clandestine efforts of Monsignor Umberto Benigni. This Italian priest, ecclesiastical historian, journalist and integralist founded the *Corrispondenza di Roma*, which changed its name to *Correspondance de Rome* in 1908. Under both titles, it served as an international agency denouncing modernism and tracing its sources. Benigni emerged as the leading opponent of all things liberal and unorthodox, orchestrating the campaign of ecclesiastical espionage and denunciation of those within the church who sought accommodation with the modern, secular world. Cardinal Pietro Maffi, archbishop of Pisa, complained of secret informants intimidating even those who had given incontrovertible proof of their faith to the Holy See, installing a virtual inquisition. Cardinal Ferrari of Milan concurred and in a pastoral letter of 1908 denounced the anti-modernist witchhunt which found the heresy everywhere and permitted Vatican inquisitors to hound those who sought to reconcile faith and science.

Benigni was considered the chief inquisitor of modernism. While an undersecretary in the secretariat of state, guided by Cardinal Merry del Val, whose conservative sentiments he shared, in 1909 Benigni founded the Sodality of St Pius V, also known as the Sodalitium pianum, or the Sapiniere, to implement the condemnations of Pius X against modernism. Serving as its president, Benigni kept files on various clergymen and laymen whom he suspected of the heresy. He transmitted writings, sermons, speeches and even conversations of figures he deemed suspect to the Holy See. The espionage network with its arbitrary methods operated in secrecy, casting doubt on the orthodoxy of several reputable Catholic scriptural scholars and theologians. While Pius X endorsed its general aims, he never issued his formal approval. Nonetheless, there were those in the curia who believed, and Cardinal Gasparri concurred with their assessment, that Pius X used it as a means of indirectly warning ecclesiastics he suspected of harbouring the heresy. Following Benigni's departure from his post in the secretariat of state in 1911, and the suppression of his *Correspondance de Rome* in 1913, the influence of the Sodalitium pianum

42 *Nôtre charge apostolique*, 25 August 1910, and *Sacrorum antistitum*, 1 September 1910, in Carlen, *PP*, I, pp. 74–5.
43 Pope John XXIII, *Journal of a Soul*, trans. Dorothy White (New York, 1965), p. 176.

steadily waned. Gasparri deplored its existence and played a part in its suppression in November 1921.[44]

The pope's war against modernism served to aggravate the tensions between the Vatican and France. There were other problems, including the anticlerical legislation of the third republic and Paris's disappointment that Cardinal Rampolla, who had worked closely with Leo XIII, had been vetoed by the Austrians during the conclave of 1903 as too Francophile. For his part, Pius frequently criticized the laws of the republic, and above all the law of associations of 1901 which struck at the religious orders. In a discourse of March 1904 to the cardinals, Pius protested that the suppression of the religious orders in France undermined the foundation of civil society. The following month, when the president of the Republic, Loubet, visited Victor Emmanuel III in Rome, the semi-official Vatican newspaper the *Osservatore Romano* criticized the insult made to the pope by the head of a Catholic nation. In response, the French government recalled its ambassador from the Vatican. On 30 July 1904 the French terminated diplomatic relations with the Vatican.

In November 1904 Pius catalogued the republic's violations of the concordat, including the curbing of religious liberty, forbidding bishops from visiting the sovereign pontiff or to correspond with him, eliminating religious orders, and demanding consecration for all its candidates, even those who were morally unworthy. In response, the French chamber drafted legislation for a complete separation of church and state in France, which secured the approval of the chamber in July 1905, and the senate later that same year. Pius protested against the separation in December 1905.

Following the promulgation of the law in January 1906, agents of the government, tax collectors, police, and even some profiteers, scurried to undertake an inventory of the goods of the more than 60,000 churches in the country, provoking an outburst of indignation. On 11 February 1906 Pius unleashed an encyclical against the law of separation, denouncing it as disastrous to society as well as religion. Recalling his battle with the modernists, Pius proclaimed 'that the state must be separate from the church is a thesis absolutely false, a most pernicious error'. Furthermore, he resented the creation of the so-called 'associations of worship' whose function it was to administer the property of the church. For these and other reasons, Pius condemned the law of separation in France as contrary to the rights and divine prerogatives of the church.[45] A decree of the sacred penitentiary imposed excommunication upon those acquiring ecclesiastical property in France.[46]

Although Pius denounced the law of separation, he did not hesitate in taking advantage of the liberty it provided by adding sixteen new bishops to the French hierarchy without consulting the republic, and personally consecrating

44 Giovanni Spadolini, ed., *Il Cardinale Gasparri e la Questione Romana (Con Brani delle Memorie Inedite)* (Florence, 1973), pp. 109–17.

45 *Vehementer nos*, 11 February 1906, *ASS*, XXXIX, pp. 3–16; *Vehementer nos*, 11 February 1906, in Carlen, *PE*, III, pp. 45–51; Giordani, *Pius X*, p. 105.

46 *ASS*, XL, pp. 249–50.

them in St Peter's. He exhorted these new members of the hierarchy to condemn the anticlerical measures of the republic and defend the rights of the church, while remaining conscious of the fact that the judgement of God and the eyes of the world were upon them.[47] Until the end of his reign, this pope continued to decry the persecution of Catholics and the war waged upon the faith in France.[48]

The Vatican's relations with Portugal were little better. After the assassination of King Carlos and the crown prince of Portugal in 1908 in the streets of Lisbon, followed by the deposition of King Manoel in 1910, the provisional government commenced a hostile campaign against the church in that Catholic country. Priests and religious were expelled, bishops were exiled, divorce introduced, religious instruction outlawed, schools deprived of their teachers, and a number of churches pillaged. In 1911 the Portuguese republic promulgated a law separating church and state along French lines. Pius denounced this transgression, which he claimed reduced the church to poverty, ignored the hierarchy, deprived priests of the rights of regulating worship, interfered with the training of seminarians, and sought to separate the church in Portugal from Rome. Declaring this legislation null and void, Pius directed the Portuguese clergy not to comply with these provisions even at the cost of forgoing the government's pensions.[49] Relations with Spain, on the other hand, improved in 1908 when the 1851 concordat was amicably modified by the Spanish government and the Vatican.

While relations between the Vatican and the republics of Portugal and France deteriorated, there was an improvement in its relations with the kingdom of Italy. Sarto, animated by a profound love of his patria, had refused to name the Francophile, anti-Italian Rampolla as his secretary of state. Unlike his predecessors, he had no nostalgia for the temporal power. Those who knew the patriarch of Venice, Cardinal Sarto, before he assumed the papacy, were aware of his determination to seek more amicable relations with Italy. He had not hesitated to receive the king and queen when they had visited Venice, and had favoured the alliance and co-operation of Catholics and moderates in local elections.

The pope also understood that Giovanni Giolitti, who dominated Italy's political life during the first decade of the twentieth century, sought accommodation rather than confrontation with the Catholics who remained outside the orbit of the parliamentary regime. It was clear that Giolitti did not share the aversion to the church shown by Giuseppe Zanardelli and Victor Emmanuel III. Indeed at the end of 1901 when the Zanardelli government presented a divorce bill, Giolitti, then minister of the interior, did not support its passage, and upon becoming prime minister in 1903 abandoned the divorce project opposed by the church. He told the German chancellor von Bülow that the

47 Merry del Val, *Memories of Pope Pius X*, p. 30.
48 *ASS*, XL, pp. 3–11, 259–62.
49 *Iamdudum*, 24 May 1911, in Carlen, *PE*, III, pp. 127–30; Cicognani, *A Symposium*, pp. 30–1, *ASS*, XLI, pp. 625–6.

religious storm brewing in France could not be duplicated in Italy, whose people and government shunned religious conflict.[50] Giolitti appreciated the pope's determination to prevent Catholics from forming their own political party, urging Catholics to focus on their religious mission.[51]

Following the disorders of the general strike in Italy in September 1904, Pius, little disposed to continue the policy of absenteeism from the country's national political life, decided that under specific conditions and in certain areas Catholics could go to the polls. Reportedly, when Pius was told of the unfortunate consequences of a continued Catholic abstention, he replied, 'Do what your conscience dictates', providing papal sanction for the lifting of the *non-expedit* which kept Catholics from the polls.[52] This was concretized in the encyclical of 11 June 1905 which allowed the bishops to decide whether Catholics in their care should participate in subsequent national elections.[53] After 1905, relations between the Giolitti government and Catholics improved, with several Catholic newspapers openly sympathetic to his government, and their number steadily increased.

In 1909 the bishops authorized Catholics in their care to go to the polls to defeat candidates who pursued a hostile policy towards the church. The relationship between the Giolitti government and Catholics grew even closer during the course of the Libyan War of 1911, which was perceived by some as a crusade against the enemy of Christianity. Indeed, the support was so broad as to prompt the Holy See to stipulate the conflict could not be labelled a religious one. Nonetheless, even Luigi Sturzo approved of the venture. 'I should very much like the president of the council to know the pain I experienced at not being able it applaud him in the chamber', Cardinal Agliardi informed a figure close to Giolitti, 'But I clapped my hands for him here, from the palace of the chancellory.'[54]

The controversy provoked by Catholic support for Giolitti during the elections of 1909 and the Libyan War was mild compared to the outcry that followed the alleged support he received from the Catholic Electoral Union during the parliamentary elections of 1913, following the concession of virtual manhood suffrage. It was charged that the astute Giolitti signed an agreement with Count Ottorino Gentiloni, president of the Catholic Electoral Union, known as the 'Gentiloni pact'. The verbose and unstable Gentiloni provoked the controversy by granting an interview to the anti-Giolittian, anticlerical *Giornale d'Italia* in which he described the role played by Catholics in the 1913 elections. Owned by Sidney Sonnino, who had for years crusaded against the

50 Giovanni Spadolini, *Giolitti e I Cattolici, 1901–1914*, 2nd edn (Florence, 1960), p. 82; Prince von Bülow, *Memoirs*, trans. Geoffrey Dunlop (Boston, 1931), II, pp. 68–9.
51 *ASS*, XL, p. 131.
52 G. Suardi, 'Quando e come I Cattolici poterono partecipare alle elezioni politiche', *Nuova Antologia*, CCCVI (November–December 1927), pp. 118–23.
53 *Il fermo proposito*, 11 June 1905, in Carlen, *PE*, III, pp. 37–44.
54 Cortesi to Giolitti, 3 November 1912, in *Dalle Carte di Giovanni Giolitti*, ed. Claudio Pavone (Milan, 1962), III, p. 76.

black or Catholic menace, the newspaper exaggerated and distorted practically everything the count said.

In fact, there was nothing insidious or even secret about the role of the Catholic Electoral Union in the elections of 1913 or its relationship with Giolitti. The Union offered its support to those candidates who agreed with their seven-point programme announced in *L'Italia* of October 1913. The entire country knew these conditions which some derided as 'the seven commandments'. Despite the outcry of diverse journals, there was nothing irregular in the electoral agreement. It was to be expected that Catholics would support those candidates who adhered to their minimum programme, but it was not true that Giolitti signed an alleged pact on behalf of the governmental party, binding his supporters to accept the 'seven commandments'. Gentiloni explained in his famous interview that 'there was no pact, no accord'.[55]

Paradoxically, while liberals such as Sonnino condemned Giolitti for allegedly betraying the liberal state, Catholics who favoured a Christian democratic course, such as the priest Luigi Sturzo, opposed Catholic support of liberal candidates, complaining it reinforced a government fundamentally antagonistic to their religious interests. Sturzo distrusted any tactic that did not break the nexus with the older parties, arguing that only an independent Catholic party could serve as a legitimate alternative to rigid absenteeism. Neither Giolitti nor Pius X concurred, preferring the interim co-operation that had evolved and brought benefits to both church and state in Italy. The pope accepted deputies who were Catholic, but not deputies of a Catholic party. Neither group, he felt, could resolve the Roman Question, whose solution was temporarily shelved. Pius X was pleased by the efforts of the Electoral Union, but renewed his prohibition against Italian clerics participating in syndicalist societies.[56]

Although the modernist crisis and relations with France, Portugal and Italy occupied much of the pope's time, he addressed other issues as well. He reconstructed the English hierarchy and was pleased to learn that in 1909 Catholics in Great Britain were accorded equal rights with other denominations; he also commended scholars to translate his works into English. Pius X supported and seconded missionary efforts worldwide and was delighted by the growth of the church in Brazil, the eucharistic congress held in Montreal, and the efforts of the Eastern clergy to effect a reunion of the churches. In 1905 he established an apostolic prefecture in the Caroline Islands.[57]

This pope communicated with the emperor of Ethiopia to provide protection for Catholic missionaries in his realm. As early as 1905, he elevated the Latin American college in Rome to a pontifical institution, granting it a new constitution, and he favoured the Society for Immigrants in Canada.

55 'Gli insegnamenti delle elezioni generali a suffragio allargato', *Civiltà Cattolica*, LXIV (1913), IV, 532–6; Il *Giornale d'Italia*, 8 November 1913.
56 *Acta Apostolicae Sedis* (Rome, 1909–) (hereafter cited as *AAS*), VI, p. 349.
57 *ASS*, XLIX, p. 165, XL, pp. 54–8, 669; *AAS*, VI, p. 132.

He honoured the church of the United States by elevating its former apostolic delegate to the cardinalate, and granting permission to have an annual collection for the Catholic University of America. Although Pius rejected Americanist or modernist-inspired conversions, he approved of the missionary work of the American hierarchy towards non-Catholics, and their special care of the Indians. In 1908 the church in the United States was removed from the congregation of propaganda and admitted into normal relations with Rome.[58] In 1914 a new apostolic delegation was created in Australia.

A son of the lower classes himself, Pius X identified with the downtrodden, and especially the Indians of South America whose treatment he deplored. In an encyclical of 1912 he sought to act on behalf of this unfortunate race, seeking to uplift them from their miserable condition. Acknowledging that slavery had been abolished, Pius deplored that pernicious customs and usages persisted, binding a substantial part of the native population in virtual servitude. He instructed the bishops to do all within their means to stop the outrages still committed against that unhappy race, preventing any further genocide in the villages and districts, which filled the pope's heart with horror. He advised the hierarchy to make certain that wherever moral instruction was given, in the schools, seminaries, colleges, and especially in the churches, the message be transmitted that Christianity requires that all men, without distinction of nation or colour, be treated as brethren who must be shown charity not only in words but also in deeds.[59]

In 1904, the year he received Theodore Herzl, he issued an apostolic constitution solemnly prohibiting the use of the veto or any lay intervention in pontifical elections as had occurred during the last conclave, and subsequently established new procedures during the election of a successor.[60] Likewise, Pius declared his intention of initiating a momentous codification of canon law, establishing the procedures in March 1904, soon after his election. In 1908 an apostolic constitution was provided the Roman curia. Pius also decreed that, beginning in 1909, the offical acts of the Holy See, including constitutions, laws, decrees of the pontiff and of the sacred congregations, would be published in the *Acta Apostolicae Sedis* to be printed by the Vatican press.[61]

The wide range of Pius's activity, his war on modernism, preoccupation to preserve the faith, and strained relations with a number of states, worked to undermine his health. In later years the drain was psychological as well as physical, for as far back as 1911 he had the premonition that Europe would be rocked by a disastrous war of horrendous consequences. As the whirlwind of modernism was ending, the spectre of world conflict cast its shadow over Europe. When asked by various diplomats how matters progressed, he inevitably

58 Carlen, *PP*, I, pp. 69, 73–4; Cicognani, *A Symposium*, pp. 33–8; *AAS*, VI, pp. 223–4.
59 *Lacrimabili statu*, 7 June 1912, in Carlen, *PE*, III, pp. 131–3.
60 *Commissum nobis*, 20 January 1904, and *Vacante Sede Apostolica*, 25 December 1904, in Carlen, *PP*, I, pp. 67–8.
61 Merry del Val, *Memories of Pope Pius X*, pp. 58–60; *Ardum sane munus*, 19 March 1904, and *Promulgandi*, 29 September 1908, in Carlen, *PP*, I, pp. 67, 74.

replied that things were going from bad to worse and the great war was approaching, making it clear that he was not referring to the Libyan War of 1911 or the Balkan Wars which followed; nor did he share his secretary of state's hope that the impending conflict could be postponed or avoided, predicting it would erupt before the end of 1914. When the Brazilian minister returned to Rio de Janeiro in 1913, Pius considered him fortunate for leaving before the cataclysm struck. In the spring of 1914 the pope warned the cardinals that war was imminent.[62] Soon thereafter, he named new members to their rank, including Monsignor Giacomo della Chiesa who would succeed him as Benedict XV.

When Austria-Hungary declared war on Serbia at the end of July, followed by Germany's declaration of war against Russia on 1 August, Pius's nightmare materialized. On 2 August, in an appeal to the faithful, the Holy Father deplored the outbreak of war in Europe and urged Catholics to pray for peace. Their prayer was not answered. The invasion of Belgium and the news of the first battles filled Pius with horror, rendering him weak and lethargic. By 18 August 1914, doctors indicated that he suffered from influenza, complicated by bronchitis which congested his lungs and provoked a high fever. His condition rapidly deteriorated. As he pondered the frightful turn of events, he expressed sympathy for his successor who would have to deal with the grave consequences to follow. Pius died on the morning of 20 August 1914, overwhelmed with grief at the war he had been unable to prevent. The states of Europe and the world sent their condolences.[63] He was canonized on 29 May 1954, some forty years after his death, the first pope since the sixteenth century designated a saint by the church.

62 Merry del Val, *Memories of Pope Pius X*, pp. 19–20; Giordani, *Pius X*, pp. 197–8; *AAS*, VI, pp. 439–56.
63 *AAS*, VI, pp. 439–56.

CHAPTER 10

Papal diplomacy and the quest for peace during and after the First World War

The conclave at the end of August 1914 assembled while war raged in Europe, and the cardinals sought a pope who could serve as a peace missionary. Both inside and outside the conclave, word spread of the need for an interventionist pope such as Leo XIII, who had addressed international concerns, rather than a pastoral and diplomatically passive one like Pius X, who had focused more on internal church issues such as modernism. Most understood the need to bypass candidates tinged by nationalist leanings, especially avoiding figures known to be sympathetic to the French or the Austrian camp. Even Cardinal Maffi of Pisa would be bypassed because he was considered too close to the Rome regime.[1]

At the end of August 1914, fifty-seven of the sixty-five cardinals gathered in Rome. Meeting when the German advance had compelled the French government to transfer from Paris to Bordeaux, and complaints mushroomed concerning the occupation of Belgium, the cardinals recognized the need to elect a pope quickly. On 3 September, and the tenth ballot, the sixty-year-old Giacomo Giambattista della Chiesa, archbishop of Bologna, was elected pope.[2] Endowed with considerable diplomatic skills, he was hailed as an ideal choice to deal with the conflict which troubled the church. Soon after the election, the German Cardinal Hartmann promised not to discuss the war, and Cardinal Gasquet from England retorted, 'Nor the Peace!'.[3]

Some believed the new pontiff, belonging to one of the oldest families in Italy, chose the name Benedict XV in honour of Benedict XIV, Prospero Lambertini, the last archbishop of Bologna to be elected pope. Others cited his long devotion to St Benedict, while some claimed the choice of his name was influenced by the recollection of Fogazzaro's hero Benedetto in *Il Santo*. Still others reported he chose the name to reveal he was a man of peace. What was clear was that the sixth child of the Marquis Giuseppe della Chiesa, of a

1 For details of the conclave of 1914 see *AAS*, VI, pp. 473–96.
2 3 September 1914, ibid., VI, p. 457.
3 Cardinal Gasquet, *A Memoir*, ed. Shane Leslie (New York, 1953), p. 16.

patrician and clerical family of Piedmont which settled in Genoa, remained both diminutive and frail. Hence his nickname, *Il piccoletto* or little one. In light of his poor health, Giacomo, born on 21 November 1854, received his first education at home. Subsequently, della Chiesa studied as a lay, day student in the diocesan seminary, and then at the university of Genoa law school, receiving a degree in civil law in 1875. Determined to enter the priesthood, his father enrolled him in the Roman seminary of the Capranica, and he studied theology, history and canon law at the Jesuit university of the Gregoriana. He was ordained a priest in December 1878, received a doctorate in theology in 1879, and another in canon law, his favourite subject, in 1880.

While in Rome training for a diplomatic career, della Chiesa impressed Monsignor Mariano Rampolla del Tindaro, who in 1882 named him an apprentice in the congregation of extraordinary affairs. A close and enduring friendship developed between the imposing Sicilian prelate and the retiring Genoese priest. At the end of 1882 when Rampolla was appointed nuncio to Spain, he took della Chiesa along as his secretary. When the archbishop was recalled to Rome as secretary of state in 1887, della Chiesa returned with him, and in 1901 was appointed undersecretary of state. In 1907 he was dispatched to the cardinalate see of Bologna,[4] but was not named cardinal until May 1914, some believed because of the opposition of Merry del Val. However, he entered the college of cardinals in the last consistory held by Pius X, receiving the red hat in time to participate in the conclave of 1914,[5] and to secure election as Benedict XV.

From the beginning of his pontificate, Benedict confronted two major problems: internationally the horror of the World War, and internally the tension within the church provoked by the integralist reaction to modernism. To assist him in these thorny issues, and as successor to Merry del Val, with whom he had not been on cordial terms, Benedict chose Cardinal Domenico Ferrata.[6] Considered a Francophile, Ferrata had served as nuncio to both Paris and Brussels. Benedict had the satisfaction of calling upon Merry del Val to vacate his apartment in the Vatican just as Pius X's influential secretary of state had earlier asked him. 'We forgive but we cannot forget', admitted the new pope.[7] No sooner had his old friend and associate Ferrata been settled in the secretariate of state, than he died from an outbreak of appendicitis. Within days Benedict selected another Francophile and disciple of Rampolla, Pietro Gasparri, who had for two decades been professor of canon law at the Catholic Institute in Paris, and the figure Pius X had placed in charge of the codification of canon law.[8]

4 *L'Osservatore Romano*, 8 October 1907.
5 Secret Consistory of 25 May 1914, *AAS*, VI, pp. 262–3.
6 Nomination of Cardinal Domenico Ferrata as Secretary of State, 4 September 1914, ibid., VI, p. 511.
7 Gasquet, *Memoir*, p. 190.
8 Nomination of Cardinal Pietro Gasparri as Secretary of State, 13 October 1914, *AAS*, VI, p. 525.

On 8 September, two days after his coronation, which was held in the Sistine Chapel rather than in St Peter's in recognition of the general sorrow unleashed by the war, Benedict released his first address to the Catholic world.[9] In this initial message the new pope expressed his determination to neglect nothing to hasten the end of the conflict he termed 'the scourge of the wrath of God'.[10] This was the first of repeated exhortations to the powers and the people, as the pope determined to use all means at his disposal to end the nightmare troubling the continent and his own psyche. Stricken by a paralyzing horror of the war, the pope prohibited chaplains from appearing in the Vatican in military uniform. He urged the faithful to implore God to end the cataclysm. Meanwhile Benedict pleaded with those who governed state affairs to abandon their discords and consider the salvation of humanity. Despite Benedict's sympathy for Catholic Austria and the religious difficulties encountered by the papacy in France and Russia, he preserved his neutrality. The pope did not believe the church should or could take sides. 'I would regret if any parish priest should take sides for one or the other belligerents', he wrote on the eve of his election, 'I have done my best to pray to God for the cessations of the war without dictating to the Almighty the way in which this terrible scourge may cease.'[11]

In October he wrote to the cardinal archbishop of Rheims regretting the spiritual and material damages inflicted by the war, noting the grave and lamentable events witnessed in the episcopal see of Rheims. That same month Benedict was heartened to hear from the archbishop of Cologne, Cardinal von Hartmann, that the German emperor, acceding to his request, had prescribed that all French priests held as prisoners of war would be treated as officers. Benedict was encouraged to ask for more, imploring charity for all captives, regardless of religion or nationality.[12]

At the opening of November 1914, Benedict issued an appeal for peace. The image of war which troubled Europe dominated the thought and action of the newly installed pontiff.[13] His soul was tortured by the brutal carnage, as the greatest and wealthiest nations competed to destroy one another with the refinements of horror. In his view the 'murderous struggle' was prompted by four disorders: the absence of mutual love, contempt for authority, unjust class strife, and the unquenchable thirst for wealth and other material objects by a deluded generation. The pope raised his voice in supplication to God for peace.[14]

Benedict reassured the cardinals he was not a modernist, and this was evident in *Ad beatissimi*. Therein, he deplored the modernist spirit which interjected

9 Coronation of 6 September 1914, ibid., VI, p. 498.
10 Benedict's first address to the Catholic World, 8 September 1914, ibid., VI, pp. 501–2.
11 'The Pope and the War', *London Times*, 6 September 1914.
12 Harry C. Koenig, ed., *Principles for Peace: Selections from Papal Documents from Leo XIII to Pius XII* (Washington, DC, 1943), pp. 128–30.
13 In this regard see G. Anaud d'Agnel, *Benoit XV et le conflit europeén* (Paris, 1916) and Anthony Brennan, *Pope Benedict XV and the War* (London, 1917).
14 *Ad Beatissimi*, 1 November 1914, *AAS*, VI, pp. 585–99.

innovation in the discussion of divine issues, in worship, and other Catholic practices.[15] The pope also rejected integralism, noting that 'Catholics should abstain from appellations . . . to distinquish one group of Catholics from another'.[16]

Benedict addressed international as well as internal problems plaguing the church, encouraging diplomatic efforts to bring the conflict to a speedy conclusion and, pending its termination, to prevent its extension. In the interim he sought to alleviate suffering among the belligerents. He had his secretary of state undertake negotiations to arrange for a truce on Christmas Day, calling upon the belligerents to suspend hostilities throughout 25 December as an act of Christian piety. Maintaining a strict impartiality, Benedict explained that the Holy See was not, and did not wish to be, neutral in the European war, but had the duty to remain impartial. The distinction was understood by neither camp, and paradoxically both accused the Holy See of favouring the other side.[17]

Moved by the relentless slaughter and suffering of the Belgians, the pope prayed for the end of their misfortunes, but hesitated condemning the German aggression.[18] His inner thoughts and moral evaluation of the invasion of Belgium he kept locked within. The holy father's cautious approach disappointed the allies, and Cardinal Mercier acknowledged the unfortunate impression created by the Vatican's failure to denounce the aggressors or to defend the cause of the ravaged nations of Belgium and Serbia.[19] This 'silence' on the part of the pope, plus the fact that he openly supported the German efforts to keep Italy neutral, angered the allied countries. Word spread that Benedict had advised Franz-Josef, by means of his nuncio in Vienna, to cede the Trentino to Italy to avert Italian intervention. Nor were the allies pleased by the pope's directive to Monsignor Pacelli, secretary of the congregation of extraordinary ecclesiastical affairs, to instruct bishops and the clergy to care for the spiritual and material welfare of prisoners of war in their countries.[20] In fact, a pamphlet produced in 1916 entitled 'The Silence of Benedict XV' claimed the pope and the church did nothing to stop the war, arguing that the 'silence' compromised Christianity in general.

The powers in both warring camps sought to influence the Vatican, hoping to utilize its voice to sway public opinion. In this competition the central powers initially enjoyed an advantage over the entente, with the Bavarian, Prussian and Austro-Hungarian envoys maintaining residence in Rome. There was no regular French representative at the Vatican as a result of the 1905 rupture in diplomatic relations, and this increased Parisian suspicion of the pope and curia. While tzarist Russia did have a minister at the papal court, his influence was limited by the Holy See's opposition to Russian religious policies

15 Ibid., VI, p. 657.
16 *Ad Beatissimi apostolorum*, in Carlen, *PE*, II, pp. 143–51.
17 'Pope Eager to Convince the World at Large of His "Absolute Impartiality" in the War', *New York Times*, 24 July 1916.
18 'The Pope's Sympathy with Belgium', *London Times*, 17 December 1914.
19 Gasquet, *Memoir*, p. 245.
20 Koenig, ed., *Principles for Peace*, pp. 140–4.

pursued in Poland. Furthermore, while Baron Vittorio Gianotti served as a go-between Italy and the Vatican, he proved unable to dispel the distrust which had accumulated over half a century between Rome and the Vatican.

Cardinal Gasquet, who regretted the lack of official communication between the British government and the pope, sought a British representative at the Vatican. Terminating over three centuries without an accredited representative, in December 1914 the British sent Henry Howard to the Vatican as a special envoy, to counter the influence which Germany was thought to exercise over the Holy See.[21] He was later succeeded by Count de Salis. The English promised the Italians they would not acquiesce to any Vatican participation in the peace conference or any discussion of the Roman Question. Sonnino was temporarily assured by the English who promised 'we don't mean to strike a bargain with the pope'.[22]

While the belligerents sought papal sanction to justify their actions, the Vatican steadfastly refused to pass judgement on either side. However, the pope did not hesitate to condemn the war in general or to urge its speedy conclusion. The theme of Benedict's Christmas allocution to the cardinals of 24 December 1914 was 'seek after peace'. Disappointed that his suggestion for a truce on Christmas Day had been disregarded, he was not discouraged, seeking to hasten the end of the war, or at least to alleviate its unfortunate consequences. The pontiff prayed that the nations would submit to arbitration, assuring a peaceful settlement of international disputes. Hoping to find a common ground among the combatants, he was not prepared to condemn one side while favouring another. At the end of the year, Benedict telegraphed the sovereigns of Austria-Hungary, Bavaria, Belgium, Germany, England and Serbia asking them to exchange prisoners incapable of further military service.[23] This proposal, like his others, remained unheeded.

The opening of the new year witnessed renewed efforts on Benedict's part to alleviate the suffering as he sought to secure an immediate end to the war. On 10 January 1915 Cardinal Gasparri revealed that the pope, deeply afflicted at the sight of a war which brought misery to families and cities, had composed a special prayer for peace, urging that it be read by the faithful worldwide.[24] The next day he renewed his request that the belligerent nations release captured civilians unfit for military service, and soon thereafter called upon the American Catholic press to co-operate in promoting a Christian peace.

The pope implored Europeans to pray for peace on 7 February 1915, asking the Catholic world to join in this chorus of prayer on 2 March 1915.[25] Benedict refused to bow to the clamour of the allied press which insisted he indict the central powers and their criminal aggression, although he created a papal commission of inquiry to investigate the subject of alleged German atrocities

21 Gasquet, *Memoir*, p. 214; Brennan, *Pope Benedict XV*, p. 3; *AVR*, pp. viii, xv, 31.
22 Sidney Sonnino, *Diario, 1914–1916*, ed. Pietro Pastorelli (Bari, 1972), p. 40.
23 Koenig, ed., *Principles for Peace*, pp. 145–8.
24 Benedict XV's Prayer for Peace, 10 January 1915, *AAS*, VII, pp. 8–10.
25 *AAS*, VII, pp. 151–4.

in Belgium. For the allies, it was too little, for the central powers, too much. Although swamped by the appeals and propaganda of the courts embroiled in the conflict, Benedict refused to take sides. In a consistorial allocution 22 January 1915, he proclaimed that the Roman pontiff, as the vicar of Christ, had to embrace all the combatants in the same sense of charity. The pope publicly lamented the suffering of the Poles and expressed deep sympathy for Belgium, praising the Red Cross for mitigating the disastrous effects of the war. Moved by their misfortune, he sent alms and assistance to both. There were frequent papal interventions on behalf of prisoners of war held by the warring nations.[26] Benedict likewise decried the plight of the unfortunate victims of the *Lusitania*, deploring the barbarism unleashed by the war.[27] Such general condemnations were deemed inadequate and unsatisfactory by both camps, which complained of the sterile universalism of the Vatican.

In the spring of 1915 the pope still nourished the hope that Italy would not become embroiled in the conflict, issuing new prayers for peace to be recited during May devotions. The nuncio in Vienna, Rafaelle Scapinelli, urged the Habsburg government to keep Italy out of the war, warning that Italian participation on the allied side would cut off relations between the Vatican and Austria and Bavaria, to the detriment of the church.[28] Matthias Erzberger, the German deputy of the Centre party, ventured to Rome in his first of three visits, to second the pope's resolve to keep Italy neutral. Unfortunately, the prime minister who succeeded Giovanni Giolitti, Antonio Salandra, was an interventionist, and following the death of San Giuliano he selected Sidney Sonnino, likewise in favour of entry into the war, as his new foreign minister. The latter, even before Italy became a belligerent, opposed papal participation in any future peace conference.[29]

The Vatican, the chamber and the great majority of Italians favoured neutrality for Italy, but by mid-April 1915 the Italian government had virtually accepted the terms of the treaty of London. Concluded on 26 April 1915, the agreement called for Italian intervention against Germany and Austria, and by article 15 prohibited the Vatican from any say or seat at the peace conference. By its terms France, Great Britain and Russia pledged their support to the Italian opposition to the Holy See's diplomatic activity for the conclusion of peace or the settlement of issues flowing from the War.[30] On 24 May 1915 Italy declared war against Austria. The next day Benedict lamented that his appeals for peace remained unanswered, and the conflict continued to bloody Europe. 'And, as if that were not enough', he added, 'the terrible conflagration has extended also to our beloved Italy . . .'[31]

26 Cardinal Gasparri to Cardinal Joseph Schutte, 29 April 1915, *ASS*, VII, pp. 224–5.
27 Gasquet, *Memoir*, p. 242.
28 Stewart A. Stehlin, 'Germany and a Proposed Vatican State, 1915–1917', *Catholic Historical Review*, LX, 3 (October 1974), pp. 406–7.
29 Sonnino, *Diario, 1914–1916*, pp. 29, 92.
30 *AVR*, p. 19.
31 Koenig, ed., *Principles for Peace*, p. 170.

Although Sonnino and the Italian government promised full liberty to the representatives of the enemy powers to the Vatican, the agents of the central powers, appreciating the difficulty of their position in Rome, abandoned the Vatican for Lugano in Switzerland. Subsequently, Germans and Austrians not protected by diplomatic immunity were ordered out of Rome, but Monsignor Rudolf Gerlach, secret chamberlain on active duty to his Holiness, asked to stay, and Benedict and the Italians allowed him to do so. Although the pope warned Gerlach to remain within the confines of the Vatican, the prelate refused to comply, and became embroiled in political intrigues on behalf of the central powers. When these revelations were brought to Benedict's attention, the pope consented to have his unruly private chamberlain transferred to Switzerland. Surrounded by one of the belligerents, the Vatican found it difficult to preserve its neutrality and its links with the universal church. In 1916 Cardinal Gasparri protested against the Italian government's confiscation of the Palazzo Venezia, the official residence of the Austrian ambassador to the Vatican, citing it as another proof of the abnormal position of the Holy See in Rome.[32]

Austria and Germany resented the loss of their direct contact with the papacy, whose moral influence they deemed useful to the various belligerents. Under these circumstances their governments supported a movement to assure international guarantees for the independence of the pope. In Germany, both the emperor and the chancellor considered a prompt solution of the Roman Question essential, and Mathias Ezberger proposed assuring the papacy a small, independent territory within Rome, to secure the Holy See from Italian pressure. By 1917, this was concretized in a draft. Although Benedict and the curia were interested in the scheme, they encouraged neither Erzberger nor his government, fearful of arousing Italian mistrust or leading them to conclude that the Vatican had ranged itself on the side of the Germanic powers in order to impose a solution to the Roman Question.[33] By 1917, Benedict had come to the conclusion that the Roman Question would have to be resolved by negotiation following a rapprochement between the Vatican and Italy, and circumstances did not permit a solution during or immediately after the war.

The pope's principal priority remained bringing the terrible war to an end. On 28 July 1915, the first anniversary of its outbreak, he issued another apostolic exhortation to the peoples at war and their leaders, inviting the combatants to end the slaughter and make a just peace.[34] In September Benedict called upon President Wilson to issue a peace appeal to the warring nations in a note transmitted by Cardinal Gibbons. The cardinal later reported that the president was gratified to hear from the pope, but responded cautiously. Word soon spread that the United States would make no overture unless it believed its mediation would be acceptable to all the belligerents. Still the cardinal spoke with Wilson for half an hour, and immediately afterwards conferred with Secretary

32 Ibid., p. 210.
33 Stehlin, 'Germany and a Proposed Vatican State', pp. 413–21, 423–6.
34 Koenig, ed., *Principles for Peace*, p. 181; *AAS*, VII, p. 376; Benedict XV to the Peoples Now at War and Their Rulers, 28 July 1915, *AAS*, VII, p. 375.

Lansing for another thirty minutes. The *New York Times* reported that the pope had asked Wilson to present the belligerents a proposal for a cessation of hostilities, hoping that in time there might be a resolution of their differences. Wilson, recalling that his good offices had been earlier rejected by the belligerents, made it clear that his standing offer of assistance remained, but he would not act until assured that the warring parties welcomed his intervention.[35]

In October the pope made inquiries through Monsignor Francesco Marchetti-Salvaggiani, his extraordinary envoy to Berne, to discuss the exchange of prisoners. The Holy See's desire to convert this temporary mission into a permanent one led the Swiss to ask whether this would create difficulties for the Italian government. Sonnino responded that he differentiated the Vatican's desire to have a nuncio in Berne from the desire to have a nuncio meddle in a peace conference which might be called in that city. While the Italian foreign minister had no objections to the former, repeating that the Holy See had the right to send representatives to all the powers, it objected to the latter, opposing papal participation in any international conference.[36] Beneath the armour of the Vatican's self-righteousness and humanitarian appeals, the Italian foreign minister believed lurked self-interest and the desire to reopen the Roman Question.

Despite Sonnino's disparagement of Vatican peace initiatives, the Italian press provided great prominence to Benedict's move for peace presented to Wilson through Cardinal Gibbons. While the Holy See preserved the strictest reserve, in his conversations with the cardinals the pope expressed his views freely, considering Wilson best able to induce the powers to discuss the issues dividing them. Benedict hoped to find a formula based on law and justice, and called upon Catholics worldwide to contribute to the peace process. Benedict indicated that President Wilson, having shown both groups of belligerents the fairness, firmness and goodwill of the American government, could address them with authority and induce them to take the preliminary steps towards a negotiated peace.[37]

At year's end, in December 1915, Benedict observed that though he had used every means to settle the discord, the fatal war continued. To bring about the cessation of the conflict yearned for by a suffering humanity, the pope pleaded for an exchange of ideas, as well as the willingness of the belligerents to make compromises.[38] These thoughts were repeated in his Christmas allocution, where benedict claimed a cloud of sadness cast a shadow over the celebration of the Nativity. Deploring the excesses and ferocity of this terrible conflict with its anti-Christian retrogresssion, he advised the faithful to seek solace in prayer.[39]

35 'Pope asks Wilson to Send Peace Appeal to the Warring Powers, but President Awaits their Call', *New York Times*, 3 September 1915.
36 Sonnino, *Diario, 1914–1916*, pp. 262–3.
37 'Pope's Efforts Continue', *New York Times*, 4 September 1915; 'Pope Says Wilson has Won the Right to Speak with Authority in Interest of Peace', ibid., 5 September 1915.
38 Benedict XV's Consistory of 6 December 1915 creating New Cardinals, *AAS*, VII, pp. 509–22.
39 *È pur troppo vero*, in Koenig, ed., *Principles for Peace*, pp. 193–7.

There was little relief in 1916 for the stricken pontiff, who continued his campaign to alleviate the suffering and slaughter, lamenting the harsh treatment of the Ruthenians as well as the bombing first of Ravenna, followed by that of Treviso, then Venice. Benedict denounced all the violations of natural law witnessed during the course of the barbaric war, which he deemed suicidal for civilized Europe. Confronted by the obstinacy of the diplomats, the pope urged the faithful to offer prayers and sacrifices during Lent, imploring God to restore peace. The children of Europe were asked to receive Communion for the holy father's intention – the restoration of peace. The pontiff placed unbounded trust in their prayers, finding more consolation therein than in the feeble diplomatic efforts undertaken to date. Benedict maintained that Christian social action had to prepare the ground for a lasting peace.

Although previous papal pleas to the powers had been unheeded, Benedict refused to remain indifferent or silent in the face of the continuing carnage he judged useless and inadmissible. He provided material as well as moral support to the suffering, sending sums of money now to Serbia, later to Lithuania, then Belgium. He urged the British government to transport food from America for the starving population of Poland, implored Italian bishops to visit Austro-Hungarian prisoners of war, and proposed that prisoners with children be released to the Swiss. Benedict's efforts were not always appreciated, so he was grateful to the women of Denmark who sensed the humanitarian effort of the Vatican and the pope's thankless interventions on behalf of humanity. Cardinal Gasparri explained that the holy father, who served as mediator between peoples, had to defend just causes and serve as the guardian of law, morality and civilization.[40]

Without pointing a finger at any one power or group of powers, the pope blamed the horrible conflict and dark tragedy of human hatred devasting Europe on the disrespect for the supreme laws which governed the mutual relations of states. There were those who hoped that Benedict would catalogue the faults and crimes committed by the aggressor nations, but the pope refused to do so, realizing that partisanship would cause profound consternation, creating animosity rather than harmony.[41] His determination to avoid taking sides very likely explains his negative reaction when the central powers – Germany, Austria, Bulgaria and Turkey – dispatched a note to the heads of government with whom they maintained relations, calling upon them to enjoin the entente powers to enter peace negotiations. The Vatican failed to respond, for it had received a note from England indicating that any intervention on the part of the pope would not be welcomed by the allies. The pope's Christmas appeal for peace, on 24 December 1916, like its predecessors, avoided any indictment.[42]

Although Benedict's please for peace were repeatedly rejected, he was not discouraged, and at the opening of 1917 he proclaimed that the attempts to

40 Koenig, ed., *Principles for Peace*, pp. 197–210; 'Justice to Belgium to be Pope's Aim', *New York Times*, 11 January 1916.
41 *AVR*, p. 6.
42 *Ancora una volta*, in Koenig, ed., *Principles for Peace*, pp. 221–2.

restore tranquillity had to be redoubled. Indeed, 1917 would witness Benedict's most substantial diplomatic effort to end the scourge of war. In April he appointed Eugenio Pacelli as nuncio to Munich, and in May his envoy presented his credentials to King Ludwig III of Bavaria, meeting with Theobald von Bethmann-Hollweg, the German chancellor, in June. In their quest for peace, the nuncio and the German chancellor discussed four points: (1) the general limitation of armaments, (2) the establishment of international courts, (3) the restoration of the independence of Belgium, (4) while agreeing that issues such as Alsace-Lorraine would be settled by the contending parties. Soon thereafter Pacelli met with William II and subsequently transmitted optimistic reports to Rome, where the pope was on the verge of launching his major peace effort. Unfortunately, Germany changed chancellors in July, and the new minister, Georg Michaelis, reflected the position of the general staff more than the peace party.

On 1 August 1917 Benedict dispatched his peace note to the belligerents, accompanied by a cover letter of Cardinal Gasparri, setting forth the pope's motivation. It encouraged the belligerents to devise just terms to end the slaughter and assure a lasting peace. Benedict's note commenced with an introductory paragraph which reiterated the three overriding aims of his pontificate towards the war: (1) to maintain an absolute impartiality, (2) to endeavour to do the utmost good without distinction of persons, nationality or religion, and (3) to omit nothing on the papacy's part to hasten the end of the calamity. Ennumerating his past appeals and endeavours of a general nature, the pope now proposed practical propositions, inviting the belligerent governments to come to some agreement upon concrete points.

Commencing with the overriding proposition that the moral force of right should be substituted for the material force of arms, the pope suggested a number of means to achieve this goal, including: (1) a simultaneous and reciprocal decrease in armaments, (2) the institution of international arbitration as a substitute for armies, (3) free intercourse of peoples and true liberty of the seas, (4) the reciprocal renunciation of war indemnities, (5) the evacuation and restoration of all occupied territories, and (6) the resolution of political and territorial claims in a spirit of equity and justice. The pope prayed that his invitation to make peace to those guiding the destinies of the belligerent nations would be accepted, noting that on their decision rested the future of numerous families and the lives and happiness of thousands of young men, whose welfare was their absolute duty.[43] Benedict suggested that these measures might be undertaken in three phases, first the suspension of the fighting, second the reduction of armaments, and finally the substitution of arbitration for combat to resolve differences. Public opinion on both sides recognized the importance of the pope's initiative, with the *Evening Post* of New York presenting it as 'a diplomatic and international event of the first rank'.[44]

43 *Des le Debut*, 1 August 1917, in Koenig, ed., *Principles for Peace*, p. 232.
44 'The Pope Acts', *Evening Post*, 14 August 1917.

In Italy, the *Giornale d'Italia* described it as the most impressive proposal addressed to the belligerents, providing the broad outline on which peace might be negotiated.

The pope's peace note made reference to the Turkish treatment of the Armenians, asking the powers to examine it in a spirit of justice and equity. Unfortunately, this invocation was virtually ignored by the various governments and the international press. Other parts of the papal proposal were not well received by the belligerents either in the entente or the central powers, who responded with scorn and derision. From Britain, Lord Balfour, while appreciative of the pope's efforts, made it clear that until the issues of restoration and reparation had been resolved, his country could not consider any move for peace. Acknowledging receipt of the proposal, Balfour claimed that Germany had not expressed her intentions with sufficient clarity to warrant negotiation. Baron Sonnino, the Italian foreign minister, proved even more dismissive, depicting the entire papal proposal as inspired by Germany, while judging its principles as entirely impractical. From France, Clemenceau denounced the Vatican proposal as directed against France, charging it would profit the violaters of justice rather than the aggrieved.[45] The proposal fared little better in the German press, which depicted Benedict as a tool of the allies.

Across the Atlantic, President Wilson did not receive the note with any greater sympathy than his European allies, and American secretary of state Robert Lansing denounced the plan as an enemy scheme. To be sure, in the letter of 27 August 1917, dispatched by his secretary of state Lansing, Wilson praised the pope's moving appeal, which was recognized as prompted by humane and generous motives. However, Wilson asserted that a peace based on the pope's note required trust in Germany, entirely lacking in the allied camp. The American response to the Vatican, coupled with the continued reluctance of Richard von Kuhlmann of the German foreign office to forthrightly proclaim Germany's intention to restore the independence of Belgium, effectively killed the pope's peace proposal.

Benedict was disappointed by the rejection of his peace offer. He sought to explain its provisions and motivation to the belligerents and their people in a series of addresses, while praising the Swiss for their abundant charity during the conflict. At the end of September, he had his secretary of state Gasparri write to the prime minister of England that international peace required a simultaneous and reciprocal suppression of compulsory military service. He again explained the reasons which restrained the Holy See from declaring which side was right and which was wrong. 'In the interest of mankind, the Holy Father, in his Letter, assumes the office of mediator, and does all that is possible to persuade the belligerent nations, each of which claims to have right on its side, to lay down their arms, to enter into conversation, and to become reconciled', Gasparri wrote. 'Now, is it, I would ask, the part of a

45 Denis Gwynn, *The Vatican and the War in Europe* (Dublin, 1941), II, p. 56; Walter H. Peters, *The Life of Benedict XV* (St Paul, 1959) p. 156; *AVR*, p. 14.

mediator to decide which of the parties concerned is wrong and which is right?'[46] Neither Gasparri nor Benedict thought so.

Early in January, President Wilson, in an address to the two houses of the American congress, introduced his famous 'fourteen points' as a basis for negotiation, drawn and elaborated from the proposals put forward by Benedict in his note of 1 August 1917. They called for: (1) agreements to be openly arrived at and the renunciation of secret diplomacy, (2) freedom of the seas in war and peace, (3) efforts for the removal of economic barriers between nations, (4) the reduction of armaments, (5) the impartial adjustment of colonial claims, (6) the evacuation and restoration of Russian territory, (7) the restoration of Belgian sovereignty, (8) the evacuation of France and the return of Alsace-Lorraine, (9) redrawing the Italian frontier along national lines, (10) autonomy for the peoples of Austria-Hungary, (11) the evacuation of Montenegro, Rumania and Serbia, providing the last with access to the sea, (12) self-determination for the peoples of the Ottoman empire and freedom of navigation through the Dardenelles, (13) establishment of an independent Poland with access to the sea, and finally (14) the creation of a general association of nations to guarantee the independence of all.[47]

Pope Benedict applauded the president's efforts which were similar to his own. Father Joseph McMahon, addressing the Catholic Library Association meeting in New York on 'The Papacy as a Peacemaker in History', proclaimed the peace terms of the pope and the president were identical, but a worldwide 'league of hatred' against the Roman Catholic church prevented this from being recognized. Father McMahon catalogued the complaints against Benedict: first, he had not pronounced which of the belligerents had right on their side, and second, he had repeatedly tried to bring these governments to some agreement by asking them to define their war aims. Finally, when the pope sought to establish guidelines on which peace could be discussed, he was attacked as being in sympathy with the central powers.[48] The pope and Cardinal Gasparri examined Wilson's address to congress and both were optimistic about its impact.

Benedict continued his efforts not only to alleviate the tragedies of the war but to hasten its end. To assist in the reconstruction of Poland, in April he appointed Achille Ratti (who in 1922 would succeed him as Pius XI) as apostolic delegate to Poland, Lithuania, and even Russia, then in the throes of revolution. In May Benedict called upon all priests to celebrate Holy Mass on 29 June 1918 to bring a speedy end to the war. Benedict continued to lament that his own attempts to bring about peace had been scandalously misinterpreted by the enemies of the church, predicting that these efforts would be appreciated

46 Cardinal Gasparri to Archbishop of Sens, 7 October 1917, in Koenig, ed., *Principles for Peace*, p. 238.
47 'The Fourteen Points', 8 January 1918, in G.A. Kertesz, ed., *Documents in the Political History of the European Continent, 1815–1939* (Oxford, 1968), pp. 347–9.
48 'Pope's Aims Like Wilson', *Evening Post*, 17 January 1918; 'Address Pleases Vatican', ibid., 15 February 1918.

and understood by all those who were fair-minded, once the war was over.[49] To assist in that endeavour Benedict authorized the publication of a papal white book which would gather all the diplomatic efforts and correspondence of the Vatican since the opening of the war, illustrating the papal views as to the settlement of the current conflict.[50] Suspicion of the papacy continued in the allied camp as the Americans and French challenged the Vatican attempt to establish diplomatic relations with China in the summer of 1918.

In his Easter message to the United States, Pope Benedict expressed the hope for a lasting settlement and the creation of a new organization of peoples and nations aspiring to a 'nobler, purer, and kinder civilization'.[51] Likewise in his talk to the delegates from Finland, Benedict proclaimed that true to its tradition, the Holy See recognized the same rights for small nations as well as the large, hoping to see this principle more universally accepted in the postwar period.[52] In November 1918, as word spread of an impending armistice, the pope implored the powers to approach the armistice proposal with goodwill, to ensure a just and honourable peace for all. Shortly thereafter, the pope rejoiced in the Austrian-Italian peace negotiations of 3 November and the armistice of 11 November 1918, which silenced the guns on the western front.

At the opening of December, Benedict crafted an encyclical on the general armistice of 11 November 1918 which finally brought about a cessation of hostilities. Benedict recognized that it was an armistice rather than a peace, but appreciated that it had suspended the slaughter, allowing a respite for a suffering humanity. Looking ahead, the pope called upon Catholics to invoke divine assistance for all those who would take part in the peace conference to produce a true peace founded on Christian principles of justice.[53] These sentiments were repeated in the pope's Christmas Eve allocution to the college of cardinals in which he prayed for God's blessing upon the Versailles peace conference. Benedict warned the peacemakers to repair the material havoc of the war as well as the moral damage. Benedict sought a peace inspired by reconciliation rather than revenge. He called for justice, charity and love, arguing that social unity and international harmony had to be based on benevolence rather than hatred. He was bound to be disappointed by what followed.

On 4 January 1919 the pope met with President Wilson, the first chief of the United States ever received by a pontiff. Benedict presented Wilson with the two volumes of the newly released canon law, on which Cardinal Gasparri and others had laboured for more than a decade. The pope and the president then discussed the prospects for a lasting peace, with the holy father expressing the hope that the hundreds of thousands of prisoners of war would be

49 Koenig, ed., *Principles for Peace*, pp. 246–54.
50 'Papal White Book Soon', *New York Times*, 2 February 1918; 'Pope Works on White Book', ibid., 10 February 1918.
51 'Papal Peace Message is Sent to America', *New York Times*, 23 March 1918.
52 Koenig, ed., *Principles for Peace*, pp. 247, 257–9.
53 *Quod Iam Diu*, in Carlen, *PE*, III, pp. 161–2; *E la Quinta Volta*, 24 December 1918, in Koenig, ed., *Principles for Peace*, pp. 261–5.

returned to their home countries as soon as possible, and the American president shared his concern. Despite rumours, the Roman Question was not broached, nor was there any effort on the pope's part to gain a seat at the impending peace negotiations. This was confirmed by the British representative at the Vatican, de Salis, who noted that Cardinal Gasparri did not try to interject himself in the peace process, revealing that the Holy See would only serve as mediator when invoked by both parties.[54]

Very likely the story of the alleged attempt of the Vatican to force itself into the negotiations was fed by the paranoia of the Italians, which was aggravated when Benedict dispatched Monsignor Bonaventura Cerretti to Versailles. However, the task of this papal envoy was to safeguard the position of the missions in the former German colonies rather than to interject the Vatican into the congress. His efforts on behalf of the missionaries were seconded by Wilson, whom Benedict thanked for helping to revise the peace and safeguard the freedom of the Catholic missions. The same concern for the missions inspired Benedict's apostolic epistle on the propagation of the faith throughout the world at the end of 1919. Benedict's pronouncement would serve as the charter of the modern missionary movement, upon which his successor Pius XI would draw. In his message on the missions in the postwar world, the holy father emphasized four fundamental principles: (1) the common missionary duty of all members of the Catholic church, (2) the promotion of the native clergy, (3) renunciation on the part of the missionaries of nationalism and condescension, and (4) an appreciation of the objective importance of the civilization of the missionary territories.[55]

The accusations that Benedict had grown increasingly rigid in his temperament and policies at the war's end were unfounded. The opposite proved true. As he witnessed the chaos and confusion in Italy, Benedict completely lifted the *non-expedit* which kept Catholics from national politics, and permitted (if he did not encourage) the formation of Don Luigi's Sturzo's Catholic Partito Popolare which Pius X had vehemently opposed. Furthermore, the pope removed the ban on visits of heads of Catholic countries to the Eternal City. He also withdrew his opposition to the vote for women. Benedict even reached out to Lenin and the Soviet Union, having his secretary of state telegraph the Soviet leader on behalf of the persecuted Orthodox, while imploring religious toleration for all faiths.[56]

Nor was the pope hostile to the projected League of Nations. Pinpointing the inability of the international configuration to resolve conflicts peacefully, as early as 1914 he proposed an alternative. In his encyclical *Ad beatissimi* of 1 November 1914, he appealed to the nations of the world to resort to some other means of resolving differences.[57] Until some new structure emerged,

54 Report on Mission to Holy See, Count de Salis to Marquis Curzon, 25 October 1922, in *AVR*, p. 12.
55 *Maximum illud.*, 30 November 1919, in Carlen, *PP*, I, p. 83.
56 Gasparri to Lenin, 12 March 1919, in Koenig, ed., *Principles for Peace*, p. 269.
57 Ibid., pp. 132, 178–9, 220–1, 238–9.

the pope demanded that the powers adhere to the existing international law. Deploring both the violation of laws and the disrespect for harmony, Benedict believed this contributed to the carnage and prayed that a new code would assure a more tranquil future.

In his Easter message to the United States of 21 March 1918, Benedict noted that the first message of the risen Saviour to his disciples after Passion week was 'Peace be unto you'. He invoked a new organization of peoples and nations united under the aegis of true religion in aspiring to a 'nobler, purer and kinder civilization'.[58] In May 1920 the pope again expressed his support for a league:

> Things being thus restored, the order required by justice and charity re-established and the nations reconciled, it is much to be desired, Venerable Brethren, that all States, putting aside mutual suspicion, should unite in one league, or rather a sort of family of peoples, calculated both to maintain their own independence and safeguard the order of human society. What specially, amongst other reasons, calls for such an association of nations, is the need generally recognized of making every effort to abolish or reduce the enormous burden of the military expenditures which States can no longer bear, in order to prevent these disastrous wars or at least to remove the danger of them as far as possible. So would each nation be assured not only of its independence but also of the integrity of its territory within its just frontiers.[59]

Rather than engineering or even gloating over the American failure to enter the League, as some suspected, Benedict regretted the turn of events.[60]

On the other hand, Benedict was less than pleased with the results of the peacemaking process. The treaties emanating from Paris did not reassure the pontiff, who feared that the conflagration was not totally extinguished as the embers of war still smoldered. The *Osservatore Romano* complained that the peace left the door open for grave political complications.[61] Above all, the Vatican worried about the territorial integrity of Germany, which it deemed central to the overall European equilibrium. Benedict also criticized the conditions imposed upon Catholic Austria, lamenting it had been reduced to a fragment of its former self. He also expressed concern that the treaties would not provide adequate protection for the Catholic missions. Finally, Benedict expressed concern about the situation in Palestine, long considered 'holy' by the Christian world and one of the great pilgrimage centres. The *Osservatore Romano* applauded the liberation of Jerusalem, judging it important for the advancement of Christian civilization.[62]

58 'Papal Peace Message is Sent to America', *New York Times*, 23 March 1918.
59 *Pacem, Dei Munus Pulcherrimum*, 23 May 1920, in Carlen, *PE*, III, p. 174.
60 Anne O'Hare McCormick, *Vatican Journal 1921–1954* (New York, 1957), pp. 20–1.
61 'Dove sono i responsabili?', *L'Osservatore Romano*, 6 November 1919; Emma Fattorini, *Germania e Santa Sede, Le nunziature di Pacelli tra la Grande guerra e la Republica di Weimar* (Bologna, 1992), p. 40.
62 'Dopo l'occupazione di Gerusalemma', *L'Osservatore Romano*, 14 December 1917; James H. Ryan, 'The Vatican's World Policy', *Current History, New York Times Magazine*, December 1922, p. 437; *Tablet*, 25 June 1921.

Although disillusioned by the treaties, Benedict did not abandon his crusade on behalf of the oppressed, distressed by the famine and disastrous conditions not only in Catholic Europe but in Orthodox Russia which had fallen under communist control. He described the horrible conditions of millions of Russians in that war-torn land, appealing to all civilized nations and Christians to help alleviate their suffering.[63] He was the first to send relief, an effort seconded by his successor, Pius XI. He telegramed the League of Nations exhorting all nations to assist Russia.

In his last year Benedict continued to champion peace worldwide. At the end of November 1921 he told the assembled cardinals that peace at home and abroad was most desired by the peoples of the world. Noting with anxiety that the solemn peace treaty had not received the seal of peace of minds, the pope cited the need for God's intervention to remedy the evils which burdened humanity. Benedict did not imply that the rulers of peoples should not attempt to use such remedies within their means to ensure the common good, but cautioned them not to rely on human effort alone. He prayed for peace in Italy, for the Irish and English to submit their differences to arbitration, and for the independence and well-being of Poland. In November 1921 the pope telegraphed President Harding of the United States on the occasion of the arms conference in Washington which addressed the thorny issue of disarmament, while in December the pontiff blessed the efforts of the First International Democratic Congress in Paris.[64] At the end of December 1921 Benedict caught a cold, which he neglected, and this developed into a serious bronchial infection and influenza. Confined to his bed on 17 January, he died five days later on 22 January 1922. Flags on Italian public buildings were flown half staff for the first time since the Italian seizure of Rome.

The death of the 67-year-old pontiff was paralleled by an erosion of the optimism that had dawned with the Enlightenment, contributing to a decline in Western faith in science, technology, progress and positivism. The ideologies which had dominated Western thought, including rationalism, liberalism, nationalism, and even democracy, were challenged in the aftermath of a suicidal war fought to the point of exhaustion. The smug confidence in European superiority over the other races, the notion of the white man's burden, the moral basis of Western imperialism, and the continuity of tradition were all shattered. While the physical damage of the conflict was quickly repaired, the psychological scars remained to haunt the subsequent generation. The World War and its aftermath witnessed the beginning of the end of bourgeois civilization in Europe and the political collapse of the continent. The world had been transformed during the course of Benedict's pontificate and his successor would have to confront the consequences.

63 Benedict to Cardinal Gasparri, 5 August 1921, in Koenig, ed., *Principles of Peace*, p. 313; Telegram of Benedict XV to the League of Nations, September 1921, ibid., p. 314.

64 Benedict XV to President Harding, 10 November 1921, and Telegram of Cardinal Gasparri to the Congres Démocratique International, 4 December 1921, ibid., pp. 315–17.

CHAPTER 11

The Vatican between the democracies and the dictatorships in the interwar period

Rome, Italy and the world beyond were surprised by the untimely death of Pope Benedict on 22 January 1922. When the conclave opened on 2 February 1922, a number of names appeared on the short-list of Vatican watchers. The following day the competition revolved between Cardinals Gasparri and La Fontaine, but neither proved able to garner the votes necessary for election. The stalemate was provoked by ideological divisions, complicated by personal animosities, rendering it impossible for either candidate to come to the fore. At this juncture a scramble commenced for a compromise candidate and pointed to the archbishop of Milan, Achille Ratti, who had the support of the more conservative clique of cardinals as well as the more progressive and Francophile forces led by Cardinal Gasparri. The latter reported in his unpublished Memoirs that Merry del Val and his chief supporter at the conclave, de Lai, both incurred excommunication for their attempt to influence the outcome of the papal election. Supposedly de Lai pledged to shift his support to Ratti if the archbishop promised not to select Gasparri as his secretary of state. Ratti rejected the offer, for following his election on 6 February 1922 he retained Gasparri as his secretary of state.[1]

Little was known about the new pope who assumed the name Pius in honour of Pius IX, during whose pontificate he was born, baptized, and commenced his ecclesiastical career, and Pius X, who called him to Rome. Born on 31 May 1857, the fourth son of a working-class family of Desio in the foothills of Lombardy, Ambrogio Damiano Achille Ratti entered the diocesan seminary in 1877, and at the end of 1879 was ordained a priest. Following his studies at the Gregorian university and the Sapienza in Rome, he was assigned to parish work in the village of Barni on Lake Como. In 1882 he began to teach at the seminary of San Carlo in Milan and was appointed to the Ambrosian library the following year, becoming its director in 1907. In 1910 he was called to Rome to serve in the Vatican library, whose prefect he became in

1 Carlo Falconi, *The Popes in the Twentieth Century: From Pius X to John XXIII*, trans. Muriel Grindrod (Boston, 1967), p. 154.

1914. Remaining aloof from contemporary controversies in the refuge of the Library, he nonetheless came to the attention of Cardinal Gasparri, Benedict's secretary of state.

At Gasparri's behest in 1918 the pope appointed Ratti apostolic visitor to Poland. This mission to Warsaw proved a decisive influence in Ratti's life. With the creation of the Polish state in 1919, Ratti was appointed nuncio and assigned the difficult task of regulating church–state relations in this Catholic country. Clearly the Polish war against Bolshevik Russia had an impact on him as the red army in 1920 approached the outskirts of Warsaw, where he was rescued only by a turn in the tide of battle. In 1921 he was transferred to the see of Milan and given the red hat, and following the death of Benedict XV the 65-year-old Ratti was elected pope. Following his coronation, he promised to dedicate his efforts for the good of the church and the pacification of peoples and nations.[2]

Pius, like Benedict, had reservations about the treaties which seemed inspired more by vengeance than reconciliation, and was disappointed when the promise of the League was not fulfilled. He was troubled by the postwar settlement and the conflicting ideologies which it unleashed. Peace could not be re-established simply by silencing the guns, nor could a purely secular league address the world's problems. Pius claimed that the *Summa Theologica* of St Thomas contained the doctrinal bases for a real 'league of nations'.[3]

In April 1922, during the Genoa peace conference in which Bolshevik Russia participated, Pius deplored the dissension between victors and vanquished. He called upon the strong powers to alleviate the world's burdens, commending the conference as a step toward international harmony. Prospects for peace rested not on a forest of bayonets, but in the creation of mutual confidence and the bonding of friendships and the reconciliation of men.[4] In May he dispatched Monsignor Pizzardo, of the secretariat of state, to Genoa to ask Russia to guarantee the complete liberty of religion and provide for the restoration of property belonging to the various religious confessions.[5] Although the Bolshevik response was negative, Pius appealed to the world's bishops for aid for the starving Russian masses. Pointing to the hardships in Russia and other parts of the world, the pope urged remedies for these disasters as he sought to bring Christian peace into the hearts of men, assuming as his motto 'the peace of Christ in the reign of Christ'.[6]

A bibliophile suspicious of party politics and conscious of the limits of diplomacy, Pius presided over a church with a broad diplomatic outreach.

2 *Discorsi di Pio XI*, ed. Domenico Bertetto (Turin, 1959), I, p. 3.
3 Anne Fremantle, ed., *The Papal Encyclicals in their Historical Context* (New York, 1956), p. 223.
4 *Con vivo piacere*, 7 April 1922 , and *Il vivissimo desiderio*, 29 April 1929, in Carlen, *PP*, I, pp. 87–8.
5 Memorandum sent by Cardinal Gasparri to the Diplomatic Representatives at the Genoa Peace Conference, in Harry C. Koenig, ed., *Principles for Peace: Selections from Papal Documents from Leo XIII to Pius XII* (Washington, DC, 1943), pp. 323–4; Edmund A. Walsh, *Why Pope Pius XI Asked Prayers for Russia on March 19, 1930* (New York, 1930), pp. 23–4.
6 *Annus fere iam est*, 10 July 1922, and *Ubi arcano Dei consilio*, 23 December 1922, both in Carlen, *PP*, I, pp. 88, 90.

At his accession, twenty-seven nations were officially represented either by ambassadors or ministers at the Vatican, while semi-official relations were maintained with China, Japan, Turkey and Lithuania. The sacred college was still dominated by the Italians – thirty-three out of a complement of sixty-four – with only six foreign cardinals in the curia.[7] For this reason, and the difficulties confronted by the American cardinals in arriving on time for the opening of a conclave, one of the first acts of the new pope was to amend the constitution *Vacante sede apostolica*, extending the time between the pope's death and the opening of a conclave.[8]

Distrustful of politics, Pius sought to withdraw the church from the political arena, preferring to have the church's interests assured by Catholic action organizations rather than organized Catholic political parties.[9] His *modus operandi* favoured concordats, through which he sought to guarantee the life of ecclesiastical organizations in the various countries. The Vatican, in turn, consecrated the new or revised states, providing recognition for their existence, while depriving Catholic minorities of cause for complaint.[10] Church–state relations in Poland were regularized by a concordat ratified in June 1925.[11] Catholic Hungary remained friendly to the Holy See even though its regent, Admiral Horthy, and many of its important political figures were Protestants. Austria, likewise, sought good relations with the Vatican, as its prime minister after 1922, Monsignor Ignaz Seipel, a Catholic priest and leader of the Christian Socialists, sought a concordat with the Holy See. Even though Vienna remained for years in the hands of the Catholic party, Pius preferred to have the Vatican's rights regularized by a formal agreement.

Early in the century the papacy had tolerated, if it had not encouraged, Catholic political parties, but Pius doubted their efficacy in upholding Catholic rights. Not surprisingly, he was not supportive of the Catholic Popular Party in Italy, even before Mussolini's accession to power at the end of October 1922. The secretary of state and the pope were upset by the charges in Mussolini's *Popolo d'Italia* that Don Sturzo wished to create a ministry of the extreme left which would prove detrimental to the church. Although Mussolini revealed his hostility to the Popular Party and the Catholic democratic movement, the Vatican appreciated fascism's restoration of order.[12] Pius believed that popular democratic governments were subject to disorder and faced the danger of being overthrown by one faction or another.[13]

7 James H. Ryan, 'The Vatican's World Policy', *Current History* (December 1922), pp. 429–38; *AVR*, pp. 76–7.
8 *Cum proxime*, 1 March 1922, in Carlen, *PP*, I, p. 87; William Henry Cardinal O'Connell, *Recollections of Seventy Years* (Boston, 1935); Robin Anderson, *Between Two Wars: The Story of Pope Pius XI (Achille Ratti) 1922–1939* (Chicago, 1977), p. 61.
9 *Discorsi di Pio XI*, I, pp. 39–40, 54–8.
10 Charles Pichon, *The Vatican and its Role in World Affairs*, trans. Jean Misrahi (New York, 1950), pp. 140–1.
11 *AVR*, pp. 51–2, 85–7.
12 *Il Popolo d'Italia*, 22 August 1922; *L'Osservatore Romano*, 1 November 1922; Eugene Beyrens, *Quatre ans à Rome* (Paris, 1934), p. 138.
13 Koenig, ed., *Principles for Peace*, pp. 334–5.

Unquestionably, the pope appreciated that Mussolini did not implement the anticlerical clauses of his party's programme but appeared to court the Vatican by invoking the name of God, restoring the crucifix to the schools and other public buildings, while rooting anticlericalism out of the universities, and freemasonry out of the party. Other concessions followed, with the Gentile educational reform of 1923 restoring religious education in the public elementary schools, while providing Catholic schools parity with the public ones. The improved climate in church–state relations encouraged Gasparri to meet secretly with Mussolini, eventually leading to negotiations for a resolution of the Roman Question. Although the papal secretary of state did not believe fascism would last more than two decades, he realized that Mussolini was capable of making concessions that his liberal predecessors judged inadmissible.[14]

The Vatican recognized that Mussolini would exact a price for his cooperation and the downpayment was the dissolution of the Catholic Popular Party. Neither Pius nor Gasparri considered the bargain unfair, having little faith in the party to provide the protection they sought while doubting it could overturn the law of guarantees. 'The Roman Question will be very difficult to resolve', confided Gasparri. 'There is only one man who could do it – and that is Benito Mussolini.'[15] When *Il Popolo*, the unofficial journal of the Popular Party, showed itself hostile to the Acerbo electoral law, a preliminary step in the establishment of the dictatorship, the Vatican's *Osservatore Romano* proved supportive. Indeed the unofficial journal of the Holy See indicated that since the regime defended Catholic interests, the Partito Populare had lost its *raison d'être*.[16] Not surprisingly, after Monsignor Enrico Pucci implied that Don Sturzo created difficulties between the church and the regime, the Sicilian priest resigned as secretary of the party, and left for London.[17]

The Vatican reciprocated fascist favours by forbidding the Italian clergy from belonging to any political party, expressly condemning Catholic collaboration with the socialists. Even more important, during the Matteotti crisis of 1924, when it appeared the regime would collapse, Mussolini received the crucial support of the church. The Holy See further betrayed its sentiments following the December 1924 assassination attempt on the life of the *duce*, as Pius praised the divine intervention which spared his life.

Relations with France were less cordial. Tension increased following the elections of 1924 which brought the anticlerical cartel des gauches to power as Edouard Herriot prepared to close the French embassy at the Vatican and pursue a policy of laicization at home. In January 1924 Pius issued an encyclical to

14 François Charles-Roux, *Huit ans au Vatican, 1932–1940* (Paris, 1947), pp. 46–8.

15 Nino Tripodi, *I Patti lateranese e il fascismo* (Bologna, 1960), p. 35.

16 'Fascismo e sindicalismo', *Civiltà Cattolica*, 3 March 1923; *L'Osservatore Romano*, 17 March 1923; 28 March 1923; 1 November 1923.

17 Stanley G. Payne, 'Spain: The Church, the Second Republic, and the Franco Regime', in Richard J. Wolff and Jorg K. Hoensch, eds, *Catholics, the State, and the European Radical Right, 1919–1945* (Boulder, 1987), p. 183; *Il Benvenuto a Voi* to the king of Spain, 19 November 1923, in Koenig, ed., *Principles for Peace*, pp. 367–8; *AVR*, p. 40; Antonio Pellicani, *Il Papa di tutti. La Chiesa Cattolica, il fascismo, e il razzismo, 1929–1945* (Milan, 1964), p. 10.

the French, listing the events provoking the present difficulties including the law of separation, and a succession of laws aimed against the freedom and rights of the church in France. A rupture with the republic was avoided when the Herriot government collapsed in the spring of 1925, providing, in the words of Gasparri, an 'Easter egg' for the Vatican.[18]

No such bonanza was forthcoming in the Holy See's difficult relationship with Soviet Russia. The cardinal secretary of state explained the church was not in principle opposed to a communist form of government, implying that in economic matters the Vatican was agnostic. It merely required the state not to interfere with the freedom of worship or its ministers' abilities to discharge their duties. Unfortunately, Vatican overtures were rebuffed. Conditions included the release of Catholics in prison or exiled in Siberia, arrangements for returning confiscated Catholic churches, the right to teach the Catechism to those under eighteen, and the liberty for the pope's representatives to communicate freely with the Catholic clergy in Russia. Although critical of the communist regime, Pius continued to invoke aid for its starving masses. The Pontifical Relief Mission's work in Moscow ended only when it was peremptorily ordered out of the country.[19]

Pius sought improved relations with the democratic French republic. Unlike Pius X, who had been sympathetic to conservative Catholics who opposed the anticlerical measures of the republic, and seemed to favour the anti-democratic, monarchical Action Française, Pius XI proved suspicious of the Action's preference of pagan over Christian culture, and attempts to use Catholicism to achieve its political agenda. Since the movement's support in the French hierarchy was broad with more than half favouring Marras's association, the pope asked Cardinal Andrieu, archbishop of Bordeaux, to condemn the movement, and he did so in August 1926. A week or two later Pius publicly supported the cardinal, emphasizing the errors of the Action Française. The pope deplored those who were Catholics not out of conviction but political interest, criticizing the mistaken sons who preached revolt against the head of the church.[20] Pius insisted that the French clergy as well as the faithful laity submit to the authority of the papacy.[21]

Although prelates of the church functioned as prime ministers of secular states in Austria (Seipel), Czechoslovakia (Sramek) and Yugoslavia (Koroshetz), while Monsignor Kaas led the German Centre party and Monsignor Nolens the majority in the Dutch chamber, Pius continued his policy of withdrawing the church from the political arena. This pope chose to rely on concordats and other bilateral arrangements to consolidate the rights of the church and the position of the Holy See. Thus, during the course of 1927 the Vatican negotiated a concordat with the Lithuanian government. Following the visit of

18 *New York Times*, 4 June 1924; *AVR*, pp. 63, 83.
19 Carlen, *PP*, I, p. 93; *AVR*, p. 68; *Discorsi di Pio XI*, pp. 380–1.
20 Carlen, *PP*, I, p. 95; *AVR*, pp. 104, 109, 119; Anthony Rhodes, *The Vatican in the Age of Dictators, 1922–1945* (New York, 1973), pp. 106–8.
21 *Discorsi di Pio XI*, I, p. 647, II, pp. 49–51.

General Averescu to Rome in September 1926, a concordat was concluded with Rumania, the only postwar accord with a predominantly Orthodox country. The six articles of the *modus vivendi* finalized with Czechoslovakia represented a compromise between those who championed a separation of church and state, and those who desired a concordat to regularize relations.[22] Negotiations with Prussia led to an agreement with its socialist government in 1929, followed by a thirteen-article accord with Baden in 1932.

Talks with the Italian government continued from 1926 through 1927, and by the end of 1927 a complete draft of an agreement with Mussolini's Italy had been elaborated. In 1928 Cardinal Gasparri felt sufficiently confident to authorize official negotiations. On 11 February 1929, on the seventh anniversary of the pope's coronation after more than thirty months of negotiation, an accord was signed by Mussolini, on behalf of the king of Italy, and Cardinal Gasparri, on behalf of the Holy See, in the Lateran palace. The agreement resolved the sixty-year-old conflict between church and state. It included three accords: a conciliation treaty which terminated the troublesome Roman Question and declared Vatican City to be the papacy's neutral and inviolable territory, demanded by Gasparri; a concordat which regulated church–state relations in Italy, on which the pope insisted; and a financial convention intended to provide some compensation for papal territory and possessions confiscated during unification, which the curia wanted.[23]

The treaty established the Holy See as a sovereign state, awarding it some 108 acres with a permanent population of 500, to which was added Castel Gondolfo, the papal summer residence. Under its terms, the Vatican secured most of the outward signs of sovereignty, including its own guards and police. Italy recognized the rights of the Holy See to send its diplomats to foreign countries and receive diplomats according to the prevailing rules of international law. By article 24, the Holy See promised to remain apart from conflicts of a temporal nature and international congresses called for their solution, unless the concerned parties appealed to its mission of peace. The concordat, on which Pius XI had insisted, defined the church's position in the Italian state. It made religious instruction in the secondary as well as the primary schools compulsory, adopted the church position that marriage was a sacrament, and sought the harmony of public policy, legislation, and moral behaviour with church teaching. The fascist state assumed the obligation of enforcing canon law upon the Catholic population, revising its civil legislation so it would be in harmony with Catholic doctrine. Article 43 provided for the immunity of Catholic action from fascist coercion, with the

22 *AVR*, pp. 114, 138; *Concordato fra la Santa Sede e la Republica del Baden*, 12 October 1932, *AAS*, XXV, pp. 177–88.

23 The text of the Lateran Accords can be found *AAS*, XXI, pp. 209–74; *Concordato fra la Santa Sede e l'Italia*, ibid., pp. 275–94; Nino Tripodi, *Patti lateranese e il fascismo* (Bologna, 1960), pp. 267–79 and in Wilfrid Parsons, *The Pope and Italy* (New York, 1929), pp. 81–114. For an analysis of the three documents see Ernesto Rossi, *Il Managnello e l'aspersorio* (Florence, 1958), pp. 227–36.

understanding that such groups refrain from all political activity.[24] The financial settlement, which included some 1,000 million lire in state bonds, gave the Holy See an important stake in the regime. For the Vatican the settlement of the Roman Question represented the preliminary step to a broader conciliation with the modern world.

Despite papal satisfaction with the accords, the devil proved to be in the details. Almost from the first the interpretation and application of the concordat provoked theoretical and practical difficulties between Catholic action and fascism based on irreconciliable differences on the nature of the state and the role of education. In the face of fascism's totalitarian philosophy and designs on education, the pope insisted on the rights of the church in instruction on the basis of both natural law and the recent accords.[25]

The fascists sought to consolidate their totalitarian state by restricting the activities of Catholic organizations and activities, charging they masked political ambitions. Pius, who was not only the 'pope of concordats' but also the 'pope of Catholic action', resented the accusations against the social and educational organizations he cherished. He responded in April 1931, condemning fascist attacks on Catholic action, stressing their non-political character, and emphasizing they were protected by article 43 of the concordat.[26] The *Non abbiamo bisogno*, which followed in June, repudiated fascist claims to dominate all associations and youth groups. 'A conception of the state which makes the young generation belong entirely to it', the holy father warned, 'cannot be reconciled by a Catholic with the Catholic doctrine . . .'[27]

Following fascist violence against Catholic action groups and the pope's spirited protest, an understanding was fashioned on 1 September 1931. Neither pope nor *duce* wanted to squander the obvious advantages derived from the Lateran Accords. The September compromise permitted Catholic action to continue its educational and recreational activities of a religious nature under diocesan control, expressly prohibiting all political action. The fascists, for their part, promised to arrange their activities so as not to interfere with Sunday religious services and other Catholic holidays. Additional restrictions were imposed on Catholic groups, but their existence and independence were not seriously compromised, despite fascist rhetoric. Differences and difficulties remained until the end of Pius's pontificate. The replacement of Cardinal Gasparri by Cardinal Pacelli as secretary of state at the end of 1930 may have changed the tone, but not the tenor of the conflict.

Although much time and effort had been allocated to the resolution of the Roman Question, the Vatican did not abandon the social question which continued to trouble the industrial world. In his longest, and in some ways

24 Carlen, *PP*, I, p. 99; Edward R. Tannenbaum, *The Fascist Experience: Italian Society and Culture, 1922–1945* (New York, 1972), p. 190.
25 *Discorsi di Pio XI*, II, pp. 75–9.
26 Carlen, *PP*, I, p. 104.
27 Fremantle, ed., *Papal Encyclicals*, p. 249.

most important encyclical, *Quadragesimo anno*, on the reconstruction of the social order, issued on the fortieth anniversary of Leo's *Rerum novarum*, Pius denounced the 'inhumanity of employers' and the 'greed of competitors', concurring with Leo that both liberalism and socialism had failed to solve the social problem. In *Quadragesimo anno* Pius returned to Leo's encyclical *Rerum novarum*.[28] Defending private property on the one hand, but refusing to accept labour as another commodity on the other, the pope urged employers and employees to work together to establish reasonable profits while providing equitable wages. Commenting on the establishment of a system of syndicates and corporations by fascist Italy, the papal encyclical championed Christian corporativism rather than the fascist variant inspired by Alfredo Rocco.

Pius had even greater reservations about the programme and policies of the Nazis in Germany, sharing many of the concerns of the German bishops who warned their people against the movement on a half dozen occasions between 1920 and 1928, with some suggesting that Catholicism and Nazism were incompatible. The bishop of Mainz went so far as to forbid the sacraments to any of his flock who joined the movement. The Vatican proved more restrained in its reaction. The Germanophile Cardinal Pacelli tooks pains to reveal that Catholic critics of the party in Germany acted on their own initiative. Hitler, for his part, appreciating the influence of the Catholic church, sent Goering to Rome in May 1931. Pius did not receive Hitler's lieutenant, who met with Monsignor Pizzardi, the undersecretary of state. The pope refused to commit himself *vis-à-vis* the Nazis, while they were simply another group grasping for power. Nonetheless, Pius was troubled by the progress of the movement, which following the elections of 1932 became the strongest party in Germany and continued to display a vulgar anticlericalism. The pope was also distressed by the suppression of the Jesuit Order by the republican government established in Spain in 1931, and the continuing hostility against the faithful and the church in Mexico and Russia.[29]

Undeniably, the Holy See worried about the march of communism, and some suggested that Pius allegedly welcomed Hitler to power as an ally in the crusade against Bolshevism. Observers at the Vatican disagreed, revealing that ecclesiastical circles in Rome responded with considerable misgivings to the accession of Hitler. The Vatican waited to see how Hitler proposed to maintain good relations with the Holy See as he promised, and how he would implement his aim of making Christianity the foundation of the moral life of the German people.[30] The pope revealed his sentiments in March 1933, when he decried the problems plaguing the church and society, engendered by an unjust and exaggerated nationalism.

28 Pius XI's Commemoration of *Rerum Novarum*, 16 May 1926, *Discorsi di Pio XI*, I, pp. 588–95; Koenig, ed., *Principles for Peace*, pp. 426–7.

29 *AVR*, pp. 234, 237; Harry C. Koenig, ed., *Principles for Peace*, pp. 467–8; *AAS*, XXV, pp. 261–74, 275–87.

30 Ibid., p. 250; 'Cronaca Contemporanea', *Civiltà Cattolica*, 10–13 March 1933 and 24 March–6 April 1933; *Discorsi di Pio XI*, II, p. 859.

The Centre party voted with the majority in providing the two-thirds vote necessary to pass the enabling act, which made the Nazi dictatorship possible. Some have seen a connection between the Centre's unanimous vote for this legislation and the Vatican's concern for concluding a concordat with the new Nazi government. Others dispute this contention, noting that the Nazis rather than Rome assumed the initiative in proposing an accord. In the spring of 1933 Franz von Papen, the vice-chancellor, visited the Eternal City and proposed an agreement.[31] The suggestion was not warmly received by Rome, as the pope's undersecretary of state noted that it hardly seemed worth the effort since eighteen of Germany's twenty million Catholics were covered by the provisions of the existing agreements. The Vatican reconsidered its position following the Nazi harassment of the organizational church.[32] Determined to preserve Catholic youth organizations in Germany, which Pius believed would best promote the interests of the faith among the young, and assure a legal rather than a political basis for the religious and educational freedom of the church in the Reich, the pope sanctioned negotiations for a concordat.

The charge that the Vatican betrayed its political supporters in Germany to obtain the agreement founders on the fact that it was clear that the Nazis did not need the concordat to dismantle the Centre. As early as June, Pacelli's private secretary, the Jesuit Father Leiber, observed that the impending collapse of the Centre rendered worthless the pope's promise to remove the clergy from politics.[33] Neither did ratification of the concordat in September 1933 imply that the Vatican sympathized with the Nazi regime. The Jesuit Father Rosa, writing in the *Civiltà Cattolica*, denied that the accord expressed approval of Hitler's government. Indeed the papal secretary of state confessed to the English chargé that he deplored the anti-Semitism of the German government, its brutal treatment of opponents, and the reign of terror it had imposed upon the nation. The Holy See had agreed to the 34-article accord only because it represented the sole means of preventing the destruction of the Catholic church in Germany.

Those who hoped the Reich concordat would function as the Magna Carta of Catholicism in Germany were disappointed. No sooner was it signed than the Reich approved a sterilization law in violation of the doctrines established by Pius XI in his encyclical on Christian marriage. Subsequently, attacks were launched against the clergy, who were charged with violation of currency laws and sexual offences. To the pope's dismay, the persecution of the church in Germany continued throughout most of 1934, increasing after 1935, when the Catholic Saar was returned.

31 'Cronoca Contemporanea', *Civiltà Cattolica*, 7–20 April 1933.

32 '*Concordato fra la Santa Sede ed il Reich Germanico*', *AAS*, 20 July 1933, XXI, pp. 389–408; 'Concordat of the Holy See and Germany', *Catholic World*, August 1933; *AVR*, p. 250; 'Cronaca Contemporanea', *Civiltà Cattolica*, 23 June–6 July 1933.

33 John Jay Hughes, 'The Pope's Pact with Hitler: Betrayal or Self-Defense?', *Journal of Church and State*, XVII (Winter 1975), p. 70; E. Rosa, 'Il Concordato della Santa Sede con la Germania', *Civiltà Cattolica*, LXXXIV (1933), IV, p. 345; Mr Kirkpatrick (the Vatican) to Sir R. Vansittart, 19 August 1933, *Documents on British Foreign Policy, 1919–1939*, series two, vol. v, n. 342, pp. 524–5.

At the end of 1935 the pope deplored events in Germany as well as Russia.[34] The holy father predicted in August 1934 that the church would survive the persecution of the Nazi regime to emerge all the stronger, repeating the message in October.[35] Still, Pius did not renounce the agreement with Hitler's government, fearing it would only aggravate the difficult position of millions of German Catholics. Unquestionably, the Nazi abuses contributed to the Vatican's reconsideration of *Anschluss*, which it had earlier favoured. The Holy See subsequently championed an independent Austria, for which the holy father expressed his love. The Vatican preferred an Austrian state which had as its symbol the cross of God and no other, concluding a concordat with it in 1934. Pius was upset by the abortive Nazi coup of 1934 and the murder of Engelbert Dollfuss, as the *Osservatore Romano* charged that the Nazis were transferring to Vienna the savage methods they employed in Munich and Berlin. The *Osservatore* suggested that National Socialism might more appropriately be dubbed national terrorism. The voice of the Vatican considered the assassination of Dollfuss an act of defiance against Europe and the civilized world. Mussolini, on the other hand, was praised for sending troops to the frontier and preserving Austrian independence in the face of Nazi aggression.[36]

The Vatican proved less supportive of Mussolini's advance into Abyssinia in 1935, urging that the difficulties between Italy and Abyssinia be resolved without recourse to war. Once the conflict opened, for prudential reasons the Holy See assumed a neutral stance. Thus, Pius did not publicly condemn the venture, but did so privately. This left the Italian clergy free to indulge in an orgy of enthusiasm, blessing the banners of departing regiments. However, the pope could not concur with Cardinal Schuster of Milan who proclaimed the conquest a virtual crusade, which opened the area to the Catholic faith and Roman civilization. Pius reportedly remarked in response, 'civilisation à coups de canon!'.[37] Pius privately disapproved of the campaign, fearing it would undermine the regime in Italy while strenthening Bolshevism there. The pope also weighed the unfortunate consequences the fascist campaign in Abyssinia had on Catholic interests in black Africa, and the missions, to which he was devoted.

Pius XI was not only the 'pope of concordats' and the 'pope of Catholic action', but also the 'pope of the missions'. In June 1922, while celebrating the third centenary of the sacred congregation of propaganda, the pope proposed extending the scope and activity of the Society for the Propagation of the Faith, providing for a global reorganization of the century-old society.[38] Pius planned for the society to be structured along national lines, with regional councils in the various countries, affiliated with the existent foreign mission

34 Koenig, ed., *Principles for Peace*, p. 488.
35 Speeches of 29 July 1934, 8 August 1934 and 8 October 1934 in *Discorsi di Pio XI*, III, pp. 183, 188, 218–19.
36 *AVR*, pp. 274–9.
37 *AVR*, p. 328.
38 *Discorsi di Pio XI*, I, pp. 24–5, 30–2.

organizations, and supervised by a general council in Rome, which would also direct its financial affairs. Concerned that the society had been too exclusively under Gallic control, he transferred much of its organization to Rome, which proved beneficial as total gifts to it virtually doubled between 1923 and 1928.

The pope took measures to bolster the position of the faith in Latin America, Southeast Asia, the Congo, as well as South and Central Africa.[39] The conversion of souls he considered a universal obligation. In April 1923, citing the need for the creation of a native clergy, he approved the plans of the Reverend William Gier, general of the Society of the Divine Word, to establish a seminary for the education of Negro priests. In 1923 the pope also erected the first native diocese of Latin rite in India, while instituting the hierarchy of the Malabar church. Fearful that the church's expansion in Asia and Africa would be identified with European imperialism, Pius warned that no religious institute should try to monopolize any mission territory, asserting that the overall direction of conversions abroad rested with the Holy See.

Pius hoped for conversions among the immense population of China,[40] deploring the persecution of the church there. On the feast of Christ the king in 1927, Pius consecrated the first Japanese bishop, Monsignor Hayosaka, and the next year recounted the work of John of Monti Corvino, the first missionary in China, emphasizing the need to establish an indigenous clergy in that vast country. Later in 1929, the pope provided for the co-ordination of missionary work. Following the thought and instructions of Pope Benedict XV, Pius warned missionaries not to succumb to nationalism, transmitting Catholicism, and that alone. Like Benedict, Pius recognized the days of the Eurocentric church were over.

Aware of the pope's effort to disassociate the spread of Catholicism from European imperialism, the Mussolini government recognized the Holy See's reluctance to be identified with the conquest of Abyssinia, and refrained from claiming its support. Pius also disapproved of the close relations between fascist Italy and Nazi Germany that commenced during the Abyssinian War and continued during the course of the civil war in Spain, as the two fascist dictatorships supported the forces of General Francisco Franco. The Vatican feared the consequences of the Rome–Berlin Axis, and the increasing European polarization to which it contributed. Mussolini's selection of the pro-German Galeazzo Ciano as his foreign minister confirmed the pontiff's concern. Internally the pope worried that the fascist regime would emulate the Nazi regime in persecuting the church.[41]

In Spain the Vatican had sought to co-operate with the republic which followed the fall of Primo de Rivera and Alfonso's abdication in 1931, despite the fact that its constitution separated church and state, and the government disbanded the religious orders. Pius protested that the church would adjust to

39 *AAS*, XXI, pp. 233–7, 485; *Discorsi di Pio XI*, I, pp. 15–18; Carlen, *PP*, I, pp. 90, 94.
40 *Discorsi di Pio XI*, I, pp. 703, 710, 735–7; II, pp. 214–15.
41 Pagnatti to Ciano, 8 October 1936, Archivo Storici del Ministero degli Affari Esteri, *busta* 29, *santa sede* 4.

any regime which recognized its rights. The constitution of 1931 was anathema not because of its republican nature but its anticlerical bias. In his encyclical of June 1933, which condemned the persecution of the church in Spain, Pius avoided an attack on the republic. To show his good faith, Pius XI recalled the conservative primate of Spain, Cardinal Segura, and hesitated offending Catholic republicans.

Despite conciliatory gestures on the part of the Vatican, the accession of the popular front government in Spain in 1936 witnessed a renewal of the anticlerical campaign. In July of that year a civil war erupted, and during the first few months of the conflict Pius was informed that republican partisans destroyed over 200 churches and massacred some 7,000 priests, religious and seminarians. Combatting the excesses of the socialists and communists, the Vatican refused to take sides, and did not recognize the Franco regime until the end of the war. 'It is quite erroneous to suppose, as do many peoples today in France and England, that there are simply two camps in the Spanish Civil War – the one the reds, the other the nationalists who are supported by the Vatican', noted the *Osservatore Romano*. This was denied by the Holy See, which explained, 'The church does not belong to any political or social camp. It is not a combatant but a martyr.'[42] For this reason the *Osservatore* supported papal neutrality in the Spanish Civil War, applauding the attempt to build a Catholic front which would steer safely between the Scylla of communism and the Charybidis of fascism.

Although the pope branded communism a grave threat,[43] he was not prepared to join forces with either fascism or Nazism in opposition to this international menace. In his radio address to the universal church at the end of 1936, he revealed that many who claimed to be defenders of civilization against communism were guided by equally false and disastrous notions. Writing in the columns of the *Civiltà Cattolica*, Father Rosa acknowledged the danger of international communism, but insisted that the Nazi reaction was no less destructive of Christian values. While the Nazi strategy differed from the Bolshevist, its neo-pagan opposition to Catholic civilization was as insidious as atheistic communism. Nazism represented the German socialist reaction against Soviet internationalism, declared another article in the Jesuit journal, and while the latter seemed to move in an opposite direction, it was aligned with the former in opposing Christianity and the Catholic church.[44]

The *Osservatore*'s assessment proved accurate as the Reich continued to restrict the rights and activities of the institutional church, imposing laws which contradicted its basic teachings. Membership in the Hitler Youth was declared compulsory for all young Germans, and even seminarians were pressured to

42 Rhodes, *The Vatican in the Age of Dictators*, p. 124.

43 *Discorsi di Pio XI*, III, p. 487; Carlen, *PP*, I, p. 110; 'Discorso inaugurale del Papa alla mostra stampa catolica', *Civiltà Cattolica*, 12 May 1936, anno 87 (1936), II, 419; Koenig, ed., *Principles for Peace*, pp. 495–7.

44 E. Rosa, 'Gli estremi opositi nella crisi della civiltà', *Civiltà Catholica*, anno 87 (1936), II, p. 91; 'L'Internazionale della Barbarie nella sua lotta contro la civiltà', ibid., III, pp. 447–8; 'Il pericolo russo e i progressi dell' invasione communistica', ibid., III, p. 266.

join their ranks, while the attacks upon the Catholic schools continued. Pius let the German ambassador know that he was 'deeply grieved and gravely displeased'.[45] The violence and intimidation persisted, to the consternation of the pope, whose resolve was reinforced by the reports of the German bishops who visited Rome. Despite the advice of Cardinal Pacelli, who hoped that a more patient Vatican policy might eventually lead to an improvement in relations with the Reich, the pope determined to act. Having condemned the persecution of the church in Spain and Russia, he felt constrained to do likewise when it occurred in Germany. On 14 March 1937 he issued the encyclical, *Mit brennender sorge*, cataloguing the abuses heaped upon the church in Germany.

On Passion Sunday the papal encyclical was read from Catholic pulpits in Germany wherein with deep anxiety and increasing dismay Pius pointed to the progressive oppression of the faithful in the Reich. Without mentioning the anti-Semitic laws of 1933, or the Nuremburg race laws of 1935, the pope proceeded to focus on the violations of the concordat. Not mincing words, Pius insisted that the believer had an inalienable right to pursue his faith and follow its dictates, observing that laws which impeded the profession and practice of this faith were against the natural law. He likewise railed against the attempts to discredit the Old Testament, charging that whoever wished to banish it from church and school blasphemed the name of God. At once exposing the fallacies of pantheism and racism, he denounced the attempts to alienate Catholics from the church in favour of state loyalty. The pope concluded by calling upon the clergy to unmask and refute error whatever its form or disguise, while urging the faithful to preserve those rights which the concordat had guaranteed the church.[46] The Hitler government considered the encyclical a 'call to battle against the Reich'.[47]

In 1938 the pope condemned the exaggerated nationalism, personified by the Hitler regime, as a veritable curse.[48] In a speech of 15 July 1938, the pope noted that this nationalism opposed the spirit of the creed and violated the teachings of the faith. The persecution distressed the holy father not only as father of the faithful but as a simple man who saw human dignity degraded and destroyed.[49] Only the intervention of Pacelli prevented a complete break with the Nazi regime. The mediation of the secretary of state did not escape the notice of the German ambassador, who advised his foreign minister that 'cardinal Pacelli constantly strives to pacify, and to exert a moderating influence on the pope, who is difficult to manage and to influence'.[50]

The pope was also dismayed by Mussolini's increasing emphasis on totalitarianism and racism as he moved closer to Hitler's Germany. 'Almost

45 *Documents on German Foreign Policy, 1918–1945 from the Archives of the German Foreign Ministry*, Series C, IV, n. 482.
46 *Mit Brennender Sorge*, 14 March 1937, in Carlen, *PE*, III, pp. 525–35.
47 *Documents on German Foreign Policy*, Series D, I, n. 633.
48 Koenig, ed., *Principles for Peace*, pp. 539–40; ibid., p. 545; *AVR*, pp. 370, 379; *Discorsi di Pio XI*, III, p. 770.
49 Koenig, ed., *Principles for Peace*, pp. 548–9.
50 *Documents on German Foreign Policy*, Series C, IV, n. 482.

everywhere it is said that everything belongs to the State, that is the totalitarian State, as it is called; nothing without the State, everything for the State', the pope complained. 'There is an error here so evident, that it is astonishing that men, otherwise serious and talented, say it and teach it to the masses . . .'[51] The pope left Rome for Castel Gandolfo early in May 1938 when Hitler visited Rome, unwilling to see either the *führer* or a cross, other than the cross of Christ, flaunted in the Holy City. The pontiff ordered the Vatican museum, which Hitler had hoped to visit, closed. Pius was angered and aroused by fascist Italy's racialist and anti-Semitic policy following the aryan manifesto issued on 14 July 1938. The pope urged Catholic action associations to combat it, initiating a chorus of opposition to the racism of the totalitarian regimes. Pius proceeded to condemn racism as contrary to the universality of the faith, while Cardinal Shuster denounced it as an international danger.[52]

In June 1938 the pope asked to see the American Jesuit John La Farge, the author of a number of books on racism. Pius XI had read and liked La Farge's *Interracial Justice* which had been published in 1937. To La Farge's surprise the pope asked him to draft an encyclical demonstrating the incompatibility of Catholicism and racism, to be delivered to the universal church. La Farge accepted the task. When he informed the general of his Order, Vladmir Ledochowski, of his assignment and the pope's desire to have the encyclical in his hands quickly, the latter suggested that he collaborate with two other Jesuits: the Frenchman Gustave Desbuquois of Action Popolaire, a social action centre in Paris, and the German Gustav Gundlach, a social theorist and professor at the Gregorian university in Rome. The three worked feverishly during the summer of 1938 to prepare a draft, and in late September placed this encyclical entitled *Humani generis unitas* (Of the unity of the human race) in the hands of Ledochowski for transmission to the pope.

While the three Jesuits met the pope's deadline for the issuance of a condemnation of racism, delay was the order of the day once it left their hands. It seems that Ledochowksi passed it on to Enrico Rosa at the *Civiltà Cattolica*, who shared it with others, but apparently not the pope. Gundlach, angry and astounded, suspected that his superiors, and especially Lodochowski, opposed the encyclical's denunciation of racism and therefore sought to scuttle it. 'An outsider might well see in all this an attempt to sabotage by dilatoriness and for tactical and diplomatic reasons the mission entrusted to you by [the Pope]', he wrote to La Farge, who had returned to the United States.[53]

The long encyclical condemned anti-Semitism as reprehensible and 'did not permit the Catholic to remain silent in the presence of racism'.[54] Even before

51 *AVR*, p. 547.
52 *New York Times*, 17 July and 22 July 1938, 12 August 1938, 8 September 1938.
53 Frederick Brown, 'The Hidden Encyclical', *New Republic*, XXVII (15 April 1996), p. 30.
54 Galleys of La Farge's copy of the encyclical *Humani Generis Unitas* preserved in the La Farge papers at Woodstock College in New York City and which was supposed to be published in *Catholic Mind* in 1973 but somehow never appeared. In 1996 the hidden encyclical was published by Georges Passelecq and Bernard Suchecky in a volume called *L'Éncyclique 'cachée' de Pie XI*. My reference is to the galleys of the encyclical for the *Catholic Mind*, p. 31, paragraph 123.

the onset of the 'final solution', the encyclical written for Pius XI noted that the struggle for racial purity 'ends by being uniquely the struggle against the Jews'.[55] Fully aware that Pius XI deplored this anti-Semitism in both Italy and Germany, the authors reported that such persecution had been censured by the Holy See in the past. 'As a result of such a persecution, millions of persons are deprived of the most elementary rights and privileges of citizens in the very land of their birth', the encyclical continued.[56] Indeed the authors warned that this anti-Semitism served as an excuse for attacking the sacred person of the Saviour himself, degenerating into a war against Christianity.

In early December 1938 Mussolini published a decree forbidding marriage between Italian Aryans with persons of another race, aligning fascist Italy with Nazi Germany, and raising the spectre of a joint persecution of the church. The pope responded in his Christmas allocution, attacking this racist measure as another violation of the concordat. This denunciation revealed that Pius XI continued to share the sentiments of the encyclical he had inspired, but no word arrived of its release. There was little opportunity to explore this with the pope, whose health was already declining and whose schedule was closely controlled and severely curtailed. Furthermore, given the hierarchical structure of the church and the quasi-military discipline of their order, none of the three Jesuits considered appealing to the pope over the heads of the superiors who were jealous of their positions and determined to preserve the lines of authority. Nonetheless, they complained about the conspiracy of silence which seemed to envelop the condemnation of racism the pope had authorized.

The new year did not bring any improvement in relations between the Vatican and the fascist regimes, as an exhausted and increasingly sick Pius was known to be working on an address on church–state relations and the Lateran Accords to be presented to the Italian bishops gathered in Rome on 11 February 1939 for the tenth anniversary of the Lateran Pacts. A rough draft of this last discourse was published by Pope John XXIII in February 1959.[57] Gundlach wondered if the draft of their encyclical would ever be presented to the pope. On 10 February 1939 Pius XI died and was succeeded in early March by Cardinal Eugenio Pacelli. Mussolini was relieved to hear of his death. Gundlach, who had known Pacelli for years, did not share the *duce*'s enthusiasm. He was not surprised when the draft of the encyclical was returned to its authors with an indication that they might publish it privately, but under their own names and only following its review by a censor. They chose not to do so, hoping that those higher up in the church would change their minds and publish it.[58] They never did, not during the course of the war, during the Holocaust, or in the postwar period.

55 Ibid., p. 33, paragraph 131.
56 Ibid., paragraph 132.
57 *AAS*, LI, pp. 129–35.
58 Brown, 'Hidden Encyclical', p. 30.

CHAPTER 12

The diplomacy and 'silence' of Pope Pius XII during the Second World War

During the last months of his pontificate, Pius XI (1922–39) feared the outbreak of another war and its impact on the church, Europe and the world. The ailing pope believed that if anyone could avert the impending catastrophe it was Eugenio Pacelli, his secretary of state since 1930. Although Pius XI relied on Pacelli for his diplomatic expertise, some saw obstacles to his succession as pope. Few papal secretaries of state had gone on to assume the tiara. Furthermore, all the pontiffs since Gregory XVI in 1831 had gone to the Vatican from an Italian see. Pacelli, on the other hand, had spent his entire clerical life in the papal secretariat of state and lacked pastoral experience. Finally, for more than 200 years, no Roman had occupied the papal throne. However, on Pacelli's birthday, 2 March 1939, the 63-member conclave, the shortest since 1623, shattered precedent and elected him pope.[1] He took the name Pius XII, in honour of his predecessor.

Eugenio Maria Giuseppe Giovanni Pacelli was born in 1876 in the shadow of the Vatican, the second child of the lawyer Ernesto Filippo Pacelli, a member of the 'black' or papal nobility, dean of the Vatican law corps, and head of the Bank of Rome. Pacelli studied at the Gregorian university and was ordained a priest in April 1899, entering the Vatican secretariat of state in 1901. Subsequently, from 1904 until 1916 he worked with Cardinal Pietro Gasparri in codifying the canon law while teaching international law at the academy of noble ecclesiastics from 1909 until 1914. In 1915 Pacelli, who spoke flawless German as well as six other languages, was sent as Benedict's envoy to Franz Josef, and two years later was dispatched as papal nuncio to Bavaria, entrusted with the pope's peace effort in the Reich. As apostolic nuncio he was stationed in Berlin in 1925, remaining there until the end of 1929 when he was recalled to Rome and given the red hat. In February 1930 he replaced his old friend and teacher Pietro Gasparri as secretary of state.[2]

1 *Conclave et Exaltio. SSMI Domini Nostri PII. XII, AAS*, XXXI, pp. 101–27.
2 *Curriculum Vitae PP. XII*, ibid., XXXI, p. 129.

As secretary of state he continued to support the pope's concordatarian policy, having negotiated agreements with Bavaria (1924), Prussia (1929), Baden (1932), Austria (1933), and Germany. The most controversial of his concordats was the one concluded with Hitler's Reich in the summer of 1933. In 1936 Pacelli made a month-long visit to the United States and was received by President Roosevelt at his family residence in Hyde Park, New York. He returned to France and the United States in 1937, and the following year ventured to Budapest where he championed a crusade of sorts against communism.

A diplomat par excellence, the secretary of state played an important part in drafting Pius XI's *Mit brennender sorge* of 14 March 1937, which condemned Nazism's myths of blood and race and the persecution of the church in Hitler's Germany, but sought to prevent a break between Berlin and the Vatican. Pacelli's close association with the former pope led most to conclude he would continue Pius XI's policies. This explains why part of the German press was unenthusiastic at the election of the aloof Pacelli, although von Plessen of the German embassy commented that 'a careful diplomat is undoubtedly better than an impulsive, irascible old man'.[3] In a radio message the day after his selection, Pius chose as his theme 'peace is the work of justice'.[4] The church and the papacy faced difficulties that were sufficient, in the words of the future John XXIII, to turn one's hair white.

Pius XII selected as his secretary of state the Neapolitan Cardinal Luigi Maglione and former nuncio to Paris, who was considered a Francophile.[5] However, from the first Pius was determined to conciliate Nazi Germany and fascist Italy. Pius perceived his democratic and anti-Axis secretary of state not as a collaborator, as he himself had been with Pius XI, but as a minister to implement the policies he outlined, especially as regards German affairs. Above all, Pacelli sought to dispel Berlin's fears that he would continue the criticism of the Reich initiated by the former pope. Following the accession of Pius XII, the German ambassador noted the relaxation of tension between the Vatican and the Reich.[6] There was a muting of the language and a modulation of the tone in the Vatican newspapers. One of Pacelli's first actions was to call together the German cardinals, revealing his intention of sending a letter to Hitler announcing his accession. Pacelli refrained from addressing the German leader as 'dearly beloved son', opting instead for *führer*.[7]

Some suspected that Pacelli's friendliness to the German people, appreciation of German culture, and desire to achieve a *modus vivendi* with the Reich, translated to support for Hitler and the Nazis. This suspicion was reinforced

3 W.A. Purdy, *The Church on the Move: The Characters and Policies of Pius XII and John XXIII* (New York, 1966), p. 27.

4 *Nuntius Radiophonicus*, 3 March 1939, *AAS*, XXXI, pp. 86–7; Carlen, *PP*, I, p. 115.

5 *AAS*, XXXI, p. 136.

6 *Records and Documents of the Holy See Relating to the Second World War: The Holy See and the War in Europe, March 1938 – August 1940* (Washington, DC, 1968), I, pp. 4, 105; *Documents of German Foreign Policy 1918–1945 from the Archives of the German Foreign Ministry*, Series D, 1937–1945 IV, nn. 473, 475.

7 Hanjakob Stehle, *Eastern Politics of the Vatican*, trans. Sandra Smith (Athens, 1981), p. 67.

in March 1939 when Hitler violated the Munich agreement and his troops occupied Prague and the remaining Czech territory, and the Vatican issued no condemnation. Instead, the pro-German, some said pro-Hitler, nuncio in Berlin, Cesare Orsenigo, blamed the 'nationalist fanaticism of the new generation'. Pius, meanwhile, refused to intervene when the Nazis pressured the Poles for a series of concessions, maintaining a strict neutrality between aggressor and aggrieved. It was the duty of the Holy See to serve truth and promote peace, he informed the college of cardinals.[8]

In an April 1939 audience, granted to a group of German pilgrims, the pope avoided the condemnations of Pius XI, substituting protestations of his sympathies for the Reich and its people. 'We have always loved Germany, where We were able to spend many years of Our life, and we love Germany even more today', Pius confided. 'For this reason, however, We desire that the rights of God and the Church be always recognized . . .'[9] German diplomats were likewise courted and given the impression that the pope was prepared to make concessions and favoured a *Burgfriede* or public truce, so long as vital church institutions and Catholic principles were not endangered.[10] As Europe veered inexorably towards war, the pope hastened to preserve the neutrality of the Holy See while serving as peacemaker and mediator. The French ambassador to the Vatican, François Charles Roux, urged Pius to make it clear that by provoking a crisis the burden of guilt would fall on Nazi Germany.[11] The pope refused to do so, antagonizing the French who resented the Vatican's placing the democracies and the totalitarian states on an equal plane, refusing to make any distinction.

At the beginning of June, Pius launched an appeal for peace, but refused to become embroiled in the territorial disputes of the rival Powers. This neutralism was reinforced by the nuncio to Paris, Cardinal Valerio Valeri, who informed the French that while the Holy See endeavoured to improve relations among nations, it could not compromise its neutrality or its mediation efforts. While the papal position won support in the axis camp, the French were furious with the 'diplomatic dance' conducted by the Vatican, while Catholics and the church were persecuted in the Reich. Conceding that all had expected some change from the course pursued by his predecessor, the French ambassador Charles Roux reported that many in France found the differences excessive.

The nuncio defended the papal position, asserting that under the grave international relations and the impending crisis, the Holy See had to preserve its contacts with the two blocs in Europe. The French ambassador responded that the Holy See could fulfil its mission in one of two ways: by relying on

8 *Records and Documents of the Holy See Relating to the Second World War*, I, pp. 93–6, 146; Harry C. Koenig, ed., *Principles for Peace: Selections from Papal Documents from Leo XIII to Pius XII* (Washington, DC, 1943), p. 555.

9 George O. Kent, 'Pope Pius XII and Germany: Some Aspects of German-Vatican Relations, 1933–1943', *American Historical Review*, LXX (October 1964), p. 65.

10 William M. Harrigan, 'Pius XII's Efforts to Effect a Detente in German-Vatican Relations, 1939–1940', *Catholic Historical Review*, XLIX, 2 (July 1963), p. 184.

11 *Records and Documents of the Holy See Relating to the Second World War*, I, p. 211.

politics and diplomacy, or by asserting and standing on the principles which the papacy and church cherished, and which were completely contrary to the fascist doctrines. The second seemed the more appropriate, but Pius thought otherwise, choosing to rely on his forty years of diplomatic experience.

The Vatican resorted to diplomatic channels to achieve its ends, and in July 1939 relied on the intervention of Mussolini and the Italian foreign service to halt the persecution of the church in the Reich, and in the recently incorporated Austria. On Monday 24 July 1939 Pius XII received Casimir Papee, the extraordinary ambassador from the beleaguered Polish state.[12] As the diplomatic situation continued to deteriorate, the Holy See received identical communications from the Berlin and Rome embassies asking the pope to submit a peace proposal for consideration by the allies. It included a thirty-day truce to organize a conference of the foreign ministers of France, Great Britain, Italy and Germany, which would resolve the Danzig question by mutual agreement. Subsequently, the British government would submit the proposed solution for Polish acceptance.[13] Neither London nor Paris was willing to coerce Warsaw into accepting a proposal that smacked of a 'second Munich'.

On the eve of the war, 31 August 1939, Pius begged the governments of Germany and Poland to avoid all incidents, refraining from any action that would aggravate the existing situation.[14] His effort failed; on 1 September 1939 German forces invaded Poland. Still preserving his impartiality, Pius failed to raise his voice to condemn the aggression.[15] Publicly Pius refused to pass judgement, insisting that as vicar of the Prince of Peace he had to remain above the fray.[16] From the first the papal failure to condemn the aggression provoked criticism. It led to an unoffical Vatican explanation that the Holy See did not wish to unleash any retaliation against the Poles, adding that its silence should not lead to the conclusion that the pope was indifferent to the plight of Poland.[17]

On 20 October 1939 Pius addressed his first encyclical to the Church, *Summi pontificatus*, on the limitations of the authority and function of the state in the modern world. In it he harped upon the 'fundamental errors' of the age. Among these Pius cited forgetfulness of the law of human solidarity, and the failure to recognize that the nations, despite their differences in development, were destined not to break the unity of the human race.[18] While the pope's

12 *Diarum Romane Curie, AAS*, XXXI, p. 322.

13 *Records and Documents of the Holy See Relating to the Second World War*, I, pp. 169, 177, 203.

14 *Records and Documents of the Holy See Relating to the Second World War*, I, pp. 183–4; Carlen, *PP*, I, p. 116; Koenig, ed., *Principles for Peace*, pp. 584–7; Letter of 31 August 1939, *AAS*, XXXI, pp, 335–6.

15 François Charles-Roux, *Huit ans au Vatican* (Paris, 1947), p. 343.

16 Allocution of 14 September 1939, *AAS*, XXXI, pp. 367–9.

17 Charles-Roux, *Huit ans au Vatican*, p. 343; *New York Times*, 1 October 1939, 15 October 1939.

18 Encyclical Letter, 20 October 1939, *AAS*, XXXI, pp. 454–80; Anne Fremantle, ed., *The Papal Encyclicals in their Historical Context* (New York, 1956), pp. 263–7; Koenig, ed., *Principles for Peace*, pp. 595–616; *Selected Documents of His Holiness Pope Pius XII: 1939–1958* (Washington, DC, n.d.), pp. 1–48; Jan Olav Smit, *Angelic Shepherd: The Life of Pope Pius XII* (New York, 1950), pp. 158–63.

encyclical rejected exaggerated nationalism and condemned the claims of absolute state authority, Pius did not abandon his prudent, diplomatic policy. His 'denunciation' of totalitarianism was general and as applicable to the Soviet Union as to Nazi Germany. The pope proved somewhat more direct in his letter of 10 November 1939 to the new minister of Haiti, proclaiming that the preservation of the peace required the renunciation of the cult of might against right. At this early date, the pope pleaded for the formation of a fruitful international organization which would assure the reciprocal independence of small and large nations, while safegarding the liberty, human dignity and prosperity of all.[19]

Across the Atlantic, President Franklin Delano Roosevelt on 24 December 1939 sent a Christmas letter to Pius XII, as head of the Roman Catholic church, expressing his intention of dispatching a personal representative to the Holy See. Subsequently, Myron C. Taylor, an Episcopalian layman, was granted the rank of extraordinary ambassador to the pope as the president's personal representative. President Roosevelt appreciated the intricate network of international representation which had the Vatican at its centre, and which could be of incalculable service to American peace efforts. It also suited the Vatican.[20]

Pius perceived the arrival of the American representative as an act of solidarity between the old world and the new against the aggressively anti-Christian tendencies threatening the fountainhead of Western civilization. Although Taylor was termed 'ambassador extraordinary', the Holy See considered him a fully fledged ambassador. To be sure, Taylor was not confirmed by the American senate, and no funds were appropriated for his mission, but he nonetheless acted as a regular diplomat. Perhaps the knowledge that the American representative would be by his side emboldened the pope to permit Vatican radio on 22 January 1940 to broadcast a detailed report on Nazi atrocities and persecution of the Poles.[21]

On 11 March 1940 the German foreign minister Joachim von Ribbentrop, accompanied by the German ambassador to the Vatican, Diego von Bergen, was received by Pius. He presented a German peace proposal that the pontiff recognized as being unacceptable to the allies. The pope, viewing the German initiative as essentially a propaganda ploy, took the opportunity to catalogue Nazi abuses against the church in the Reich and cited reports he had received of the inhuman treatment of civilians in the occupied territories. Distressed by the diplomatic, although obviously critical position of the papacy, Hermann Wilhelm Goering, Reich minister of aviation, asked Alfieri how the Vatican would react should Italy enter the war. The Italian ambassador to the Vatican

19 Allocution to Minister of Haiti, 10 November 1939, in *AAS*, XXXI, pp. 674–6.

20 Koenig, ed., *Principles for Peace,* p. 640.

21 Myron C. Taylor, ed., *Wartime Correspondence between President Roosevelt and Pope Pius XII* (New York, 1947), pp. 22–3, 33; Carlen, *PP*, I, p. 117; George A. Flynn, 'Franklin Roosevelt and the Vatican: The Myron Taylor Appointment', *Catholic Historical Review*, LVIII, 2 (July 1972), pp. 185–7.

revealed the reaction would be unfavourable. Goering worried that this negative attitude might affect public opinion in the United States, but reassured the Italians the war would be short.[22]

Mussolini, inching towards intervention, was spurred by the Nazi invasion of Denmark and Norway in April, and the subsequent British withdrawal from Norway, but deterred by the opposition of the king, the Vatican and Italian public opinion. Early in the morning on 10 May 1940, German forces crossed the borders of the Netherlands, Belgium and Luxemburg as the Vatican had been forewarned by Father Robert Leiber. The Holy See had alerted Italy's Crown Prince Umberto, whose wife was a Belgian, to the impending invasion. Tardini drafted a papal letter dated 13 March 1940 implicitly condemning the German invasion of neutral Belgium, Holland and Luxemburg, but the pope chose not to release it. By mid-month the Germans pushed into France. Pius responded by sending messages of condolence to the victims, expressing his regret to Belgium's King Leopold that his people again had their homeland subjected to the cruelties of war. Similar regrets were dispatched to Queen Wilhelmina of Holland, and to the Grand Duchess Charlotte of Luxemburg, as the pope implored God to hasten their deliverance. Although the Germans were not mentioned, this represented the most courageous papal criticism of aggression, leading some to hope that Pius would say more. He hesitated in doing so.[23]

The pope's telegrams of sympathy did not pinpoint the responsibility of the Nazis or condemn their aggression, much to the discomfort and bewilderment of the French ambassador, François Charles Roux, who regretted the failure to specify the crime and the criminals. Nonetheless, they angered Mussolini, who was on the verge of entering the conflict, anxious to share in the spoils. The *duce*, having determined to send Alfieri from the Vatican to Berlin, had his departing envoy convey his extreme displeasure to the pope over the telegrams, hindering the distribution of the *Osservatore Romano* in which they were printed. The holy father found the *duce*'s irritation incomprehensible inasmuch as the aggression had been the work of Hitler not Mussolini, adding that he had done no more than his duty, and while he did not wish to give offence to anyone, he could not remain silent when his conscience and apostolic ministry constrained him to speak.[24] When Mussolini entered the conflict in June 1940, the *Osservatore Romano* published the declaration of war without any comment.

Unable to stop the spread of the war, during the remainder of 1940 the pope harped upon many of the themes Benedict XV had proclaimed during the First World War, including the conviction that real peace was virtually

22 Smit, *Angelic Shepherd*, p. 215; Oscar Halecki, *Eugenio Pacelli: Pope of Peace* (New York, 1951), pp. 143–4; Dino Alfieri, *Dictators Face to Face*, trans. David Moore (Westport, CT, 1978), pp. 9–11, 26.

23 Carlo Felice Casula, *Domenico Tardini (1888–1961). L'Azione della Santa Sede nella crisis fra le due guerre* (Rome, 1989), p. 163; Koenig, ed., *Principles for Peace*, pp. 668–9.

24 Alfieri, *Dictators Face to Face*, pp. 16–17; *Records and Documents of the Holy See Relating to the Second World War*, I, pp. 75–7.

impossible outside the rules of justice and charity promulgated by the Gospel.[25] During the course of 1940 and more so in 1941, the Vatican received detailed reports of Nazi atrocities in the occupied territories as well as vivid accounts of their persecution of the church. The pope lamented the suffering unleashed by modern warfare and the evils weighing upon entire populations. His oblique criticism failed to satisfy those horrified by the Nazi atrocities. It was charged that in his mania for neutrality Pius failed to act as the conscience of a troubled world, undermining the spiritual and moral mission of the papacy.

Taylor and his assistant Harold Titmann repeatedly warned the Holy See of the danger to its moral leadership posed by the failure to denounce the notorious Nazi violations of the moral and natural law. The pope did not heed the advice and continued to move cautiously, preserving an even-handed position between the axis and the allies. Even when the Vatican received reports of the euthanasia programme in Germany at the end of 1940, no formal protest was lodged. Various voices, including a number of cardinals close to the Holy See, urged Pius XII to follow the example of Pius XI and publicly denounce the Nazi persecution of the church in Germany. His silence, they argued, caused confusion and consternation among the faithful. Pius disagreed, and continued to pursue his diplomatic approach, carefully watching his words following the German invasion of the Soviet Union on 22 June 1941. In a *note verbale* from the secretariat of state to the German embassy, the Vatican decried the violations of the concordat of 1933 and the Nazi attacks upon the divine, natural and positive law. However, the tone of the message was moderate and its focus restricted.[26]

President Roosevelt asked the Vatican to moderate its anti-communist stance. The American president concluded that the survival of Russia would prove less dangerous to religious life than the survival of the Nazi dictatorship.[27] Pius disagreed. Despite his possession of facts which contradicted Roosevelt's optimistic appraisal of communist policy, the pope did not openly challenge the Americans on whom he increasingly relied. In fact, Pius issued instructions that his predecessor's March 1937 encyclical on communism, *Divini redemptoris*, might be interpreted broadly. Shortly thereafter, Archbishop John McNicholas of Cincinnati drafted a letter which drew a distinction between Catholic sympathy for the Russian people during their time of trouble, and continuing Catholic opposition to communism. In this fashion the Vatican provided support for Roosevelt's lend-lease programme for the Soviet Union.[28]

Vatican sensitivity to American sentiments did not prevent it from resuming talks with the Japanese imperial government about opening diplomatic relations. These negotiations were still in progress when the Japanese attacked

25 Koenig, ed., *Principles for Peace*, pp. 670–9, 684–704.
26 Kent, 'Pope Pius XII', pp. 67, 71; *Documents on German Foreign Policy*, Series C, I, n. 501; Carlo Falconi, *The Silence of Pius XII*, trans. Bernard Wall (Boston, 1970), p. 247.
27 Taylor, *Wartime Correspondence*, p. 61.
28 John S. Conway, 'A German National Reich Church and American War Propaganda', *Catholic Historical Review*, LXIII, 3 (July 1976), pp. 469–70.

the United States at Pearl Harbor, and continued even as the United States declared war on Japan, and Nazi Germany and fascist Italy declared war on the United States. At the end of March 1942, Japan and the Vatican established diplomatic relations. This created considerable ill-will in the United States, where the move was perceived as providing legitimacy for the warlike regime. By this time, the three major axis states had diplomatic relations with the Vatican, whereas neither of the Anglo-Saxon powers maintained regular relations with the Holy See.

On the other hand, the Vatican steadfastly refused to support the Nazi invasion of Russia or to denounce 'allied atrocities'. The pope informed Attolico that if he had to denounce the Bolshevik violations, he would feel constrained to denounce those of the Nazis as well. He threatened that were he to speak out one day, he would have to say everything. Monsignor Domenico Tardini reported that although communism was the worst enemy of the church, it was not the only one, because the Nazis continued their persecution. Observing that the swastika was hardly a crusader's cross, Tardini added if the Holy See had to call attention to the horrors of communism, it would have likewise to denounce those of Nazism. He preferred to see these 'demons' exorcise one another.[29]

The Vatican, likewise, revealed its independence of the totalitarian dictators on the Croatian question, opposing the forced conversions of the Serbs in Croatia. Nor did the Holy See hesitate to protest Slovakia's deportation of Jews. It encouraged the Slovak bishops to dispatch a protest (7 October 1941) to Father Tiso the Slovak president, denouncing the Jewish code. When this priest replied that he perceived no conflict between Nazi principles and Catholic doctrine, the papal undersecretary of state retorted he might have to remove Tiso's name from the list of *monsignori*. This strategy proved successful. The Vatican and the Slovak hierarchy, working together, halted the deportation of Jews.[30]

A quiet papal diplomacy also intervened on behalf of the Jews in Rumania. No sooner were the first racial laws promulgated there in July 1940, than the nuncio, Andrea Cassulo, objected and managed to wring concessions for baptized Jews from the Antonescu government. By 1941, the nuncio broadened his efforts, and in October of that year appealed not only on behalf of converted Jews but the non-converted as well. His pleas went unanswered, and the following year the Antonescu government made plans to deport Jews, prompting new protests in August and September 1942. As a consequence of these and other developments, the Rumanian government did not implement the threatened deportations. 'For two long years, when the deportation of Rumanian

29 Attolico to Ciano, 16 September 1941, *I Documenti Diplomatici Italiani*, series IX, vol. 7 (Rome, 1987), pp. 580–1; Stehle, *Eastern Politics*, p. 209.
30 Falconi, *The Silence of Pius XII*, p. 304; Pinchas Lapide, *Three Popes and the Jews* (New York, 1967), p. 138; Richard J. Wolff, 'The Catholic Church and the Dictatorships in Slovakia and Croatia, 1939–1945', *Records of the American Catholic Historical Society of Philadelphia* (1978), pp. 10–12.

Jewry was already decided and about to be carried out', wrote the chief rabbi of Rumania, 'the high moral authority of the Nuncio saved us . . . he prevailed so that the deportations should not take place . . .'[31]

The Holy See proved more cautious and circumspect in resisting Hitler, whose power was greater than that of the 'little dictators', and who could do great harm to the church and to the millions subject to his whim. The persistent refusal of the Nazi government to answer the Holy See's queries and appeals led the pope to conclude that even less would be obtained by public denunciations, for these might render more brutal the *Kulturkampf* confronted by the church in Nazi-occupied Europe. In one of his radio addresses, the pope sought to explain to the faithful, and perhaps to himself, why Divine Providence permitted the indescribable suffering caused by the fury and brutalization of the war. 'Can an omnipotent God, infinitely wise and infinitely good, possibly allow so many evils which He might so easily prevent?', he asked. How could He allow the apparent triumph of such evil by His silence? Pius responded that man must trust in God, who sees and judges not in the short-sighted vision of times and proximate causes, but in their remote effects. In Pius's words, such trust in God 'means believing that God can permit at times . . . the tormenting of innocent, peaceful, undefended, helpless men'.[32]

In his Christmas message of 1942, the pope came closest to openly revealing his sympathy for those 'who without fault on their part, sometimes only because of race or nationality, have been consigned to death or to a slow decline'.[33] In May 1942 Pius was informed of the mass extermination of Jews from Germany, Poland and the Ukraine, with more than 100,000 murdered in the Ukraine alone. Nonetheless, Pius still refused to publicly condemn the horror, fearing the consequences of such denunciations for those subject to the Nazi occupation and the well-being of the organizational church. Vatican officials defended this stance, claiming that the Holy See could not condemn Nazi atrocities without denouncing Bolshevik brutalities.[34]

During the last years of the war, the pope skirted many of the issues plaguing mankind as a result of the brutal Nazi war, occupation, and the genocide of the Jews. In a letter of 30 April 1943 to the bishop of Berlin, Count Conrad von Preysing, who had earlier pressed the pope to issue an appeal on behalf of the persecuted Jews, Pius claimed that his Christmas message of December 1942 had denounced what was being done to the non-Aryans under German occupation.[35] That he did not speak more openly and frankly was due to his desire to prevent greater evil.

Many in the church and the curia begged the pope to abandon his prudence and reserve, follow the path of Pius XI, and openly denounce the persecution

31 John F. Morley, *Vatican Diplomacy and the Jews During the Holocaust, 1939–1943* (New York, 1980), pp. 45–6.
32 Koenig, ed., *Principles for Peace*, pp. 734–5.
33 Ibid., p. 804; *AAS*, XXXV, p. 23.
34 Kent, 'Pope Pius XII', p. 71.
35 Radio Message of 24 December 1942, *AAS*, XXXV, p. 23.

and atrocities. They cited the danger to papal moral leadership should he continue to ignore the widespread suffering among Christians and Jews. Others supported the prudent, diplomatic course of the pontiff, noting that (1) the Holy See could not condemn Nazi atrocities without also criticizing Russian cruelties, (2) the Vatican would have to investigate the charges first, (3) the difficulties of assembling evidence of violations would be enormous, (4) the danger of making errors in the heat of war was great, (5) the pope had already condemned major offences against morality in wartime, (6) when members of the hierarchy spoke they did so on behalf of the pope, (7) such a condemnation of Nazi atrocities would only worsen the precarious position of Catholics in these areas.[36]

In response to Charles-Roux's incomprehension of papal silence regarding both the Nazi and Soviet invasion of Poland, Monsignor Montini replied, 'Every word against Germany and Russia would be bitterly paid for by the Catholics who are subject to the regimes in these countries'.[37] This was confirmed by Monsignor Jean Bernard, bishop of Luxemburg, who was detained at Dachau. A. Wolfsson, who managed to escape from Rome because of the Vatican's quiet intervention, later wrote that he understood and appreciated the Holy See's low public profile, claiming 'it was much better that the Pope kept silent'.[38]

Throughout 1943 as the war raged and the brutality increased, Pius sought refuge in institutional affairs, outlining general conditions of peace.[39] These angered even the Germans, who accused the Vatican of being steeped in a 'moral-political fog' in which it hid. During the course of 1943, the pope addressed such issues as the uses of atomic energy, drafting encyclicals on the Mystical Body of Christ, and the promotion of biblical studies, among other issues. In his 1943 Christmas message to the world, he deplored the continuing international strife and proposed the lesson of Bethlehem to the disillusioned and hopeless.[40] Meanwhile, the axis forces ceased fighting in North Africa in May 1943, abandoning it to the British and Americans.

The Vatican feared the consequences of the North African campaign and the Anglo-American diplomacy which flowed from it. Pius was particularly disturbed by the allied demand for unconditional surrender at the Casablanca conference in January 1943. He foresaw it would rouse a desperate German resistance, bringing the Soviets into central Europe. The Vatican focused on the projected allied invasion of Italy with the possibility of an occupation of the Eternal City. On 1 March 1943 the pope received Galeazzo Ciano, the new Italian ambassador to the Holy See.[41] In May the pope moved closer

36 Kent, 'Pope Pius XII', pp. 71–2.
37 Stehle, *Eastern Politics*, p. 195.
38 Lapide, *Three Popes and the Jews*, p. 263.
39 *AAS*, XXXV, pp. 165–79.
40 Carlen, *PP*, I, p. 121; *TESP*, pp. 1162–223; *Selected Documents of His Holiness Pope Pius XII: 1939–1958*, pp. 3–49.
41 *Diarium Romane Curiae, AAS*, XXXV, pp. 93, 160.

to the royal family by personally administering confirmation on Maria Pia of Savoy.[42] On 18 May 1943 Pius XII reminded President Roosevelt of Taylor's promise that the Italian people would be treated with consideration and understanding. Promising to limit the war to military targets, Roosevelt indicated that allied aviators would scrupulously avoid the bombardment of Vatican City.

The successful allied invasion of Sicily on 10 July 1943, of which the pope was informed by another letter from President Roosevelt, was followed by the massive bombardment of Rome's railroad yards on 18–19 July, which also struck several houses, demolished the Basilica of San Lorenzo, and damaged the adjacent cemetery.[43] Some 500 Romans were killed and more were wounded. The pope, personally touched when he learned that several of the bombs had torn up a number of graves of his own family members, visited the sites. The invasion of Sicily pushed the pope from his neutrality and reserve, as the Vatican quietly let it be known that it favoured a change of regime in Italy that would initiate negotiations with the invaders. In fact, the Holy See had discussed the matter with the Americans, advising them that the Italian people remained attached to the monarchy, and Victor Emmanuel III should be allowed to appoint a successor to Mussolini. On 24 July the Fascist Grand Council asked for Mussolini's resignation. The following day, the *duce* was dismissed by the king and placed under house arrest. Marshal Pietro Badoglio formed a caretaker government under the direction of Victor Emmanuel III. The Vatican prepared for the transition to the post-fascist regime.

Italy surrendered on 8 September 1843, prompting a German push into the peninsula from the north and occupation of Rome on 10 September. When the king, the Badoglio government and the general staff fled to the south to avoid capture, Pius remained behind. To some, it confirmed Hitler's analysis of the Italian situation when he indicated that there were three powers in Italy, the duce, the king and the pope – and of the three, the pope was the strongest.[44] The pontiff's subsequent behaviour led many to question the *führer*'s assessment. Among other things, the Germans ordered the arrest of the Jews in the Eternal City in October 1943 and began to transport them to Mauthausen, the Austrian concentration camp, for liquidation. In response, the pope instructed Monsignor Hudal, the rector of Santa Maria dell' Anima, to complain to the German commander, General Stahel, while his secretary of state, Cardinal Maglione, summoned the German ambassador to whom he protested about the deportation of the Jews from Rome. Although the arrests had occurred under his windows, the pope failed to denounce the outrage against humanity and the sanctity of the Eternal City. He instructed the monasteries and convents in Rome, which enjoyed an 'extraterritorial status', to provide refuge

42 Epistle of 20 July 1943, ibid., XXXV, pp. 252–4.
43 John Lucas, 'The Diplomacy of the Holy See during World War II', *The Catholic Historical Review*, LX (July 1974), pp. 271–8. Kent, pp. 277–8, idem., 'Pope Pius XII', p. 78.
44 For a defence of Pius XII's actions see the Allocution of Paul VI of 10 January 1975, *AAS*, LXVII, p. 95.

for the Jews. Some 5,000 of the 8,000-member Jewish community in the capital found shelter in this fashion.[45]

Meanwhile the slow advance of the allied forces in the peninsula, the fall of Cassino on 18 May 1944, and the piercing of the German line in the Alban hills, paved the way for an allied liberation of Rome. The German commander, General Albert Kesselring, proposed that Rome be declared an open city and withdrew his forces, as Pius reviewed the afflictions of Rome. On 4 June 1944 the allies entered Rome, confronting only sporadic resistance, the first of the European capitals to be liberated. Half a million Romans flocked to St Peter's to cheer the pope as *defensor civitatis*, defender of the city. Persisting in his neutrality, the pope addressed the crowd in St Peter's, praising God that the capital had been spared.[46]

While Rome had been liberated, the pope worried about the rest of Italy, the fate of Europe, and the expansionism of the Soviet Union and its communist ideology following the collapse of Nazi Germany. The curia shared his concerns. Before his death, Cardinal Maglione warned the British of the dangers of Russian hegemony in Europe, a supremacy he viewed as more terrible than that of Nazi Germany. His apprehension was shared by Monsignor Tardini, who predicted the war would end with a predominant Russian victory in Europe, leading to a rapid diffusion of communism throughout the greater part of the continent, to the detriment of European civilization and Christian culture. Even if the allied armies remained in Europe, Tardini continued, the ensuing peace would rest only on the mutual fear their forces inspired.[47]

The pope contributed to the campaign against the 'communist menace and the cold war'. On 1 September 1944, the fifth anniversary of the outbreak of the war, he issued a radio appeal calling for the reconstruction of the world on a Christian foundation. In it he postulated that Christians could not accept a social order which denies the right to possess private property, insisting that the survival of civilization required adherence to the eternal principles of justice. He returned to these themes in his Christmas message of 24 December 1944, in which he called for a complete halt to the bloodletting, without regard to war guilt, reparations, or balance of forces.[48] Although Pius XII proclaimed the church the guardian of man's dignity,[49] many believed this pope failed to exemplify this mission.

Pacelli, whose relations with Roosevelt had cooled following the 19 July 1943 bombardment of Rome, contested what he felt to be the president's excessive optimism towards Stalin and the Soviet Union. He deplored the actions of the Soviets in Poland and suspected their intentions in the whole of Eastern Europe. Long opposed to unconditional surrender, Pius and the curia

45 Carlen, *PP*, I, p. 121; Halecki, *Eugenio Pacelli*, pp. 205–6.
46 Halecki, *Eugenio Pacelli*, pp. 205–6.
47 Stehle, *Eastern Politics*, pp. 238–9.
48 *Selected Documents of His Holiness Pope Pius XII: 1939–1958*, pp. 1–15.
49 *The Major Addresses of Pope Pius XII: Christmas Messages*, ed. Vincent Yzermans (St Paul, 1961), II, pp. 87–8.

had strong reservations about the Yalta agreements (February 1945) which contemplated a world organization based on the principles of the grand alliance of the allied powers. The *Osservatore Romano* noted that its provisions would continue the distinction between great and small, victor and vanquished, perpetuating the errors and discriminations of the League of Nations. It also had reservations about the prominent part accorded the Soviet Union in the projected postwar settlement.[50]

The Vatican's reservations about the postwar settlement in general, and the influence exercised by the Soviet Union in particular, would be expressed more strongly in the years after the Second World War and play a part in the subsequent cold war.

50 Carlo Falconi, *The Popes in the Twentieth Century* (Boston, 1967), p. 265.

CHAPTER 13

The Holy See and the cold war in transition

In April 1945 Pope Pius XII issued another appeal for peace. His prayer was finally answered when an unconditional surrender was signed at General Eisenhower's headquarters at Rheims on 7 May 1945. The pope applauded the peace which brought six years of suffering to an end.[1] Only at this juncture did the pope speak out plainly, exposing the satanic spectre of National Socialism, and the horror of the death camps. After years of diplomatic finesse and studied neutrality, the loquacious pope branded Nazism 'the arrogant apostasy from Jesus Christ, the denial of His doctrine and of His work of redemption, the cult of violence, the idolatry of race and blood, the overthrow of human liberty and dignity'.[2] It represented a belated public acknowledgement of the moral rectitude of his predecessor's position, which Pacelli had restrained.[3] There were those who appreciated Pius XII's quiet diplomacy and behind-the-scene activities. At the war's end, a group of seventy representatives of Jews liberated from the camps visited the pope to thank him for his support when they were persecuted. For some the Vatican was not really silent, and they pointed to the catalogue of direct and indirect diplomatic protests found in the Vatican archives, the diocesan authorities, and the Nazi foreign ministry.[4] In the judgement of others, the pope said too little, too late.

During the latter half of the 1940s the pope dedicated himself to the reconstruction of Europe and the reconstitution of the church worldwide, initiating an effort to bring it into the twentieth century. He was very preoccupied by the victory of the Soviet Union and the march of communism. For this, among other reasons, the pope questioned Stalin's attempt to normalize relations with the Vatican in the late spring of 1944, recalling that Stalin had already destroyed the structure of the institutional church in Russia, and feared

1 *Epistula Encyclica*, 15 April 1945, *AAS*, XXXVII, pp. 97–100; *Nuntius Radiophonicus*, 9 May 1945, ibid., XXXVII, pp. 129–31.
2 J.S. Conway, *The Nazi Persecution of the Churches, 1933–1945* (London, 1968), p. 326.
3 *Allocutio*, 2 June 1945, *AAS*, XXXVIII, pp. 159–68.
4 Jeno Lavai, *Hungarian Jewry and the Papacy* (London, 1967), p. x.

he would attempt to do the same in Eastern Europe. Pius foresaw the need to prepare the church and the world community to confront the impending communist menace. His encyclical of December 1945, on the 350th anniversary of the reunion of the Ruthenian church with the Apostolic See, condemned its current persecution by the Soviets. A pronouncement early in 1946 denounced Stalin's forced assimilation of the Catholic Uniate church into the Russian Orthodox church.[5]

In the summer of 1946 Pius called for Catholic and world reconstruction. He continued the efforts of his immediate predecessors to make the church more universal, affirming that the Catholic church did not identify with any particular culture. Stressing the supra-national character of the church in 1946, Pius named thirty-two new cardinals, the largest number announced at any single seating, selecting many non-Italians and a number of non-Europeans for the red hat, and creating the first Chinese cardinal. By these steps, the conservative Pius XII altered the balance of power in the college of cardinals. Before 1946 there had been twenty-three Italian cardinals and fifteen from the other nationalities; afterward there were twenty-eight Italians and forty-two from the rest of the world.[6] In order to make room for the non-Italians, this pope reduced the number of cardinals in the curia. Pius considered the impact of the postwar transformation among the greatest since the collapse of the Roman empire.[7]

A number of conservative cardinals, most notably Ernesto Ruffini, archbishop of Palermo, and Alfredo Ottaviani, assessor of the Holy Office, persuaded Pius that the difficulties facing the church might best be confronted by the convocation of a church council. This would deal with the problems caused by the recent war and the march of communism, update the code of canon law, provide new directions for Catholic action, and clarify a number of social questions. The convocation of a council appealed to the pope insofar as it would facilitate the achievement of his major goals. Throughout 1948 he seriously considered calling one, and established five secret commissions to undertake preparatory studies. Although Pius appreciated the need to strengthen the church during an age of transition, this secretive and authoritarian pontiff did not relish the thought of having to share power with the bishops. Furthermore, the pope's health was not good, and he feared that he would not be able to bring the council to a successful conclusion. Thus, after almost three years of preparation, Pius abandoned the project in 1950. He unilaterally defined the Assumption of Mary into heaven, and condemned contemporary errors in his encyclical *Humani generis* of August 1950.

5 Carlen, *PP*, I, p. 123; Peter Nichols, *The Politics of the Vatican* (New York, 1968), pp. 140–1; Dennis J. Dunn, 'Stalinism and the Catholic Church during the Era of World War II', *Catholic Historical Review*, LIX, 3 (October 1973), p. 404.

6 Allocution of 9 March 1956, *AAS*, XXXXVIII, p. 211; Sermon of 24 December 1945, ibid., XXXVIII, pp. 67–99; *Consistorium Secretum*, 23 February 1946, ibid., XXXVIII, pp. 101–35; Carlen, *PP*, I, p. 124.

7 Talk of 15 September 1948, *AAS*, XL, p. 410.

The Assumption was the first, and to date the only, exercise of papal infallibility as proclaimed by the first Vatican council.[8] Some perceived it as an additional, and unnecessary, barrier to Christian unity. The work undertaken by the speculative theology commission, in anticipation of Pius XII's abortive council, found its way into *Humani generis* (Of the human race). This encyclical challenged recent theological and pastoral trends in the church, particularly as espoused by French theologians, while asserting that earlier papal pronouncements had closed the theological debate on hitherto open issues.[9] Some disagreed with both contentions of the encyclical. *Humani generis* cast suspicion on the *nouvelle theologie* or new theology at a time when the church and the papacy still had difficulties in accepting anything modern in theological matters. Those associated with the attempt to break through the rigid categorization of Catholic dogma and introduce a more ecumenical dimension were deprived of their teaching positions, and some were even forbidden to write or lecture. 'From the beginning of 1947 to the end of 1956', Father Congar recalls of his dealings with Pius XII and his curia, 'I knew nothing from that quarter [Rome] but an uninterrupted series of denunciations, warnings, restrictive or discriminatory measures and mistrustful interventions.'[10] Theologians such as Congar and his fellow dominican Father Marie-Dominique Chenu believed that the church had undermined its ability to address the contemporary world. The pope disagreed, and sought to overcome opposition by appealing directly to the faithful.

By 1948, Vatican radio was broadcasting in nineteen languages. In his 1948 Christmas radio message, Pius proclaimed that the church, battered by the World War, had preserved its integrity and vitality.[11] During the last decade of his pontificate from 1948 to 1958, Pius dedicated himself to a number of his own interests, withdrawing from the day-to-day activities confronting the church and the papacy. Critics charged this paved the way for nepotism and intrigue. Few criticized his confessor, the learned Jesuit Father Augustin Bea, rector of the Biblical Institute, who Pius appointed to the Holy Office.[12] However, the pope's long-time housekeeper Josefine Lehnert, known as Sister Pasqualina, was not spared. She was dubbed *Virgo Potens* or the powerful virgin and La papessa because she allegedly controlled access to the pope, oversaw his diet and medication, and virtually organized his life. Some charged that the pope, who retained a partiality for all things German and spoke to her in German, even though she had become fluent in Italian, consulted her on vital church matters including the selection of cardinals. Reportedly, she set the pope's daily agenda and determined the duration of papal audiences.[13]

8 *Munificentissimus Deus*, 1 November 1950, *AAS*, XXXXII, pp. 753–71 and consistory of 30 October 1950, *AAS*, XXXXII, pp. 774–82.
9 *Humani Generis*, 12 August 1950, *AAS*, XXXXII, pp. 561–78.
10 Peter Steinfels, 'Beliefs', *New York Times*, 12 August 1995.
11 Radio message of December 1948, *AAS*, XXXXI, pp. 7–8.
12 *AAS*, XXXXI, p. 198.
13 Vittorio Gorresio, *The New Mission of Pope John XXIII*, trans. Charles Lam Markmann (New York, 1969), p. 39.

Sister Pasqualina had been by Pacelli's side for some forty years since the 23-year-old nun had encountered the 41-year-old prelate in her Order's mother house in Rorschack, Switzerland. In 1917, when he moved to Munich as papal envoy, she accompanied him as his housekeeper, remaining at his side both in Munich and Berlin. She returned with him to Rome once he was selected as Pius XI's secretary of state in 1930, and during the conclave of 1939 was allowed to serve Pacelli his meals. Following his election, Sister Pasqualina moved into the pontifical apartments and loyally served the pope. There was little if any gossip about her personal relationship to Pius, few suspecting the ascetic and sickly pope of any carnality, but many resented her influence. Trusted by the pope as few other figures or prelates, she often drafted confidential letters, made telephone calls, and even undertook visits on his behalf.[14]

Sister Pasqualina's authority was checked by a number of tough-minded Italian cardinals collectively called Il pentagono. Meanwhile, the pope focused on such issues as the communist peril, Mary's role in the faith, the missions, the reform of the liturgy, and the impact of science and technology on the modern world. Throughout the postwar period, Pius XII rejected communism as a social system which violated Christian doctrine and the fundamentals of natural law.[15]

Initially, the Soviet dictator did not attack the Latin rite church in the Baltic states, Poland, and throughout much of Eastern Europe. In fact, from 1945 to 1948 the policy of Stalin's satellites in Eastern Europe was non-persecutory if not benevolent. However, by 1948 there was a radical shift in the dictator's course, prompted by the growing cold war and the Vatican's rejection of reconciliation on Soviet terms.[16] As Stalin consolidated his stranglehold on Eastern Europe, which early in 1949 led to the condemnation and arrest of the primate of Hungary, Cardinal Josef Mindszenty, Pius denounced the trial, condemnation, and the false accusations hurled against the church. Four days later in a speech to the Romans, the pope noted that he could not remain silent when a minority regime took total control of education and suppressed dioceses and deposed bishops. Deploring the crude attempts to prohibit religion, the pope launched a counter-attack against the unbelievers who sought to subvert the faith.[17]

In the summer of 1949 Pius published the decree *Responsa ad dubbia de communismo*, which attacked Stalin's attempt to impose totalitarianism on Eastern Europe and elsewhere. It authorized the Holy Office to prescribe excommunication for those who voted for, joined, or even collaborated with the godless communists or their materialistic allies.[18] In the years from 1945 to 1948, the communists in Czechoslovakia pursued a moderate policy towards the Roman

14 Paul Hofmann, *O Vatican! A Slightly Wicked View of the Holy See* (New York, 1984), pp. 133–5; Peter Hebblethwaite, *John XXIII, Pope of the Council* (London, 1984), p. 27.
15 Radio message of 24 December 1955, *AAS*, XXXXVIII, p. 33.
16 Dunn, 'Stalinism and the Catholic Church', pp. 425–7.
17 Allocution of 16 February 1949, in *AAS*, XXXXI, pp. 73–4; Address of 20 February 1949, ibid., XXXXI, pp. 74–6.
18 *Decretum*, 1 July 1949, *AAS*, XXXXI, p. 334; Hebblethwaite, *John XXIII*, p. 225.

Catholic Church, and in July 1946 Pius accepted the credentials of the extraordinary minister of the Czech republic. This changed following the *putsch* of 25 February 1948, which introduced a brutal persecution of the church and religion. Pius XII denounced these actions and the attempt to separate Czech Catholics from Rome. In June 1949 the Holy Office condemned Catholic action in Czechoslovakia as schismatic.[19]

At home, as primate of Italy, Pius XII perceived communism as the principal threat to the position of the church in Italian society. The pope long had been concerned about the prospect of a communist takeover of Italy, a fear that increased following the collapse of fascism and during the ensuing civil war.[20] To prevent the establishment of such an 'atheistic regime', the Holy See warned the faithful that one could not be a Catholic and communist at the same time.[21] It was a stance reminiscent of the one assumed by a number of German bishops who preached the incompatibility of Catholics supporting the Nazis, but was repudiated by then secretary of state Pacelli. Now that the enemy was communism, and the battleground was Italy, Pacelli assessed things differently. He also abandoned the notion that the church remain extraneous to partisan politics.

Following the formation of de Gasperi's Christian Democratic government at the end of 1945, Pius interjected the church into the political life of postwar Italy, harping upon the right of the clergy to instruct the public. At the same time, the Vatican worked to secure the inclusion of the Lateran Accords of 1929 within the postwar constitutional structure. Once this was attained, the Vatican openly intervened in the Italian elections of 1948, co-ordinating its activities with the parish clergy and the three million members of Catholic action organizations. Stressing the importance of the Italian elections of 1948, Pius alerted the clergy of their right to prepare the faithful to vote responsibly. Thus, the pope invoked candidates committed to preserving their Catholic religion and defending it against known enemies.[22]

Paradoxically, the *Civiltà Cattolica* justified this intervention by claiming that since the concordat of the Lateran Pacts assured the church a public presence, it had the obligation to oppose those parties that challenged its principles and position.[23] In July 1949 the congregation of the Holy Office warned the faithful that those who supported the anti-Christian doctrine of communism incurred an automatic excommunication. In 1952, when it appeared that the Christian Democrats might prove unable to win the administrative elections in Rome, Luigi Gedda, president of Catholic action, proposed a Christian Democratic alliance with the parties of the right. Although the plan had the support of the pope, de Gasperi rejected it, creating a rift between Pius XII and the Italian

19 *Acta SS. Congregationum*, 20 June 1949, *AAS*, XXXXI, p. 333.
20 *Actes et documents du Saint Siège relatif à la seconde guerre mondiale*, ed. Pierre Blett et al. (Vatican City, 1965–82), VII, pp. 237–9.
21 *L'Osservatore Romano*, 23 July 1944.
22 *New York Times*, 17 March 1946; *Le benemerenze del Clero di Roma*, 10 March 1948, *ASS*, XV, pp. 119–20.
23 *La Civiltà Cattolica*, 30 July 1949.

prime minister. Thereafter, Vatican intervention in Italian political affairs steadily declined, although it was not eliminated.[24]

Pius XII had recourse to diplomacy and was prepared to negotiate even with the communist regimes he condemned; agreement was possible only when he deemed the conditions acceptable. In 1950 he pronounced the forty-two 'patriotic' bishops appointed by the Chinese communist government to be in schism. However, that same year he reached a *modus vivendi* with the Polish government, which provided the pope would remain supreme authority within the church on matters of faith and ecclesiastical jurisdiction, but had to accept the Polish government's insistence on a separation of church and state. No understanding was possible with the Chinese, and in 1951 Mao Tse-tung expelled the papal nuncio. In his encyclical to the Catholic churches of the east at the end of 1952, Pius reaffirmed Rome's desire for unity and deplored the exclusion of God from their lives.

During the course of January 1954, Pius fell seriously ill and was diagnosed as suffering from cancer. Illness increased the isolation of the already aloof pontiff, who saw few figures other than Sister Pasqualina, his doctors, Montini and Tardini. He survived with the assistance of an expensive treatment of live cell therapy administered by Dr Paul Niehans, whom a grateful pope inducted into the papal academy of science.[25] The anti-communist, pro-western position of the Holy See led President Harry Truman in 1950 to attempt to open full diplomatic relations with it, proposing General Mack Clark as ambassador. The suggestion aroused anti-Catholic agitation in America, forcing Truman to withdraw the nomination. Nonetheless, the pope continued to support the efforts of the Americans against the march of communism, and sympathized with Cardinals Mindszenty, Alojzije Stepinac and Stefan Wysznsksi and the entire clergy and laity that endured persecution in Eastern Europe.[26] In 1956 he denounced the Soviet invasion of Hungary and railed against co-existence.[27]

Preoccupied by the cold war and its consequences for the church, Pius, dubbed by some the pope of the Atlantic alliance, never allowed his anti-communism to become an obsession causing him to neglect issues such as European integration, which he favoured.[28] Devoted to the missions, Pius regretted their neglect during the course of the Second World War. Even during that catastrophic conflict, he consecrated twelve missionary bishops in 1939 and 1940, and recalled the mission agreement between the Holy See and the Portuguese signed hundreds of years earlier. He urged the Portuguese to continue their centuries-long missionary activity. He conveyed similar sentiments to Vladimir Ledochowski on the fourth centenary of the founding of the Society of Jesus, stressing the Order's missionary role in the past and

24 Elisa Carrillo, 'The Italian Catholic Church and Communism, 1943–1963', *Catholic Historical Review*, LXXVII, 4 (October 1991), pp. 649–51.

25 Hans Kugler, 'Live Cell Therapy: Rejuvenation Breakthrough', *Journal of Longevity Research*, 1996, I, 11, pp. 13–14.

26 *Epistula Apostolica*, 29 June 1956, *AAS*, XXXXVIII, pp. 549–54.

27 *Lucticosissimi eventas*, 28 October 1956, ibid., XXXXVIII, pp. 741–4.

28 Allocution of 11 November 1948, ibid., XL, pp. 508–9.

hoping it would continue its efforts in the future. After the war, the pope praised the contributions of the missionaries in Canada, Africa, Asia and the Far East, and on a number of occasions pointed to the contribution of the Society of African Missions.[29]

Pius XII, like Pius IX, showed particular devotion to Jesus's mother, and had frequent recourse to her intervention during the course of the World War. He also pondered the question of issuing a formal declaration of the Assumption of the Virgin Mary, asserting as a dogma of faith that her body was taken to heaven upon her death. After the war, the pope consulted the bishops on the Assumption of Mary which Benedict XIV had earlier pronounced a probable opinion, but had not declared an article of faith. The consensus of those consulted concurred with the pope's sentiments, as Pius prepared to proclaim the dogma. In anticipation, the pope named 1950 a Holy Year of Jubilee. In November 1950, in his dogmatic bull *Munificentissimus Deus*,[30] Pius examined the historical background of the dogma, approaches to the definition, and then announced the offical definition. Pronounced *ex-cathedra*, it proclaimed that Mary's body was raised from the grave shortly after her death and transported up to heaven. Some complained that it posed a barrier to ecumenism. For his role in the definition and for proclaiming 1954 a Marian year, Pius was perceived not only as the pope of the missions but also as the 'Marian pope'.

Pius XII might also be dubbed the pope of science and technology, for he had a profound interest in the sciences, and the interaction of faith and science. He labelled the postwar period the age of technology.[31] From the first days of his pontificate and in his first message to the Catholic world. Pius made use of the radio address, even more so than did President Roosevelt. He viewed it as 'a weapon of truth'. He also explored the impact of motion pictures, and later he recognized the importance of television. Applauding the work of Marconi, he appreciated the social significance of telecommunications. In 1951 he named the Archangel Gabriel the patron of telecommunications, just as earlier he had proclaimed St Albert the Great the patron of the natural sciences.[32] In 1951 Pius brought the Holy See into the International Union of Telecommunications and the Universal Postal Union.

Aware that both science and technology could be abused, Pius took pains to explain that the abuse of God's gifts and man's discoveries did not devalue them, denying that the church or the papacy were opposed to technological progress. He subsequently addressed the question of atomic energy, which could be a boon to humanity, although Pius deplored its destructive power when applied to weapons, the pollution of the environment, and its potential as a pathogenic menace to all human organisms. Condemning its destructive use, Pius championed its peaceful applications. In 1956 he brought the Holy

29 Carlen, *PP*, I, pp. 116–18, 127–40; Jan Olav Smit, *Angelic Shepherd: The Life of Pope Pius XII* (New York, 1950), p. 196.
30 *AAS*, XXXXII, pp. 753–71.
31 Talk of 12 September 1948, ibid., XL, p. 411.
32 Carlen, *PP*, I, pp. 119, 140, 155, 171.

See into the International Agency for Atomic Energy. He made it clear that the 'second technological revolution', while recognizing human reality and progress, had to respect and understand the undeniable limits of human nature.[33]

Pius XII concurred with Pius IX and Pius X in rejecting the notion that Catholic doctrine had to be altered to render it acceptable to the modern mind, and resisted all efforts to free dogma from established terminology and scholastic concepts. Nonetheless, he recognized the obligation of ecclesiastical institutions to further the progress of the sciences, while preserving Catholic truth. Indeed, he paid tribute to the services provided by science to humanity and the church.[34] He did not perceive a conflict between science and the church, and cited St Thomas's philosophical proofs for the existence of God in the light of modern natural science. This pope stressed the harmony between scientific findings and revelation.

In his 1955 Easter message, Pius proposed a synthesis of religion and life as a solution to current problems, as he commended the achievements of scientific progress. The frail pontiff attributed the historical separation of science and philosophy to mutual ill-will, incompetence, and the failure to recognize their synthesis and mutual responsibilities. In his address to the fourth International Thomistic Congress, he again denied the existence of any conflict between science and philosophy and urged philosophers to study science. Similar sentiments were conveyed to the tenth International Congress of Historical Sciences, held in 1955. The pope refuted the contention that the church opposed the historical sciences, noting the accessibility of the Vatican archives. Pius proclaimed that the research stimulated by Leo XIII's opening of these records had redounded to the justification and even honour of the church. 'The serious scholar reflects that faith does not fear reason', he told a group of Fulbright scholars who visited him in the last year of his pontificate, adding, 'Dogma is not afraid of scientific research.'[35] In the postwar years, Pius outlined the fundamentals of various sciences, examining their relationship to psychology, philosophy and revelation, cataloguing both their positive and negative aspects.[36]

Pius XII, more than any other pontiff before him, sought to achieve an accommodation between Catholic civilization and the new technological society. The theme of his message to the participants of the Brussels World's Fair of 1958 was human progress and the things of God, an issue to which he devoted a good part of the postwar pontificate. 'We live in an age of technology', he said shortly thereafter. 'As far as the Church is concerned she can live and fulfil her mission under every civilization.'[37] His pontificate sought and achieved a reconciliation between Catholicism and contemporary scientific developments. Intrigued by the march of technology and the transformation

33 *Scienze speculative e scienze praticale*, 8 February 1948, *AAS*, XL, p. 78; Carlen, *PP*, I, pp. 135–6, 180, 183, 192.
34 *Humani generis*, 12 August 1950, and *Quoniam*, 12 January 1950, Carlen, *PP*, I, pp. 136, 140.
35 Carlen, *PP*, I, p. 195.
36 Ibid., I, pp. 152, 156, 160, 165, 170, 178, 181, 189, 207.
37 Ibid., I, p. 206.

it wrought, Pius applauded human progress which did not seek to denigrate spiritual values.

Although criticized as austere and authoritarian, Pius continued the papal commitment to social justice, writing in the first year of his pontificate that 'the goods are created by God for all men should in the same way reach all, justice guiding and charity helping'.[38] He also proved open to an increased role of the laity in the church, convening the first World Congress of the Lay Apostolate in 1951. In his address to the second such congress, he commented on the increasing shortage of priests and the need for the formation of a lay apostolate to fill the slack. On a number of occasions this pope expressed disapproval of the clerical monopoly in the church. Consequently, it is not surprising that Pius XII appealed to the laity to combat the weakness and decline within the institution.[39] Perhaps more surprisingly, he encouraged Catholic women to reach out beyond their traditional sphere in the home, urging them to be more active outside their family life and to assume a greater political role. In April 1943 Pius XII addressed the changed role of women in society, appreciated the transformation of feminine models, and examined future prospects for women.[40]

Pius's programme represented a judicious synthesis of conservation and liberalism, and justified the use of modern methods of linguistic and cultural research as well as historical discoveries to achieve a broader and better understanding of the faith. His *Divino afflante spiritu* (With the help of the Divine Spirit) of 1943 liberated biblical scholars from many anti-modernist proscriptions, and permitted them to consider the study of literary forms in their historical setting. He authorized, under special circumstances, the ordination of married men in the Latin church, while approving the use of the 'rhythm method' for avoiding procreation when there were good medical, eugenic or economic reasons. His encyclical *Mediator dei* (Mediator of God) of 1947 sought to restore the communal character of public worship. Pius, likewise, sanctioned liturgical changes such as the introduction of evening masses and revised Easter observances, while encouraging a new Latin translation for use in the church's liturgy. He set the stage for the second Vatican council, and predicted his successor would convoke it.

Pius XII's personality and policies made him an enigma for many. In 1953 he pleased conservatives and upset liberals by suppressing the priest workers in France, even as he pleased liberals and angered conservatives by changing the rules for the period of fasting before receiving communion, and taking steps to make evening masses possible. Likewise, his denunciation of atomic weaponry provoked a mixed reaction from the left and right, as did his 1956 establishment of the Latin American Episcopal Council. He challenged the conservative Vatican bureaucracy which he once likened to the Bourbons who

38 Encyclical Epistle to the hierarchy of the United States, 1 November 1939, *AAS*, XXXI, p. 653.
39 Carlen, *PP*, I, pp. 125, 143, 191.
40 Allocution of 24 April 1943, *AAS*, XXXV, pp. 136–43.

'learned little and forget nothing', but he failed to reform it radically. He even challenged the clericalism which had dominated the church, telling the laity 'You are the church'.[41]

Pius XII's reforms did not endear him to the masses. He remained a cold and distant personality for many, and during his pontificate which lasted almost twenty years, he created an inaccessible atmosphere in Rome. Because of his solitary nature and dislike of personal contacts, which he considered more of a burden than a blessing, his leadership tended towards isolation rather than collegiality. Tardini noted that Pacelli had a slight stammer when he engaged in private conversation, which disappeared when he spoke to a crowd.[42] Perhaps this was due to his uneasiness in interpersonal relations. Pacelli was also criticized for the 1933 concordat with Nazi Germany, which he defended after the war. He continued to favour concordats with repressive as well as democratic regimes, signing one with Franco's Spain in 1953[43] and another with Trujillo's Dominican Republic in 1954.

Although Pius XII was willing to collaborate with dictatorial regimes, he did not allow the postwar church, much less the Vatican, to become subordinate to them, as is illustrated in the case of Argentina. During the Second World War the Argentian church, without opposition from the pope, adhered to the military government of Juan Peron which emerged in 1943–44. Shortly thereafter, in 1945, cordial relations were established between Buenos Aires and Rome.[44] Subsequently, the church received a privilege it had been unable to exact from previous governments – the law of religious education which provided for religious instruction in the public schools under church administration. The church also enjoyed state subsidies as federal and provincial governments built churches and supported all sorts of religious activities. In return, the hierarchy in Argentina issued a pastoral letter which aided Peron in the electoral campaign of 1945–46, issuing another in 1951 which again sustained the Peronist party.[45]

There were difficulties between the church and the Peron regime during his first administration of 1946–51, but on the whole Pius XII preserved close relations with Argentina.[46] The hierarchy, however, resented Eva Duarte Peron's far-reaching welfare organization, the Eva Peron Foundation, which overshadowed the church's traditional role in charity. Perhaps this played a part in her failure to receive the insignia of the Supreme Order of Christ when she visited Rome. In 1949 and 1951 Eva sought the honour, only to be rebuffed by Pius XII. Nonetheless Eva remained devoted to Rome. Her death in 1952

41 Peter Hebblethwaite, *Paul VI: The First Modern Pope* (New York, 1993), p. 207.
42 For a picture of Pius XII from one of the few figures close to him, see Cardinal Domenico Tardini, *Pio XII* (Rome, 1960).
43 Julio Gorricho, 'El Concordato Espanol de 1953. Notas para su historia', *Lumen*, XXIII (January–February 1974), pp. 3–26.
44 *Allocutio*, 27 November 1945, *AAS*, XXXVII, pp. 314–17.
45 Virginia W. Leonard, 'Education and the Church–State Clash in Argentina, 1954–1955', *Catholic Historical Review*, LXVI, 2 (January 1980), pp. 34–5.
46 *Clero et Populo Argentinae Republicae*, 1 February 1948, *AAS*, XL, pp. 85–7.

allowed anti-Catholic tensions within the Peronist party to surface, compounded by Juan Peron's clumsy pressure to have the Vatican proclaim Evita a saint. Pius XII in Rome, and the hierarchy at home, also resented Juan Peron's attempt to increase state control over the nation's youth. In 1953 his ministry of education formed the Union de Estudiantes Secundarios (UES), which attracted secondary school students throughout Argentina. In September 1954 Argentina's Catholic action organization attacked both the UES and the ministry of education, and in October 1954 Peron counter-attacked by sanctioning a campaign against the church. At this juncture, the Peron government began an active persecution of the church, arresting clerics and prohibiting religious processions. In December 1954 the government terminated its financial support for Catholic schools, and in May 1955 Peron had his congress terminate religious instruction in the public schools.

These provocative measures were intensified when the congress ended the church's tax exempt status, and levies were imposed on religious schools, convents and other religious institutions. Following the government's interference with a Corpus Christi celebration on 11 June 1955, on 16 June Peron was excommunicated. Conservative Catholic naval officers almost immediately led an abortive coup against Peron's government. Although they failed, on 16 September General Eduardo Lonardi, a devout Catholic, successfully deposed Peron, and his provisional government restored the educational and economic privileges that the church had earlier enjoyed.[47] The Vatican was determined to safeguard the Catholic action organization and the church's role in education, if not yet prepared to defend human rights *vis-à-vis* oppressive regimes.

Although Pius made broad use of the radio and other media, his style always remained public and never became personal. He did not have much contact with the Catholic hierarchy and even abolished the scheduled audiences with responsible figures in the Roman curia. Only his canary kept him company. He read his speeches out in full, confiding that when he spoke he only saw the pages before him. Reports also circulated of the pope's visions. Supposedly, at the end of October and the beginning of November 1950 Pius XII saw the Virgin Mary to whom he was devoted, and the vision was repeated two or three times during the course of 1951. At the end of 1954, while Pius was suffering from an abdominal hernia, he believed Jesus entered his room, an encounter that was reported a year later in the *Osservatore Romano* of December 1955. In 1957, a year before his death, word spread that the pope had bestowed sight on a little girl born blind.[48] Such a pope might inspire some, but never encouraged familiarity. Even his private secretary, the Jesuit Robert Leiber, found him difficult to approach and a solitary figure. Not surprisingly, he treated subordinates as extensions of his will, seeking executants rather than collaborators. With few exceptions, he was more respected than loved.

47 Leonard, 'Education', pp. 36–7, 45–51.
48 *Osservatore Romano*, 11 December 1955.

The controversial assessment and image of Pius XII was compounded by his 'silence' during the course of the Second World War, a picture that was reinforced by the appearance of Rolf Hochhuth's *The Deputy* in 1963, which portrayed Pius XII as insensitive and aloof to Jewish suffering during the Holocaust, and preoccupied with the narrow, clerical interests of the institutional church. Montini, who later became Paul VI, denied Hochhuth's charge that the pope's conduct was inspired by calculating political opportunism or moral inertia. Praising his 'courage and goodness' in protecting Rome, he claimed that 'Pius XII did what was humanly possible to save human lives and alleviate unspeakable suffering'. Further condemnations on the pope's part, Montini insisted, would have been 'not only futile but harmful'.[49] He thus praised Pius for measuring his words to avoid reprisals. The controversy on the 'silence' and the entire pontificate continues.[50]

49 Hebblethwaite, *Paul VI*, p. 195.
50 José M. Sanchez, 'The Enigma of Pius XII', *America*, 14 September 1996, pp. 18–21.

CHAPTER 14

Aggiornamento *and the opening of Vatican II: reconciliation of the papacy with the modern world*

Pius XII's death on 9 October 1958 brought the cardinals to Rome to elect a successor; on 25 October they entered the conclave. The Italians, who constituted eighteen out of the fifty-one cardinals, represented the largest and most important bloc, followed by the French, who formed the second largest group. Since Pius XII (1939–58) had not convoked the cardinals for consultation, they did not know one another well, giving Angelo Roncalli, known by both the Italians and the French cardinals, an advantage. The average age of the cardinals was seventy-four, so Roncalli was not deemed particularly old.[1] Indeed when the archbishop of Florence, Ellia dalla Costa, earlier suggested he would make a good pope, and Roncalli objected that he was seventy-six, dalla Costa replied, 'That's ten years younger than me'.[2] Some considered Roncalli's age a benefit, convinced that the church needed a transitional pope who would not live long enough to introduce dangerous innovations.

Roncalli, who was elected on 28 October, announced he would be called John, knowing that no pope had assumed that name for some 400 years and all of the legitimate predecessors bearing the name had relatively short pontificates. He favoured the name because it was that of his father, the church in which he was baptized, as well as the Lateran Basilica, the pope's cathedral. Perhaps he also assumed the name because he wanted to be a new John the Baptist for the church.[3] The rotund John – he weighed over 200 pounds at the time of his election – stood in stark contrast to his ascetic and inaccessible predecessor, Pius XII. The new pope was an optimist and extrovert. John gesticulated and radiated warmth and sincerity, and was far more gregarious than Pius, who ate all his meals alone. As early as 1898, Roncalli had observed that he had a tendency to talk too much, hoping to attain 'prudence and sobriety in speech'.[4]

1 *Disposizioni per la chiusura delle cerimonie e custodia del conclave*, 15 October 1958, *AAS*, L, pp. 865–6; *Instrumento della chiusura esterna del conclave, AAS*, L, pp. 870–89.
2 Peter Hebblethwaite, *Pope John XXIII, Pope of the Council* (London, 1984), p. 272.
3 *Electo Summi Pontificis*, 28 October 1958, *AAS*, L, p. 877; Hebblethwaite, *Pope John XXIII*, p. 286; Carlen, *PP*, I, p. 211.
4 Pope John XXIII, *Journal of a Soul*, trans. Dorothy White (New York, 1965), p. 43.

He had scrutinized the scriptures, John remarked, and had found not one single word on the pope having his meals in seclusion. This was tantamount to a personal revolution, with others to follow.[5]

Angelo Giuseppe Roncalli was born on 25 November 1881, the third of thirteen children of Giovanni Battista Roncalli and Mariana Mazzolo of Sotto il Monte, outside of Bergamo. Sharecroppers, the family was poor, but adequately fed and housed. He attended elementary school in town, and in 1892 entered the minor seminary of Bergamo, followed by attendance at the major seminary from 1895 to 1900. In 1895 he received the clerical habit and commenced keeping a diary. In 1901, as Giovanni Giolitti and Giuseppe Zanardelli assumed control of Italy's political life, Angelo enrolled in the Roman Seminary of the Apolinare, receiving a degree in theology shortly thereafter. At the end of the year he reported to the military barracks in Bergamo for his compulsory military service. At the end of 1902, following his year of service, Angelo returned to the seminary.

In 1903 Roncalli was ordained deacon and the following year he received a doctorate in sacred theology and was ordained a priest. Early in 1905, when Giacomo Radini-Tedeschi was appointed bishop of Bergamo, Angelo was named his secretary, accompanying him on a pilgrimage to Lourdes that same year, followed by one to Palestine. Angelo worked alongside this social-minded prelate for nine years, sharing his concern for the problems of the working classes. In 1915, when Italy entered the World War, Angelo was recalled to service, remaining in the military until the end of 1918. He returned to serve as spiritual director of Bergamo's seminary, but at the end of 1920 was summoned to Rome to serve as the director of the Italian section of propaganda fide. Roncalli travelled throughout Italy, followed by tours of France, Belgium, Holland and Germany. At the end of 1924 he was appointed professor of patrology at the Lateran university.[6]

In 1925 he was appointed apostolic visitor to Bulgaria. 'The Church is making me a Bishop in order to send me to Bulgaria, to fulfil there, as apostolic visitor, a mission of peace', he jotted in his diary in March.[7] Transferred to Turkey and Greece in 1934, during the Second World War he established an office in Istanbul for locating prisoners of war and assisting Jewish refugees in German-controlled territories.

Late in 1944 General de Gaulle, consolidating his powers as chief of state, refused to accept the presence of Valerio Valeri, who had served as nuncio in Vichy. Faced with the need to have a nuncio in Paris quickly, Pius XII pressed Roncalli into service. There was surprise bordering on shock in the curia, and Monsignor Domenico Tardini confided as much to Roncalli, assuring him that the decision was made by the holy father. Some claimed that Pius, angry with de Gaulle, decided to dispatch a second echelon diplomat as nuncio.

5 Paul Hofmann, *O Vatican! A Slightly Wicked View of the Holy See* (New York, 1984), p. 27.
6 Pope John XXIII, *Journal of a Soul*, pp. xxxvii–xli; Hebblethwaite, *Pope John XXIII*, pp. 5–11, 33–50; Carlen, *PE*, V, pp. 3–4.
7 Pope John XXIII, *Journal of a Soul*, pp. 205–6.

Supposedly, Pius quipped, 'If they don't want an aristocrat [Valeri], then let them have a peasant! [Roncalli]'.[8] It was a mean-spirited evaluation, which ignored the fund of diplomatic experience, personal warmth and great tact displayed by Roncalli in a series of difficult posts.

Roncalli served Rome well in Paris, resisting French attempts to expel thirty-three French bishops from their sees as collaborators with the Pétain regime, so that ultimately only a handful were recalled. In 1951 he was appointed Vatican observer to UNESCO, the following year Pius rewarded him with the red hat, and in 1953 named him patriarch of Venice. No less than eight former French prime ministers attended the departing nuncio's farewell dinner, providing another proof of his personal magnetism. Roncalli expected to spend the remaining years of his life in Venice, where he took pride in serving as *pastor et pater* (shepherd and father), but in October 1958 left for Rome to take part in the conclave which elected him pope. From the first, he caused some sensation, making the novel decision to preach a homily at his coronation mass on 4 November 1958.[9] He again broke with tradition in creating twenty-three new cardinals, exceeding the number of seventy set by Sixtus V (1585–90) and creating the first cardinals from the Philippines, Japan, Mexico and Africa, in continuation of the internationalization of the college commenced by Pius XII.[10] His visit to the Regina Coeli or Queen of Heaven prison in Rome by the Tiber, in December, was another first in the modern period, and John's embrace of its convicts brought him support in Italy and abroad.

The new pope projected the updating or *aggiornamento* of the church, as well as an *aperturismo* or opening up of the institution, even as he selected the conservative Domenico Tardini, who had been Pius XII's undersecretary for external affairs, as his secretary of state.[11] Both Tardini and Giovanni Battista Montini were granted the red hat that had eluded them during the pontificate of his predecessor. Although Tardini was far more cautious than his master, his selection served to reassure the curia, which Tardini knew so well. While John, like his predessor, lived in the apostolic palace on the right of St Peter's square on the same floor of the secretariat of state, he refused to remain a recluse, looking towards the world beyond, with which he sought an accommodation. John believed that the church, while remaining true to its principles, had to reach an accord with contemporary civilization.

Roncalli had first used the term *aggiornamento* during the diocesan synod of Venice in November 1957, and during his pontificate it was to become his slogan and trade-mark. John perceived synods and councils as the constitutional means to renew the church. Early on, he conceived the notion of calling a council, the twenty-first of the church, to effect the *aggiornamento* he deemed necessary. Paradoxically, the need for a council was shared by conservatives

8 Wilton Wynn, *Keepers of the Keys: John XXIII, Paul VI, and John Paul II: Three Who Changed the Church* (New York, 1988), p. 19.
9 John's Coronation Homily, 4 November 1958, *AAS*, L, pp. 884–9.
10 *Sacra Concistoria*, 15 December 1958, *AAS*, L, pp. 981–97.
11 Nomination of Tardini as Secretary of State, *AAS*, L, pp. 905–6; Carlen, *PP*, I, p. 212.

such as Cardinal Alfredo Ottaviani and Cardinal Ernesto Ruffini, who had encouraged Pius XII to convoke one and raised the issue with Roncalli during the conclave prior to his selection as pope.[12] In January the pope broached the prospect of a Roman synod, the calling of an ecumenical council, and the updating or *aggiornamento* of the code of canon law with his secretary of state, Tardini. John appeared uncertain and felt the need for affirmation. The conservative Tardini enthusiastically endorsed the project.

Tardini, Ruffini and Ottaviani shared a vision different from that of the pope on the scope and agenda of the projected council. When John announced his decision to call a council during a meeting with the curia at the Benedictine Monastery of St Paul on 25 January 1959, its agenda remained uncertain.[13] Would it be a council of reform and renewal as John seemed to posit, or one called to refute contemporary errors, as some of the conservatives desired? Unfortunately, John transmitted mixed signals, appointing Tardini president of the preparatory commission for the council, pleasing conservatives, as did his decision that the president of each subcommission would be the prefect of the corresponding Roman congregation, thus giving the curia considerable sway in its workings. Furthermore, the admission that he was inspired to call the council by the example of Pope Pius IX frightened others.[14]

On the other hand, John spoke of transforming the church and using the council as the mechanism to do so. He hoped it would demonstrate the striking diversity of rites within the unshakeable unity of the faith.[15] In a consistory naming eight new cardinals, the pope predicted the council would provide for the future of the faithful and humanity as a whole. Subsequently, he saw the forthcoming council as an instrument for unity, as the church's response to modernity, and the mechanism of *aggiornamento*.[16]

In May 1959 a preparatory commission was created, assuming the task of consulting the world's bishops and archbishops, male superiors of religious orders, and theological faculties of Catholic universities, regarding matters to be considered. While the inspiration and programme of the council remained unknown, and a vast administrative and consultative machinery was devised for its functioning,[17] a number of writers sought to influence it. In 1959, the year the council was announced, Lorenz Jaeger, archbishop of Paderborn, produced a study entitled *The Ecumenical Council of the Church and Christendom.* It denied the existence of a fixed or prescribed historical model that had to be pursued, while favouring some form of lay participation. In 1960 another German-speaking theologian, the Swiss born Hans Küng, produced a book

12 *Annuario Pontificio per l'anno 1964* (Città del Vaticano, 1964), pp. 48, 66.

13 *Homilia*, 25 January 1959, *AAS*, LI, pp. 70–4; Carlen, *PP*, I, p. 216.

14 *Talk of 24 December 1960*, *AAS*, LIII, p. 35.

15 *Epistula Apostolica*, 19 March 1961, ibid., LIII, pp. 210–11; Allocution of 16 April 1961, ibid., LIII, pp. 266–8.

16 Pope John XXIII, *Journal of a Soul*, pp. 229, 232, 234; Peter Hebblethwaite, *Paul VI: The First Modern Pope* (New York, 1993), p. 1.

17 *Motu propio*, 5 June 1960, *AAS*, LII, pp. 433–7, and Allocution of 5 June 1960, ibid., pp. 517–24.

called *The Council, Reform and Reunion*, proclaiming the overriding need for reform of the church. Tardini, in his press conference of 30 October 1959, saw things differently.

It was not until Giovanni Montini's Lenten pastoral of 1962 entitled *Pensiamo al Concilio*[18] (Let us think about the council), followed by John's September 1962 broadcast on Vatican radio, that it became clear what direction the pope wanted the council to take. Whether he would be able to keep the council on a reformist course was another matter, as Romans joked that Tardini reigned, Ottaviani governed, and John blessed. The death of Tardini in 1961 did not change matters appreciably, for John replaced him with the equally cautious Amleto Giovanni Cicognani, who had been apostolic delegate to Washington for some twenty-five years.

John was aware of the awesome responsibility he had assumed in calling the council, recognizing he might not be able to see it to a conclusion. 'When on 28 October, 1958, the Cardinals of the Holy Roman Church chose me to assume the supreme responsibility of ruling the universal flock of Jesus Christ, at seventy-seven years of age, everyone was convinced that I would be a provisional and transitional Pope', he wrote in his diary in August 1961. 'Yet here I am, already on the eve of the fourth year of my pontificate, with an immense programme of work in front of me to be carried out before the eyes of the whole world, which is watching and waiting.'[19] Perceiving the difficult road ahead, John never lost his good nature or sense of humour. Thus, when asked how many people worked at the Vatican he responded, 'less than half'.

On 11 October 1962 the council officially opened.[20] John set the tone for the half million people in St Peter's square, and the seventy-nine nations that were represented in one form or another in the first of the four sessions. That evening he spoke to the crowd assembled in St Peter's square for a torch-light procession. A few days later, Archbishop Giovanni Montini of Milan, considered the alter-ego of the pope by some, and granted apartments in the Vatican during the sessions, issued a tentative programme for the council. Montini hoped it would deal with the issue of collegiality – the relationship between the pope and bishops. He proposed the first session of the council focus on the nature of the church, exploring what the church does during the course of the second session, while a third session would be needed to examine the church's relationships with other groups. Montini perceived the main business as renewal and *aggiornamento*, a positive rather than a punitive council. Predicting it would have a great spiritual impact, he foresaw it would be truly 'catholic', reaching out towards the entire world and all civil society. Some suggested that Montini's key role in establishing the council's agenda made him John's chosen and logical successor.

18 Giovanni Battista Montini, *Pensiamo al Concilio* (Milan, 1962).

19 Pope John XXIII, *Journal of a Soul*, p. 303.

20 *Concilium Oecumenicum Vaticanum Il Sollemniter Ichoatur*, 11 October 1962, *AAS*, LIV, pp. 85–805.

John's *aggiornamento* sought to make the church relevant to the world in which it was housed, adapting it to the changed times; the council was to be the means to that end. As early as his first public address of 29 October 1958, John harped on the themes of his pontificate. First, a concern with the needs of the persecuted church where pastors could not preform their duties in freedom, leading him to have recourse to his so-called *Ostpolitik* or opening to the Eastern bloc and particularly Moscow. Second, he called for unity between east and west, Catholics and Orthodox Christians. Finally, he called for justice and harmony that included the need to address the social question in the industrialized world and the need to assist the third world by missionary and other efforts. Departing from the thunderous denunciations of his predecessors, he harped on unity in the church and peace in the secular order. He, even more than Pius XII, deplored the way wealth was squandered on the arms race rather than being used to uplift the downtrodden at home and abroad.[21]

John sought to bridge the gap between the church and the world which had developed since the French Revolution. Something had been done by his predecessors to improve the church's relations with the modern state system and secular society, but this pope felt more was needed. During the course of the diocesan synod of Rome, John referred to the adaptability of the church in incidentals, something that he had believed from the time he had introduced a few Turkish words into the worship while in Istanbul. 'It does not suffice to study religious truths or to reflect on them', he confided to a group of French university students in March 1959. 'One must do something about them.'[22] He had expressed similar sentiments in his journal as early as 1898 when he wrote, 'I must remember that it is my duty not only to shun evil but also to do good'.[23]

John's vision from the first was global and catholic, noting in his diary in February 1900 that all men on earth bore in themselves the image of God, and if all men were made in his likeness, 'should I not love them all, why should I despise them'.[24] Convinced of the common unity of the human race, he announced at the mass preceding his coronation his intention to serve as pastor of the whole flock. He returned to this theme when he celebrated the anniversary of his coronation, referring to the ancient tradition of the papal role as universal shepherd, uniting humanity. This was the theme of his Christmas message of 1959, in which he summarized the nineteen Christmas messages of his predecessor Pius XII in two words: unity and peace.[25] He shared his desire for unity and universal peace, expressing special concern for the oppressed of humanity. He regarded the whole world as his family, citing

21 Carlen, *PP*, I, p. 211; Hebblethwaite, *Pope John XXIII*, p. 292.
22 Carlen, *PP*, I, p. 219.
23 Pope John XXIII, *Journal of a Soul*, p. 37.
24 Ibid., p. 66.
25 *Eccoci a Natale*, 25 December 1959, *AAS*, LII, pp. 27–35.

the need for global welfare while applauding the work of the United Nations in assisting refugees.[26]

For John, a crucial aspect of the council was to promote unity. This was reflected in his selection of the Jesuit Cardinal Augustin Bea, for years the rector of the Pontifical Biblical Institute, as well as confessor to Pius XII, as head of the new secretariat for promoting Christian unity. Among other things, the new secretariat aimed to make contact with the 'separated brethren', preparing the way for the participation of observers of other Christian communities in the council, the promotion of ecumenism within the Roman Catholic church, as well as proposing a statement against the age-old discrimination against the Jews. John provided an example by meeting with the observers representing the non-Catholic communities, receiving the archbishop of Canterbury, and altering the Easter liturgy which made reference to the 'perfidious Jews'.

John also sought an accommodation with the Eastern bloc, despite the hesitation of his first secretary of state, Tardini. Drawing a distinction between communism as an atheistic creed, with which the church could not compromise, and communism as a social, political and economic theory, which Pope John deemed a reality that had to be confronted, he was prepared to negotiate on the latter basis. Rather than continuing Pius XII's anti-communist crusade, he was prepared to adopt a pragmatic approach to the communist regimes. Relying on the archbishop of Vienna, Cardinal Franz Koenig, and his personal secretary Monsignor Loris Capovilla, he informed Moscow that the Vatican sought improved relations. He utilized Monsignor Agostino Casaroli, his new secretary of state, to reach accommodations with a number of communist governments, enabling him to obtain the liberation of imprisoned ecclesiastics from Eastern Europe while filling a series of long vacant bishoprics there. The Yugoslav government, meanwhile, granted permission for the public funeral of Cardinal Alojzije Stepinac.[27]

The thawing of Vatican–Moscow relations could be seen in the September 1961 publication of Nikita Khrushchev's interview with *Pravda*, which paid tribute to Pope John's reasonableness. Relations were further improved in November 1961, following Khrushchev's telegram congratulating John on his eightieth birthday, which also expressed support for his efforts to solve international problems by negotiation. The pope responded warmly, thanking the Soviet leader for his greetings and promising to pray for the people of his vast state. Benefits soon followed as the Vatican utilized the Soviet ambassador to Turkey to facilitate the participation of the bishops from Eastern Europe in the council, and Moscow complied. Assured that the council would not condemn communism, Khrushchev gave permission for Russian Orthodox observers to attend and some ninety bishops from the communist countries of Eastern Europe to participate. Early in February 1962, Pope John received

26 Carlen, *PP*, I, pp. 212, 214, 225, 230, 243, 251; Pope John XXIII, *Journal of a Soul*, p. 299.
27 Carlen, *PP*, I, pp. 212–13, 235; Hofmann, *O Vatican!*, p. 29.

Luis Amado-Blanco y Fernandez, the extraordinary ambassador and minister plenipotentiary of Castro's Cuba.[28]

The thaw between the Vatican and Moscow continued even as the Cuban missile crisis of October 1962 threatened the peace of the world. Urged to intervene by President John Kennedy, on 25 October 1962 the pope implored both superpowers not to ignore humanity's cry for peace. The fact that the papal peace message was given front-page coverage in *Pravda* represented the first signal that the Soviets were prepared to negotiate a peaceful resolution of the conflict. Subsequently, Moscow sought regular, though private, contacts with the Vatican, and released Cardinal Josyf Slipyj, primate of Ukranian Catholics, from prison, in deference to John. In December 1962 Norman Cousins hand-delivered a Christmas message from Khrushchev to Pope John, congratulating him for his efforts on behalf of peace and the well-being of the whole of humanity, while in February 1963 the pope received Alexis Adzhubei, the editor of *Izvestia*, and his wife, Rada, Khrushchev's daughter.

While John focused on the council and improved relations with the Eastern bloc, he did not neglect the social question which he considered equally important. In his first encyclical of 29 June 1959 he not only referred to plans to summon an ecumenical council but discussed three objectives: truth, unity and peace.[29] On the issue of unity, he noted that God created men as brothers, and this led him to discuss the social question indicating that all should enjoy the earth's fruits and the necessities of life. In his words, a harmonious unity had to be sought not only among peoples and nations but also among the various classes, and he cited the great disparity in the possession of material goods and the threat of underemployment or unemployment. Expressing his sympathy for the poor who were dissatisfied with their lot in life, he revealed the church was sensitive to their plight and needs.[30]

John returned to the theme of social justice and the union of mankind in his encyclical of September 1959. Soon, thereafter, he addressed a delegation of the second national convention on the dignity of labour, in which he urged workers to seek a synthesis of Christian ideals with the conditions of the working world. In October he praised those who sought a peaceful resolution of the social question.[31] He informed a group of workers from Naples that being guided by Christian principles did not mean being reconciled to stagnation or restricted to obsolete positions, nor did it require that one abandon all efforts to achieve progress. On the contrary, John's church encouraged humanity to improve its living standard, fostering temporal prosperity and happiness. Likewise, in his Easter message of 17 April 1960, he sympathized with those who suffered because of race or economic conditions. In a May 1960 radio message, he defined work as 'the intelligent and effective collaboration of man with God', offering St Joseph as an example to those whose lives were

28 *Diarum Romane Curiae, AAS*, LIV, p. 120.
29 *Ad Petri Cathedram*, 29 June 1959, *AAS*, LI, pp. 497–531.
30 Carlen, *PE, 1958–1981*, V, p. 17.
31 Talk of 17 October 1959, *AAS*, LI, p. 821.

conditioned by the laws of work. Meanwhile, John supported the worldwide 'campaign against Hunger' undertaken by the United Nations Food and Agricultural Organization, and interested himself in the migration provoked by poverty.[32]

At the end of December 1960 John expressed his concern over world conditions and social problems, revealing his intention of releasing an encyclical on the seventieth anniversary of Leo's *Rerum novarum*. *Historia magistra veritas*, or history is the teacher of truth, John argued. In May 1961 John issued *Mater et magistra*, on the church as mother and teacher of all nations, pinpointing the role of Christianity in social progress. Commending Leo's *Rerum novarum*, John claimed it initiated the process by which the church and papacy sought to champion and restore the rights of the working class. In his view, Leo's encyclical represented a synthesis of social principles and a compendium of Catholic social and economic teaching.[33]

John concurred with Leo that work was not simply a commodity, but a specifically human activity, and while private property was a right, it entailed social obligations. Consequently, the state could not remain aloof from economic matters, but had to ensure that the terms of employment were regulated by justice and equity, while safeguarding the dignity of workers. Distressed by the sorry spectacle of millions of workers, on diverse continents, condemned through inadequate wages to subsist in subhuman conditions, often offset by the enormous wealth and unbridled luxury of the privileged few, the pope sought redress. John concluded that remuneration for work could not be left either to the 'laws' of the marketplace or the will of the powerful, decrying the sums squandered on ill-conceived national prestige and armaments to the disadvantage of hard-working men.

John also concurred with the findings of Pius XI in his *Quadragesimo anno*, issued forty years after the publication of *Rerum novarum*. He believed it fallacious to ascribe to property or to work alone whatever had been attained through the combined effort of the two, insisting that while a just share of the profits of production be permitted to accumulate in the hands of the wealthy, sufficient compensation had to be provided to the workers. In his view, the relationship between wages and profits had to be determined by the common good. Probing the demands of the common good he concluded:

> On the national level they include: employment of the greatest possible number of workers; care lest privileged classes arise, even among the workers; maintenance of equilibrium between wages and prices; the need to make goods and services accessible to the greatest number; elimination, or at least the restriction, of inequalities in the various branches of the economy . . .
>
> The demands of the common good on the international level include: the avoidance of all forms of unfair competition between the economies of different countries; the fostering of mutual collaboration and good will;

32 Carlen, *PP*, I, pp. 229, 237–9.
33 *Mater et Magistra*, 15 May 1961, *AAS*, LIII, pp. 401–64.

and effective co-operation in the development of economically less advanced countries.[34]

While John, like Pius XI, refused to accept communism or socialism, whose objectives, he claimed, failed to transcend material well-being, he acknowledged the lawfulness of state and public ownership of productive goods. He conceded that often the exigencies of the common good virtually required that public authority broaden its scope, keeping in mind the Creator's plan that all of the world's goods are primarily intended for the support of the entire human race. *Mater et magistra* assigned an extraordinary responsibility to the state in providing social security. In this fashion, John's encyclical accepted the welfare state as an expression of the common good. It welcomed the increase in social relationships among the nations, peoples and classes of the world's powers. Thus, John was prepared to sanction 'socialization' while he rejected socialism and communism. John deplored the glaring economic and social imbalances internally and internationally, citing the responsibility of those who were blessed with worldly goods to assist those individuals, classes and nations not as well provided.[35]

John's call for social and international justice was repeated in his last encyclical *Pacem in terris* of 11 April 1963, on universal peace in truth, justice, charity and liberty.[36] Unlike some of his predecessors who decried contemporary developments, John appraised the modern world positively. Rather than anathematize the progress of modern research and the discoveries of technology, he concluded, as did Pius XII, that in proper perspective they reflected the infinite greatness of God. In this encyclical the papacy came to terms with the individualism introduced by the revolutionary movement in Europe, and particularly France, but within a Christian context. It catalogued the political, economic, social, cultural and religious rights of man, including the right to bodily integrity, food, clothing, medical care and the necessary social services. John also cited the natural right to share in the benefits of culture and to receive a good general education. Most interestingly, he departed from his predecessors' denunciations of latitudinarianism, asserting man's right to worship God in accordance with the dictates of his own conscience, and 'to profess his religion both in private and in public'.[37]

Pacem in terris also reached an accord with democracy by insisting on man's personal dignity, entailing the right to active participation in public life while contributing to the welfare of his fellow citizens. John's encyclical cited three characteristics of the modern age. In the first place, it listed the progressive improvement in the economic and social conditions of working people, who rightly insist on being treated as human beings involved in every sphere of human society including the socio-economic, the governmental, and the realm

34 *Mater et Magistra*, 15 May 1961, in Carlen, *PE*, V, p. 68.
35 Ibid., V, pp. 59–90.
36 *Litterae Encyclicae Pacem in Terris*, 11 April 1963, *AAS*, LV, pp. 257–304.
37 *Pacem in Terris*, 11 April 1963, in Carlen, *PE, 1958–1981*, V, p. 108.

of learning and culture. Second, it emphasized the increased role of women in the society's life. Aware of their natural dignity, women rightfully demanded in domestic and public life, the rights and duties of all human beings. Finally, Pope John denounced imperialism as an anachronism, as the people of the globe either attained political independence or were in the process of achieving it. Foreign domination was superseded, as was class and gender subordination, as the conviction grew that all were equal in natural dignity. The pope proved to be 'politically correct' on social issues, the women's question, and in his denunciation of imperialism.

John argued that the natural law governing individual life, likewise, regulated the relations of political communities with one another. In his view, these international relations had to be ordered by truth and justice. The first required the elimination of every trace of racial discrimination, and the recognition of the principle that all states are by nature equal in dignity. Justice mandated their relations be governed by mutual rights and duties, and the fact that some had acquired a superior degree of scientific, cultural and economic development did not entitle them to exert political domination over others. Calling for a cessation of the arms race, John pleaded that disputes between nations be resolved by negotiation rather than recourse to arms. In light of the emergence of worldwide problems, the moral order required the establishment of some general form of public authority. John thus applauded the formation of the United Nations, with its 'special aim of maintaining and strengthening peace between nations and entrusted with highly important international functions in the economic, social, cultural, educational and health fields'.

Pope John recognized that the struggle for reform required the co-operation of Catholics with Christians who were separated from the Holy See, and even with non-Christians. The pope advised Catholics to be animated by a spirit of understanding, ready to co-operate in achieving positive objectives. He seemed to support the 'opening to the left' in Italy, and even co-operation with communist regimes, when he wrote that one had to distinguish between error and one who falls into error – repeating that a man who has fallen into error does not cease to be a man. Likewise, John made a clear distinction between 'a false philosophy of the nature, origin and purpose of men and the world' and the political and socio-economic changes, which might have drawn their inspiration from that philosophy.[38]

John's global vision, reflected in the convocation of the council, his social encyclicals, and his support of international organizations, also encouraged the work of the missions. As pope, he frequently praised missionary work, now applauding the missionary spirit of the Belgians, then that of the Irish. He likewise complimented Italian missionaries.[39] In October 1959 he took great delight in presenting crucifixes to over 400 Catholic missionaries in St Peter's

38 Ibid., V, pp. 123–5.
39 Carlen, *PP*, I, pp. 221–2; *Allocutiones*, 26 April 1959, *AAS*, LI, pp. 339–52.

Basilica as they prepared to leave their homes to bring Christianity to distant peoples.[40]

In November 1959, on the fortieth anniversary of Benedict XV's *Maximum illud* on the missions, John issued *Princeps pastorum*, his counterpart on the missions, the native clergy and lay participation.[41] In the forty years following Benedict's apostolic letter, the missions flourished, bringing the church to the entire world, with the first bishop of east Asian origins consecrated in 1923, and the first vicars apostolic of African Negro descent named in 1939. John announced that by 1959 there were sixty-eight Asian and twenty-five African bishops, but claimed that the Christian communities to which missionaries devoted their zeal still required assistance. Observing that the church had historically been identified with Western civilization, John preached that it did not identify with any one culture, welcoming anything that redounds to the honour of the human mind. Missionaries from Europe had therefore to shed their Western cultural accretions. In this regard, the pope warned that their contribution must be carefully attuned to local conditions and needs, urging the local clergy to select from among its ranks those capable of governing, forming and educating their own seminarians. John conveyed a similar message to the second world congress of Negro writers and artists in June 1959, positing that since the church's goal was the salvation of humanity, it could not identify with any single culture.[42]

There was a missionary component in *Mater et magistra* of 15 May 1961, wherein John taught that the church was the mother and teacher of all nations. In it John also applauded the collapse of imperialism and the independence of the peoples of Asia and Africa, while condemning the international disparity of wealth. He wrote that 'the solidarity of the human race and Christian brotherhood demanded the elimination, as far as possible, of these discrepancies'.[43] In *Pacem in terris* of 1963, John returned to the theme of the unity of the human family and the imperative to promote its common good. Clerical missionaries had a role to play in evangelization, but so did lay Catholics, as the pope applauded Papal Volunteers for Latin America (PAVLA).

When the mass on 8 December 1962 closed the first session of the second Vatican council,[44] the expectations aroused had yet to be fulfilled. Although John applauded the Christian unity which emerged, during the course of the two crowded months of the first session, which fired the imagination of the world, no overall plan or structure had emerged, and no decrees had been approved.[45] John, whose cancer was advanced, had barely six months to live, and would not be able to see the council to its successful conclusion. When he

40 *Diletti Figli Missionari! AAS*, LI, pp. 349–52.
41 *Princeps Pastorum*, 28 November 1959, ibid., LI, pp. 833–64.
42 *Princeps Pastorum*, in Carlen, *PE*, V, pp. 43–57; Peter Nichols, *The Politics of the Vatican* (New York, 1968), p. 212; Carlen, *PP*, I, p. 219.
43 Carlen, *PE*, V, p. 77.
44 *Ad Patres Conciliares in Vaticana Basilica adunotas*, 7 December 1962, *AAS*, LV, pp. 33–41.
45 Talk of 22 December 1962, *AAS*, LV, p. 17.

died on 3 June 1963, much was left undone.[46] John had lived for eighty-one and a half years, had been a priest for fifty-eight years, a bishop for thirty-eight, and a pope for less than five years. In his last will and testament, John confessed that his sense of unworthiness had served him well, keeping him humble. Having been born poor, he was happy to die poor, dispensing his personal effects to various charities.[47]

During his short pontificate, more than thirty monarchs and heads of state visited him. His death was mourned by much of the world; Khrushchev's Soviet Union and Janos Kadar's Hungary joined the other powers in sending condolences. Representatives from throughout the world attended his funeral mass. He had been awarded the International Peace Prize of the Eugenio Balzan Foundation in March 1963,[48] and had been selected *Time* magazine's 'man of the year' for 1962. 'Within his greatness were embodied qualities of goodness that impressed all the peoples of the world, who feel a profound loss at his passing', wrote the American secretary of state Dean Rusk. He concluded that 'The world is a smaller place without him . . .'.[49]

John's popularity stemmed not only from his personal warmth and human style, but also from his willingness to take risks – convoking the council was one, the improvement of relations with the Soviet Union and the Eastern bloc represented another, while his determination to keep the Holy See out of Italian politics was yet another. He dared do what no other pope had done: visit President Antonio Segni in the Quirinale Palace, embracing him and Italy in the process. In April 1963 John conferred the Supreme Order of Christ on the president of the Italian Republic. Prior to his death, he planned to open formal diplomatic relations with Israel, according to Rabbi Marc Tanenbaum.[50] Not all were pleased. Likewise his reconciliation with Jews, Protestants, Muslims, and even non-believers, and his advancement of the social question, spawned criticism as well as acclaim. Conservative Catholics held him responsible for opening the floodgates of change in Rome. Consciously or unconsciously, John had unleashed liberal sentiments in the church which prompted calls for ecclesiastical reforms.

46 *Estrema Aegrotatio, obitus, Funebria, AAS*, LV, pp. 465–9.
47 *AAS*, LX, pp. 508–10.
48 Ibid., LV, pp. 448–55, 497–507, 536–55.
49 Ibid., LV, p. 529.
50 *Diarum Romanae Curiae*, ibid., LV, p. 464; Jim Castelli, 'Says John Planned to Recognize Israel', *National Catholic Reporter*, 5 January 1973, p. 3.

CHAPTER 15

The papacy in an age of transition: the pontificate of Paul VI

When the conclave of 19 June 1963 opened, the candidate of the conservatives was Cardinal Ildebrando Atoniutti, champion of *Opus Dei*, the Spanish organization which enjoyed the special support of the Holy Office. Giovanni Battista Enrico Antonio Maria Montini, the cardinal archbishop of Milan, emerged as the liberal choice. Conservatives opposed Montini because he had opposed the Lateran Accords with Mussolini's Italy, and in the post Second World War period had not favoured Luigi Gedda's interventionism in Italian political life. They also charged that he followed the philosophical precepts of Jacques Maritain, and was thought to support the priest-worker movement. Clerics of the right also disliked the left-leaning tendencies of Studium, the Montini-sponsored publishing house, and suspected the archbishop was inclined to accept an 'opening to the left' in Italian politics. The first five ballots proved inconclusive, but on the sixth ballot cast on 21 June, the 65-year-old Montini was elected the 259th successor to St Peter. He assumed the name Paul, announcing his determination to reach out to the modern gentiles.[1]

Unlike other popes who were little known in Rome, the frail Montini was universally known. Born to a prominent bourgeois family of Brescia, his father Giorgio was a bank lawyer who controlled the Catholic newspaper *Il Cittadino*, and was active in politics, having been elected to the Chamber of Deputies for Don Sturzo's Popular Party. He had been president of the Unione Popolare. His mother Giuditta Alghisi served as president of the women's association of Brescia. Montini received his early education from the Jesuits at the Cesare Arici school, but poor health forced him to complete his education privately. Even after entering the seminary in 1916, his fragile condition conspired to keep him at home. Some suspected that his ailments and bouts of irregular heartbeat contributed to his introversion. Following his ordination in 1920, he was sent to Rome to study at the Gregorian university and the university of Rome. In 1922, through the intervention of Cardinal Pietro Gasparri, he was transferred to the accademia dei nobili ecclesiastici to study diplomacy.

1 *Electio Summi Pontificus, AAS*, LV, p. 612.

Appointed attaché to the nunciature in Warsaw in 1923, within one year he returned to Rome, unable to withstand the rigours of the Polish climate. Assigned to the secretariat of state, and serving as ecclesiastical assistant or chaplain to the Italian Association of Catholic University Students in Rome (Federazione Universitaria Cattolica Italiana), he caught the attention of Cardinal Eugenio Pacelli, who made him undersecretary for ordinary affairs, and furthered his career. When Pacelli became pope in 1939, Montini functioned as pro-secretary of state, thus serving over thirty years in the secretariat of state, and judged the most important figure in the Vatican after Pius XII. During that time, he made two brief visits to the United States, and some speculated that Pius XII, to whom Montini was devoted, wanted him to succeed to the papacy.[2]

Such did not prove to be the case. In the consistory of 1953, when Pius named his new cardinals, neither Montini nor Tardini appeared on the list; according to Pius both had refused the offer. Shortly thereafter, Montini, who had served Pius long and loyally, was dispatched to Milan as archbishop, a move perceived as exile from Rome. Such speculation was reinforced by the fact that during the course of the next four years Pius did not name Montini a cardinal, as was customary for the head of the most prestigious see of Italy, and thus he was ineligible for the papal throne in 1958. This was remedied by Pope John, whose friendship with Montini dated back to 1925. John arranged matters so that the archbishop would play an important role in the council, and early on believed that Montini would succeed him. Thus it was not surprising that Montini, who headed the list of new cardinals created in 1958, was invited to collaborate in drafting some of John's major speeches.[3]

When Paul became pope only one, inconclusive session of the council had been completed. Six days after his election, Paul proclaimed that the council would be continued, announcing the date of 29 September 1963 for its resumption.[4] Subsequently, in a September allocution to the cardinals and curia, Paul invoked *aggiornamento* and renewal.[5] His *aggiornamento* included the need to revise the canon law, reform the curia, while continuing his commitment to the social justice enunciated in his predecessor's encyclicals. Thus he made it clear that the main programme of his pontificate would be the completion, followed by the implemention, of the council's decisions. Although Paul shared many of John's goals, including his global vision, he was far more Roman and diplomatic than his predecessor. However, he fully shared John's conviction that peace ultimately depended on justice, love and liberty, and likewise sought to avoid persecutions, admonitions and suppressions. To reassure hard-core

2 *Curriculum Vitae Pauli, PP,* VI. ibid., LV, pp. 643–4; Richard J. Wolff, 'Giovanni Battista Montini and Italian Politics, 1897–1933: The Early Life of Pope Paul VI', *Catholic Historical Review*, LXXXI, 2 (April 1985), pp. 228–47.

3 Peter Hebblethwaite, *Paul VI: The First Modern Pope* (New York, 1993), pp. 319, 326–31; idem, *Pope John XXIII, Pope of the Council* (London, 1984), p. 345; Carlen, *PP*, I, p. 211.

4 *Sacrosanctum Oecumenicum Concilium Vaticanum II*, 27 June 1963, *AAS*, LV, p. 581.

5 Allocution of 21 September 1963, ibid., LV, pp. 796–7.

conservatives, he confirmed Amleto Cigognani as his secretary of state.[6] Paul's task was to perpetuate John's reformism without allowing it to degenerate into revolution.

Early in July 1963, Paul received President Kennedy, who wanted to discuss Vietnam and the Vatican's position towards the countries of Eastern Europe. Paul, in turn, commended the achievements of the United States in race relations, citing the harmony of the president's statements and programme with John's *Pacem in terris*. 'We are ever mindful in our prayers of the efforts to ensure to all your citizens the equal benefits of citizenship, which have as their foundation the equality of all men because of their dignity as persons and children of God', the pope told the American president.[7]

Soon thereafter, Paul expressed his esteem for the United Nations, comparing its temporal universality with the spiritual universality of the church:

> In recent years, the voices of the Popes, Our Predecessors, was among the first to augur the formation of a body such as that of which you, Mister U Thant, guide its activities. In his own time, Pope Benedict the fifteenth desired it; its fundamental criteria were traced with happy foresight by Pope Pius the twelvth in his Christmas message of nineteen hundred and thirty-nine, and that of September, nineteen hundred and forty-four; then its importantance was underlined and its increasingly perfect functioning was encouraged by Pope John the twenty-third in his last Encyclical Letter, 'Pacem in terris', the text of which, bearing the autograph signature of the Pontiff, was consigned to you, Mister Secretary, by Cardinal Suenens.[8]

In August 1963 he focused on John's social teaching in *Mater et magistra*, while deploring the difficulties faced by the people of Vietnam. Paul hoped for better days, applauding the treaty banning nuclear experiments.[9] As September neared, and the time approached for convoking the second session of the council, Paul outlined new directives, including the admission of lay Catholics, extending invitations to non-Catholic observers, and appointing cardinal moderators. In mid-September, while issuing invitations to the council's second session, he restated its task of renewal. Later, at the opening of this second session, he recalled the council's four goals: awareness of the church, renewal, Christian unity, and dialogue with the modern world. The council, he informed non-Catholic observers, called for encounter and true dialogue, praying together as well as listening and loving one another.[10]

The second session lasted sixty-seven days from 29 September to 4 December 1963, during whose course there were more than forty working sessions, and over 600 speeches delivered. Paul struggled to persuade the Roman curia

6 *Nomina Pontificia di Cardinale Amleto Giovanni Cicognani*, *AAS*, LV, pp. 582–3; Carlen, *PP*, I, p. 295.

7 Pope Paul VI to President John F. Kennedy, 2 June 1963, *AAS*, LV, p. 650.

8 *Ad Excellentissimum Virum U Thant*, 11 July 1963, ibid., LV, p. 653.

9 *Ad populum vietnamensem*, 30 August 1963, *AAS*, LV, p. 759; *Nuntius Telegraphicus*, 5 August 1963, ibid., LV, p. 760.

10 *Summi Pontificis Allocutio*, 29 September 1963, *AAS*, LV, pp. 841–59; Carlen, *PP*, I, pp. 300–2.

and the council to collaborate. He pressed the bishops to exercise their rights to govern the church with him, encouraging them to create conditions for ecumenical encounters with non-Catholics. At the close of this second session, Paul expressed gratitude for the results achieved and referred explicitly to the proclamation of the constitution on the liturgy, *Sacrosanctum concilium*,[11] and the decree on the means of social communication, *Inter mirificia*. In reforming the liturgy, the church fathers sought 'to adapt more closely to the needs of our age those institutions which are subject to change; to foster whatever can promote union among all who believe in Christ; to strengthen whatever can help to call all mankind into the church's fold'.[12]

Aware that much remained to be done, in December Paul forecast the agenda for the third session, announcing his intention to undertake a pilgrimage to the Holy Land early in 1964. The first pope to fly in an airplane, and first to visit the Holy Land, Paul met Athenagoras II, the ecumenical patriarch of Constantinople there, as well as the Armenian patriarch of Jerusalem and the Anglican archbishop of the City. His message during his 4–6 January 1964 visit was one of peace and unity – a message he transmitted to King Hussein of Jordan and President Zalman Shazar of Israel. Paul recognized the historic significance of the first meeting between pope and patriarch since the schism of 1054, convinced that the Jerusalem meeting marked the beginning of a new era in the relations between the Holy See and the ecumenical patriarchate.[13] In March 1964 Pope Paul received a delegation from the German Social Democratic Party, despite the opposition of the nuncio in Berlin and the disapproval of the German bishops. Marking the end of almost a century of hostility between the Vatican and social democracy, the visit paved the way for the Social Democratic assumption of power in 1969.[14] Some saw this as a precursor for papal approval of 'an opening to the left' in Italy.

As Paul prepared for the third session of the council scheduled to convene in mid-September 1964, he invoked the need for unity which had moved him to visit the Holy Land and which inspired the council.[15] In August he issued his first encyclical letter *Ecclesiam suam*, indicating his intention of continuing the dialogue within the church, with non-Catholic Christians, with non-Christians, and with the entire contemporary world.[16] Paul's first encyclical sought to heal the rift between the church and the modern world which had persisted since the French Revolution.

11 *Ad Patres Conciliares habita*, 4 December 1963, *AAS*, LVI, pp. 31–40; *Sacrosanctum Concilium Decumenicum Vaticanum II*, 4 December 1963, ibid., LVI, pp. 97–134.

12 Austin Flannery, ed., *Vatican Council II: The Conciliar and Post Conciliar Documents* (Grand Rapids, MI, 1992), I, p. 1.

13 *Summi Pontificis Peregrinato in Palestinum, AAS*, LVI, pp. 158–82; Carlen, *PP*, I, pp. 308–11, 317.

14 Paul R. Waibel, 'The Politics of Accommodation: The SPD Visit to the Vatican, March 5, 1964', *Catholic Historical Review*, LXV, 2 (April 1979), pp. 238–9.

15 *Vitale svolgimento del Concilio Ecumenico*, 23 June 1964, *AAS*, LVI, pp. 583–4.

16 *Ecclesiam Suam*, 6 August 1964, *AAS*, LVI, pp. 609–59.

In September 1964 Paul prepared for the opening of the third session of the council, allowing some women to attend as auditors, although they were not accorded the right to speak or vote during the debates. At the opening of this session, Paul indicated the council had many important matters to decide but the most delicate concerned the nature of the episcopate.[17] Soon, thereafter, he told the non-Catholic Christians, who likewise attended as observers, that the church was prepared to participate in ecumenical dialogue. By 21 November, when the third session closed, three important decrees had been approved: *Lumen gentium*, on the dogmatic constitution of the church, explaining the relationship of the pope, the bishops, priests and laity within the church; *Orientalium ecclesiaum*, the decree on the Catholic eastern churches; and *Unitatis redintegratio*, the decree on ecumenism.[18]

At the end of 1964, Pope Paul ventured to Bombay, India, to be present at the thirty-eighth International Eucharistic Congress. Upon returning to Rome Paul planned for the fourth session of the council, which he envisioned as the last. In January 1965 he revealed his intention of naming twenty-seven new cardinals, proclaiming the need to make the college more universal and appointing the four major Eastern patriarchs to it. When the complete list appeared in February, it included a broad spectrum of nations, a variety of ecclesiastical rites, and an impressive array of talent. A number of problems continued to haunt the church, including the birth control issue which John had assigned to a commision of six members. Paul expanded the membership of this special commission, although its task remained delicate and difficult. In March he reminded its members of the urgency of the situation and the need for an unambiguous direction for the church.[19] Unfortunately, he received conflicting messages.

In June 1965, addressing the college of cardinals, Paul provided a broad survey of the difficulties confonting the church including collegiality, the reform of canon law, mixed marriages, birth control, world peace, and concluding the council. The latter remained a matter of concern due to the number, seriousness and complexity of subjects under consideration. Paul foresaw the immense problems that would follow its conclusion, recognizing the spirit of expectation and eagerness that it had aroused among the faithful. Nonetheless, at the opening of the fourth session on 14 September, Paul did not discuss the themes to be examined, preferring to leave the church fathers freedom on such matters. The following day, however, Paul announced that the Vatican council had motivated him to establish a synod of bishops to collaborate with him in an advisory capacity in the governance of the church.[20] It represented the first tentative step towards a more collegial governance of the church with the bishops balancing the Roman curia.

17 Allocution of 14 September 1964, ibid., LVI, pp. 805–16.
18 In Vaticana Basilica ad Conciliares Patres habita, 21 November 1964, *AAS*, LVI, pp. 1007–18; Flannery, ed., *Vatican Council II*, pp. 350–426, 441–51, 452–70.
19 Carlen, *PP*, I, p. 338.
20 Ibid., I, pp. 342, 344, 346.

Pope Paul, who supported the United Nations' quest for disarmament and fight against hunger, agreed to address that body on the occasion of its twentieth anniversary in October 1965. His message was a simple one. It was 'no more war, war never again'. The pope's plan had four major elements. First, relations between states should be governed by reason, justice, law and negotiation rather than by fear, violence, deceit or war. This required disarmament. The money saved from the stockpiling of weapons could, and should, be utilized to assist the developing nations, and solving the problems of hunger and poverty. Finally, the pope saw the need to protect fundamental human rights and freedom, and above all religious liberty. Paul's programme represented an elaboration of Benedict XV's peace proposal.

The day that Paul returned from his peace mission, the council was discussing the final chapter of *Gaudium et spes* on war and peace. If this represented a measure that pleased liberals, Paul's decision to withdraw the issue of clerical celibacy from conciliar debate was not, as celibacy joined contraception as another subject removed from the council's agenda. On 28 October 1965 Paul promulgated five important council documents: one on the pastoral office of bishops in the church, a second on the adaptation and renewal of religious life, a third on the training of priests, a fourth on Christian education, and finally *Nostra aetate*, on the church's attitude toward non-Christian religions. In the last document, the church reproved and deplored 'all hatreds, persecutions, displays of anti-Semitism levelled at any time or from any source against the Jews'.[21] It represented a belated condemnation of Nazi anti-Semitism which Pius XII had failed to censure clearly and publicly during the Holocaust.

In mid-November 1965 Paul spoke of implementing the norms on the dogmatic constitution on divine revelation and the decree on the apostolate of lay people, as the council neared its end. As it drew to a conclusion on 7 December, a joint declaration issued by Pope Paul VI and Partiarch Athenogoras I, read at Rome and Istanbul simultaneously, nullified the Catholic–Orthodox exchange of excommunications issued in 1054, stipulating that they did not break the ecclesiastical communion between the sees of Rome and Constantinople. That same day, there was promulgated a declaration on religious liberty, one on the church's missionary activity, another on the ministry and life of priests, and finally *Gaudium et spes* or the pastoral constitution on the church in the modern world. The pope thanked the diplomatic delegates who attended the closing ceremonies of Vatican council II, pleased by their appreciation of its importance. On 8 December 1965 Paul declared the council closed.[22] The results proved mixed and the implementation of its liturgical innovations particularly difficult, with some wishing to forge ahead while others urged caution and restraint. The council's impact on the church, and its place in the modern world, had just begun.

21 Flannery, ed., *Vatican Council II*, I, p. 741.
22 Carlen, *PP*, I, p. 355.

The year following the council, 1966, and in some respects the subsequent decade, were dominated by a continuing discussion of issues raised by that body and the need to implement its decrees and decisions. Some cynically argued *aggiornamento si, ma cambiamento, no!* (updating yes, but change, no!). The difficulties of the *dopoconcilio* (post-conciliar age) proved as troubling as those confronted during its sessions. Paul recognized that the documents promulgated could not affect change unless they were implemented, and therefore established post-conciliar commissions to continue its work, as well as yearly meetings to be held in Rome to continue the dialogue. He provided encouragement to the commission for implementing the constitution on the liturgy, while proposing a real and continuous Catholic–Jewish dialogue.[23]

Perhaps the encyclical that most pleased liberals within and outside the church, and established Paul's progressive position, was his social encyclical *Populorum progressio* of 26 March 1967, on the development of peoples. Deemed by some a *magna carta* for justice and peace, Paul revealed his concern for those attempting to escape the ravages of hunger, poverty, endemic disease and ignorance, making a plea for social justice and fundamental improvement for the impoverished masses and emerging nations of the third world. Citing Leo's *Rerum novarum*, Pius XI's *Quadragesimo anno* and John XXIII's *Mater et magistra* and *Pacem in terris*, as well as his own trips to Latin America (1960) and Africa (1962), he addressed the perplexing problems of these continents. Observing that each individual belongs to a community, he cited their responsibility to further the development of human society as a whole, indicating that the earth belongs to all, not just the rich. Issuing four commandments for the contemporary world order, he instructed its members to free the enslaved, educate the masses, provide health care for the poor, and feed the hungry. Paul insisted that when private gain and basic community needs were in conflict, the public authorities had to find an equitable solution. 'You are not making a gift of what is yours to the poor man', he wrote, quoting St Ambrose, 'but you are giving back what is his.'[24] Some have seen this as Paul's endorsement of liberation theology for the third world, pleasing liberals and alarming conservatives.

Paul's subsequent encyclical of 24 June 1967, on priestly celibacy, distressed liberals while comforting conservatives. Using arguments from theology and scripture, as well as an assessment of historical, sociological, psychological and pastoral views, he reaffirmed the church's traditional position of mandating priestly celibacy. 'We consider that the present law of celibacy should continue to be linked to the ecclesiastical ministry', Paul wrote.[25] While he shared the council's conviction that the church had to draw closer to the

23 Ibid., I, pp. 358–9, 364–5, 378; *Orientations et Suggestions pour l'Application de la Declaration Conciliare 'Nostra Aetate', AAS*, LXVII, pp. 74–8.
24 *Populorum Progressio*, 26 March 1967, in Carlen, *PE*, V, p. 187.
25 *Sacerdotalis Caelibatus*, 24 June 1967, ibid., V, p. 205.

world, he indicated that there was a wrong and right way to do so.[26] Even his reform of the Roman curia later in the year did not compensate for what some deemed his 'reactionary' position on celibacy.

Nor was the papal attempt at conciliation furthered by Paul's long-awaited pronouncement on birth control, provided in *Humanae vitae* in July 1968. It was hoped by some that the commission on this question first created by John, and then enlarged by Paul, would encourage the Vatican to modify its traditional position on physical and chemical methods of contraception. Expectations were fuelled by the fact that the commission reportedly advised Paul that church teaching on birth control could, and should, be changed. Paul, however, rejected such suggestions. Having examined the Commission report, he condemned as unlawful 'the use of means which directly prevent conception, even when the reasons given for the latter practice may appear to be upright and serious'.[27] Unwilling to accept the notion that the responsibility of procreating life should be left to the arbitrary action of men, Paul asserted in his encyclical that there were limits to humanity's control over the body and its natural functions.

Conscious of the fact that some viewed birth control as a means of dealing with poverty, Paul refused to hold divine Providence responsible for 'misguided governmental policies, of an insufficient sense of social justice'.[28] In this fashion Paul VI tied the issue of birth control to the disequilibrium of wealth between the industrial North and the dependent South. The pope opposed the northern solution of curbing population to preserve its privileged position, advocating instead a more equitable distribution of the world's wealth. His position unleashed a torrent of criticism, particularly in North America and Europe, with the more radical Jesuits challenging the validity of *Humanae vitae*. Nonetheless, Paul remained steadfast.

In 1968 Paul flew to Bogota and Medellin Colombia, the first visit of a pope to Latin America, to address the opening of the Latin American Bishops Conference and conclude the Eucharistic Congress in Bogota. In Latin America his support of the third world in *Populorum progressio* was appreciated, as was his condemnation of the unequal distribution of the world's goods catalogued in *Humanae vitae*, a disequilibrium which spurred the industrial world to press for population control. At Madellin, the Latin American bishops indicated their church would dedicate itself to preach the gospel to the poor and neglected, stressing liberation not only from individual sins but the sinful structures of society, thus laying the foundation for liberation theology. Citing Paul's *Populorum progressio* as well as the council's *Gaudium et spes*, the bishops charged that governments that supported repressive economic systems which exploited the poor were guilty of violence. They latched on to the pope's address which stressed human rights and social justice, considering it a confirmation of their liberation theology. Frightened by the radicalism of part of the Latin American

26 *Uno dei risultati*, of 12 July 1967, and *Noi divevamo*, of 19 July 1967, in Carlen *PP*, I, p. 404.
27 *Humanae vitae*, 25 July 1968, in Carlen, *PE*, V, p. 227.
28 Ibid., V, p. 230.

clergy, Paul had later to moderate their excessive zeal and use of Marxism to champion their cause.

Some critics of the pope charged that Paul, in his attempt to maintain a balance between extremes in the church, proved indecisive, and referred to him as the 'Hamlet of the papacy'. Paul was aware of such criticism, asking 'What is my state of mind? Am I Hamlet? Or Don Quixote? On the Left? On the right? I don't feel I have been properly understood.'[29] These questions increased during the later years of his pontificate. While he insisted that the reforms of Vatican II be implemented, he distinguished between reform and revolution. Tradition, he told the cardinals and the curia, was the key to the church, but while some believed it enclosed it in a tomb, in reality it served as the secret of the church's mysterious vitality.[30] While preserving the traditionalist posture on priestly celibacy and contraception, he continued to be influenced by the new French Catholic philosophy and theology of Jacques Maritain and others, and made the French Cardinal Gabriel-Marie Garrone prefect of the congregation for Catholic education. In 1969 he made Jean Villot his secretary of state, the first non-Italian to hold the post since Cardinal Merry del Val, who served Pius X. A good part of the thirty-five new cardinals he named that year were non-Italians, giving the college of cardinals a more international outlook.

Paul continued to pursue his *via media*, encouraging the extraordinary synod at the end of 1969 to explore the relationship between papal primacy and episcopal collegiality. In 1970 he ruled that bishops must submit their resignation when they reached seventy-five, and that cardinals after their eightieth year could no longer take part in a conclave. Some suggested that the pope himself should retire, but Paul continued to preside over the church and travel on behalf of peace and social justice. In 1969 he visited Africa, again the first pope to do so, while in 1970 he visited Australia, Indonesia and the Philippines where the Bolivian painter Benjamin Mendoza made an attempt against his life in Manila. Undaunted, the pope continued his spiritual leadership and his *Ostpolitik* of seeking a reconcilation of sorts with the communist regimes of Eastern Europe. Abandoning anathemas for dialogue, the Vatican established diplomatic relations with Yugoslavia in 1971, and improved relations with Hungary to the point that Cardinal Mindszenty was released that same year. Utilizing traditional diplomacy, Paul sought to improve the religious position of millions of Catholics controlled by the communist regimes of Eastern Europe.

Throughout these difficult years, the pope continued to inject the Vatican into international affairs, supporting peace in Vietnam and upholding the cause of the United Nations. Speaking before that body in 1965, Paul proposed the admission of 'red' China and two years later suggested that Taiwan establish diplomatic relations with the mainland government.[31] Unlike Pius XII, who had often maintained a diplomatic silence, Paul was outspoken, denouncing

29 Hebblethwaite, *Paul VI*, p. 7.
30 Address to the Cardinals, 23 December 1974, *AAS*, LXVII, p. 50.
31 Peter Hebblethwaite, *The Year of Three Popes* (New York, 1979), p. 36.

the genocide in Biafra and the bombing of civilians in Vietnam. At the end of 1967 President Johnson visited Paul in the Vatican, and the following spring the Americans announced a pause in their bombing of North Vietnam. In 1968 the Vatican acted as an intermediary for the Paris peace talks. Paul described peace as the sun of the world.[32] In July 1972 the Holy See participated in the conference on security and co-operation in Europe at Helsinki as a participant and not simply as an observer. It marked the first full participation in an international conference since the congress of Vienna of 1815. Cardinal Casaroli, who was at Helsinki, followed this by a visit to Moscow in 1972, the first Vatican official to travel there in an official capacity. Subsequently, he travelled to Castro's Cuba, and invoked a just and peaceful solution to the sad situation in Northern Ireland.[33] In 1973 Paul established a 'study commission on the role of women in church and society' but warned from the outset that the ordination of women would be excluded, a prohibition repeated in 1977. Paul appreciated the changed role that women played in society, and acknowledged that the new condition was not entirely negative.[34] In January 1973 he met with Golda Meir and talked with the Israeli prime minister for over an hour.[35] His audience to Betty Friedan, author of *The Feminine Mystique*, in 1974, like his earlier proclamation of Mary as mother of the church, or his appointment of the first woman to the pontifical academy of sciences, did not placate the feminists. In turn, homosexuals deplored his declaration 'on certain problems of social ethics' of 1975, which branded sexual relations between persons of the same sex as necessarily disordered.

Paul, who reached his eightieth year in September 1977, was not in the best of health. His policies continued to confound observers and provoke criticism from both the left and the right – from Hans Küng who charged that the pope sought to return the church to a pre-conciliar theology, and Marcel Lefebvre who decried Paul's rejection of traditional practices. His last audience in 1978 was for the socialist president of Italy, and his last letter was dispatched to Giuseppe Prezzolini, a non-believer. In March Paul caught a persistent cold, and he died at Castel Gandolfo on 6 August 1978 after a massive heart attack. He asked that his funeral be simple and no monument be placed over his grave.

Straddling the twentieth century and having had to cope with modernism, futurism, fascism, Nazism, communism and feminism among other ideologies and movements, Paul has been labelled the first modern pope and one of the most talented figures to occupy the chair of Peter in the twentieth century. The last pope to be crowned, he not only brought John's council to a successful conclusion, he continued his work of *aggiornamento* and reconciliation with the modern world. He managed to dismantle the papal court and reform the Roman curia without alienating either, introducing collegiality in the church

32 Paul's Address of 1 January 1975, *AAS*, LXVII, p. 55.
33 Paul's Address to Irish Ambassador, 19 December 1974, ibid., LXVII, p. 47.
34 *Allocutiones*, 7 December 1974, ibid., LXVII, pp. 35–6.
35 'Meir Sees Pope Amid Controversy', *National Catholic Reporter*, 15 January 1973, p. 3.

without undermining papal primacy. Paul internationalized the college of cardinals, offering the red hat to individuals from Karachi in Pakistan, Osaka in Japan, Nairobi in Kenya, Seoul in Korea, and Hanoc in Vietnam. Travelling more than all of his predecessors combined, Pope Paul's visits to all five continents earned him the title of the pilgrim pope and rendered the papacy far more international and much less Eurocentric. He visited the Holy Land, India, Turkey, the United Nations in New York, Latin America, the Philippines, Australia and Portugal among other places.

Paul helped to make the church in Africa more native, and implemented the use of modern languages in the liturgy. These and other achievements were overshadowed by the sharp divisions within the church on the issue of reform and continuity, tormenting Paul and rendering his last years difficult. For conservatives, he had gone too far; for liberals, his reformism remained incomplete. While conservatives found his stance against communism and theological revolt too timid, liberals criticized his position on birth control and gender issues as too rigid. The church at Paul's death was divided into a right wing, a left wing, and the *via media* pursued by the pope. The destruction of most of Paul's personal papers on his orders only compounded the confusion surrounding the man and his contribution. The bitter controversy provoked by the implementation of the council's directives led some to predict that the church and papacy could not preserve their precarious balance and would either revert to reaction or be overwhelmed by revolution. To Paul's credit, neither occurred.

CHAPTER 16

The year of three popes and beyond: the contemporary papacy

Despite the success of the second Vatican council (1962–65), in 1978 the Catholic church remained divided. Critics of conciliar reform, with Archbishop Marcel Lefebvre among the most prominent, denounced the innovations and moved to restore the traditional discipline. Meanwhile, liberals lamented that Paul VI's attempts to implement the *aggiornamento* of his predecessor and the council were half-hearted. These divisions found their way into the college of cardinals, which numbered 111 in 1978, the largest it had ever been. The rules for the conclave were set by Paul's *Romano pontifici eligendo*, which barred cardinals over eighty from voting.[1] Those who wished bishops and priests, and perhaps even the laity to participate in the election, and called for an end to the shroud of secrecy, denounced the changes in the electoral process as 'trivial'. Others railed against the exclusion of the older cardinals. Ideological divisions were compounded by national rivalries. The Italians, who constituted about half of the fifty-seven European cardinals, expected that the 455-year-old tradition continue, and the next pope be Italian. Others claimed the time had arrived to smash this lock on the papacy, as non-Italian names were seriously pondered.

The first ballots cast on 26 August 1978 proved inconclusive, but the fourth yielded the name of the 262nd successor of St Peter: Cardinal Albino Luciani, archbishop and patriarch of Venice. Determined to implement the initiatives of the second Vatican council supported by his two immediate predecessors, Luciano broke with tradition by choosing two names, John Paul. In his inaugural message, following the mass celebrated in the Sistine Chapel for his pontificate, he promised to continue the work of Pope Paul, and his predecessor, Pope John XXIII.[2]

Characterized by an uncluttered faith, the new pontiff explained why he had assumed the name of John Paul I. Admiring the 'wisdom of heart' of John, as well as the 'preparation and learning' of Paul, he shared their vision

1 This constitution upheld the provisions of Paul VI's previous *motu proprio Ingravescentem aetatem* II. See *AAS*, LXVII, pp. 609–45.
2 Carlen, *PP*, II, p. 843.

to serve the church.[3] Outside Venice, Luciani was virtually unknown, unlike his predecessor Montini, who had an international reputation. True enough, he had written a book entitled *Illustrissimi*, which contained a series of letters to fictional and historical personages, in which he chatted with historical and literary figures, such as Mark Twain, Pinocchio, King David, Guglielmo Marconi and others, but its circulation was limited.[4]

Albino Luciano was born on 17 October 1912 in a small village in the Dolomites, outside of Belluno. His mother, a scullery maid, was devoted to the church, and his father, a seasonal labourer, found it necessary to travel to France, Switzerland and Germany to support his two daughters from his first marriage, and his three children from his second. When ten, Luciano entered the minor seminary at Feltre and progressed to the major seminary at Belluno, after a brief period of military service. He was ordained at Belluno in July 1935, and sent by his bishop to the Gregorian university in Rome, where he received a doctorate in theology, having studied the theology of Antonio Rosmini. In 1937 he was appointed vice-rector of the seminary at Belluno, where he remained until 1958, when he was named bishop of Vittorio-Veneto by Pope John XXIII. In 1969 Pope Paul VI named him patriarch of Venice, and in 1973 conferred the cardinal's hat. In Venice, as in Vittorio-Veneto, the public appreciated his simplicity, goodness, directness and humour, as well as his determination to serve the poorest of the poor.

As pope, John Paul I remained unpretentious. In his message of August 1978 to the cardinals, John Paul I revealed his commitment to the council's heritage.[5] Discarding pomp and ceremony, he perceived the church as existing for the welfare of others and especially the poor. It was not surprising that this priest and bishop who had chosen *Humilitas* (humility) as his motto, refused to be crowned as a monarch, insisting on being installed as bishop of Rome with a pontifical mass celebrated in St Peter's Square. Thus on 3 September 1978 he received the symbol of his authority, the *pallium*, a mantle of lamb's wool. Dispensing with the imperial 'we' used by his predecessors, John Paul I utilized the simpler 'I' and addressed the public as 'brothers and sisters' rather than 'sons and daughters'. He sought to abolish the use of the *sedia gestatoria* or portable throne on which pontiffs were borne, preferring to walk, until pilgrims complained they could not see him. From the first, his pontificate promised to be more pastoral than authoritarian. The existence of bad catholics, bad priests, bad popes, he related did not mean the Gospel had been applied, but rather it had not.[6]

Although John Paul confirmed Cardinal Jean Villot as secretary of state while retaining most of the dignitaries in the curia, he faced enormous responsibilities.

3 Albino Luciani, *Illustrisimi: Letters from Pope John Paul I*, trans. William Weaver (Boston, 1976).
4 Peter Hebblethwaite, *The Year of Three Popes* (New York, 1979), pp. 44–6, 71; Gordon Thomas and Max Morgan-Witts, *Pontiff* (Garden City, NY, 1983), pp. 94–6, 109–11.
5 John Paul I to the cardinals and the world, 27 August 1978, in Albino Luciani, *The Message of John Paul I* (Boston, 1978), pp. 25–40.
6 Luciani, *Letters from Pope John Paul I*, p. 78.

He relied on the cardinals who administered the departments to confront the daily cares of church government, acknowledging his inexperience in these sectors of church life.[7] John Paul I wished to further the internationalization of the curia commenced by Paul, while introducing younger figures in its ranks. At the same time, he continued his commitment to the poor, serving as the advocate for the dispossessed, oppressed and disadvantaged of the world. While he appreciated the importance of the production of wealth, he cautioned humanity not to become too attached to it, and insisted that wealth be shared, removing the serious inequities of the day.[8]

John Paul I stressed the need for prayers to assist the talks then being held at Camp David, as he sought a satisfactory solution to the problems of the Palestinians, the security of Israel, and the well-being of the city of Jerusalem. The Israeli-Arab conflict he considered a malady which infected the neighbouring countries with unfortunate consequences.[9] Recognizing he did not possess miraculous solutions for the problems of the age, he hoped to contribute the spirit of universal charity and openness to transcendent values. The church, he explained, had to address the problems of freedom, justice, peace and development, while promoting friendship between individuals and peoples. With love, one could do everything.[10]

The challenge of the papacy proved a heavy burden for John Paul I. His long days taxed his stamina and undermined the tenuous health of the smiling, humble and serene pope. He had suffered from a tubercular condition early in life, complicated by phlebitis, aggravated by the series of minor heart attacks he had endured during the past years. John Paul I confided that he had been in the hospital eight times and had endured four operations. 'When you were little, you were very ill', his mother had told him when he was a boy, adding, 'I had to take you from one doctor to another and watch over you whole nights.'[11] Still, his cheerful disposition hid the gravity of his condition and the enormous burdens imposed by the papacy. Thus, when he died in September after only thirty-three days in office, the public suspected the worst. These suspicions were fuelled when the curia refused to authorize an autopsy, and further enhanced when a major financial crisis appeared to engulf the Holy See, seemingly involving a figure who was mysterious to many, Monsignor Paul Marcinkus.

In the second conclave of 1978, which opened on 14 October, the bloc of twenty-seven Italian cardinals were hopelessly divided between the ultraconservative Giuseppe Siri and the liberal Giovanni Benelli. The Italians split on the issue of continuing the reforms of Vatican II, or attempting some

7 John Paul I to the Sacred College of Cardinals, 30 August 1978, in Luciani, *Message of John Paul I*, pp. 45–7.

8 Luciani, *Letters from Pope John Paul I*, p. 209.

9 John Paul's talk to a general audience on 6 September 1978, in Albino Luciani, *Message of John Paul I*, pp. 89–90.

10 Carlen, *PP*, II, pp. 845–8.

11 John Paul I to a general audience, 13 September 1978, in Luciani, *Message of John Paul I*, p. 105.

curtailment. These divisions prevented the election of a pope in the early ballots until 16 October, when Cardinal Karol Wojtyla, archbishop of Krakow, was elected. The selection of the first non-Italian since Hadrian VI of Utrecht in 1522 commenced a new era for the church. Only fifty-eight, Wojtyla was the youngest pope since the election of Pius IX in 1846. Wojtyla's decision to be called John Paul II revealed his commitment to continue the work of the council.

Karol Wojtyla was born in a small village outside Krakow on 18 May 1920. The son of a retired army lieutenant, his mother and brother died while he was young, leaving him a motherless only child.[12] He attended state schools in Poland, joined a troupe of actors, and had entered the University of Krakow when the Nazi invasion shut down the school system. During the conflict, he found shelter in the episcopal palace of Cardinal Adam Sapiha, the archbishop of Krakow, where he secretly studied for the priesthood, perceiving the spiritual life an antidote to the dehumanization of the modern age.[13] He was ordained on 1 November 1946. During the occupation, he had been hit by a German army lorry which required his hospitalization. Sent to Rome by his bishop after the war, he spent two years in the Holy City where he received his doctorate in theology, before returning to Poland. Consecrated auxiliary bishop of Krakow in September 1958, at the age of thirty-eight, he was one of the last bishops appointed by Pius XII. He published some of his poems and other literary works under the pseudonym of Andrzez Jawien.[14] At the age of forty-four he became archbishop of Krakow in 1964, proving a formidable rival of the repressive communist regime. Three years later, Pope Paul made him the youngest cardinal in Poland's history.

Wojtyla had participated in all four sessions of the second Vatican council and four subsequent meetings of the synod of bishops between 1969 and 1977. Although his interventions at the council were few, he has been credited with the compromise which produced the pastoral constitution 'On the Church in the Modern World', which sustained the dignity of marriage and the family in the contemporary world.[15] As archbishop he maintained close and cordial relations with the city's Jewish community.[16]

Following his election, the young and athletic new pope assumed the name John Paul II. He combined the charisma of John XXIII with the administrative agility of Paul VI. On 21 October, only five days following his election, John Paul held a press conference for some 2,000 journalists in the Vatican, and later in the day addressed the members of the diplomatic corps. In both speeches the pope revealed his desire for dialogue with all nations. To achieve

12 André Frossard, *'Be Not Afraid': Pope John Paul Speaks Out on his Life, his Beliefs, and his Inspiring Vision for Humanity*, trans. J.R. Foster (New York, 1984), pp. 13–14, 23.

13 Speech of 20 March 1993, *AAS*, LXXXVI, pp. 73–4.

14 Mieczyslaw Malinski, *Pope John Paul II: The Life of Karol Wojtyla*, trans. P.S. Fall (New York, 1979), pp. 38, 48.

15 Letter of 13 March 1994, *AAS*, LXXXVI, p. 643.

16 Pope John Paul II, *Crossing the Threshold of Hope*, ed. Vittorio Messori (New York, 1994), p. 98.

this goal, he was prepared to assume a broader political role than any of his modern predecessors. In his investiture homily, the pope called for the opening of the frontiers of states as well as political and economic systems.

Although John Paul II retained Villot as secretary of state, he did not hesitate to bypass his minister in the pursuit of his global goals. Convinced that communism stood simply for the perpetuation of power, he foresaw its inevitable demise. In December he dispatched a letter to the bishops of Hungary, highlighting the role the Catholic church played in shaping its history and image.[17] On 23 October 1978 the pope received Henryk Jablonski, titular head of the Polish state. Towards the end of November, he met with a number of black liberation leaders from Africa, all of whom challenged the establishment. Towards the end of the year, as Chile and Argentina veered towards war over their dispute over the Beagle Channel and the islands of Neuva, Picton and Lennox, the pope dispatched Cardinal Antonio Samore of the Vatican secretariat of state to Buenos Aires and Santiago, initiating talks in nearby neutral Montevideo that culminated in January 1979 in a peaceful resolution which demilitarized the area and provided the binding arbitration of papal envoys.[18]

Subsequently, the pope left for Mexico, with a one-day stopover in Santo Domingo on 25–26 January, where he implored a more just and humane international order. Declaring himself a pilgrim of peace and hope, in Mexico he met President Lopez Portillo and formally inaugurated the Latin American bishops conference at Puebla. The pope refused to accept a liberation theology based on a non-Christian ideology, reminding the clergy their first obligation was to preach liberation from sin rather than espouse socio-political doctrines and radical ideologies. He sympathized with the plight of the workers of town and country, supporting their call for justice, a fair wage, social security, and the opportunity to improve their lot. However, he rejected liberation reduced to narrow economic and political dimensions, which neglected liberation from sin and evil. In his words, the real liberation of man demanded profound changes in the modes of thinking, evaluating and acting.[19] He defended both the sacrament of penance and the adoration of the crucifix.[20] The pope also insisted that the Jesuits end their criticism of papal policy and their conflict with the church, exacting such a promise from their dying general, Pedro Arrupe.

John Paul II showed himself no more inclined to tolerate 'deviations' from the right than from the left. Thus Marcel Lefebvre, the seventy-year-old archbishop who continued to question the changes introduced by the second Vatican council, while challenging the authority of the pope, was summoned to Rome. Charging that the archbishop's attempt to turn back the clock and

17 Daughters of St Paul (ed.), *USA: The Message of Justice, Peace and Love* (*Messages of John Paul II*) (Boston, 1979), II, pp. 15–16; 'The Pope: A See Change', *The Economist*, 29 April 1995.

18 Malachi Martin, *The Keys of this Blood: The Struggle for World Dominion Between Pope John Paul II, Mikail Gorbachev, and the Capitalist West* (New York, 1990), pp. 60–9, 141.

19 *Messages of John Paul II*, II, pp. 212–18, 274–81; Malinski, *Pope John Paul II*, p. 241; Frossard, *'Be Not Afraid'*, p. 207.

20 *AAS*, LXXXVI, pp. 81, 83.

refusal to implement the recent reforms undermined the papal authority he claimed to uphold, the pope ordered him and his followers to desist their public attacks on the Vatican's innovations and the new mass, or face excommunication. John Paul II warned he would not tolerate any further attempt to use the media to spread his archaic ideas or promote his book, *I Accuse*. Lefebvre capitulated, and remained silent in his secluded Swiss seminary.

In April, following the death of Villot, John Paul named Agostino Casaroli, who had helped to orchestrate John's and Paul's *Ostpolitik*, his new secretary of state. Casaroli was one of fourteen new cardinals selected to replace the fourteen members over the age of eighty who were barred from voting in papal elections. The new inductees included five other Italians, as well as Joseph-Marie Trinh Van Can, who headed the diocese of Hanoi, Joseph Asajiro Satowaki, president of Japan's episcopal conference and archbishop of Nagasaki, Roger Etchegaray, archbishop of Marseilles, Tomas O'Fiaich, archbishop of Armagh and primate of Ireland, and two Poles: Franciszek Marcharski, archbishop of Krakow, and Wlayslaw Rubin, secretary general of the synod of bishops.[21]

With the co-operation, if not the support, of Gromyko, whom the pope had met at the beginning of June 1979, John Paul returned to his homeland to preside over the plenary meeting of the 77-member Polish hierarchy, the first of three visits (1979, 1983 and 1987) before the opening of Eastern Europe. As in Mexico, the pope attracted huge crowds that proved even more embarrassing for the atheistic regime in Poland than for the anticlerical one in Mexico. Although the visit from 2 to 11 June was religious rather than political, it had political overtones. It revealed the fragile hold of the regime on the minds and hearts of the Polish people, exposing it not only as unloved but inconsequential. During the mass celebrated at Auschwitz on 7 June 1979, he invited the congregation to commemorate a people doomed to total extermination, the descendants of Abraham, father of the faith.[22] The American CIA considered the visit a serious setback for Polish communism. Upon returning home in July, John Paul sent a message to Lech Walesa in Gdansk approving his solidarity movement.[23]

In October 1979 the pope arrived in the United States for a seven-day visit. From the moment of his arrival in Boston, John Paul II, who continued to attract huge crowds, cited the need for obedience, assuming a conservative stance on such issues as divorce, birth control, clerical celibacy,[24] abortion, and the position of women within the church. At the same time, the pope decried the emphasis on materialism, permissiveness, drugs and violence, using his popularity and magnetic personality to reinforce his orthodox positions. John Paul repeated similar messages in New York, where he addressed the

21 'Pope Names 14 New Cardinals Including 6 Italians and 2 Poles', *New York Times*, 27 May 1979.
22 Frossard, '*Be Not Afraid*', p. 213.
23 Martin, *The Keys of this Blood*, pp. 111–12; Malinski, *Pope John Paul II*, p. 267.
24 Address of 6 July 1993, *AAS*, LXXXVI, p. 413.

United Nations, and Washington, where he was received by President Carter at the White House. During his 1979 visit as well as subsequent ones, John Paul deplored the hostility to claims of certainty and the pressure to compromise church teaching.[25]

In Washington he was confronted by Sister Theresa Kane, president of the leadership conference of women religious, who pleaded on behalf of women in the church. The pope, who on a number of occasions observed there were no women at the Last Supper, was little inclined to support their ordination. The response proved disappointing to women religious.[26] The selection of the conservative Cardinal Oddi Silvio as prefect of the sacred congregation for the clergy made it clear that there would be no married priests and no ordination of women during his tenure.

John Paul expressed his views on the role of the church in the world in his first encyclical released in March 1979 *Redemptor hominis* (The redeemer of man). The pope insisted that the pressing problems of the world, including hunger, the violation of human rights, war and violence, as well as economic oppression and political persecution, could only be resolved by implementing Christ's revelation as announced by the church. These themes were repeated in his second encyclical of December 1980.[27] In 1980 when liberals challenged his suspension of Hans Küng, the pope responded by reaffirming the dogma of papal infallibility. In a letter to the German bishops, the pope presented the Vatican's justification for the suspension. 'Has a theolgican who does not accept the integral doctrine of the church the right to teach in the name of the church and on the basis of a special mission received from the church?'[28] The pope thought not.

In August 1980, when John Paul II learned that the Russians were seriously considering ordering the Polish regime to purge the Solidarity leadership under the threat of military intervention, he personally assumed direction of Vatican-Polish relations. He wrote to President Leonid Brezhnev about the impending Soviet invasion, supposedly warning that should it materialize he would relinquish the throne of St Peter and stand at the barricades with his fellow Poles. Some believe the threat helped to broker the agreement reached between Solidarity and the Polish regime, precluding the prospect of a Russian intervention. Others suspect it prompted the assassination attempt on his life on 13 May 1981, when Mehemet Ali Agca shot the pope in the stomach, the right arm and right hand in St Peter's Square. Vatican circles were convinced that Kremlin masterminds ordered the assassination, considering the pope a destabilizing factor in the whole of Eastern Europe. The sturdy pontiff

25 Speech of 20 March 1993, *AAS*, LXXXVI, p. 75.

26 Annie Lally Milhaven, *The Inside Story: 13 Valiant Women Challenging the Church* (Mystic, CT, 1987), pp. 5–6; *National Catholic Reporter*, 19 October 1979; *New York Times*, 8 October 1979; *Newsweek*, 15 October 1979; *America*, 17 November 1979.

27 J. Michael Miller has collected and edited the official texts in English of John Paul's encyclicals in the volume *The Encyclicals of John Paul II* (Huntington, IN, 1996); Pope John Paul II, *Crossing the Threshold of Hope*, p. 48.

28 Daniela Iacono, 'Censure of Hans Kueng Discussed by Pope John', *The Tablet*, 31 May 1980.

survived, and by October 1981 resumed his hectic schedule. One hand fired the bullet, the pope philosophied, but another guided it.[29] For the moment further visits abroad had to be curtailed. He subsequently resumed his travels, averaging some four major trips per year, travelling more than any of his predecessors, indeed more than all of them combined. At the end of 1984, two days before Christmas, the pope met and forgave the man who gunned him down.

In 1984 the pope agreed to a revision of the concordat that had been concluded between Pope Pius XI and the Mussolini government in 1929. By the terms of the new agreement, the Vatican recognized the separation of church and state in Italy, stipulating in article 1, 'The Italian Republic and the Holy See reaffirm that the State and the Catholic Church, each in its own order, are independent and sovereign'.[30] It thus took a Polish pope to come to terms with the Rome government, and permit the separation of church and state condemned by Pius IX and his Italian successors.

In September 1981, while still convalescing, he issued his third enycyclical *Laborem exercens* ('by means of labour', commonly called 'on human work') commemorating Leo XIII's *Rerum novarum*. Focusing on economic and social problems, John Paul II defended the workers' right to organize, and called for a new economic order which avoided the excesses of unrestrained capitalism and ideological Marxism. On 7 June 1982 he met with President Ronald Reagan, who like John Paul II had escaped an assassination attempt, discussing Israel's invasion of Lebanon and the Soviet domination of Eastern Europe. According to Richard Allen, Reagan's first national security adviser, the two plotted to 'hasten the dissolution of the communist empire'. Reportedly the United States and the Vatican co-operated to keep the outlawed Solidarity movement alive following the proclamation of martial law in December 1981. Drawing from a network that owed as much to the Vatican as the CIA, money and material was supplied to the Poles, while information was filtered to the West about the Polish regime and its relations with Moscow.[31] Early in 1984 President Reagan announced that William A. Wilson of California, who had served as personal representative to the pope, would be appointed ambassador to the Holy See. By 1985, American-Vatican co-operation had frustrated the communist regime's campaign to suppress Solidarity.

In the interim the pope again met with Soviet foreign minister Andrei Gromyko on 27 February 1985, discovering that the accession of Gorbachev brought new initiatives into Soviet foreign policy. Gorbachev favoured *glasnost*, a policy of 'openness', removing bureacratic restrictions from the flow of information, democratization, and *perestroika*, a socio-economic restructuring of Soviet society, rendering communism more human and economically feasible.

29 Thomas and Morgan-Witts, *Pontiff*, pp. 406–7; Frossard, '*Be Not Afraid*', p. 251.
30 Maria Elisabetta de Franciscis, *Italy and the Vatican: The 1984 Concordat Between Church and State* (New York, 1989), p. 225.
31 Carl Bernstein, 'The Holy Alliance', *Time*, 24 February 1992, p. 28. Also see Carl Bernstein and Marco Politi, *His Holiness: John Paul II and the Hidden History of Our Times* (New York, 1996).

Gromyko's successor, Eduard Shevardnadze, early on warned Gorbachev that much was rotten in the Soviet Union and required change.[32] Perhaps this played a part in Warsaw's 1987 pledge to reopen a dialogue with the Catholic church, which in turn encouraged President Reagan to lift the American sanctions against the Polish regime. On the other hand, the pope was not entirely pleased with developments in the United States. During the course of his second visit, he condemned the propensity of some American Catholics for a cafeteria-style Catholicism, picking and choosing to adhere to certain church teaching while ignoring or violating others. 'Selectivity in adhering to authoritative Church teaching', he warned the American bishops in 1987, was 'incompatible with being a "good Catholic".'[33]

In 1988, to commemorate the 1,000th anniversary of the birth of Christianity in the Ukraine, Gorbachev decided to celebrate by inviting the religious leaders of the various Christian churches to Moscow. By means of intermediaries an invitation was dispatched to Pope John Paul, who agreed to go only if he were allowed to visit the Catholics of Lithuania. When his request was refused, the pope sent a delegation of seven cardinals led by secretary of state Cardinal Casaroli, who carried a catalogue of complaints. In February 1989 the Soviets restored the cathedral of Vilnius, long used as an art museum, to the Catholics, and permitted expansion of the Catholic hierarchy. By April, the government promised to legalize Solidarity and called for open parliamentary elections in June of 1989. In July 1989 Poland was the first of the communist-bloc nations to establish diplomatic relations with the Holy See, facilitating the dramatic changes that occurred from 1989 to 1992.

In July 1989 Gorbachev conveyed another positive signal to John Paul II, allowing him to appoint a Catholic bishop in Byelorussia – the first in more than six decades. In August President Bush's new ambassador to the Vatican, Thomas Patrick Melady, arrived in Rome.[34] In December 1989 Gorbachev went to Italy on a state visit and expressed the desire to meet with the pope. That historic visit occurred on 1 December 1989, during which the two men discussed the plight of the four million or so Catholics in the western Ukraine, whose hierarchy had been dissolved by Stalin, and whose churches had been handed over to the Orthodox church. The major problem flowed not from Gorbachev's hostility to Catholicism, but his fear of alienating Russian orthodoxy and stirring the nationalist fervour still linked with religion. The pope, even more clearly than Gorbachev, foresaw the revival of Christianity in the Soviet Union to fill the void left by the failure of the Soviet experiment.

In December 1990 Lech Walesa became president of Poland and the Russian hold on Eastern Europe ended. By 1991 the communist system in the Soviet

32 Eduard Shevardnadze, *The Future Belongs to Freedom* (New York, 1991), pp. 36–7.
33 Speech of 20 March 1993, *AAS*, LXXXVI, p. 75.
34 Thomas Patrick Melady, *The Ambassador's Story: The United States and the Vatican in World Affairs* (Huntington, IN, 1994), p. 11.

Union was crumbling as governments in the Russian republics refused to follow the directives of Moscow.[35] Near the end of 1991, Pope John Paul II convoked a synod of European bishops, both from the East and West, to assess the opportunities presented by the political changes to promote a new evangelization of Europe.[36] On 20 December 1991 President Boris N. Yeltsin of Russia visited Pope John Paul II in Rome.[37] By Christmas 1991 the Holy See witnessed the collapse of the Soviet Union, the end of Gorbachev's leadership, and the transition to a 'commonwealth' of independent states of precarious existence. Subsequently, in an interview, the ousted Soviet leader Gorbachev concluded that Pope John Paul II had played 'a major political role' in undermining communism in Eastern Europe.

In 1991 Pope John Paul II issued a major encyclical *Centisimus annus* (The hundredth year) marking the 100th anniversary of Leo XIII's *Rerum novarum*. In it the pope warned the capitalist countries that the collapse of communism should not blind them to the need to repair injustices in their own economic systems, and the dangers of excessive consumerism, materialism and alienation. In addition to identifying weaknesses in democracy and defending the universal norms of human rights, the pope stressed the need for the world to find an alternative for military action to resolve difficulties.[38] Rejecting the attempt to achieve 'an impossible compromise between Marxism and Christianity', thus condemning the excesses of liberation theology, he was likewise critical of the exploitation and quasi-servitude found in large parts of the globe, and particularly the third world.

When the former Yugoslavia disintegrated into its component parts and witnessed fierce ethnic and religious rivalry, the pope urged negotiation rather than war to resolve their differences. Appalled by the Serb destruction of churches and hospitals in Croatia, in mid-January 1992 the Vatican unilaterally recognized the independence of both Croatia and Slovenia, underscoring its support for these two predominantly Roman Catholic republics. As the war spread into Bosnia-Herzegovina, and reports circulated of ethnic cleansing and genocide, the Vatican favoured United Nations intervention to stop these Nazi-style abuses.

While the Croats called for papal intervention in the form of diplomatic recognition, anti-abortion groups in the United States petitioned Pope John to excommunicate Catholic American lawmakers supporting abortion rights opposed by the Vatican. The pope did not answer the last appeal. Nonetheless, there were differences between the Vatican and the United States on the Gulf War as the pope pleaded with President Bush not to resort to arms to redress Iraq's movement into Kuwait. On 13 January 1991 John Paul had called for an Iraqi withdrawal from Kuwait and the convocation of a peace conference in

35 Michael Mandelbaum, 'Coup de Grace: The End of the Soviet Union', *Foreign Affairs*, 71 (Spring 1992), pp. 164–82; Shevardnadze, *The Future Belongs to Freedom*, pp. 25–7.
36 Allocution of 16 April 1993, *AAS*, LXXXVI, pp. 227–9.
37 Melady, *The Ambassador's Story*, p. 25.
38 Ibid., pp. 158–60; 'The Pope: A See Change', p. 24.

the Middle East. There were also differences in their attitude towards Israel, which the Vatican did not officially recognize early in the 1990s.

The opening of the Madrid conference had an important impact on the Holy See's attitude towards Israel, with Rome hoping that it would signal the commencement of improved relations between the Jewish state and her Arab neighbours and permit the normalization of relations between the Holy See and Israel. Early in 1992 Cardinal John O'Connor visited the Middle East and met with both King Hussein of Jordan and prime minister Yitzak Shamir of Israel. The Vatican no longer demanded internationalization of Jerusalem, asking only for international guarantees of access to the holy sites. This was confirmed in the summer of 1992 when the Holy See commenced talks with Israeli officials for the creation of a joint commission to study the issue of full diplomatic relations, which were established at the end of 1993 on the basis of a fifteen-point agreement. To reassure Arab countries with Christian minorities, the Vatican promised a similar accord with Jordan. In the interim, the pope had a historic meeting with the chief rabbi of Israel, like the pope, a Pole.[39]

During the years from 1992 to 1998, Pope John Paul II resumed his hectic travel schedule, targeting the developing world which housed more than half the world's Catholics and looked to the dawning of a new missionary age.[40] John Paul made these journeys in fulfilment of his apostolic ministry, explaining the practice was commenced by two of his predecessors, the popes of Vatican II, John XXIII and especially Paul VI. John Paul II saw the need to continue it. In 1992 the pope visited Santo Domingo to celebrate the 500th anniversary of Columbus's landing in the new world and the opening of the fourth Latin American bishops conference. Although the pope reiterated the church's 'preferential option for the poor' as called for by the Latin American bishops at their meetings in Medellin, Colombia, and Puebla, Mexico, the pope cautioned the Latin American clergy not to forget their spiritual mission while battling economic, social and political injustices.

In the summer of 1993 the pope travelled to Denver, Colorado, for world youth day, following such gatherings in Spain in 1989 and Poland in 1991.[41] In Denver, the pope adhered to his traditionalist theological outlook, refusing to have church doctrines determined by public opinion polls. The pope opposed all attempts to redefine marriage or accept 'domestic partnerships'.[42] In September 1993, following his visit to the United States, the pope returned to the issues of sexual ethics and moral relativism, which he perceived as a threat to Western civilization, in his long encyclical *Veritatis splendor* (The splendour of truth). Arguing that morality cannot be situational, he rejected not only abortion and euthanasia, but contraception, artificial insemination, homosexual conduct, and premarital sex. The encyclical condemned birth control as

39 Melady, *The Ambassador's Story*, p. 136.
40 *Ad Ganae episcopas*, 22 February 1993, *AAS*, LXXXVI, p. 52.
41 John Paul II's Address of 21 September to North American Bishops, *AAS*, LXXXVI, p. 342.
42 John Paul II's Address to North American Bishops, 8 June 1993, *AAS*, LXXXVI, p. 342.

'intrinsically evil' and denounced those who live by the flesh. Early in 1994 the pope established a pontifical institute for the defence of life.[43] The media, Pope John Paul II warned, conditioned society to listen to what it wants to hear, and worse still, some moralists actually ally themselves with their message. This pope deplored the damage inflicted on individuals and society by their misguided message.[44]

During the course of 1993, Pope John Paul apologized for the church's collaboration in the enslavement of African men, women and children, following the Vatican's belated vindication of Galileo, but did not budge on moral and theological issues. He assailed the resolution of the European parliament which proposed that homosexual couples should be allowed to marry and adopt children. The pope also indicated his displeasure with the social policies supported by the Clinton administration which he judged seriously wrong.[45] In June 1994 the American pro-choice president met with the pro-life pope to discuss the draft for the international conference on population and development to be held in September in Cairo. Disturbed that it called for massive contraception programmes worldwide, the Vatican issued a document criticizing the 'contraceptive imperialism' of the modernized world *vis-à-vis* the third world. Despite the pope's unpopular position on birth control, abortion, gay rights, divorce and the ordination of women priests in liberal circles, in December 1994 Pope John Paul II was selected as *Time* magazine's man of the year, for the Vatican's presence in Cairo.

In the autumn of 1994, the pope appointed thirty new cardinals. In keeping with his vision of a universal church, these hailed from twenty-four countries, including two from the United States: William Henry Keeler, the archbishop of Baltimore, and Adam Joseph Maida, the archbishop of Detroit. There were candidates from countries where Catholics live under communist rule such as Monsignor Jaime Lucas Ortega y Alalimo from Cuba and Paul Joseph Pham Din Dung from Vietnam, while his selection of the archbishop of Sarajevo, Monsignor Vinko Puljic, underlined the pope's quest for peace in the Balkans. Additional cardinals were appointed from Lebanon, the Czech Republic, Italy, Japan, Chile, Scotland, Mexico, Indonesia, Belgium, France, Switzerland, Uganda, Canada, Peru, Spain, Madagascar, Ecuador, Belarus, Albania and Germany. The Italians, once the dominant element in the college, were whittled down to twenty out of 120 cardinal electors.[46]

In March 1995 John Paul II issued his eleventh encyclical letter *Evangelium vitae* (The gospel of life). Defending life and the onslaught made against it in strong language, the pope restated the church's opposition to contraception, abortion, euthanasia and capital punishment. Noting that the passing of unjust

43 *Statuto della Pontifica per la Vita, AAS*, LXXXVI, pp. 388–93.

44 Address to Pontifical Council for Social Communications, 12 March 1993, *AAS*, LXXXVI, p. 71.

45 Melady, *The Ambassador's Story*, p. 174.

46 Alan Cowell, 'Pope Appoints 30 Cardinals, 2 from U.S.', *New York Times*, 31 October 1994.

laws created problems of conscience for morally upright people who have a right not to be implicated in such evil actions, the pope warned that 'each individual in fact has moral responsibility for the acts which he personally performs; no one can be exempted from this responsibility, and on the basis of it everyone will be judged by God himself'.[47] Some Jewish, Muslim and Catholic leaders applauded the pope's courage in denouncing the 'culture of death' and defending the sanctity of life.

John Paul II's *Evangelium vitae*, on the value and inviolability of human life, was addressed not only to the Catholic clergy and the lay faithful, but to all people of goodwill. It reflected his determination to re-Christianize a world which he perceived had lost its moral mission and was seriously undermined by relativism. Not all agreed with him, even within his church. Social conservatives who concurred with the pope's message on sexual ethics were less likely to be comfortable with his critique of the death penalty, capitalism, inequality, and self-centredness of the industrialized world. In turn, many who agreed with his social pronouncements found his teaching on moral matters restrictive and retrograde. Nonetheless, a broad consensus emerged that the pope's convictions entailed a world-view and a moral authority displayed by few others.[48]

John Paul's policies have inspired both ardent support and bitter criticism. Ironically, the pope who has preached that 'politics' was not the business of the church, has practiced it successfully. A number of writers have claimed that Pope John II not only worked with President Ronald Reagan to keep the banned Solidarity union alive, but in the process played a key role in breaking the communist grip on Poland. 'Nobody believed the collapse of communism would happen this fast or on this timetable', one of the pope's closest advisers confided, 'But in their first meeting, the Holy Father and the president committed themselves and the institutions of the church and America to such a goal.'[49] Other papal tours have emboldened the opposition to a broad array of oppressive rulers, including Joal Baptista Figueiredo of Brazil, Ferdinand Marcos of the Philippines, Augusto Pinochet of Chile, and the Argentine junta and South Korean generals, among others.[50] Despite the enormous pressure of Catholic Argentina contesting control of the Falkland Islands with Britain, Pope John Paul II visited that Protestant country – the first post-Reformation pope to do so.

Michael Novak, who in 1994 was awarded the Templeton Prize for Progress in Religion, in an address at Westminster Abbey in London, ranked this pope among the greatest in the long history of the papacy. His opinion is not shared by Sinead O'Connor, who tore a picture of the pontiff on national American television, or one of his doctors who pronounced him 'psychologically

47 'Pope's Letter: A Sinister World Has Led to Crimes Against Life', *New York Times*, 31 March 1995.
48 'The Pope: A See Change'.
49 Bernstein, 'The Holy Alliance', p. 35.
50 'The Pope: A See Change', p. 23.

unbalanced'.[51] Equally critical were the more than 400 Catholic theologians who signed the 'Cologne declaration' of 1989, which charged that in requiring blind obedience from the bishops, clergy and theologians, John Paul II was denying the church's historical practice of constructive questioning, overstepping papal competence. Whether he will be judged by history as the pope who had the largest audience of the century, or the one who proved least heeded, remains to be seen.[52]

51 Carl Eifert, 'Religion Prize Winner Michael Novak Says John Paul is Among Best Popes', *The Tablet*, 9 July 1994; Janice C. Simpson, 'Watch Out: An Unrepentant Sinead O'Connor Blasts the Catholic Church . . .', *Time*, 9 November 1992; Kieran Crowley, 'Pope's Doc Calls him "Unbalanced"', *New York Post*, 6 October 1994.
52 'The Pope: A See Change', pp. 23–4.

CHAPTER 17

Conclusion: the modern papacy in historical perspective

The intellectual climate in the West since the age of revolution has often been hostile to the papacy, which has been constrained to demonstrate its legitimacy and relevance. The pontificate of John Paul II reflects the accommodation and confrontation of the papacy with developments from the onset of the French Revolution to the end of the cold war. Like his predecessors over the past two centuries, the present pope has espoused traditionalist views on certain matters, while seeking accommodation on others. John Paul II inherited the difficulties confronted by Pope Paul VI, who sought to implement the reforms of the second Vatican council, while restraining those who pressed for 'excessive' innovations. During an audience of December 1968, an anguished Pope Paul criticized Catholics who rejected his *via media*. Departing from his prepared text, Paul preached that the effort to dress the church message in modern garb did not entail abandoning basic doctrines. The pontiff warned that the refusal to accept papal pronouncements would provoke a crisis of authority.[1]

The papacy's role remains controversial, with progressives in the church pushing for a decentralization of the hierarchical structure, and the more conservative insisting on Rome's final authority. Although proclaiming itself the custodian of an unchangeable dogma and an unyielding moral vision, during the past two centuries the papacy has not been a fixed and monolithic reality. Indeed, it has never been static or frozen in one form. Since its inception, the papacy's willingness to accommodate itself and the church to diverse governments and times have made it one of the most resilient institutions in the world. Diversity in continuity has been Rome's hallmark. It is the extent and direction of change that is debated and remains contentious as it confronts the challenge of modernity. There has been a tendency for some observers to focus on popes such as Leo XIII, John XXIII and John Paul II for their innovations, forgetting that Gregory XVI, Pius IX, Pius XI and Pius XII likewise introduced changes of tremendous historical impact.

1 'Pope Paul Scores Dissident Clergy', *New York Times*, 5 December 1968.

Hostile ideologies, social and political revolution, and economic modernization have challenged the papacy during the nineteenth and twentieth centuries. Pius VI and Pius VIII had to confront Napoleon; Pius IX had to confront Napoleon III, Cavour and Bismarck; Pius XI confronted Mussolini and Hitler; and Pius XII confronted Hitler and Stalin; while the present pontiff has met with Gorbachev as well as Reagan. During the turmoil of the revolutionary and Napoleonic period there were those who predicted the collapse of the papacy, which was derided as outmoded; likewise some contemporary critics believe its days are numbered. Just as some eighteenth-century revolutionaries were convinced that the papacy would not survive the nineteenth century, some contemporary critics predict its collapse during the course of the twenty-first century.

Despite difficulties, the Holy See remains an active member of the international community, maintaining one of the largest diplomatic establishments. Although its primary realm is that of conscience with spiritual ends and objectives, this does not prevent, and indeed enables, the Holy See to wield considerable influence in diplomatic affairs and global relations. Its authority does not flow from exercising control over the diminutive state of Vatican City, the smallest in the world, but as the representative of the universal Catholic church and as mediator between the secular and spiritual spheres.[2] The United States, no less than Russia, seeks relations with the pope as a religious figure rather than as head of tiny Vatican City. Indeed, the Holy See has assumed the lead in establishing that a territorial base is no longer a pre-condition for a subject of international law. Presently, other institutions such as the United Nations enjoy juridical identity and immunities while performing essential functions in world affairs, without possessing territory.[3]

Every age craves guidance, and this helps to explain why the papacy has preserved its position. It is true that Benedict XV's invocations for peace during the course of the great war were largely unheeded; nonetheless, his effort was not without impact. Many of the suggestions in Benedict's peace plan of 1917 were echoed in Wilson's fourteen points, and the League of Nations and the United Nations borrowed from papal pronouncements calling for some other mechanism besides war to resolve international disputes. Later, much of the Vatican's proposed solution for the troublesome reparations issue found its way into the Dawes Plan of 1924, which enabled Germany to fulfil her treaty obligations from 1924 to 1929.[4] The influence of the Holy See is exercised both through diplomacy as well as broader moral mechanisms.

2 Agostino Casaroli, 'The Unique Role of the Holy See in the International Community', *Paths to Peace. Documents of the Holy See to the International Community* (New York, 1987), pp. xxvii–xxx.
3 Robert A. Graham, S.J., 'Introduction: Reflections on Vatican Diplomacy', in Peter C. Kent and John F. Pollard, eds, *Papal Diplomacy in the Modern Age* (Westport, CT, 1994), pp. 4–5.
4 Stewart A. Stehlin, 'The Emergence of a New Vatican Diplomacy during the Great War and its Aftermath', in Kent and Pollard, eds, *Papal Diplomacy in the Modern Age*, p. 80.

Papal representatives to the accredited countries, the nuncios, differ from traditional ambassadors. The latter have a single mission in relation to the host government. The nuncio, however, is not only accredited to the host country but is charged with overseeing the life of the church there and advising Rome.[5] In its operation in the diplomatic order, the Holy See has tended to focus on social and economic issues with a moral basis.[6]

From time to time the moral mission of the Holy See has constrained it to assume a defiant political stance. Pius VII refused to accept Napoleon's dictates or join his continental system, closing Europe's ports to British commerce, despite threats and an invasion of his states. In 1839 Gregory XVI condemned slavery. Popes Gregory XVI and Pius IX denounced the revolutionary upheavals in Europe from 1831 to 1870, as both proved unwilling to sanction the notion that national self-determination justified aggression against legitimately constituted authority. Popes Leo XIII, Pius X and Benedict XV all had serious reservations about the new imperialism ushered in after 1870, and the recourse to arms to resolve national differences from the emergence of the German empire to the outbreak of the First World War. In 1937, during the turmoil of the Spanish Civil War, Pius XI launched his encyclical *Divini redemptoris* which condemned communism and called for its containment.[7] The five points of Pope Pius XII's Christmas speech of 1939 anticipated by some two years the Atlantic Charter.[8] During the course of the cold war, the Vatican assumed a decidely anti-Soviet stance, and was a key player in the collapse of communism in Poland, the Eastern bloc, and ultimately the Soviet Union.[9] More recently, it has posed a series of demands on Castro's Cuba, including the lifting of the ban on foreign priests, access to the state media, and freedom of action for Catholic charities.

On occasion the Vatican has been critical of right-wing oppressive regimes as well as dictatorships of the left. Papal support of the Filipino church's opposition to the flagrant electoral fraud of 1986 contributed to the civil disobedience against, and the ultimate collapse of, the Marcos regime.[10] The Vatican has also interjected itself in the Middle East. In November 1975, April 1976, December 1978 and March–April 1980, four papal missions were dispatched to Lebanon, during the course of which papal representatives met with Yassir Arafat, providing a sort of recognition by the Holy See of the PLO.[11] To be sure the papacy has had to confront problems posed by secularism, individualism, fascism, nationalism, racism, imperialism, materialism and socialism in

5 Graham, 'Reflections on Vatican Diplomacy', p. 6.

6 Casaroli, *Paths to Peace*, pp. xxviii–xxx.

7 James Kurth, 'The Vatican's Foreign Policy', *National Interest*, XXXII (Summer 1993), pp. 40–3.

8 Luigi Sturzo, 'The Vatican's Position in Europe', *Foreign Affairs*, January 1945, p. 220.

9 In this regard see Carl Bernstein and Marco Piloti, *His Holiness: John Paul II and the Hidden History of Our Time* (New York, 1996).

10 For a good account of Catholic and papal opposition to the Marcos regime see Robert L. Youngblood, *Marcos Against the Church: Economic Development and Political Repression in the Philippines* (Ithaca, 1991).

11 George E. Irani, 'Diplomats in a Quandary: The Vatican and the Lebanon War', *American-Arab Affairs* (Fall 1990), pp. 29–37.

the broader society, as well as issues of democracy, collegiality, ecumenism, liberation theology, feminism, laicism and celibacy within the church. These developments inside and outside the church are often interrelated.

During the last two centuries, when the state arrogated increasing power to itself, culminating in the creation of the 'ethical state' and Soviet totalitarianism, it provoked tensions with the universal church while prompting a counter-centralization from within, making it more papal, hierarchical and Roman. The new imperialism of the powers after 1870 was countered by renewed missionary efforts in the Americas, Asia and Africa. In 1919 Benedict XV issued his missionary encyclical invoking the creation of a native clergy while insisting that Western missionaries respect and appreciate the indigenous culture. His successor Pius XI issued a series of directives to European missionaries not to impose their European civilization, warning that would prove detrimental to church interests in the non-Western world.[12] In a sense the universal church transcending borders has functioned as a countervailing force to the pretensions of the national state. Vatican policy has served to counteract the influence of unrestrained nationalism while counterbalancing militarism with mediation, resisting the claim that force is the sole means of resolving international disputes. For many the unity and direction of the church was centred in the papacy, to which both the clergy and laity rallied.

Paradoxically, the onset of the French and the industrial revolutions at the end of the eighteenth century, which some predicted would undermine the papacy, served instead to strengthen it. Pius VI and Pius VII provided moral opposition to the Napoleonic imperium, and during the restoration Rome was courted as a valuable ally against the revolutionaries.[13] In an age of nationalism, Rome remained an inspiration for the universalists. Even as its temporal power totally collapsed in 1870, with the Italian acquisition of the Eternal City, the first Vatican council proclaimed papal infallibility while assuring that papal power remained intact. The power of the pope within the church was confirmed by the code of canon law promulgated by Benedict XV in 1917, which exalted the position of the papacy in the ecclesiastical legal structure. Subsequently, the second Vatican council reaffirmed papal power and primacy over both pastors and peoples.

One view of the papacy following the age of the industrial and French revolutions emphasizes the papal demonization of the modern world, whose condemnations reached a high-point during the pontificate of Pius IX (1846–78). Within this political and ideological framework, Popes Leo XIII (1878–1903) and Benedict XV (1914–22) are seen to assume a more subtle strategy, but they no less than Pius X (1903–14) proved critical of the contemporary developments that Pius X condemned as modernism. These 'liberal popes' no less than their conservative counterparts supposedly sought to bring the world into harmony with church teaching. In this regard Pius XI (1922–39)

12 Stehlin, 'Emergence of a New Vatican Diplomacy', p. 77.

13 Alan J. Reinerman, 'The Vatican and the Austrian Empire during the Restoration, 1814–1846', in Kent and Pollard, eds, *Papal Diplomacy in the Modern Age*, pp. 23–31.

and Pius XII (1939–58) are depicted as transitional popes, paving the way for the *aggiornamento* of John XXIII (1958–63) and Paul VI (1963–78). This interpretation remains a one-sided picture of papal policy, neglecting important religious, cultural and social considerations.

One might also note that the dual impact of the French and industrial revolutions brought lay people into closer contact and collaboration with the hierarchy and the papacy. Popes Leo XIII, Pius X and Benedict XV all recognized the laity's contribution to stem the tide of secularism. Pius XI, who followed, encouraged lay participation in the apostolate of the hierarchy in the organization of Catholic action. He concluded a host of concordats to assure the security of Catholic organizations and activities in democratic and fascist regimes. This orientation was furthered by Pius XII, who exhorted the laity to enter the apostolic field by providing the ecclesiastical hierarchy with their active co-operation. His successor John XXIII, who expressed a heightened appreciation of mankind, envisioned an even broader role for the laity.

The industrial revolution, which introduced astounding changes in communication, eliminated many of the barriers that had earlier hindered the voice, image and action of the popes, thereby broadening the range of papal influence. The medium of photography played a part in transforming Pius IX, 'the prisoner of the Vatican', into a graphic image and 'icon' of universalism enjoyed by no former pope.[14] The transportation revolution has enabled Pope John Paul II to make more than seventy trips outside of Italy and over one hundred within. In turn, the communication revolution ushered in by the telegraph, telephone, radio and television has allowed the Holy See to maintain a close and continuous contact with the faithful worldwide. By 1996 the Vatican daily information bulletin of papal speeches and official announcement was 'on line'.

Finally, the papacy has provided its own solution to the social question provoked by the industrial transformation, offering an alternative differing from both socialism and capitalism. Aware of the negative impact of industrialization on the masses of Europe, the papacy rejected both unrepentent capitalism and atheistic socialism. Inspired by Christian principles, the social encyclicals of the popes from Leo XIII to John Paul II introduced a third way to uplift the masses of humanity. This social awareness and call for justice has appealed not only to the Catholic masses of the globe, but has won the allegiance and the respect of non-Catholics in the industrial world as well as in 'third world' countries.

The nineteenth-century popes rejected unbridled liberalism which focused on the maximization of the individual, while rejecting the canonization of capitalism. The Vatican recognized that the emancipation of the person which provided freedom, also led to alienation and loneliness, provoking unfortunate personal and political consequences. The papacy contended that an increase in wealth did not necessarily lead to an increase in well-being. In 1824 Pope Leo

14 Peter C. Kent and John F. Pollard, 'A Diplomacy Unlike Any Other: Papal Diplomacy in the Nineteenth and Twentieth Centuries', in ibid., p. 16.

XII issued *Ubi primum*, which denounced contemporary errors such as liberalism and the de-Christianization of society.[15] Gregory XVI condemned the relentless pursuit of wealth masquerading as God's will in his *Mirari vos* of 1832. Pius IX followed his example in his encyclical *Quanta cura* and the attached Syllabus of Errors of 1864, which likewise attacked the excesses of economic liberalism as well as those of socialism and nationalism. Leo XIII continued this tradition in his *Rerum novarum* of 1891, which criticized the 'unbridled greed of competitors' and denounced the yoke imposed upon the propertyless workers.

Leo did more than issue denunciations of the liberal notions of progress, suggesting in his *Rerum novarum* that the church understood the social and economic problems plaguing the contemporary world, and proposing Christian solutions. Perceiving both socialism and liberal capitalism as incomplete in their outlook, and flawed in their ideologies, a *via media* was deemed necessary. This pope insisted that government had a moral responsibility to regulate working hours and conditions, while approving the workers' right to form and join their own associations. Some saw this encyclical as inaugurating modern Catholic social teaching.

During the course of the twentieth century, the popes continued their critique of unrestrained capitalism as well as socialism. In 1931 Pius XI issued his *Quadragesimo anno*, marking the fortieth aniversary of *Rerum novarum*. In it Pius rejected socialism as a means for resolving the social question provoked by the greed of capitalism. He suggested a vocational and corporativist solution, proposing the formation of councils bringing together the representatives of management and workers to resolve disputes peacefully. In his vision, neither strikes nor lockouts would be sanctioned, while the public authority would facilitate the resolution of outstanding differences. The positive role expected of government was also emphasized in John XXIII's *Mater et magistra* of 1961, issued on the seventieth anniversary of *Rerum novarum*. John's encyclical introduced the principle of socialization, which appreciated that lower levels of organization or government often proved incapable of addressing complex problems transcending local boundaries. Thus, the Holy See stressed the need for governmental intervention and action.

Pope Paul's VI's *Populorum progressio* of 1967 not only addressed the church's concern with the iniquitous distribution of wealth between rich and poor within the various states, but confronted the inequities in the distribution of wealth among the various nations of the world. Proclaiming that God intended the goods of the world to be enjoyed by all, it warned that the growing disparity between the wealthy, modernized nations of the West and the underdeveloped, impoverished lands of the third world, frustrated the design of Providence. To rectify the situation, Pope Paul VI called upon the privileged nations to aid the needy, proposing that trade relations recognize the principle

15 Frank J. Coppa, 'The Diplomacy of Intransigence: Vatican Policy during the *Risorgimento*', in ibid., p. 34.

of social justice. It encouraged the adherents of liberation theology which arose in Latin America as a moral reaction against the widespread and collective suffering of that region's poor and oppressed. Pope Paul's critique of the relations between the wealthy industrialized Western nations and the poor countries of the underdeveloped world also bolstered the dependency theory followed by the third world countries rather than the liberal classicism of the West, or the Marxist doctrine of the Soviets. Paul VI's position paralleled that of social scientists who have discerned a world system with dominant core societies, intermediate semi-peripheral ones, and dependent peripheral societies.[16]

John Paul II's third encyclical letter *Laborem exercens* of 1981 marked the ninetieth anniversary of *Rerum novarum*. Rejecting the doctrines of a rigid and narrow capitalism, which perceived private ownership an untouchable dogma of economic life, the pope proclaimed the common use of goods the first principle of the ethical and social order. In his encyclical on the international political economy of 1987, Pope John Paul II focused on the negative consequences of liberal capitalism for third world countries. Like his predecessor, John Paul recognized the danger inherent in the Western world's almost total monopoly of economic wealth and political power.

Although Vatican documents in 1984 and 1986 deplored liberation theology's borrowing of Marxist concepts such as class struggle, and the prospect of reducing faith to politics, they nonetheless recognized the legitimacy of liberation as a theological theme. Rejecting the dialectical vision flowing from Hegel and Marx, and the policies of Lenin and Stalin, the pope recognized the validity of aspects of the critique of capitalism both within states and internationally. In a 1986 letter to the bishops of Brazil, Pope John Paul II, who has maintained a traditional stance on birth control, abortion, homosexuality and women's ordination, cited the 'useful and necessary' character of liberation theology.[17] The popes from Pius XII to John Paul II have all realized that Hilaire Belloc's dictum that the 'church is Europe and Europe is the church' is no longer so. Walter Buhlmann reported in *The Coming of the Third Church* (1974) that by the 1970s the 367 million Catholics of Latin America, Africa and Asia outnumbered the 318 million of Europe and North America.[18] In response, the Holy See has sought to demonstrate that the church is a universal institution, not to be identified with any specific geographic or cultural area.[19]

In 1991, the year John Paul II designated as one of Catholic social teaching, he issued *Centesimus annus*, on the 100th anniversary of *Rerum novarum*. It presented a distinctly Catholic conception of a just social order for the world, and reinforced the social teaching of the church which emphasized the priority of labour over capital and the call for a just wage allowing the full development

16 Daniel Chirot, *Social Change in the Modern Era* (New York, 1986), p. 6.
17 Paul J. Wojda, 'Liberation theology', *The Harper Collins Encyclopedia of Catholicism*, ed. Richard P. McBrien (San Francisco, 1995), pp. 768–9.
18 John Taylor, 'The Future of Christianity', in *The Oxford Illustrated History of Christianity* (Oxford, 1992), p. 637.
19 Irani, 'Diplomats in a Quandary', p. 29.

of the human person. In the papacy's position the 'preferential love for the poor' requires the elimination of poverty worldwide. In August 1988 John Paul II published the first papal treatise devoted exclusively to the question of feminism, rejecting the patriarchal reading of the scriptures and the misogynist tradition within the church.[20]

The papacy has also been embroiled in diplomacy. Benedict XV sought to bring peace to a troubled continent during the course of the First World War and argued for a peace without victory to assure tranquillity in its aftermath. Popes Pius XI and Pius XII attempted to prevent the outbreak of a Second World War, and sought to restore peace once it erupted. During the course of the Second World War the papacy again played a crucial role in the international relief effort, helping to feed the hungry and resettle the homeless. Some have suggested that it could have, and should have, done more to assist the Jews and combat the genocide practiced by the Third Reich. Indeed, the muted response of Pius XII to the horrors of the Holocaust, dubbed the 'silence', remains one of the gravest historical burdens recently endured by the papacy.[21] It has had an impact on the institution, for John XXIII, Paul VI and John Paul II have not hesitated to denounce racism, genocide, weapons such as the neutron bomb, the terrifying nuclear threat, and the recourse of war to resolve differences between states and people. Pope John Paul II has condemned the genocide in Bosnia as well as that in East Timor, Rwanda and Burundi. The Vatican pursued an interventionist course on behalf of peace during the Cuban missile crisis of 1962, in the closing years of the Vietnam war, and during the Persian Gulf conflict.[22]

Furthermore, the papal presence has become more pervasive. During the age of the modern papacy, Pius VI visited Vienna in 1782, and his successor Pius VII travelled to Paris in 1804 for the coronation of Napoleon. Both popes were forcibly removed from the Eternal City by the French, Pius VI in 1799 and Pius VII in 1809, and held captive. Pius IX abandoned Rome in 1848, and only returned in 1850. Following the Italian seizure of Rome in September 1870, Pius IX closed himself in the Vatican, refusing to venture outside its walls. His example was followed by his successors Leo XIII, Pius X, Benedict XV and Pius XI, until the Lateran Accords of 1929 resolved the Roman Question. Pope Paul VI began the papal process of travelling worldwide, in his determination to bring the Gospel to all nations. He visited four continents and has been dubbed the pilgrim pope. His global travels have been continued by John Paul II, who is the most travelled pope in history.

Since Paul's *Populorum progressio* of 1967, the papacy has displayed a persistent concern with the needs of the underdeveloped, third world. Pope Paul VI

20 Richard L. Camp, 'From Passive Subordination to Complementary Partnership: The Papal Conception of a Woman's Place in the Church and Society since 1878', *Catholic Historical Review*, LXXXVI, 3 (July 1990), p. 523.
21 John S. Conway, 'The Vatican, Germany and the Holocaust', in Kent and Pollard, eds, *Papal Diplomacy in the Modern Age*, pp. 105–20.
22 Kent and Pollard, 'A Diplomacy Unlike Any Other', p. 14.

also dramatically favoured the internationalization of the college of cardinals, not only increasing the size of the college – he created 144 cardinals – but diversifying its membership by nominating prelates from Asia, Africa, Oceania, and North and South America. He was one of two popes within the past two centuries to appoint a non-Italian papal secretary of state, the Frenchman Jean Villot (1969–79). Pius X appointed the other, the Anglo-Spanish Merry del Val (1903–14). At Paul's death, the majority of cardinals were no longer European.

During the two decades of his pontificate, John Paul II has continued the papal commitment to the universal church, making more than seventy trips outside of Italy, travelling often to Africa and Latin America, which both in terms of numbers and culture are the most Catholic of the world's regions. On two of his trips to the United States, Pope John Paul II addressed the United Nations, revealing his commitment to that international peacekeeping institution.

An observer at the United Nations and UNESCO, the papacy has spoken forcefully on a series of economic and social issues troubling humanity since industrialization. John Paul II revealed serious reservations about the Gulf War, denounced the 'scandalous arms trade', defended the land rights of aborigines, and pleaded for the wealthy creditor nations to consider forgetting the burdensome third-world debts. This option in favour of the third, non-Western world is also reflected in John Paul's choice of cardinals, which has continued Paul's policy, with an increasing number being drawn from outside the Western orbit.[23] Furthermore, the position assumed by the papacy at international conferences has not always attained Western support. During the course of the 1994 United Nation's Cairo conference on population and development, the Vatican representative Joaquin Navarro objected to references in the draft statement to reproductive health, sensing it provided implicit recognition and legitimization of abortion as one means of curbing population growth. John Paul II insisted that his apostolic ministry constrained him to address difficult and complex moral issues.[24]

The conflict between continuity and reform in the papacy and the church is reflected in the recently released Catholic Catechism.[25] Recommended by an international synod of bishops in 1985 to confront the vast changes in the church unleashed by the second Vatican council two decades earlier, some have seen it as an attempt on the part of the church to update the ten commandments for the modern world, while others have seen it as an attempt to curtail contempory influences. Promulgated by Pope John Paul II at the end of 1992, the Catechism elaborates the church position on problems confronting Catholics in the industrialized, urbanized world as well as those in the underdeveloped, third world.

Some have criticized the new Catechism not so much for what it says as for what it purportedly attempts to do – increase the power of the pope and the

23 'The Pope: A See Change', *The Economist*, 29 April 1995.
24 Address to Bishops of New Zealand, 21 October 1993, *AAS*, LXXXVI, p. 600.
25 Address to Bishops of Canada, 16 September 1993, *AAS*, LXXXVI, p. 492.

Vatican at the expense of local churches. The papacy has also been accused of being a discordant factor in the search for ecumenism and religious unity, sought by church fathers with increased vigour since the second Vatican council's degree on ecumenism of 1964. A Roman Catholic dialogue has been conducted with Anglicans, Lutherans, Calvinists and other Protestant groups, but the results have been more symbolic than substantive.[26]

The papacy and papal primacy, recognition of the pope's supreme authority over the unified Christian church, has been perceived as one of the major stumbling blocks for Christian unity, evoking anxieties among Protestants about the misuse of power and authority. Catholics and even some popes have acknowledged this reality. Catholic theologians such as Hans Küng have opposed infallibility, linking it to the emergence of an absolutist pope.[27] 'The Pope, as we all know', Paul VI wrote in 1967, 'is undoubtedly the gravest obstacle in the path of ecumenism.'[28] While the pontificate of Pope John XXIII emphasized the prospects of a collegial and pastoral exercise of the Petrine office, and led those outside and within the faith to appreciate the potential of the papacy for promoting peace and harmony worldwide, the controversial mantle of papal infallibility continues to engender suspicion. The Vatican's pronouncement at the end of 1995 that the ban on female ordination must be accepted as an 'infallible' truth rather than a procedural norm aroused old doubts and persistent concerns.

In response to the Vatican's claim that the ban on the ordination of woman was an infallible doctrine, the *London Tablet*[29] harped on the pope's failure to consult with the bishops and the lay faithful, concluding that often the invocation of authority represents an admission of weakness. The contention of the *London Tablet* was supported by two Jesuits: Father Ladislau Orsy, an expert on the canon law, and Father Francis A. Sullivan, a theologian widely regarded as an expert on the church's teaching authority. In the 9 December 1995 issue of *America*, they cited the criteria for infallibility, including 'consultation with all the bishops, the universal and constant consensus of Catholic theologians, and the common adherence of the faithful'.[30] In October 1996, when John Paul II virtually accepted the theory of evolution, he pleased those who sought to reconcile religion and science, but angered and aroused creationists.

The reaction of the various Protestant denominations towards the papacy has evolved, with the Anglicans, who have accepted the ordination of women, speaking of a 'limited papal primacy' in which the pope would exercise 'a primacy of love', implying both honour and service. Others envision the pope as a first among equals, invoking a leadership based on persuasion rather than authority. Among Lutherans the response has varied, with some viewing

26 Antonio Gaspari, 'For the Sake of Unity, Can the Papacy Change?', *Inside the Vatican*, June–July 1995, pp. 7–10.
27 Peter Chirico, 'Infallibility: Rapprochement between Küng and the Official Church?', *Theological Studies*, 42 (December 1981), pp. 531–2.
28 Peter Hebblethwaite, *Paul VI: The First Modern Pope* (New York, 1993), p. 9.
29 *The London Tablet*, 25 November 1995.
30 'Women's Ordination and Infallibility', *The Tablet*, 9 November 1995.

the pope as an outdated symbol of monarchy, while others believe that a reformed papacy might prove acceptable. The Calvinists continue to be the most dismissive, reminding Catholics that John Calvin could find no mention of the papacy in scripture.

Pope John Paul II has expressed the hope that all Christians might welcome in the new century united, recognizing the tasks facing the church in the third millenium as immense and arduous.[31] On Good Friday 1995 the pope made an impassioned plea for the unity of Christians in a service attended by senior Orthodox prelates and representatives of the Anglican church. He also offered reconciliation towards Jews whom he called the 'elder brothers' in the faith. Unity was also the message of his pastoral letter *Orientale lumen* of 2 May 1995.

On 30 May 1995 Pope John Paul II, in one of his longest encyclicals *Ut unum sint* (That they may all be one), indicated his willingness to discuss the future role of the papacy with other Christian denominations. Recognizing that an agreement among Catholics, Protestants, Anglicans and the Orthodox church on the role of the papacy would prove difficult, he urged patient dialogue. While John Paul II did not elaborate his conception of a reformed papacy, he reported that in the early church the institution served as a moderator to resolve differences and preserve unity. In this encyclical the pope made it clear that he is a direct heir of Vatican II's position on the need for ecumenism and Christian unity. On the other hand, the pope reasserted the contention that Christ chose and formed Peter to lead the church, and the pope has inherited his mission. How the pope will do so in the third millenium remains in contention and under discussion.[32]

31 Address to the Bishops of New Zealand, 21 October 1993, *AAS*, LXXXVI, p. 602.
32 Gaspari, 'For the Sake of Unity', pp. 8–10.

Notes on Vatican sources

Below the reader will find some of the primary sources useful for a study of the papacy for the period examined within the pages of this volume. Primary material that has a more specific chronological or thematic focus will be found, along with secondary sources, in the Select Bibliography which follows.

Archivio di Stato di Roma (ASR)

Among the useful papers of the state archives of Rome are the papers of the Consiglio di Stato and those of the Carte Miscellanea Politche O Riservate.

Archivio Segreto del Vaticano, or the Secret Vatican Archives (ASV)

This remains a crucial primary source for a study of the papacy. Deemed secret because the first nucleus of this present collection originated in the *bibliotheca secreta* of Sixtus IV (1471–84), it was initially open to select scholars. Pope Leo XIII in 1880 opened it for general consultation. Although its usage was originally restricted to the early modern period, it is presently open through the pontificate of Benedict XV (1914–22). Much can be learned about papal foreign and domestic policy from the Archivio di Stato Esteri and the Archivii delle nunziature, especially the Fondo Archivio della nunziature di Vienna.

Acta Apostolicae Sedis, or Acts of the Apostolic See (*AAS*)

This is the offical journal of the Holy See containing laws, pronouncements and addresses of the pope as well as the major documents issued by the various departments of the Vatican. Following Pius X's constitution *Promulgandi* of 29 September 1908, the *AAS* has appeared since January 1909 as the official publication of the Holy See. It followed and replaced the *Acta Sanctae Sedis*, which served a similar function but did not enjoy its official character. Decisions and decrees published in it are officially promulgated, becoming effective three months from the date of issue.

Acta Sanctae Sedis, or Compendium of Documents Produced by the Holy See (*ASS*)

Beginning in 1865, this monthly journal was published in Rome, but not by the Holy See, until 1908 when it was replaced by the *AAS*. Like its successor it contained the legislative and administrative acts produced by the Holy See but lacked its official character until 1904 when Pius X made it authentic and official. It was superseded by the *AAS* at the end of 1908.

Annuario Pontificio, or Papal Yearbook or Annual Papal Directory

Presently published by the Libreria Editrice Vaticana, and printed by the Vatican Polyglot Press, some have traced the *Annuario* back to the compendium *Notizie*, first put out by the Holy See during the pontificate of Clement XI (1700–21). During the pontificate of Pius IX (1846–78), it was rechristened the *Annuario Pontificio* and termed the *Annuaire pontifical catholique* in the later 1890s. It later was returned to Rome with its earlier name. Declared an official publication during the pontificate of Leo XIII (1878–1903), this reference was ended in 1924, but it is still deemed essential for an understanding of yearly developments in the church. It provides a wealth of statistical information regarding the church, the biography and acts of the reigning pope, the cardinals and their sees, as well as biographical notes. Each yearly edition provides a list of members of the hierarchy and officials. Its articles are valuable for historical as well as ecclesiastical information.

Bullarii romani continuatio (Bull Rom Cont)

This continues the publication of papal bulls and other important letters and documents in chronological order of the *Magnum Bullarium Romanum*, which lists letters of popes from Leo X (1513–21) to Benedict XIII (1724–30). The *Bullarii romani continuatio* was published from 1835 to 1857, edited by Andreas Barberi and published in Rome by the Camera Apostolicae.

Carlen, Sister M. Claudia, ed., *The Papal Encyclicals*, 5 volumes, 1740–1878; 1878–1903; 1903–39; 1939–58; 1958–81. Wilmington, NC: McGrath Publishing Co., 1981.

In these five volumes published in 1981 the editor has included the formal circular letters written by, or under the authority of, the modern popes from 1740 to 1981. Presently these encyclicals are almost exclusively papal documents. These letters and epistles are addressed explicitly to the patriarchs, primates, archbishops and bishops of the universal church in communion with the Holy See and thus to the faithful. Since the pontificate of John XXIII, some of these letters have also been addressed to all persons of goodwill. By and large the epistles are addressed to a specific issue, and often focus on a problem in a particular country. The letters generally have a broader audience. Sister Carlen also has produced a guide to the more recent encyclicals.

Carlen, Sister M. Claudia, ed., *Papal Pronouncements. A Guide: 1740–1978.* Volume I: *Benedict XIV to Paul VI*; Volume II: *Paul VI to John Paul I.* Ann Arbor, MI: Pieran Press, 1990.

These two volumes provide an authoritative guide not only to the encyclicals of the popes since the mid-eighteenth century to the present, but also many of their published allocutions – addresses delivered by the pope from the throne to the cardinals in secret consistory – as well as many sermons, *motu proprios* or papal decrees, and homilies and sermons, and even some radio messages. Listed in chronological order, the entry indicates the classification of the document, estimated length, the occasion for its publication or its addressee, as well as an abstract of its contents. Within its almost 1,000 pages are included more than 5,000 documents shedding light on the history of the modern papacy.

Civiltà Cattolica

This forthnightly review is a semi-official journal of the Vatican under the direction of the Society of Jesus. Founded in Naples by Father Carlo M. Curci, assisted by Fathers Bresciani, Liberatore, and Zaparelli, with the blessing of Pius IX, it moved to Rome in 1853. It maintained a continuous publication there from 1853 to 1870, moving to Florence at the end of 1870 to protest the Italian seizure of the Eternal City. The *Civiltà* returned to Rome in 1888, establishing its offices in the Via di Ripetta where it has remained. The articles in this review provide insights into papal thought and policy on social, religious and political issues, for the editors have remained consistently loyal to the Vatican.

Fremantle, Anne, ed., *The Papal Encyclicals in their Historical Context.* New York: G.P. Putnam's Sons, 1956.

This collection includes portions of some of the most important social and political encyclicals issued by the modern popes. The editor has placed them within their historical and political perspective, providing valuable information about the popes and the times. There is an Introduction by Gustave Weigel which also explains the significance of these papal missives.

Momigliano, Eucardio, ed., *Tutte le encicliche dei sommi Pontefici* (*TESP*). Milan: dall 'Oglio, editore, 1959.

This one volume compilation of encyclicals in Italian includes those from the pontificate of Benedict XIV (1740–58) through some of the early encyclicals of Pope Paul VI (1963–78). It has an analytical index, arranged alphabetically, which includes the various topics and subjects included within the various encyclicals.

Osservatore Romano

The *Roman Observer* is considered the daily newspaper of the Holy See and has existed in its present form since 1861, when a group of laymen felt the need for its presence. It had predecessors in 1849 and 1851, but only functioned as a daily since 1861. Since that time it has served as an important source of information on the activities and actions of the pontiff, justifying its position as the 'official' newspaper of the papacy. Although begun as an independent organ, after 1870 it functioned as the authoritative, but unofficial organ of the Holy See, printing the texts of papal speeches as pronouncements and announcements. Its editors are appointed by the papal secretariat of state. Printed in Italian every day of the week except Sunday, there are weekly editions in English, German, Spanish, French and other languages. There is an Italian Sunday edition published separately known as *L'Osservatore della Domenica*. It has been published in Vatican City since the Lateran Accords of 1929.

Select bibliography

Abbot, Walter, S.J. *The Documents of Vatican II*. New York/London, 1966.

Acta Pii IX. Pontificis Maximi. Para prima acta exhibens quae ad Ecclesiam universam spectant (1846–1854). Rome, 1855.

Acta Summi Pontificis Joannis XXIII. Vatican City, 1960, 1964.

Actes de Benoit XV: Encycliques, motu proprio, brefs, allocutions, actes des dicastres. Paris, 1926–34.

Actes de Leon XIII: Encycliques, motu proprio, brefs, allocutions, actes de dicasteres, etc. Paris, 1931–37.

Actes de S.S. Pie XI: Encycliques, motu proprio, brefs, allocutions, actes de dicasteres, etc. Paris, 1932–36.

Actes et documents du Saint Siège relatifs à la seconde guerre mondiale, 11 vols, ed. Piere Blet et al. Vatican City, 1965–82.

Adornato, Giselda, ed. *Giovanni Battista Montini. Archvescovo di Milano. Al Mondo del Lavaro. Discorso e scritti (1954–1963)*. Rome, 1988.

Akten deutscher Bischofe uber die Loge der Kirche 1933–1945, Volume II: 1934 1935. Mainz, 1976.

Alberigo, Giuseppe, ed. *Papa Giovanni*. Rome, 1987.

Albini, Crosta Maddalena. *Compendio della Vita di Pio X*. Milan, 1914.

Alfieri, Dino. *Dictators Face to Face*, trans. David Moore. Westport, CT, 1978.

Althann, Robert. 'Papal Mediation during the First World War', *Studies (of Ireland)*, LXI, 243 (1972), 219–40.

Althaus, Friedrich, ed. *The Roman Journals of Ferdinand Gregorovius, 1852–1874*. London, 1906.

Alvarez, David J. 'The Papacy in the Diplomacy of the American Civil War', *Catholic Historical Review*, LXIX, 2 (April 1983), 227–48.

Alvarez, David J. 'The Department of State and the Abortive Papal Mission to China, August 1918', *Catholic Historical Review*, LXII, 3 (1976), 455–63.

Anderson, Robin. *Between Two Wars: The Story of Pope Pius XI*. Chicago, 1977.

Aretin, Karl Otmar von. *The Papacy and the Modern World*, trans. Roland Hill. New York, 1970.

Andreu, Francesco. *Un aspetto inedito nel raporto Ventura-Lamennais*. Florence, 1991.

Angelozzi, Garibaldi. *Pio XII, Hitler e Mussolini*. Milan, 1988.

Anni e Opere di Paolo VI, ed. *Nello Vian*, introd. Arturo C. Jemolo. Rome, 1978.

Appeals for Peace of Pope Benedict XV and Pope Pius XI. Washington, DC, 1931.

Appleby, R. Scott. *'Church and Age Unite': The Modernist Impulse in American Catholicism*. Notre Dame, IN, 1992.

Aradi, Zsolt. *Pius XI: The Pope and the Man*. Garden City, NY, 1958.

Aradi, Zsolt et al. *Pope John XXIII: An Authoritative Biography*. New York, 1954.

Archivio di Stato di Roma. Among useful archives contained therein are the *Fondo Famiglia Antonelli*, the *Carte Miscellanea Politche O Riservate*, the *Fondo Repubblica Romana*, the papers of the *Consiglio di Stato* and those of the *Consulta di Stato*.

Ardali, Paolo. *Mussolini e Pio XI*. Mantore, 1926.

Ataud de Montor, Alexis François. *Histoire du Pape Pie VII*, 2nd edn, 2 vols. Paris, 1837.

Atti del Sommo Pontefice Pio IX, Felicemente Regnante. Parte seconda che comprende I Motu-proprii, chirografi editti, notificazione, ed. per lo stato pontificio. Rome, 1857.

Aubert, Roger. *The Church in a Secularized Society*. Volume V: *The Christian Centuries*. New York, 1978.

Aubert, Roger et al. *The Church Between Revolution and Restoration*. New York, 1981.

Aubert, Roger. 'Il primo Concilio Vaticano', *Studi Romani*, XVIII (1970), 318–39.

Aubert, Roger. *Le Pontificate de Pie IX*. Paris, 1967.

Aulard, Alphonse. *Recueil des actes du comite de salut public*. Paris, 1889.

Babis, Daniel G. and Anthony J. Maceli, *A United States Ambassador to the Vatican*. New York, 1952.

Baisnee, Jules A. *France and the Establishment of the American Catholic Hierarchy: The Myth of French Interference (1783–1784)*. Baltimore, 1934.

Barmann, Lawrence. 'Friedrich von Hugel as Modernist and More than Modernist', *Catholic Historical Review*, LXXV, 2 (April 1989), 211–32.

Barthel, Manfred. *The Jesuits: History and Legend of the Society of Jesus*, trans. Mark Howson. New York, 1984.

Bartocinni, Fiorella. *Roma nel Ottocento*. Bologna, 1985.

Bartocinni, Fiorella. *La 'Roma dei Romani'*. Rome, 1971.

Bazin, Rene. *Pius X*. London, 1928.

Bea, Cardinal Augustin. *The Unity of Christians*. New York, 1963.

Belvederi, Raffaele. *Il papato di fronte alla rivoluzione ed alle consequenze del Congresso di Vienna*. Bologna, 1965.

Bernstein, Carl. 'The Holy Alliance', *Time*, 8 (24 February 1992), 28–35.

Beyer, Jean, S.J., ed. *John Paul II Speaks to Religious*. Baltimore, 1988.
Biggini, Alberto. *Storia inedita della conciliazione*. Milan, 1942.
Binchy, D.A. *Church and State in Fascist Italy*. New York, 1941.
Blakiston, Noel, ed. *The Roman Question: Extracts from the Dispatches of Odo Russell from Rome 1858–1870*. London, 1962.
Bland, Joan, SND de N. *The Pastoral Vision of John Paul II, Books I–IV*. Chicago, 1982–86.
Boettner, Lorraine, *Roman Catholicism*. Philadelphia, 1962.
Bonaparte, Napoleon. *Correspondance de Napoleon Ier*. Paris, 1859.
Bonaparte, Napoleon. *The Corsican, A Diary of Napoleon's Life in his Own Words*, ed. R.M. Johnston. Boston, 1910.
Bonnot, Bernard R. *Pope John XXIII: An Astute Pastor*. New York, 1979.
Booke, Bernard, ed. *The Papacy and the Church in the United States*. New York, 1989.
Bourassa, Henri. *Le Pape Arbitre de la Paix*. Montreal, 1918.
Bourgeois, Émile, and E. Clermont. *Rome et Napoleon III (1849–1870)*. Paris, 1907.
Brady, Joseph A. *Rome and the Neapolitan Revolution of 1820–1821: A Study in Papal Neutrality*. New York, 1976.
Brady, W. Maziere, ed. *Anglo-Roman Papers. Volume III: Memoirs of Cardinal Erskine, Papal Envoy to the Court of George III*. London, 1890.
Brennan, Anthony. *Pope Benedict XV and the War*. London, 1917.
Broderick, Francis L. 'The Encyclicals and Social Action: Is John A. Ryan Typical?', *Catholic Historical Review*, LV (April 1969), 1–6.
Broglio, Francesco Margiotto. *Italia e Santa Sede dalla grande guerra alla conciliazione*. Bari, 1966.
Brown-Olf, Lillian. *Their Name is Pius: Portraits of Five Great Modern Popes*. Milwaukee, 1941.
Browne-Olf, Lillian. *Pius XI: Apostle of Peace*. New York, 1938.
Buonaiuti, Ernesto. *Pio XII*. Florence, 1958.
Burton, Katherine. *Leo the Thirteenth: The First Modern Pope*. New York, 1962.
Burton, Katerine. *The Great Mantle: The Life of Giuseppe Melchiore Sarto, Pope Pius X*. New York, 1950.
Buschkuhl, Matthias. *Great Britain and the Holy See, 1746–1870*. Dublin, 1982.
Butler, Cuthbert. *The Vatican Council: The Story Told from Inside in Bishop Ullathorne's Letters*. New York, 1930.
Camp, Richard L. 'From a Passive Subordination to Complementary Partnership: The Papal Conception of a Woman's Place in the Church and Society since 1878', *Catholic Historical Review*, LXXXVI, 3 (July 1990), 506–25.
Canapa, Andrew. 'Pope Pius X and the Jews: A Reappraisal', *Church History* (September 1992), 362–72.
Capello, Maggiornino. *Papa Pio X. Aneddoti e ricordi*. Turin, 1935.
Capovilla, Loris. *Ite Missa Est*. Padua, 1983.
Capovilla, Loris. *The Heart and Mind of John XXIII. His Secretary's Intimate Reflection*. New York, 1964.

Capovilla, Loris. *Giovanni XXIII, Quindici Letture*. Rome, 1970.
Capovilla, Loris. *Giovanni XXIII*. Vatican City, 1963.
Caprara, Cardinal Jean. *Concordat, et recueil des bulles et brefs de N.S.P. le Pape Pie VII, sur les affaires actuelles de l'Eglise de France*. Liege, 1802.
Caprile, Giovanni. 'Pio XII e un nuovo progetto di Concilio Ecumenico', *Civiltà Cattolica*, 6 August 1966, pp. 209–27.
Caprile, Giovanni, ed. *Il Concilio Vaticano II*, 5 vols, *Civiltà Cattolica*, 1965.
Caprile, Giovanni, ed. *Il Sinodo dei vescovi. Interventi e documentazione*. Rome, 1992.
Caprile, Giovanni, ed. *Karol Wojthla e il Sinodo dei Vescovi*. Vatican Press, 1980.
Cardinale, Igino. *The Holy See and the International Order*. Gerrards Cross, 1976.
Carillo, Elisa A. 'Alcide De Gaspari and the Lateran Pacts', *Catholic Historical Review*, XVIX, 4 (January 1964), 532–9.
Cassi, Gellio. *Il Cardinale Consalvi ed e prime anni della restariazione pontificia, 1815–1819*. Milan, 1931.
Cerio F. Diaz de, and M.F. Nunez y Monez, eds. *Instrucciones secretas a los nuncios de Espana en el siglio XIX (1847–1907)*. Rome, 1989.
Chadwick, Owen. *Britain and the Vatican during the Second World War*. Cambridge, 1986.
Chadwick, Owen. 'The Pope and the Jews in 1942', in *Persecution and Toleration, Studies in Church History*, 21, ed. W.J. Sheils, The Ecclesiastical History Society. Oxford, 1984.
Chadwick, Owen. *The Popes and European Revolution*. Oxford, 1981.
Charles-Roux. *Huit ans au Vatican, 1932–1940*. Paris, 1947.
Chassin, C.L., ed. *Les élections et les Cahiers de Paris en 1789*. Paris, 1888.
Cianfarra, Camille M. *The War and the Vatican*. London, 1945.
Ciano, Galeazzo. *Diario*. Milan, 1950.
Ciano, Galeazzo. *L'Europa verso la Catasrofe*. Verona, 1948.
Cicognani, Amleto Giovanni. *A Symposium on the Life and Work of Pope Pius X*. Washington, DC, 1946.
Clancy, John G. *Apostle for Our Time: Pope Paul VI*. London, 1964.
Clermont, Émile and E. Bourgeois. *Rome et Napoleon III (1849–1870)*. Paris, 1907.
Clonmore, William Cecil James Philip John Paul Howard, Lord. *Pope Pius XI and World Peace*. New York, 1938.
Codex Iuris Canonici Pii X. Rome, 1947.
Colapietra, Raffaele. 'Il Diario Brunelli del Conclave del 1823', *Archvio Storico Italiano*, CXX (1962), 76–146.
Colapietra, Rafaele. 'Il Diario del Conclave del 1829', *Critica Storica*, I (1962), 517–41.
Colapietra, Raffaele. *La chiesa tra Lamennais e Metternich. Il Pontificato di Leone XII*. Brescia, 1963.
Colapietra, Raffaele. *La formazione diplomatica di Leone XII*. Rome, 1966.
Colleville, Comte de. *Pio X intime*. Paris, 1904.

Collins, Joseph B., ed. *Chatechetical Documents of Pope Pius X*. New York, 1946.
Confalonieri, C. *Pio XI Visto da vicino*. Turin, 1957.
Confessore, Ornella. *L'Americanismo cattolico in Italia*. Rome, 1984.
Congar, Yves-Maries. *Dialogue between Christians*. London, 1966.
Consalvi, Ercole. 'Le Memorie sul concalve tenuto in Venezia' di Ercole Consalvi', *Archivum Historiae Pontificiae*, III (1965), 239–308.
Consular Relations between the United States and the Papal States; Instructions and Despatches, ed. Leo Francis Stock. Washington, DC, 1945.
Conway, J.S. *The Nazi Persecution of the Churches, 1933–1945*. London, 1968.
Copernico, Galilei e la Chiesa: Fine della controversia (1820), gli atti del Sant'Uffizio, ed. Walter Brandmuller and Egon Johannes Greipl. Florence, 1992.
Coppa, Frank J. 'Cardinal Antonelli, the Papal States and the Counter-Risorgimento', *Journal of Church and State*, XVI (Autumn 1974), 453–71.
Coppa, Frank J. 'Cardinal Giacomo Antonelli: An Accommodating Personality in the Politics of Confrontation', *Biography II* (Fall 1979), 283–302.
Coppa, Frank J. *Cardinal Giacomo Antonelli and Papal Politics in European Affairs*. New York, 1990.
Coppa, Frank J. 'Giacomo Antonelli', *Clio* (of Rome), IX (April/June 1973), 183–210.
Coppa, Frank J. 'Giolitti and the Gentiloni Pact between Myth and Reality', *Catholic Historical Review*, LIII, 2 (July 1967), 217–28.
Coppa, Frank J. 'Pessimism and Traditionalism in the Personality and Policies of Pio Nono', *Journal of Italian History*, II (Autumn 1979), 209–17.
Coppa, Frank J. *Pope Pius IX: Crusader in a Secular Age*. Boston, 1979.
Coppa, Frank J. 'Realpolitik and Conviction in the Conflict between Piedmont and the Papacy during the Risorgimento', *Catholic Historical Review*, LIV (January 1969), 592–3.
Coppa, Frank J. *The Origins of the Italian Wars of Independence*. London, 1992.
Cornwell, John. *A Thief in the Night: The Death of Pope John Paul I*. London, 1989.
Correspondence between President Truman and Pope Pius XII, with an Introduction by Myron C. Taylor, Personal Representative of the President of the United States to His Holiness Pope Pius XII. New York, 1952.
Correspondence Between President Roosevelt and Pope Pius XII. New York, 1947.
Corrigan, Raymond. *The Church and the Nineteenth Century*. Milwaukee, 1938.
Cretineau-Joly, J., ed. *Mémoires du Cardinal Consalvi, secretaire d'état du Pape Pie II, avec un introduction et des notes*. Paris, 1864.
Crews, Clyde. *English Catholic Modernism*. Notre Dame, 1984.
Crispolti, Filippo. *Pio IX, Leone XIII, Pio X, Benedetto XV. Ricordi Personali*. Milan, 1932.
Curran, Robert Emmett. 'The McGlynn Affair and the Shaping of the New Conservatism in American Catholicism, 1886–1894', *Catholic Historical Review*, LXVI, 2 (April 1980), 184–204.
Curran, Robert Emmett. *Michael Augustine Corrigan and the Shaping of Conservative Catholicism in America, 1878–1902*. New York, 1978.

Cushing, Cardinal Richard James. *Pope Pius XII*. Boston, 1959.
D'Agnel, Anaud. *Benoit XV et le conflit europeen*. Paris, 1916.
Daim, Wilfred. *The Vatican and Eastern Europe*. New York, 1970.
Dalla Torre, Paolo. *Pio IX e Vittorio Emmucle II. Dal loro carteggio privato negli anni del dilaceramento (1865–1878)*. Rome, 1972.
Daly, Gabriel. 'Catholicism and Modernity', *Journal of the American Academy of Religion*, LIII (December 1985), 773–96.
Daniel-Rops, Henri. *The Church in an Age of Revolution 1789–1870*. Garden City, NY, 1967.
Daniel-Rops, H. *The Church in the Eighteenth Century*. Garden City, NY, 1966.
Daughters of St Paul, eds. *Messages of John Paul II*. Boston, 1979.
De Cesare, Raffaele. *The Last Days of Papal Rome*. London, 1909.
De Cigalo, Albim. *Vie intime de Pie X*. Paris, 1904.
De Ecclesia: The Constitution on the Church of Vatican Council II proclaimed by Pope Paul VI. Glen Rock, NJ, 1965.
De Felice, Renzo. *Storia degli ebrei italiani sotto il fascismo*. Turin, 1961.
De Franciscis, Maria Elisabeta. *Italy and the Vatican: The 1984 Concordat Between Church and State*. New York, 1989.
De Franciscis, Pasquale, ed. *Discorsi del Sommo Pontefice Pio IX Pronunziati in Vaticano ai fedeli di Roma e dell orbe dal principio della sua prigionia fino al presente*, 4 vols. Rome, 1872–78.
De Gasperi, Alcide. *Lettere sul Concordato*. Brescia, 1970.
De la Bedoyere, Michael. *The Life of Baron von Hugel*. London, 1951.
De Laubier, Patrick. *Il pensiero sociale della Chiesa Cattolica*. Milan, 1986
De Maistre, Joseph. *St Petersburg Dialogues*, ed. Richard A. Lebrun. Montreal, 1993.
De Rosa, Gabriele. *Storia del movimento cattolico in Italia. Dalla restaurazione all 'età giolittiana*. Bari, 1966.
Delattre, A.J. *Un Catholicisme Americaine*. Namur, 1898.
Delzell, Charles F., ed. *The Papacy and Totalitarianism Between the Two World Wars*. New York, 1974.
Delzell, Charles F. 'Pius XII, Italy, and the Outbreak of War', *Journal of Contemporary History*, II, 4 (October 1967), 137–61.
Di Nolfo, Ennio, ed. *Vaticano e Stati Uniti 1939–1952. Dalle carte di Myron C. Taylor*. Milan, 1978.
Dimitriu-Snagov, Ion. *La Romania nella diplomazia Vaticana, 1939–1944*. Rome, 1987.
Discorsi di Pio XI, ed. Domenico Bertone *Vol. I: 1922–28; Vol. II: 1929–33; Vol. III: 1934–39*. Turin, 1959.
Discorsi e Radio messagi di Sua Santita Pio XII, 2 vols. Milan, 1941.
Discorsi, messaggi, colloqui del Santo Padre Giovanni XXIII, 5 vols. Vatican City, 1961–67.
Discourses of the Popes from Pius XI to John Paul II to the Pontifical Academy of Sciences, 1936–1986. Vatican City, 1986.

Doing the Truth in Charity: Statements of Pope Paul VI, John Paul I, and John Paul II, ed. John B. Sheerin. New York, 1982.
Dolan, Jay. *The American Catholic Experience*. New York, 1985.
Dorr, Donal. *Option for the Poor: A Hundred Years of Vatican Social Teaching*. New York, 1983.
Dougherty, M. Patricia. 'The Rise and Fall of *L'Ami de la Religion*: History, Purpose, and Readership of a French Catholic Newspaper', *Catholic Historical Review*, LXXXVII, 2 (January 1991), 21–41.
Dreyfus, Paul. *Jean XXIII*. Paris, 1979.
Duerm, Charles van. *Un peu plus de lumiere sur le conclave de Venise et sur le commencements du pontificat de Pie VII, 1799–1800*. Louvain, 1896.
Duerm, Charles van, ed. *Correspondance du Cardinal Hercule Consalvi avec le Prince Clement de Metternich*. Louvain, 1899.
Dunn, Dennis J. *The Catholic Church and the Soviet Government, 1939–1949*. New York, 1977.
Dupuy, André. *La Diplomatie du Saint-Siège*. Paris, 1980.
Elliot, Lawrence. *I will be called John*. London, 1974.
Elliott, Walter. *The Life of Father Hecker*. New York, 1894.
Ellis, John Tracey. *Cardinal Consalvi and Anglo-Papal Relations, 1814–1824*. Washington, DC, 1942.
Enchiridion delle Encicliche, Vol. 1–7. Bologna, 1994.
Eppstein, John. *The Catholic Tradition of the Law of Nations*. Washington, DC, 1935.
Falconi, Carlo. *Il Cardinale Antonelli. Vita e carriera del Richelieu italiano nella chiesa di Pio IX*. Milan, 1983.
Falconi, Carlo. *The Popes in the Twentieth Century*. Boston, 1967.
Falconi, Carlo. *The Silence of Pius XII*, trans. Bernard Wall. Boston, 1970.
Farina, John. *An American Experience of God: The Spirituality of Isaac Hecker* New York, 1981.
Farini, Luigi Carlo. *Lo stato romano dell' anno 1815 al 1850*. Florence, 1853.
Fattorini, Emma. *Germania e Santa Sede. La Nunziature di Pacelli tra la Grande Guerra e la Repubblica di Weimar*. Milan, 1992.
Felici, Pericle. *Il Lungo Cammino del Concilio*. Milan, 1967.
Ferrari, Liliana. *Una storia dell 'Azione Cattolica. Gli Ordimamenti Statutari da Pio IX a Pio XII*. Genoa, 1989.
Filipuzzi, Angelo. *Pio IX e la politica Austriaca in Italia dal 1815 al 1848*. Florence, 1958.
Flannery, Austin, ed. *Vatican Council II: The Conciliar and Post Conciliar Documents*. Grand Rapids, 1992.
Flathe, Teodoro. *Il periodo della resaurazione e della rivoluzione, 1815–1851*. Milan, 1889.
Flint, James. 'The Attempt of the British Government to Influence the Choice of the Second Archbishop of Westminister', *Catholic Historical Review*, LXXVII, 1 (January 1991), 42–55.

Floridid, Alexis U. *Moscow and the Vatican*. Ann Arbor, 1986.
Flynn, George Q. 'Franklin Roosevelt and the Vatican: The Myron Taylor Appointment', *Catholic Historical Review*, XVIII, 2 (July 1972), 171–94.
Fogarty, Gerald P. *The Vatican and the American Hierarchy from 1870 to 1965*. Wilmington, 1985.
Fogarty, Gerald P. *The Vatican and the Americanist Crisis: Denis J. O'Connell, American Agent in Rome, 1885–1903*. Rome, 1974.
Fontenelle, René. *His Holiness Pope Pius XII*. London, 1938.
Forbes, F.A. *Life of Pius X*. London, 1918.
Foundations for Peace: Letters of Pope Pius XII and President Roosevelt. London, 1941.
Friedlander, Saul. *Pius XII and the Third Reich*. New York, 1966.
Frossard, André, ed. *'Be Not Afraid': Pope John Paul speaks Out on his Life, his Beliefs, and his Inspiring Vision for Humanity*, trans. J.R. Foster. New York, 1984.
Fulani, Silvio. 'La Santa Sede i il Congresso di Verona', *Nouva Rivista Storica*, XXIX (1955), 465–91.
Furey, Francis T. *Life of Leo XIII and History of His Pontificate*. New York, 1903.
Fusi-Pecci, Odo. *La vita del Papa Pio VIII*. Rome, 1965.
Gabriele, Mariano, ed. *Il Carteggio Antonelli-Sacconi (1850–1860)*. Rome, 1962.
Gajani, Guglielmo. *The Roman Exile*. Boston, 1856.
Gargan, Edward T. *Leo XIII and the Modern World*. New York, 1961.
Garzia, Italo. *Pio XII et l'Italia nella seconda guerra mondiale*. Brescia, 1988.
Gasquet, Cardinal Aiden. *Great Britain and the Holy See, 1772–1806: A Chapter in the History of Diplomatic Relations between England and Rome*. Rome, 1919.
Gasquet, Cardinal. *A Memoir*. New York, 1953.
Gilkey, Langdon Brown. *Catholicism Confronts Modernity: A Protestant View*. New York, 1975.
Gilson, Etiene, ed. *The Church Speaks to the Modern World: The Social Teachings of Leo XIII*. New York, 1954.
Gioberti, Vincenzo. *Del primato morale e civile degli Italiani*. Turin, 1932.
Giolitti, Giovanni. *Memorie della mia vita*, 2 vols. Milan, 1922.
Giordani, Igino. *Pius X: A Country Priest*. Milwaukee, 1954.
Giordani, Igino. *Pio XII. Un grande Papa*. Turin, 1961.
Giovanni e Paolo, due Papi. Saggio di corrispondenza (1925–1962). Brescia, 1983.
Giovanni XXIII, Il Giornale dell'Anima, ed. Loris Capovilla. Rome, 1968.
Giovanni XXIII, Lettere 1958–1963, ed. Loris Capovilla. Rome, 1978.
Giovanni XXIII, Papa di Transzione, ed. Loris Capovilla. Rome, 1979.
Giovanni XXIII, Il Pastore, ed. Giambattista Busetti. Padua, 1980.
Giovanni XXIII, Lettere di familiari, ed. Loris Capovilla. Rome, 1968.
Giuntella, Vittorio E. *La religione amica della Democrazia. I cattolici democratici del Triennio rivoluzionrio (1796–1799)*. Rome, 1990.
Gladstone, W.E. *The Vatican Decrees in their Bearing on Civil Allegiance: A Political Expostulation*. New York, 1875.

Godechot, Jacques. *La Contra-Revolution. Doctine et action, 1789–1804*. Paris, 1961.
Gonella, Guido. *A World to Reconstruct. Pius XII on Peace and Reconstruction*. Milwaukee, 1944.
Gontard, Friedrich. *The Chair of Peter, A History of the Papacy*. New York, 1964.
Gonzalez, James L. *Paul VI*. Boston, 1964.
Gorresio, Vittorio. *Risorgimento scomunicato*. Florence, 1958.
Gorresio, Vittorio, ed. *Stato e Chiesa*. Bari, 1957.
Gorresio, Vittorio. *The New Mission of Pope John XXIII*, trans. Charles Lam Markmann. New York, 1969.
Gough, Austin. *Paris and Rome: The Gallican Church and the Ultramontane Campaign, 1848–1853*. Oxford, 1986.
Graham, Robert A. *Vatican Diplomacy: A Study of Church and State on the International Plane*. Princeton, 1959.
Graham, Robert. *Pius XII's Defense of Jews and Others*. Milwaukee, 1987.
Graham, Robert. 'Quale pace cercava Pio XII?', *Civiltà Cattolica*, 1 May 1982, 218–33.
Granfield, Patrick. *The Limits of the Papacy*. New York, 1987.
Graubert, Judah. 'The Vatican and the Jews: Cynicism and Indifference'. *Judaism*, XXIV, 2 (Spring 1975), 53–64.
Greeley, Andrew M. *The Making of the Popes 1978*. Kansas City, 1978.
Grissell, Hartwell de La Garde. *Sede Vacante, Being a Diary Written During the Conclave of 1903*. London, 1903.
Guilday, Peter, ed. *The Catholic Church in Contemporary Europe 1919–1931, Vol. 2*. New York, 1932.
Guitton, Jean. *Dialogues avec Paul VI*. Paris, 1967.
Guitton, Jean. *Paul VI Secret*. Paris, 1979.
Gutierrez, Gustavo. *A Theology of Liberation*. Maryknoll, NY, 1973.
Gwynn, Denis. *The Vatican and the War in Europe*. London, 1941.
Habiger, Matthew, O.S.B. *Papal Teaching on Private Property, 1891–1981*. Lanham, MD, 1990.
Hachey, Thomas I., ed. *Anglo-Vatican Relations 1914–1939: Confidential Reports to the British Minister to the Holy See*. Boston, 1972.
Halecki, Oscar. *Eugenio Pacelli: Pope of Peace*. New York, 1951.
Hales, E.E.Y. *The Catholic Church in the Modern World*. Garden City, NY, 1958.
Hales, E.E.Y. *Revolution and Papacy, 1769–1846*. Notre Dame, IN, 1966.
Hales, E.E.Y. *The Emperor and the Pope: The Story of Napoleon and Pius VII*. Garden City, NY, 1961.
Hales, E.E.Y. *Pio Nono: A Study in European Politics and Religion in the Nineteenth Century*. Garden City, NY, 1962.
Hales, E.E.Y. *Pope John and His Revolution*. London, 1965.
Halperin, Samuel W. *The Separation of Church and State in Italian thought from Cavour to Mussolini*. Chicago, 1937.

Hanson, Erik O. *The Catholic Church in World Politics*. Princeton, NJ, 1987.
Hasler, August. *How the Pope became Infallible*. Garden City, NY, 1981.
Hatch, Alden. *A Man Named John: The Life of Pope John XXIII*. New York, 1963.
Hearley, John. *Pope or Mussolini*. New York, 1929.
Hebblethwaite, Peter. *John XIII, Shepherd of the Modern World*. New York, 1985.
Hebblethwaite, Peter. *John XXIII, Pope of the Council*. London, 1984.
Hebblethwaite, Peter. *Paul VI: The First Modern Pope*. New York, 1993.
Hebblethwaite, Peter. *The Year of Three Popes*. New York, 1979.
Hebblethwaite, Peter. *Understanding the Synod*. Dublin, 1968.
Hecker, Isaac T. *The Aspirations of Nature*. New York, 1857.
Hecker, Isaac T. *The Church and the Age*. New York, 1887.
Helmreich, Ernst. *The German Churches under Hitler*. Detroit, 1979.
Henriot, Peter J., ed. *Catholic Social Teaching*. New York, 1988.
Herber, Charles. 'Eugenio Pacelli's Mission to Germany and the Papal Peace Proposal of 1917', *Catholic Historical Review*, LXV, 1 (1979), 20–48.
Hergenrother, Giuseppe. *Storia universale della Chiesa*. Florence, 1911.
Herzer, Ivo, ed. *The Italian Refuge: Rescue of Jews During the Holocaust*. Washington, DC, 1989.
Hilberg, Raul. *The Destruction of the European Jews*. Chicago, 1961.
Hitchcock, James. *Catholicism and Modernity: Confrontation or Capitulation*. New York, 1979.
Hoare, F.R. *The Papacy and the Modern State: An Essay on the Political History of the Catholic Church*. London, 1940.
Hofmann, Paul. *O Vatican! A Slightly Wicked View of the Holy See*. New York, 1984.
Hollis, Christopher. *The Papacy*. New York, 1964.
Holmes, J. Derek. *The Triumph of the Holy See: A Short History of the Papacy in the Nineteenth Century*. London, 1978.
Holmes, Derek J. *The Papacy in the Modern World, 1914–1978*. London, 1986.
Houtin, Albert. *L'Americanisme*. Paris, 1904.
Huber, R.M., ed. *A Symposium On the Life and Work of Pope Pius X*. Washington, DC, 1946.
Hughes, John Jay. *Pontiffs, People who Shaped History*. Huntingdon, IN, 1994.
Hughes, John Jay. 'The Pope's Pact with Hitler: Betrayal or Self-Defense?', *Journal of Church and State*, XVII (Winter 1975).
Hughes, Philip. *The Popes' New Order: A Systematic Summary of the Social Encyclicals and Addresses from Leo XIII to Pius XII*. New York, 1944.
Hughes, Philip. *Pope Pius XI*. New York, 1937.
Hull, R.R. *The Syllabus of Errors of Pope Pius IX: The Scourge of Liberalism*. Huntington, IN, 1926.
Husselien, Joseph Casper, ed. *Social Wellsprings: Eighteen Encyclicals of Social Reconstruction by Pope Pius XI*. Milwaukee, 1942.
Il Congresso di Vienna del 1815 e la Precedenza dei Rappresentati pontificii nel corpo diplomatico. Relazioni del Cardinale Ercole Consalvi Segret. di Stato e Ministro

Plenipotentiziario del Sommo Pontifice Pio VII al Cardinale B. Pacca Camerlengo di S.R.C. Pro-Secretari di Stato. Rome, 1899.
Insegnamenti di Paolo VI, 16 vols. Vatican City, 1963–77.
Jaeger, Lorenz. *The Ecumenical Council, the Church, and Christendom*. London, 1961.
Jemolo, Arturo Carlo. *Church and State in Italy, 1850–1950*, trans. David Moore. Philadelphia, 1961.
John Paul II. *Crossing the Threshold of Hope*, ed. Vittorio Messori. New York, 1994.
John Paul II. *Pilgrim of Peace: Homilies and Addresses*. New York, 1987.
John Paul II. *Speeches and Selections*. Warsaw, 1991.
Johnson, Paul. *Pope John XXIII*. London, 1974.
Johnson, Paul. *Pope John Paul II and the Catholic Restoration*. London, 1982.
Kaiser, Robert B. *Council and World, the Story of Vatican II*. New York, 1963.
Katz, Robert. *Death in Rome*. New York, 1967.
Kelly, John N.D. *The Oxford Dictionary of Popes*. Oxford, 1986.
Kent, Peter C. *The Pope and the Duce*. New York, 1981.
Kent, George O. 'Pope Pius XII and Germany: Some Aspects of German-Vatican Relations, 1933–1943', *American Historical Review*, LXX (October 1964), 59–78.
Kiefer, William J. *Leo XIII: A Light from Heaven*. Milwaukee, 1960.
Kiernan, T.J. *Pope Pius XII*. Dublin, 1958.
Kinsman, Frederick. *Americanism and Catholicism*. New York, 1924.
Klaiber, Jeffrey S.J. *The Catholic Church in Peru, 1821–1985*. Washington, DC, 1992.
Klein, Felix. *Americanism: A Phantom Heresy*. Atchison, KS, 1951.
Koenig, Harry C., ed. *Principles for Peace: Selections from Papal Documents from Leo XIII to Pius XII*. Washington, DC, 1943.
Küng, Hans. *Christianity: Essence, History and Future*. New York, 1995.
Kurth, James. 'The Vatican's Foreign Policy', *National Interest*, XXXII (Summer 1993), 40–52.
Kurtz, Lester. *The Politics of Heresy: The Modernist Crisis in Roman Catholicism*. Berkeley, 1980.
Lai, Benny. *Les secrets du Vatican*. Paris, 1983.
Lapide, Pinchas. *Three Popes and the Jews*. New York, 1967.
La Separation de l'Église et del l'état en France: Expose et Documents, Supplement to the Acta Sanctae Sedis, volume XXXVIII. Rome, 1906.
Latreille, Andre. *Napoleon et le Saint-Siège (1801–1808)*. Paris, 1935.
Latreille, André. *L'Eglise catholique et la Revolution française. I: Le pontificat de Pie VI et la crise française (1775–1799)*. Paris, 1946.
Lawler, Ronald D., O.F.M. *The Christian Personalism of John Paul II*. Chicago, 1980.
Leflon, Jean. *Pie VII. Des Abbayes bénédictines a la Papauté*. Paris, 1958.
Lehnert, Pascalina. *Pio XII. Il privilegio di servirlo*. Milan, 1984.
Leonis XIII Pontificis Maximi Acta, 23 vols. Rome, 1881–1905.

Leprieur, François. *Quand Rome condamne*. Paris, 1989.
Lettres apostoliques de S.S. Pie X. Encycliques, motu proprio, brefs, allocutions, etc., 8 vols. Paris, 1930–36.
Levai, Jeno. *Hungarian Jewry and the Papacy*. London, 1968.
Lewy, Guenter. *The Catholic Church and Nazi Germany*. New York, 1964.
Liberati, Luigi Bruti. *La Santa Sede e la origini dell'impero americano. La guerra del 1896*. Milan, 1984.
Longford, Frank Pakenham. *John Paul II: An Authorized Biography*. London, 1982.
Looms, Thomas Michael. *Liberal Catholicism, Reform Catholicism Modernism: A Contribution to a New Orientation in Modernist Research*. Mainz, 1979.
L'Opera della Santa Sede nella Guerra Europea. Raccolta dei documenti (Agosto 1914–Luglio 1916). Rome, 1916.
Luciani, Albino. *The Message of John Paul I*. Boston, 1978.
Luciani, Albino. *Illustrisimi: Letters from Pope John I*, trans. William Weaver. Boston, 1976.
Lukcas, Lajos, ed. *The Vatican and Hungary 1846–1878: Reports and Correspondence on Hungary of the Apostolic Nuncios in Vienna*, trans. Esofia Karmos. Budapest, 1981.
MacCaffrey, James. *History of the Catholic Church in the Nineteenth Century*, 2 vols. Dublin, 1909.
Maccarrone, Michele. 'L'Apertura degli archivi della Santa Sede per i Pontificati di Pio X e di Benedetto XV (1903–1922)', *Rivista di Storia della Chiesa in Italia*, XXXIX, 2 (1985), 341–8.
Magister, Sandro. *La politica vaticana e l'Italia 1943–1978*. Rome, 1979.
Maguire, John Francis. *Rome: Its Rulers and its Institutions*. London, 1857.
Maier, Hans. *Revolution and Church: The Early History of Christian Democracy*, trans. Emily M. Schossberger. Notre Dame, 1969.
Maioli, Giovanni. *Pio IX da vescovo a Pontefice. Lettere al Card. Luigi Amat. agosto 1839–luglio 1848*. Modena, 1943.
Manuscript of *Breve relazione al Cile dal Canonico Giovanni Mastai-Ferretti di Singigaglia*, Sala Studio Manoscritti of the Vatican Library.
Malinski, Mieczyslaw. *Pope John Paul II: The Life of Karol Wojtyla*, trans. P.S. Fall. New York, 1979.
Mandelbaum, Michael. 'Coup de Grace: The End of the Soviet Union', *Foreign Affairs*, LXXI (Spring 1992), 164–82.
Manzo, Michele. *Papa Gioianni vescovo di Roma. Sinodo e pastorale diocesana nell'episcopato romano di Roncalli*. Cinsello Balsamo, 1991.
Marchsan, Angelo. *Pio X nella sua vita, nella sua parola, e nelle sue opere*, 3rd edn. Rome, 1910.
Martin, Malachi. *The Jesuits: The Society of Jesus and the Betrayal of the Roman Catholic Church*. New York, 1988.
Martin, Malachi. *The Keys of this Blood: The Struggle for World Dominion Between Pope John Paul II, Mikail Gorbachev, and the Capitalist West*. New York, 1990.
Martina, Giacomo. *Pio IX. Chiesa e mondo moderno*. Rome, 1976.

Martina, Giacomo, ed. *Pio IX e Leopoldo II*. Rome, 1967.
Martina, Giacomo. *Pio IX (1846–1850)*. Rome, 1974. *Pio IX (1851–1866)*. Rome, 1986. *Pio IX (1867–1878)*. Rome, 1990.
Matheson, Peter, ed. *The Third Reich and the Christian Churches*. Grand Rapids, 1981.
May, William. *Vatican Authority and American Catholic Dissent*. New York, 1987.
Mazzini, Joseph. *Italy, Austria, and the Pope: A Letter to Sir James Graham Bart*. London, 1845.
McAvoy, Thomas. *The American Heresy in Catholicism*. Notre Dame, 1953.
McCormick, Anne O'Hare. *Vatican Journal 1921–1954*. New York, 1957.
McDermott, John M., S.J., ed. *The Thought of Pope John Paul II*. Rome, 1993.
McKnight, John P. *The Papacy: A New Appraisal*. London, 1953.
McManners, John. *The French Revolution and the Church*. New York, 1970.
Mecham, Lloyd J. *Church and State in Latin America: A History of Politico-Ecclesiastical Relations*. Chapel Hill, 1966.
Melady, Thomas Patrick. *The Ambassador's Story: The United States and the Vatican in World Affairs*. Huntington, IN, 1994.
Meltzer, Milton. *Rescue: The Story of How Gentiles Saved Jews in the Holocaust*. New York, 1988.
Meneguzzi, Rostangi, Carla, ed. *Il Carteggio Antonelli-Barili, 1859–1861*. Rome, 1973.
Menozzi, Daniele, ed. *La chiesa italiana e la rivoluzione francese*. Bologna, 1990.
Merry del Val, Cardinal. *Memories of Pope Pius X*. London, 1939.
Metternich, Klemens von. *Mémoires, documents et écrits divers laissés par le prince de Metternich*, ed. M.A. Klinkowstroem, 8 vols. Paris, 1880–84.
Metternich-Winneburg, Prince Richard, ed. *Memoirs of Prince Metternich, 1773–1815*. New York, 1970.
Meurthe, Boulay de la, ed. *Documents sur la négociation du concordat et sur les autres rapports de la France avec le Saint-Siège en 1800 et a 1801*. Paris, 1891–1905.
Miller, David C. 'A.G. Camus and the Civil Constitution of the Clergy'. *Catholic Historical Review*, LXXVI, 3 (July 1990), 481–505.
Molony, John N. *The Emergence of Political Catholicism in Italy: Partito populare 1919–1926*. London, 1977.
Monti, Antonio. *Pio IX nel Risorgimento Italiano con documenti inediti*. Bari, 1928.
Monticone, Ronald C. *The Catholic Church in Communist Poland, 1945–1985*. New York, 1986.
Montini, Giovanni Battista. *Pensiamo al Concilio*. Milan, 1962.
Montini, Giovanni Battista, *Lettere ai Familiari 1919–1943*, ed. Nello Vian, Brescia, 1986.
Montini, Giovanni Battista. *La Chiesa*. Montreal, 1964.
Montini, Giovanni Battista. *Discorsi e scritti sul Concilio (1959–1963)*. Rome, 1983.
Montour, François Alexis Artaud de. *Histoire du pape Pie VII*, 2nd edn. Paris, 1837.

Morelli, Anna. 'Cattolici liberali belgi e gli ideali mennaissiani', *Gioacchino Ventura e il pensiero politico d'inspirazione cristiana dell 'ottocento*. Florence, 1991.

Morgan, Thomas B. *A Reporter at the Papal Court: A Narrative of the Reign of Pope Pius XI*. New York, 1937.

Morgan, Thomas B. *The Listening Post, Eighteen Years on Vatican Hill*. New York, 1944.

Morley, John F. *Vatican Diplomacy and the Jews During the Holocaust 1939–1943*. New York, 1980.

Morse, Arthur D. *While Six Million Died*. New York, 1968.

Mourret, Fernand. *Le concile du Vatican d'après des Documents inedits*. Paris, 1919.

Murphy, Francis X. *The Papacy Today*. New York, 1981.

Napoleon in Exile or a Voice from St Helena: The Opinions and Reflections of Napoleon, ed. Barry O'Meara. New York, 1922.

Naughton, James W. *Pius XII on World Problems*. New York, 1943.

Nichols, Peter. *The Politics of the Vatican*. New York, 1968.

Nichols, Peter. *The Pope's Divisions: The Roman Catholic Church Today*. New York, 1981.

Nielson, Fredrik. *The History of the Papacy in the XIX Century*. London, 1906.

Nippold, Friedrich. *The Papacy in the 19th Century*. New York, 1900.

Novelli, Angelo. *The Life of Pius XI*, trans. by P.T. Lombardo. Yonkers, NY, 1925.

O'Carroll, Michael. *Pius XII, Greatness Dishonoured: A Documented Study*. Chicago, 1980.

O'Carroll, Michael. *Poland and Pope John Paul II*. Dublin, 1979.

O'Connell, Denis J. *A New Idea in the Life of Father Hecker*. Freiburg, 1897.

O'Connell, Marvin. *Critics of Trial: An Introduction to the Catholic Modernist Crisis*. Washington, DC, 1994.

O'Donnell, J. Dean. 'Cardinal Charles Lavigerie: The Politics of Getting a Red Hat', *Catholic Historical Review*, LXIII, 2 (April 1977), 185–203.

O'Dwyer, Margaret. *The Papacy in the Age of Napoleon and the Restoration: Pius VII, 1800–1823*. New York, 1985.

Official German Documents Relating to the World War. New York, 1923.

Olf, Lilian. *Pius XI: Apostle of Peace*. New York, 1938.

O'Malley, John. *Tradition and Transition: Historical Perspectives on Vatican II*. Wilmington, DE, 1989.

Oncken, Gugliemo. *L' Epoca della Rivoluzione, dell 'Impero e delle Guerre D'Indipendenza, 1789–1815*. Milan, 1887.

O'Reilly, Bernard. *A Life of Pius IX Down to the Episcopal Jubilee of 1877*, 8th edn. New York, 1878.

O'Reilly, Bernard. *Life of Leo XIII. From an Authentic Memoir Furnished by His Order*. London, 1903.

Our Name is Peter: An Anthology of Key Teachings of Pope Paul VI. ed. Sean O'Reilly. Chicago, 1977.

Pacca, Bartolomeo. *Historical Memories*, trans. George Head, 2 vols. London, 1850.

Pacelli, Eugenio. *Discorsi e Panegirici*, 2nd edn. Milan, 1939.
Pacelli, Francesco. *Diario della Conciliazione*. Città del Vaticano, 1959.
Padellaro, Nazareno. *Portrait of Pius XII*. London, 1956.
Palazzini, Pietro. *Il Clero e l'occupazione di Roma*. Rome, 1995.
Palmer, Robert R. *The Age of the Democratic Revolution*, 2 vols. Princeton, 1964.
Paolo VI, *Discorsi e documenti sul Concilio (1963–1965)*. Brescia, 1986.
Papa, Egidio. *Il Sillabo di Pio IX e la stampa francese, inglese e italiana*. Rome, 1968.
Papal Teachings. Education: Selected and Arranged by the Benedictine Monks of Solesmes, trans. Aldo Rebeschini. Boston, 1960.
Papal Teachings. Matrimony: Selected and Arranged by the Benedictine Monks of Solesmes, trans. Michael J. Byrnes. Boston, 1963.
Parolin, Giuseppe. *Compendio della vita di Pio X*. Turin, 1931.
Parsons, Wilfrid. *The Pope and Italy*. New York, 1929.
Pasolini, Giuseppe. *Memorie. 1815–1876*. Turin, 1887.
Pastor, Ludwig Freiherr von. *The History of the Popes. XV: Pius VI (1755–1799)*. St Louis, MO, 1953.
Pasztor, Lajos. 'Le "Memorie sul conclave tenuto in Venezia" di Ercole Consalvi', *Archivum Historiae Pontificiae*, III (1965), 239–308.
Paulus PP. VI (1963–1978). Elenchus Bibliographicus, ed. Paolo Vian. Brescia, 1981.
Pellicani, Antonio. *Il Papa di tutti, La Chiesa Cattolica, il fascismo, e il razzismo, 1929–1945*. Milan, 1964.
Peters, Walter H. *The Life of Benedict XV*. Saint Paul, 1959.
Petrocchi, Massimo. *La restaurazione, il Cardinale Consalvi, e la riforma del 1816*. Florence, 1941.
Pichon, Charles. *The Vatican and its Role in World Affairs*, trans. Jean Misrahi. New York, 1950.
Pierami, Benedetto. *Vita del servo di Pio X publicata a cura della postulazione*. Turin, 1925.
Pii X Pontificis Maximi Acta or Acta Pii X, 5 vols. Rome, 1905–14.
Pistolesi, Erasmo. *Vita del Sommo Pontefice Pio VII*. Rome, 1824.
Pius XII and Technology, compiled by Leo J. Haigerty. Milwaukee, 1982.
Poliakov, L. 'The Vatican and the Jewish Question', *Commentary*, X, 5 (November 1950), 439–49.
Pollard, Peter C. and John F. Kent, eds. *Papal Diplomacy in the Modern Age*. Westport, CT, 1994.
Pollard, John F. *The Vatican and Italian Fascism, 1929–1932: A Study in Conflict*. Cambridge, 1985.
Pollock, Robert C. ed. *The Mind of Pius XII*. New York, 1955.
Portier, William L. *Isaac Hecker and the First Vatican Council*. New York, 1985.
Prima romana synodus A.D. 1960. Vatican City, 1960.
Proclaiming Justice and Peace: Documents from John XXIII to John Paul II. London, 1984.

Purdy, W.A. *The Church on the Move: The Character and Policies of Pius XII and John XXIII*. New York, 1966.

Quardt, Robert. *The Master Diplomat: From the Life of Leo XIII*. New York, 1964.

Quindicesimo anniversario della morte di Papa Giovanni, ed. Loris Capovilla. Rome, 1978.

Radice, Gianfranco. *Pio IX e Antonio Rosmini*. Vatican City, 1974.

Ramati, Alexander. *While the Pope Kept Silent*. London, 1978.

Ratte, John. *The Modernists: Alfred Loisy, George Tyrrell, William L. Sullivan*. New York, 1967.

Ratti, Achille. *Essays in History*. Freeport, NY, 1967.

Ratzinger, Joseph Cardinal. *Turning Point for Europe*. San Francisco, 1993.

Rebichini, Andrea. *Chiesa e Stato in Cecoslovachia, 1948–1968*. Padua, 1977.

Records and Documents of the Holy See Relating to the Second World War: The Holy See and the War in Europe, March 1939–August 1940. Washington, DC, 1968.

Reinerman, Alan. 'Metternich and the Papal Condemnation of the Carbonari, 1821', *Catholic Historical Review*, LIV (April 1968), 55–69.

Reinerman, Alan J. *Austria and the Papacy in the Age of Metternich: Revolution and Reaction, 1830–1838*. Washington, DC, 1989.

Rhodes, Anthony. *The Vatican in the Age of Dictators, 1922–1945*. New York, 1973.

Riccardi, Andrea, ed. *Pio XII*. Rome, 1984.

Rinieri, Ilario, ed. *Corrispondenza inedita dei Cardinali Consalvi e Pacca*. Turin, 1903.

Rinieri, Ilario. *Il concordato tra Pio VII e il primo console, 1800–1802*. Rome, 1902.

Rinieri, Ilario, ed. *Il Congresso di Vienna e la Santa Sede, 1813–1815*. Rome, 1904.

Rinieri, Ilario, ed. *Napoleone e Pio VII, 1803–1813*. Turin, 1906.

Rivoluzione francese (1787–1799). Repertorio delle fonti archivisitche e delle fonti . . . conservate in Italia e nella Città del Vaticano, 4 vols. Rome, 1991.

Robinet, Jean François Eugene. *Le mouvement réligieux à Paris pendant la Révolution (1789–1801)*. New York, 1974.

Rocca, Roberto Morozzo della. *Le Nazioni non muoiono. Russia rivoluzionaria, Polonia indipendente e Santa Sede*. Bologna, 1992.

Rocca, Roberto Morozzo della. '*L'Osservatore Romano* durante la prima guerra mondiale', *Rassegna Storia del Risorgimento*, LXXVI, 3 (1989), 349–66.

Rodocanachi, E. *Pie VII a Paris*. Paris, 1900.

Romana Beatificationis et Canonisationis Servi Dei Pii Papae X. Disquisitio circa quasdam obiectiones modum agendi Servi Dei respicientes in modernismi debellatione. Vatican City, 1950.

Romanato, Gianpaolo. *Pio X. La Vita di papa Sarto*. Milan, 1992.

Romero, Oscar Archbishop. *A Shepherds Diary*. Cincinnati, 1986.

Roncalli, Angelo. *In memoria di monsignore Giacomo Radini Tedeschi, vescovo di Bergamo*. Bergamo, 1916.

Roncalli, Angelo. *Mission to France 1944–1953*. London, 1966.

Roncalli, Angelo. 'Memorie e Appunti 1919', *Humanitas* (June 1973), 428–87.
Roncalli, Angelo. *Scritti e discorsi 1953–1958*, 4 vols. Rome, 1959–62.
Rope, Henry E.G. *Benedict XV, the Pope of Peace*. London, 1941.
Rosmini, Antonio. *Della missione a Roma*. Turin, 1854.
Rossi, Ernesto. *Il Sillabo*. Florence, 1957.
Roveri, Alessandro, ed. *La missione Consalvi e il Congresso di Vienna*, 3 vols. Rome, 1970–73.
Rusak, Stephen T. 'The Canadian Concordat of 1897', *Catholic Historical Review*, LXXVII, 2 (April 1991), 209–34.
Ryan, Edwin. 'Papal Concordats in Modern Times', *Catholic Historical Review*, XVI (October 1930), 302–10.
Schaefer, Mary C. *A Papal Peace Mosaic, 1878–1936: Excerpts from the messages of Popes Leo XIII, Pius X, Benedict XV and Pius XI*. Washington, DC, 1936.
Schall, James V., S.J. *The Church and State in the Thought of John Paul II*. Chicago, 1982.
Schmidt, Erich. *Der Kulturkampf in Deutschland, 1871–1890*. Gottingen, 1962.
Schmitz, E. *Life of Pius X*. New York, 1907.
Schuck, Michael. *That They Be One: The Social Teaching of the Papal Encyclicals, 1740–1989*. Washington, DC, 1991.
Schultenover, David. *A View From Rome: On the Eve of the Modernist Crisis*. New York, 1993.
Scott, Ivan. *The Roman Question and the Powers, 1848–1865*. The Hague, 1969.
Selected Documents of His Holiness Pope Pius XII: 1939–1958. Washington, DC.
Serafini, Alberto. *Pio Nono. Giovanni Maria Mastai Ferretti dalla giovinezza alla morte nei suoi scritti e discorsi editi e inediti*. Vatican City, 1958.
Shea, John Gilmary. *The Life of Pope Pius IX and the Great Events in the History of the Church during his Pontificate*. New York, 1878.
Shevardnadze, Eduard. *The Future Belongs to Freedom*. New York, 1991.
Sixteen Encyclicals of His Holiness Pope Pius XI, 1926–1937. Washington, DC, 1938.
Smit, Olav. *Pope Pius XII*. London, 1951.
Smith, Janet E. *Humanae Vitae, A Generation Later*. Washington, DC, 1991.
Soderini, Eduardo. *Leo III, Italy and France*. London, 1935.
Sonnino, Sidney. *Diario, 1914–1916*. Bari, 1972.
Souvenirs d'un nonce: Cahiers de France, 1944–1953. Rome, 1963.
Spadolini, Giovanni, ed. *Il Cardinale Gasparri e la Questione Romana (Con Brani delle Memorie Inedite)*. Florence, 1973.
Spadolini, Giovanni. *Giolitti e I Cattolici, 1901–1914*, 2nd edn. Florence, 1960.
Staaf, Giles. *The Dignity of Man in Modern Papal Doctrines: Leo XIII to Pius XII*. Washington, DC, 1957.
Stehle, Hansjakob. *Eastern Politics of the Vatican, 1917–1979*, trans. Sandra Smith. Athens, 1981.
Stehlin, Stewart A. 'Germany and a Proposed Vatican State, 1915–1917', *Catholic Historical Review*, LX, 3 (1974), 402–26.
Stehlin, Stewart A. *Weimar and the Vatican 1919–1933*. Princeton, 1983.

Suardi, G. 'Quando e come I Cattolici poterono partecipare alle elezioni politiche', *Nuova Antologia*, CCCVI (November–December 1927), 118–23.
Sugrue, Francis. *Popes in the Modern World*. New York, 1961.
Sweeney, David F. 'Herman Schell, 1850–1906: A German Dimension to the Americanist Controversy', *Catholic Historical Review*, LXXXVI, 1 (January 1990), 44–70.
Szulc, Tad. *John Paul II: The Biography*. New York, 1995.
Talbot, James F. *Pope Leo XIII. His Life and Letters*. Boston, 1886.
Talks of Pual VI, John Paul I, and John Paul II to the Hierarchy of the United States. Boston, 1979.
Tardini, Cardinal Domenico. *Pio XII*. Rome, 1960.
Taylor, Myron C., ed. *Wartime Correspondence between President Roosevelt and Pope Pius XII*. New York, 1947.
Teeling, William. *Pope Pius XI and World Affairs*. New York, 1937.
The Encyclicals and Other Messages of John XXIII. Washington, 1964.
The Pope and the People: Select Letters and Addresses on Social Questions by Pope Leo XIII, Pope Pius X, Pope Benedict XV, and Pope Pius XI. London, 1932.
The Pope Speaks: The Words of Pius XII. New York, 1940.
The Teachings of Pope Paul VI. Vatican City, 1968.
Theiner, Agustin. *Histoire des deux concordats de la république française et de la république cisalpine*. Paris, 1869.
Thiers, Adolphe. *History of the Consulate and the Empire of France under Napoleon*. Philadelphia, 1861.
Thomas, Gordan and Max Morgan-Witts. *Pontiff*. New York, 1983
Thomas, Louis, ed. *Journal d'un Conclave*. Paris, 1913.
Townsend, Walter. *The Biography of His Holiness Pope Pius XI*. London, 1930.
Tramontin, Silvio. *Un secolo di storia della Chiesa. Da Leone XIII al Concilio Vaticano II*. Rome, 1980.
Trevor, Meriol. *Pope John*. London, 1967.
Tripodi, Nino. *I Patti lateranese e il fascismo*. Bologna, 1960.
Vaillancourt, Jean-Guy. *Papal Power: A Study of Vatican Control over Lay Catholic Elites*. Berkeley, 1980.
Van den Heuvel, J. *The Statesmanship of Benedict XV*, trans. J.C. Burns. New York, 1923.
Vercesi, Ernesto. *Tre secretari di stato. Consalvi, Rampolla del Tindaro, Gasparri*. Venice, 1932.
Veuillot, Pierre, ed. *Notre Sacerdoce, Documents Pontificaux de Pie X à nos jours*. Paris, 1954.
Vidler, Alexander. *A Variety of Catholic Modernists*. London, 1970.
Wallace, Lillian Parker. *Leo XIII and the Rise of Socialism*. Durham, NC, 1966.
Wallace, Lillian Parker. *The Papacy and European Diplomacy, 1869–1878*. Chapel Hill, NC, 1959.
Walsh, Henry H. *The Concordat of 1801: A Study of the Problem of Nationalism in the Relations of Church and State*. New York, 1977.
Weaver, Mary Jo, ed. *Newman and the Modernists*. Lanham, MD, 1985.

Webster, Richard. *Christian Democracy in Italy, 1860–1960*. London, 1961.
Webster, Richard A. *The Cross and the Fasces*. Stanford, 1960.
Weigel, George. *Freedom and its Discontents: Catholicism Confronts Modernity*. Lanham, MD, 1991.
Weigel, George, ed. *A New World Order: John Paul II and Human Freedom*. Lanham, MD, 1992.
Wenger, Antoine. *Vatican II. Chronique de la premiere session*. Paris, 1963.
Whale, John, ed. *The Man Who Leads the Church: An Assessment of John Paul II*. New York, 1980.
Williams, George Hunston. *The Contours of Church and State in the Thought of John Paul II*. Waco, 1983.
Williams, George Huntston. *The Mind of John Paul I*. New York, 1985.
Wiseman, Cardinal Nicholas Patrick. *Recollections of the Last Four Popes and of Rome in their Times*. New York, 1858.
Wojtyla, Karol. *Person and Community: Selected Essays by Karol Wojtyla*, trans. Theresa Sandok, O.S.M. New York, 1993.
Wolff, Richard J. and Jorg K. Hoensch, eds. *Catholics, the State, and the European Radical Right, 1919–1945*. Boulder, CO, 1987.
Wolff, Richard J. *Between Pope and Duce: Catholic Students in Fascist Italy, Studies in Modern European History*, ed. Frank J. Coppa. New York, 1990.
Wolff, Richard J. 'Giovanni Battista Montini and Italian Politics, 1897–1933: The Early Life of Pope Paul VI', *Catholic Historical Review*, LXXXI, 2 (April 1985), 228–47.
Wolff, Richard J. 'The University under Mussolini: The Fascist-Catholic Struggle for Italian Youth, 1922–1943', *History of Higher Education Annual*, I (1981), 132–47.
Wycislo, Aloysius J. *Vatican II Revisited: Reflections by One Who Was There*. New York, 1987.
Wynn, Wilton. *Keepers of the Keys: John XXIII, Paul VI, and John Paul II: Three Who Changed the Church*. New York, 1988.
Wynne, John J., ed. *The Great Encyclical Letters of Pope Leo XIII*. New York, 1903.
Youngblood, Robert L. *Marcos Against the Church: Economic Development and Political Repression in the Phillippines*. Ithaca, 1991.
Yzermans, Vincent A., ed. *All Things in Christ: Encyclicals and Selected Documents of Saint Pius X*. New York, 1954.
Zanetti, Francesco. *Pio X*. Rome, 1937.
Zuccotti, Susan. *The Italians and the Holocaust*. New York, 1987.

Maps

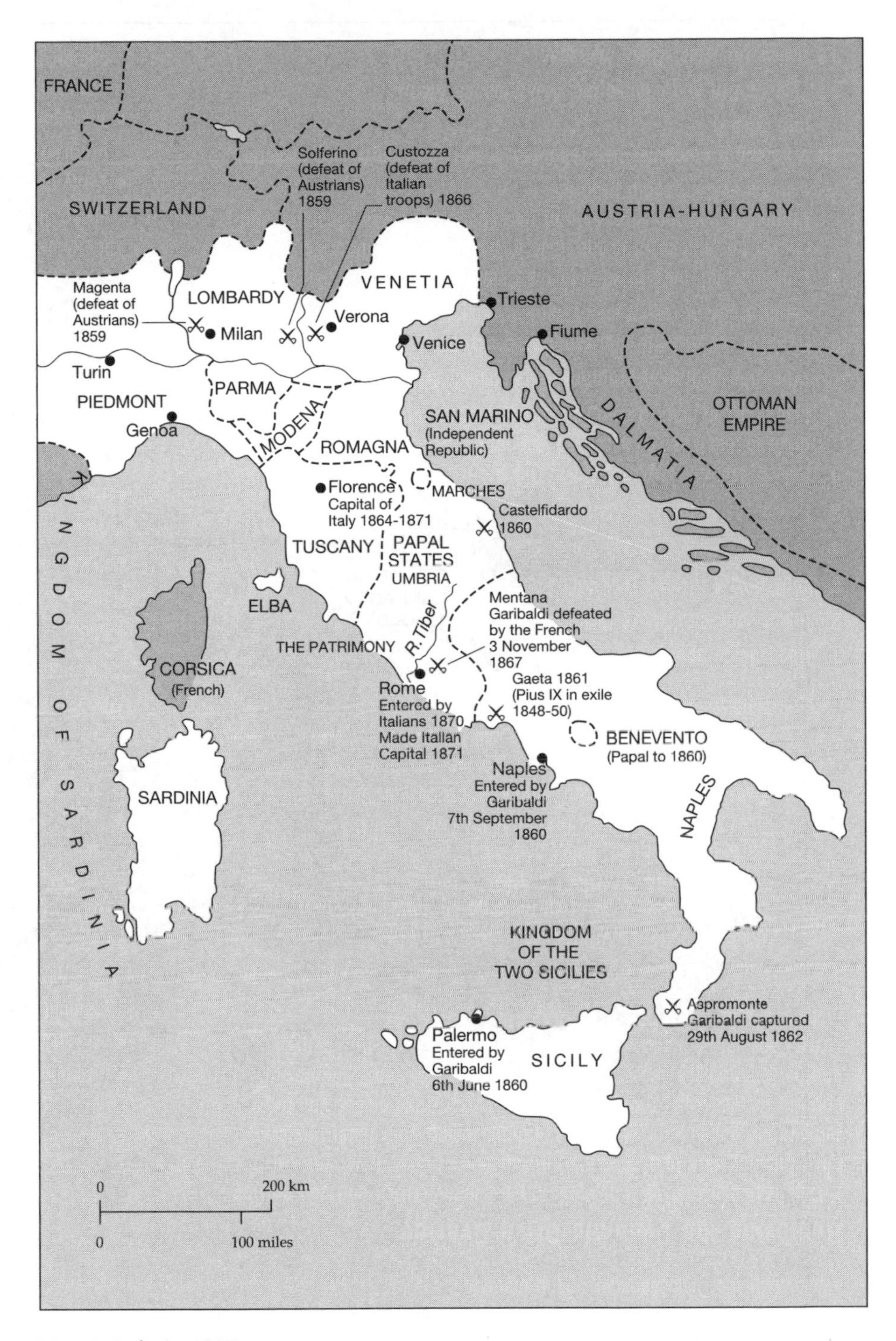

Map 1: Italy in 1815
After Karl Ottmar von Arentin *The Papacy and the Modern World*, translated by Roland Hill (Toronto, 1970), p. 81.

Map 2: Catholicism in modern Europe
After Karl Ottmar von Arentin *The Papacy and the Modern World*, translated by Roland Hill (Toronto, 1970), p. XX.

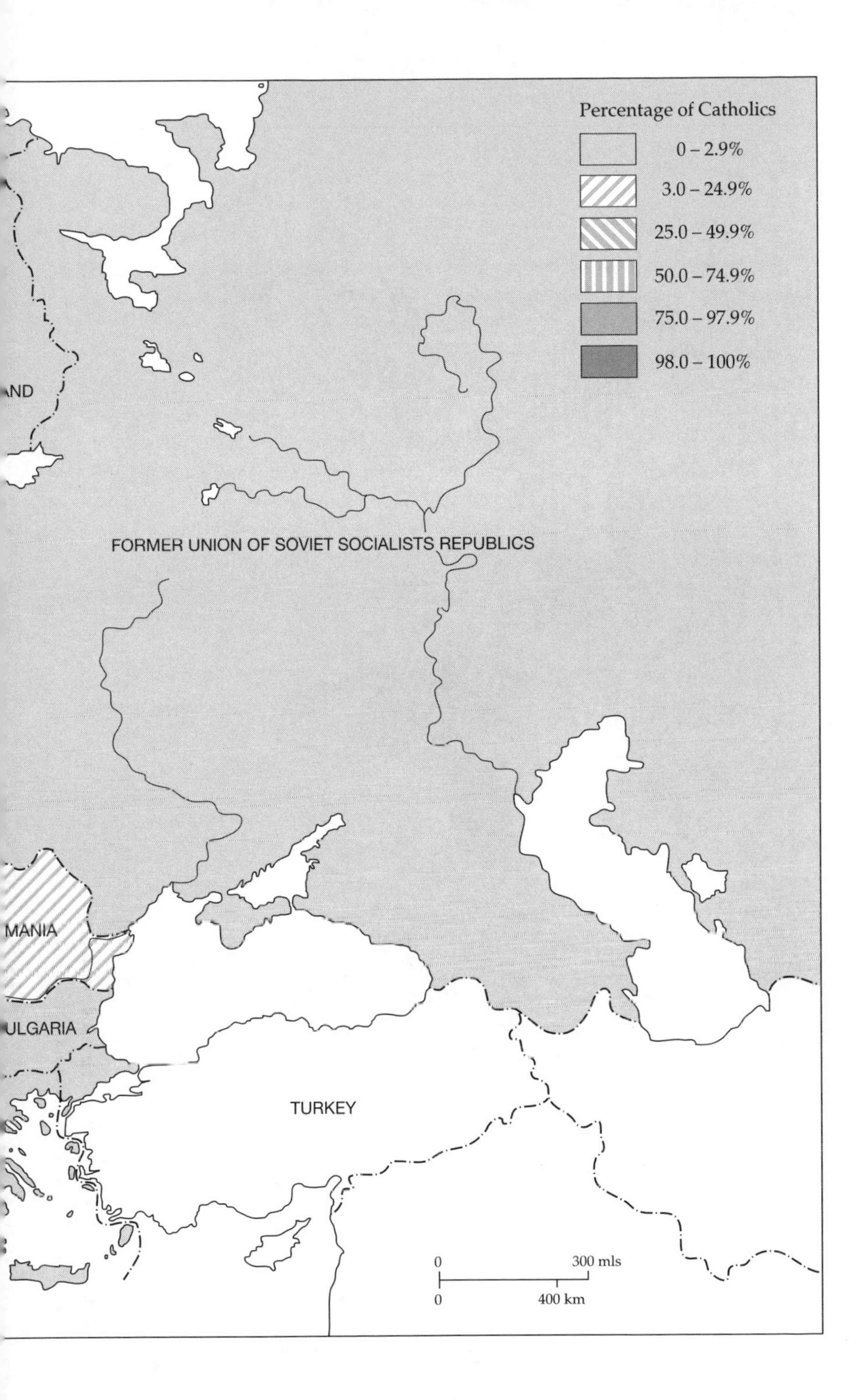
Percentage of Catholics
0 – 2.9%
3.0 – 24.9%
25.0 – 49.9%
50.0 – 74.9%
75.0 – 97.9%
98.0 – 100%
ND
FORMER UNION OF SOVIET SOCIALISTS REPUBLICS
MANIA
ULGARIA
TURKEY
0
300 mls
0
400 km

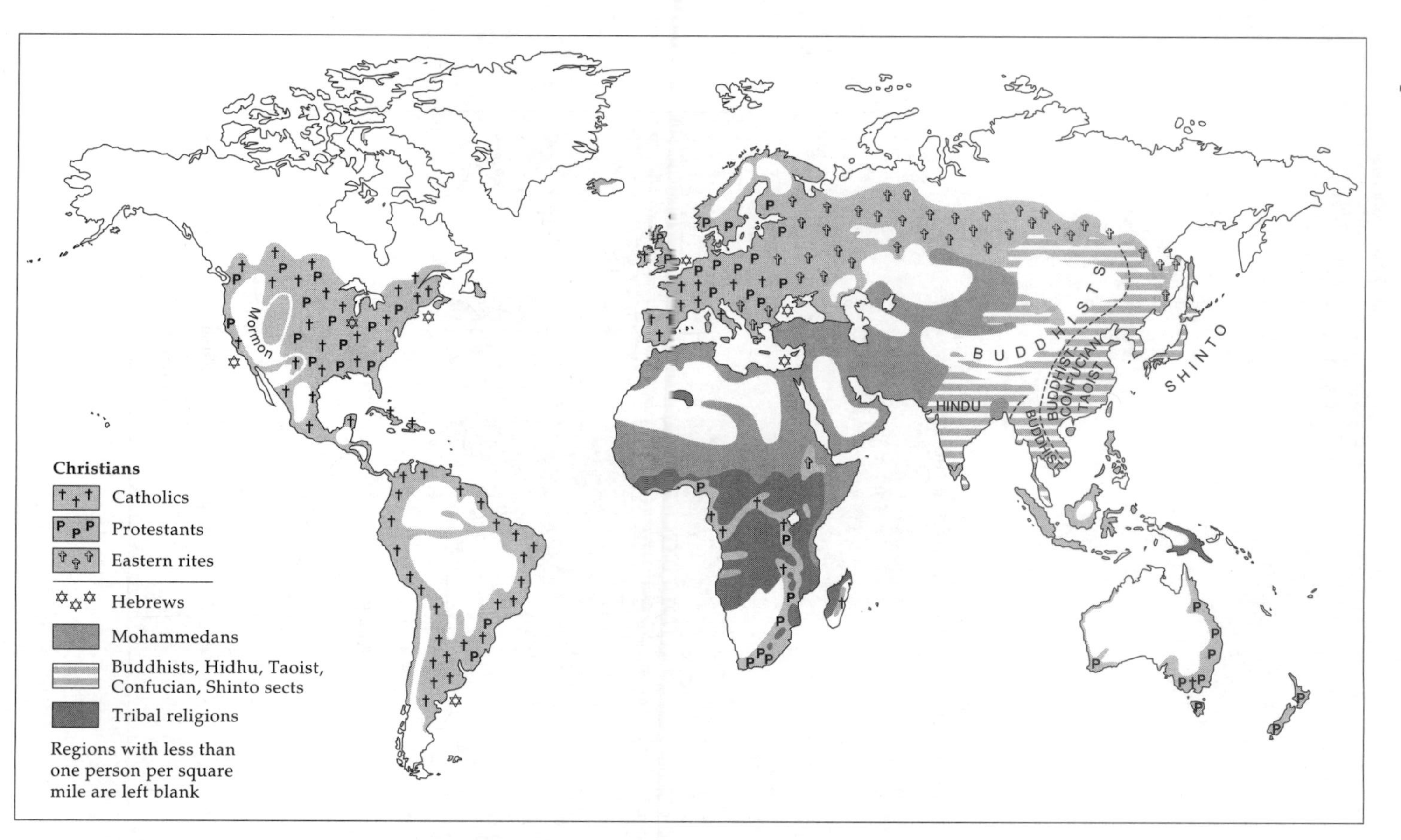

Map 3: The spread of Catholicism in the modern world
After Hammond World Atlas for Students (New Jersey), p. vi.

Index